Making High School Work

Lessons from the Open School

Making High School Work

Lessons from the Open School

Tom Gregory
INDIANA UNIVERSITY

Teachers College, Columbia University
New York and London

Published by Teachers College Press, 1234 Amsterdam Avenue
New York, New York

Library of Congress Cataloging-in-Publication Data

Gregory, Thomas B., 1940–
    Making high school work : lessons from the open school / Tom
Gregory.
        p.   cm.
    Includes bibliographical references (p.   ).
    ISBN 0-8077-3294-X
    1. Open plan schools—Colorado—Jefferson County—Case studies.
2. Jefferson County Open High School—History.   I. Title.
LB1029.06G74   1993
373.788'84—dc20   93-31309

Printed on acid-free paper

Manufactured in the United States of America

99 98 97 96 95 94 93   8 7 6 5 4 3 2 1

To Toby May
whom I never got to know

Contents

Acknowledgments

The study on which this book is based was funded by two sources: The Maris and Mary Proffitt Endowment of the School of Education at Indiana University supported most of the data collection, and the Lilly Endowment provided a generous fellowship that enabled me to spend an entire academic year at the Open School.

I'd like to thank the data collection team—Liz Collins, Larry Embree, Greg Lomme, Valerie Solof, and Mary Beth Teitelbaum—which I formed at the school, for its work. These five "insiders" contributed in many ways to the depth and substance of this description of the school.

Two individuals outside the school—Arnie Langberg and Mary Ellen Sweeney—played key roles in helping me understand the school and what I was trying to say about it. No "outsider" is more familiar with the school than Arnie, its first principal, and Mary Ellen conducted her own qualitative study of the school in 1983. She still lived in Evergreen and taught elsewhere in the Jefferson County Schools when I conducted my study, and she has maintained a close relationship with the school over the years. Mary Ellen's and Arnie's counsel was invaluable as I attempted to establish my interpretation of what I was experiencing.

I wish to thank many people for their assistance and support. Let me start with Toby May's mother; I call her Linda May in the book. Her comments about the Toby May chapter were most helpful and added much depth to the description of a boy I never got to know. Ruth Steele read several drafts of each chapter and eliminated embarrassing errors of fact before they reached a more public forum. Many other Open School staff members and students also reacted to various drafts of the manuscript. More than two dozen others—among them, Jerry Smith, Leslie Bloom, Rick Lear, Fran Rains, Richard Powell, Hornfay Cherng, Greg True, Jim Sears, Elizabeth Lion, Debbie Woodward, Arnie and Dag Langberg, Mary Ellen Sweeney, Mary Anne Raywid, and Joyce McDonald—read and provided helpful suggestions to drafts of one or more chapters. My wife, Diane Gregory, carefully proofread and brought a fresh eye to the final draft.

I want to thank Egon Guba, a valued colleague and teacher. Besides reading and reacting to parts of the book, he also did a great deal to make this, my first attempt at a qualitative study, whatever success it has been. He shares no blame for its shortcomings.

I—and particularly readers of this book—owe a special thank you to Judy Troy, who edited early drafts of it and did her best to transform a pretty good technical writer into a passable writer of what some call "nonfictive" prose. The book has changed in major ways since the manuscript last benefitted from her masterful touch, but her imprint on the book is still clear.

Lastly, I'd like to thank my family and particularly my wife, Diane, who held house and home together alone for most of a year while I followed my bliss.

Portions of chapter 14 appear in altered form in *Public Schools That Work: Creating Community*, edited by Gregory A. Smith and published by Routledge, New York, 1993.

Making High School Work

Lessons from the Open School

Can This Be a Public School?

I made my first visit to the Jefferson County Open High School on a crisp, sunny November day in 1981. The school was then located in Evergreen, Colorado, about 30 miles west of Denver and 2,000 feet higher in elevation. Evergreen's small business district is nestled in the bottom of a canyon. The school was south of the heart of town, on Highway 73—a winding two-lane road. The Open School was housed in a small, single-story, cream-colored building that was built in the 1950s, when Evergreen was still a small mountain town. By 1981 it had become an affluent bedroom community of Denver. The school looked older than its years, in some ways more time-worn than the old Evergreen High School with which it shared a parking lot. The old high school—a turn-of-the-century red brick building with a steep green gable roof—housed a branch office of the County Sheriff on its ground floor; the upper portion of the building had been condemned. The old high school had a substantial look. It was probably the most important building in Evergreen in its day. The Open School's building, just a few yards away, conveyed a different message. It was the sort of basic shelter that results when the city fathers' quest is not for ennobling architecture, but for more square feet.

The Open School's principal in 1981 was Arnie Langberg. His office was inside the entry to the left of the foyer beyond the anteroom that served as the office of the school's secretary, Marilyn Wittebort. On the day I was there, Marilyn, a fashionable woman in her fifties, was wearing jeans and a handsome, close-fitting sweater. Her desk had the look of control central for the whole school. The bulletin board beside it was a haphazard collage of memorabilia and office humor. Signs proclaimed that "An Uncluttered Desk Is the Sign of a Sick Mind!" and "I Know I'm Efficient, Tell Me I'm Beautiful." One of several photographs showed Marilyn posing defiantly at her desk with one foot up on her chair, wearing punk rocker gear.

In the few minutes that I watched her as I waited for Arnie, she deftly fielded a dozen inquiries and requests from the shifting collection of kids and teachers that surrounded her: "Don't you *dare* walk

1

away from this desk with my scissors." "The legal-size paper is on the top shelf of the supply closet—put your hand in that drawer and you lose it—behind the pink eight-and-a-half by eleven." "Students are not allowed in the safe, Ciery.[1] The Surgeon General has even determined that it's *un*safe for them to go in the safe."

During a lull in the action, Marilyn stuck her head in Arnie's office—he was in a meeting—to confer about where to send me first. Then she called to a tall, red-headed boy named Curtis who was talking to friends out in the foyer. She asked him if he could spare a moment to take me to Patrick Headley's class in the Turkey Farm. As we walked, Curtis explained that the Turkey Farm was a classroom on the far side of the school. He didn't know how it had acquired the name. Curtis's long hair was topped by an old felt fedora. He wore a University of Colorado sweatshirt and khaki pants—what we used to call paratrooper pants when I was a kid—that had big, boxy pockets on them at mid-thigh. Curtis's paratrooper pants stopped just above his ankles, revealing a pair of well-worn, black high-top sneakers.

The building was a square with a gym in the middle. A stage that once opened onto the gym had been walled off and converted into a science room. The other three sides of the gym were bordered by corridors that served the classrooms that were lined up around the building's perimeter. Curtis explained that most people cut through the gym, since it was the shortest route to almost anywhere else. We took the long way around, past the sounds of laughing children in the preschool classroom that was—and still is—an adjunct to the school's program. Curtis mentioned that some Open School students do internships in the preschool. As we turned a corner of the square, I said, "I thought the Celtics were the only people who could still find shoes like that."

Curtis grinned. "You can get 'em, if you work at it."

I asked him how it was that he didn't have a class at that time of day. He explained that he only had one class on Tuesdays—in the afternoon. On Tuesday mornings he worked on his Transcript. "We don't have grades," he said, "so we each write these Transcripts. They're long papers describing what we've done in high school. Mine's 25 pages so far. That's what we send to colleges we're applying to."

"Do colleges actually read something that long?" I asked.

Curtis shrugged his shoulders. "They must," he said. "We get in." He dropped me at the Turkey Farm and then cut through the gym, heading back to his friends in the foyer. Pat Headley's class, Colonial American History, was already in progress. Close to 20 students were engaged in all sorts of activities—consulting maps, preparing food lists, and poring over assorted history and travel books and old *National Geographics*.

"The class is in the final stage of preparation for a 17-day, 6,000-mile trip through colonial America," Pat said. He sounded as though he had done it all before. He had, the previous year. This time, though, he and this group of kids had shortened the trip a bit. The southward leg of the previous Evergreen to Boston to St. Augustine triangle would be truncated at Virginia.

"Trips longer than two weeks work okay as long as you're staying put in one spot," he said, "but people begin to wear down when they're constantly on the road."

"How do you pay for all this?" I asked.

"The school district pays for the nine-passenger vans we use and for most of the fuel and maintenance expenses," Pat explained. "It's money that would be spent on coaches and shoulder pads in other high schools. The kids—and staff—have to come up with the money for their food. We buy it in bulk and at discount to keep costs down." He explained that trip groups either camped out or arranged to sleep in schools or homes along the way. He nodded toward a boy and girl at typewriters. "They're writing to alternative schools along our route asking if we can sleep in their schools or in kids' homes when we're in their area. Lodging is free that way, and the kids from both schools learn a lot just talking to each other."

Pat's class put away its materials a little before noon and headed for a temporary building—the "tin building"—next to the school that functioned as an annex. The students and staff ate lunch together. The main course was chiles rellenos. I sat next to Joy Jensen, a heavy-set staff member whose dark hair framed a beautiful face. A native Californian, Joy had been with the school since 1977. The preparation of lunch was an integral part of the school's program, Joy explained, and running "munchie," as the lunch program was called, was her primary responsibility. Munchie relied on pitch-in help from students. They planned the menu, prepared and served the meal, and washed the dishes; if nobody volunteered to cook on a particular day, nobody ate.

As we talked, I learned other things about the school. The curriculum contained only two required courses.[2] Joy explained that every student had an advisor. "Staff members are asked to keep about a third of their time free to meet with students individually," she said.

As a boy began wiping off tables that had been vacated, Joy continued describing the day-to-day routine of the school. "The staff shares the responsibilities of running the school," she said. "We meet every Wednesday morning from 8:00 to 10:30." She explained that the school day started at 9:15; for an hour and 15 minutes every Wednesday, the school ran without teachers. Joy excused herself to check on how dish-washing was proceeding and I headed back to the main building.

I wandered around the school by myself in the afternoon. I passed the open doors of several classes. Informal conversations spilled out into the hall. Kids sat in small groups on the hall's carpeted floor, mostly just talking but occasionally discussing school-related issues: a protest demonstration that had occurred near Boulder the previous Sunday, and where the assigned reading for a literature class was located in the school's library. There were several Apple computers scattered throughout the building, all being used by kids doing word processing. One of the things I knew about the school before my visit was that it took on all comers, regardless of their motivational or ability levels or past school history. Not all the kids I was encountering looked busy, but there was no hint, even when the idle saw me approaching, that they thought they were doing anything wrong.

Near the end of the school day I visited Susie Bogard's art class. Her door, like all the others, was open. Disorganized piles of student projects and art materials occupied almost every available surface in the crowded room. Susie noticed me and came over. We stood in the quiet of the hall just outside the door, but I had no sense that she had taken up that position in order to keep an eye on the kids.

"There are a lot of things about this school I can't believe," I said. "Tell me more about these trips."

"They're the core of a number of classes each year," she told me, as she nodded hello to a couple of passing girls. "They make learning a personal venture rather than someone else's assignment." Her eyes were still following the two girls. She seemed to be collecting and filing away some piece of information about them even as we talked. One girl was tall, wearing a bright print dress and hose and low heels. The other was short and wore an old Eisenhower jacket that was several sizes too big. Its shoulder insignia displayed the big white "1" of the First Division. The girl's well-worn Levis had probably once belonged to a boy: the threadbare outline of a billfold still showed on a now-empty hip pocket. Susie continued talking as the girls moved off down the hall.

"I've got a class that's beginning to fall apart right now because the group has just determined that the trip it's been planning isn't going to happen," she said. Her gaze once again returned to me. "It's going to cost too much to go to China."

The Study and the School

I remember the day I first learned of the Open School. I felt as though I'd found *my* school. To be accurate, the school had found me. Arnie Langberg and his wife, Dag, walked into my office at Indiana. Arnie was of average build and had wiry brown hair. Wire-rimmed glasses framed alert eyes. I had surmised that Dag was Scandinavian, mostly because of Arnie's reference to a period he and Dag had spent in Sweden. But Dag was short for Dagnija, not Dagmar, and she was born in Latvia. The exact day of their visit is easy to remember. The previous evening, Indiana had just won its fourth NCAA basketball championship and Ronald Reagan had been shot on the steps of the Washington Hilton. The regulars down at Smittie's were making bets about which event would be headlined when Bloomington's *Herald Telephone* hit the newsstands. (The Hurryin' Hoosiers got the nod.) I wouldn't know it for years, but the seed of the idea to study the Open School intensely had most certainly been planted that day.

The Langbergs and I had just begun to talk when *Newsweek* called trying to track down Arnie for an interview. John Hinckley, Jr. — Reagan's would-be assassin — was from Evergreen. The reporter's previous call had confirmed that Hinckley hadn't gone to Evergreen High and had referred the reporter to the Open School. Arnie informed him that Hinckley hadn't attended the Open School either and hung up. The call amused Arnie; he joked that someone in town probably concluded that anyone as crazy as Hinckley *must* have attended the Open School, and that was why the reporter had been set on Arnie's trail.

MY GOAL in writing this book is to involve readers in the life of the Open School, much as I was for an entire school year. I hope the story of the school comes through in these pages. It is a compelling story; the school challenges most people's conceptions of a public high school. I also hope that readers will learn some important lessons from the school, just as I most certainly have. In an attempt to facilitate that process, I have clustered the descriptions of events that occurred in the life of the school during my year in it into six groups. I call each of these groups of vignettes a "lesson" because that is what each represents for me—a collection of experiences that challenged one concept I embraced about how to educate teenagers, just as I suspect each of these lessons will challenge the concepts held by many readers of this book.

General Procedures

I spent the entire 1987–88 school year as an unpaid, "half-time" staff member at the school. I carried a load of six advisees, taught classes, attended all staff meetings, served on several school committees, and participated in four school trips. I would describe my presence in the school as being much closer to full-time than half-time, however; only on rare occasions was I able to steal away for a half-day of uninterrupted writing.

My research observations were seldom formally arranged; rather, I experienced events in the school in much the same way as any other member of the school community, as part of my day-to-day work in the school.

I interviewed every full-time staff member and several part-time staff members and volunteer teachers for an hour or more. Details of my interviewing procedures are described in the Appendix. Some staff members were interviewed as many as four times. All told, I conducted 30 interviews with 23 individuals who worked in the school. Included in this group were two volunteer teachers, an intern, and a student teacher. Staff members knew from the outset that I might use their real names in this book, but only if—after inspecting the review copy of the manuscript—they voted unanimously by secret ballot to permit it.

Forty-two students were also interviewed individually. In several cases, particularly with my six advisees, I conducted two or three interviews, months apart. Most of the student interviews, however, were conducted by a research team that I assembled from within the school community. My interest in enlisting "insiders"—and particularly students—was that their intimate view of the school would lend these interviews a flavor that I could not hope to create. I hired a team of five individuals—two staff members and three graduating seniors—and then trained them in standard interviewing techniques.[1] The team and I then constructed an interview guide that ensured that each interviewee's views on several key issues would be collected. A summary of that guide is located in the Appendix. My own interviews with students generally occurred in situations where I was interested in collecting their versions of particular events that had become of interest to me. Occasionally I also interviewed students in small groups about an experience that they had all shared. All told, approximately 20 students were interviewed in small groups.

I also interviewed six educational professionals, including three Jefferson County Schools administrators who had varying degrees of contact with or knowledge of the school, but no continuous involvement in it. Although I interviewed a few parents and had dozens of less formal interchanges with parents throughout the year, the systematic collection of parents' views of the school was beyond the scope of the study.

Throughout the text, material quoted from any of the interviews will be cited parenthetically by date, in the form: "(Int. 3/88)."

My Background and Biases

I make no claims of objectivity. I may be able to contain my biases, but I cannot eliminate them. Because in this study I was the primary instrument for the collection of information about the school, readers may find some information about me useful in judging the veracity of my descriptions of events. Because my biases influenced what I judged to be important information about the school, let me share them, as I understand them.

I began my year in the school very much looking forward to the experience; in a way it would be the consummation of a 6-year love affair with the school that started with that first visit in 1981. But I also began the year with considerable trepidation. I had not taught teenagers since 1967, when I left the suburbs of Cleveland to pursue a doctorate at the University of Texas. Indeed, my lengthening hiatus from public school teaching had become an awkward reality that loomed larger with each passing year. As the public schools changed, teaching undergraduates how to be effective agents in them had begun to feel more and more like a charade. During my first years at Indiana, when a student would occasionally challenge my views, I could always retreat—as a last resort—to the lame justification, "I've been there." I had increasingly avoided that defense as the probability grew that some student might snicker, "When?" The Open School would be a year-long refresher course for me.

I could have undergone that kind of professional overhaul almost anywhere, even at Bloomington High School South, where my two sons sometimes flourished, sometimes languished in pursuing what passes for a good American high school education. But I wanted more. I wanted to learn as much from my year as I could, not only about myself as a retreaded teacher of adolescents, but about the potential of the schooling process. No school I could identify anywhere in the country presented more promise in that respect than the Open School. I saw my year in the school as an opportunity not only to reload my pedagogical guns but also to improve their aim. And I would do it in a setting that a visiting evaluator once called "the future."[2] My own view of the school, then and now, is tersely summarized in the assessment of one Open School student, who once described it as "a real logical way to have a school" (Sweeney, 1983, p. 238).

And so I began my experience wondering if any school could really be as good as I thought this one was. I was prepared for some disappointments; I knew the Open School wasn't Utopia. But in the months leading up to my departure for Evergreen I still heard myself from time to time describing the Open School to friends as the most interesting high school—even as the *best* public high school—in the country, usually being careful to confine my comparison to the few hundred schools of which I had some direct knowledge. I had built a trap for myself from which only an extraordinary school could free me.

Before my year in the school my contacts with it had been few, but I had always felt as though I belonged among its people, and I began my year again feeling very welcome. I'd never been around a group of professionals whose values and style were so compatible with my own, who seemed to accept me so unconditionally. During my entire year in the school, that feeling never left me for long.

The Setting

The Jefferson County Public School District, called "Jeffco" for short, was created in 1950 when 39 small rural, mountain, and suburban Denver districts were consolidated into one county-wide district covering almost 800 square miles.[3] Jeffco grew at a breakneck pace in the early 1960s, an era in which Washington was spending lots of money on education. The atmosphere led Lawrence M. Watts, then Jeffco's assistant superintendent, to boast:

> Jeffco isn't going to build just an experimental school. We want to build an experimental school system. Most schools don't like to go all the way. They want to leave things as they are, and then add special programs for the gifted or the disadvantaged. Whatever we try out we expect to use for every student. We're going to get a different kind of kid with a different

kind of attitude. None of us fully understand [sic] it, but that's what's going to happen. (Schrag, 1965, p. 242)

Peter Schrag spent four months of 1965 touring the country, visiting and writing about the nation's schools in all their diversity. After his travels, he wrote that Jeffco "may well be the most exciting public school system in the United States" (p. 242). The Open School was created near the end of this heady period in the district's history.

I've already described the Open School's building. Readers also may wish to gain some sense of the town of Evergreen, where the school was located until 1989. The school and the town had an unusual relationship. In some ways the school was very much a part of the town. The Open School was started at the behest of parents of the Evergreen Open Living School—a prekindergarten through ninth-grade program that was started in the early 1970s. (The school's name was changed to Tanglewood Open Living School when it was moved in 1978 to Golden, 25 miles east of Evergreen.)[4] Many of the parents who were most active in starting the high school in 1975 were from the Evergreen area. Seeking to have their children's informal mode of education continue beyond ninth grade, they approached the Jeffco school board about starting a high school and received permission to conduct a national search for a principal. They found Arnie, an MIT-trained engineer who became a teacher to avoid the Korean War draft and got hooked on working with kids. He was principal of a public alternative school in Great Neck, Long Island.

A second national search, this one for teachers, produced over 200 applicants whom Arnie and a group of 25 parents, teachers, and students eventually winnowed down to the school's first six teachers. The school's close ties to the Evergreen community were maintained in several ways—particularly through the many community service efforts that Open School students performed in and around Evergreen—until the school moved to Lakewood after this study was conducted.

But in other ways the school stood apart from the community. Most of its students—about 60%—came to this public school of choice from elsewhere in Jefferson County, an area two-thirds the size of Rhode Island. Some students rode school buses for over 4 hours a day to commute to the school, which I took to be a most tangible sign of their commitment to the program. The relationships between many of these "commuters" and the community of Evergreen may have been little more than what each saw of the other through school bus windows or in local fast-food restaurants.

The school's location in this affluent town often led those just learning of the school to presume that it was a place for rich kids, an elite private school masquerading in public school garb. That convenient but demonstrably incorrect image of the school was reinforced when they learned of the school's extraordinary trips. The school's demographics, however, paint a very different picture. At the time of the study, for example, school district personnel estimated that, by the time they left high school, 70% of Jeffco's students no longer lived with both natural parents.[5] Rick Lopez, who handled applications and maintained school records and therefore probably knew the Open School's demographics better than any other staff member, estimated that the school's broken-family rate was closer to 85%.[6] Many of these homes were strong, supportive places, but others were chaotic in one way or another. All of them were different from the traditional nuclear family that existed in the era when the idea of big comprehensive high schools was conceived. So an image of the school's students as products of affluent, stable, suburban families is unfounded. Very few of the Evergreen kids who attended the school at the time of the study were from the town's more affluent families; it may have been that those upper middle-class parents who knew about the school at all viewed it as a dubious path to the high aspirations they held for their children.

The town itself is distinctive. I remember the immediate impressions of it that I formed on my first visit as I drove over the ridge on Highway 74, down the hill and around the bend, along the shore of Evergreen Lake, and into a narrow canyon with Main Street crowded into it. Evergreen had a quaintness that held a strange familiarity for me; I had seen it before. It took a few moments for me to make the connection, but I was looking at a model railroad layout like the one that had gradually taken over my small room when I was a boy. The layout had grown over the years; the room hadn't. With space at a premium I had to pack buildings and roads and additional right-of-way and a lake into very tight quarters. As I ran out of room for expansion, I exploited the space above my plywood plain by creating steep mountains that seemed to defy the laws of gravity and the forces of erosion. These steep slopes became the sites of tunnels and waterfalls and buildings precariously perched on rock outcroppings high above the town. While each object in the landscape—crafted with a discerning eye toward detail—looked real, the impact of the whole as it climbed toward my ceiling did not. The mountain terrain in which Evergreen's Main Street exists had confined and shaped the growth of the street as surely as the four walls of my bedroom had confined and shaped my railroad layout, and the results were not dissimilar. Each building looked realistic, but the totality of the scene had that same sense of unreality for me.

It was the Colorado gold rush of 1858 that first drew white men to Evergreen.[7] They would stop there on their way up the old Soda Creek toll road from the railhead at Morrison. Some would stay long enough to accumulate a grubstake, often working in one of the area's six saw-mills, and then head up to Clear Creek or South Fork or South Park to try their luck with pan or pick. Others would take a liking to life in Evergreen and trade their dreams of untold riches for a dry roof over their heads and steady pay. They'd lay claim to a 160-acre tract of some of Evergreen's less vertical terrain and establish homesteads.

In 1987, Main Street still bore the remnants of that turn-of-the-century ranching and lumbering town of 200 inhabitants. But even the remnants were slowly disappearing. A fire in 1926 had wiped out a major portion of old Evergreen. Contemporary kitsch was gradually destroying the rest. Main Street competed for the scarce canyon bottom with Bear Creek, which until Amos Post moved his general store there, some time around 1870, had had the town's tight mountain canyon all to itself. The street had become a narrow thoroughfare of commercial establishments: gift and curio shops that catered to the weekend tourist trade, more mundane businesses like the AutoPro parts store and the Bell Telephone building, and franchise operations like Baskin and Robbins. The stream still ambled through granite boulders and pine trees in spots, right alongside the street. But in other places, it was forced underground beneath asphalt parking lots and drive-through banking facilities. Despite being a universally treasured remnant of the town's historic ambience, Bear Creek couldn't repel the unrelenting march of commerce. Any model railroader understands the problem.

The canyon was so tight that no cross streets were possible for most of the course of the business district. Some houses, on short cross alleys, were built not so much behind the business fronts of Main Street as above them. Two intersections less than a mile apart effectively marked the two ends of the commercial strip. In either direction out of town along Bear Creek, one passed 50- and 60-year-old houses that once were the summer retreats of Denver's upper class. A few of Evergreen's old summer homes fronted by formidable gates that were closed with the first September snows still served as seasonal retreats. But as improved roads—especially the completion of Interstate 70—and reliable automobiles expanded the scope of Denver's influence, most of these grand old homes became year-round residences. Built of the granite and timber that surround them, they looked a part of the landscape. They had been joined, in recent years, by hundreds of new houses, as ranch after ranch in the Evergreen area gave way to yet another suburban subdivision. Crowded onto tiny lots on the mountain slopes, these new interlopers, many built in ski-lodge cliché, were an ever-present reminder of what Evergreen had become. Over the past century a town that had been shaped by the hands of ranchers and mountain people was transformed by the hands of real estate developers into an upscale bedroom community of Denver with a population of 20,000.

The Open School at the time of the study was part of this ever-changing Evergreen, but it also stood apart from it in numerous ways. The school also stood apart from the high schools with which most of us are familiar. It is those differences—really the differences between this school and almost every other public high school in America—that made it such a fascinating place for me to study and to learn from.

Columbus in the New World

It would be inaccurate to say that when I was first confronted with the Open School in 1981 I glimpsed my ideal school. Many things going on at the Open School—extended trips, the abandonment of not only grades but graduation credits, kids constituting majorities on key committees—weren't features of my ideal. I'd never considered them as possibilities. In that sense the school was a disorienting experience; it was as though a switch had been thrown that day that permanently changed my understanding of *school*. I thought often about the school over the months following that first visit, never quite reconciling it with everything else that I knew about schools. A breakthrough of sorts occurred when I reread James Herndon's book about life in a junior high school, *How to Survive in Your Native Land* (1971), and I made an unlikely connection between my disorientation that day at the Open School and Herndon's account of Christopher Columbus in the New World. Because it became a recurring metaphor during my year-long struggle to understand the school, I share it here.

Herndon describes the way the great explorer, thinking he had reached India, tried to figure out why the strangers he was encountering weren't acting like Indians. It drove him crazy. He finally gave up on finding spices and silks and looked for gold. Columbus figured—in Herndon's words—"from Old World premises that [the Carib and Arawak chiefs] knew where the gold was [hidden] but naturally wouldn't tell him. It never penetrated his mind that they really didn't have any" (pp. 36–37). When, during a sailing trip far from land, Columbus came across some large canoes full of elaborately and brightly dressed natives, he again didn't know what to make of them.

> [Columbus] knew that the natives of the New World didn't go out of sight of land. He mentioned them in dispatches as an oddity, something else trying to drive him out of his mind, intimated that they were crazy, and forgot them. . . . I don't think that Columbus ever found out that those seagoing businessmen were most likely Aztecs, possessors in nearby Mexico City of all the gold in the world. (p. 37)

It occurred to me that, like Columbus trying to understand the New World using Old World rules, I hadn't coped well with my introduction to the Open School because I thought I was visiting a school. I wasn't, really. At least it wasn't any semblance of a school that I had ever seen. But if I conceived that initial experience at the school as that of an explorer in a New World, it somehow became easier to understand the setting and consequently to learn from it. Seen from that perspective the school began to make sense to me, at least intellectually—from the eyebrows up. But periodically throughout the year I continued to struggle to make the crazy things that the school did feel okay from the viscera down. At those times I would again think of Columbus and remind myself that in some ways the culture of this little school was markedly different from that of any other school I had ever experienced.

Most visitors to the Open School face a similar challenge: trying to understand its culture without judging it by the values of the schools with which they are familiar. In many ways a visitor enters a new world just as Christopher Columbus did when he landed in the midst of a group of tropical islands that he would do his best to rationalize as India.

Lesson 1

(RE)CONNECTING

Human beings have strong needs to belong, to feel as though they are part of something bigger than themselves. These needs are even stronger among adolescents. Schools—even that subset that we might identify as small, informal schools—differ widely in the effort they expend in inducting newcomers into the school community. For some of these schools, entry is little more than a processing, the completion of impersonal forms; perhaps the school secretary softens the procedure with a welcoming smile. Other schools conduct orientation sessions or make sure that an older student shows the newcomer around.

The Open School, in contrast, expended great effort—more than any other school I've seen—in attempting to bond new students to the school and to at least one key adult, the student's advisor. Bonding was accomplished through the Wilderness Backpacking Trip, a required experience for all beginning students. The importance the staff placed on these four days spent hiking above the 9,000-foot level is evidenced by the fact that it was one of the school's very few universal requirements. In this section we will follow one trail group that begins the year as a collection of strangers and first plans and then undergoes the trial entailed in this experience. Our attention will focus on one new student, Inge Pedersen, as she tries to define her place in the Open School community.

The more different a school's program is from the norm, the more consciously it must strive to orient new students to its modes of operation. The Open School devoted almost the entire first block—8 weeks—of the school year to this task. "Beginnings," the school's name for its orientation to the New World, was the Open School's only required class. Some staff members viewed it as a disorientation, a process of throwing off old habits—passivity, docility, and an acceptance of depersonalization—learned in other schools. Beginnings attempted to convey one overarching concept to new students: what it means to be a self-directed learner.

15

For many years the Open School structured a student's first experiences in the school around *two* required courses. Beginnings, as it was then structured, grouped students by Advising group. The Wilderness Backpacking Trip was the course's central activity. Its primary goal was to help kids build an attachment to a small group of students and to one staff member—their temporary advisor—and thus bond to the school. Beginnings lasted only a few weeks. The second required course—Self-Directed Learning, or S.D.L.—followed directly on the heels of Beginnings. Two Advising groups and their advisors would combine forces for S.D.L. so that kids could begin broadening their connections to the school. My impression is that the old S.D.L.'s content focused much more on the individual student as a learner than did the interest groups that were being tried for the first time during my year in the school. S.D.L. classes, as staff members described them to me, were introspective experiences that included much self-analysis: What do I want out of a high school education? How do I learn best? What am I already good at? Kids would discover their learning styles and become aware of the habits that helped or hindered them in learning.

The Beginnings that I was part of was structured as several interest groups—Adventure (physical challenge), Performance (music, drama, dance), The City (culture, social service agencies, and government), and Spaces and Places, the group that Bruce Andrews, Susie Bogard, and I taught. Each of the other groups was also team-taught. Each new student elected to be in one of these groups or classes. While our focus in Spaces and Places was on building things, our class, like each of the others, was a means to a more important end. Our real goal was to help new kids who had pretty much been told what to do and when to do it through most of their schooling careers begin the sometimes frustrating process of becoming self-directed learners.

But to undo in 8 weeks what had taken the school's newcomers 9 or more years to learn about themselves as students was a major undertaking. Indeed, none of the many approaches to Beginnings that have been tried over the years has been completely successful. And so it was with our attempt. The central activity of the 7-week experience that was Spaces and Places was a 5-day trip to Cortez, Colorado in the four-corners area, where we helped in the ongoing excavation and restoration of a small Anasazi kiva. (Kivas are circular subterranean chambers that the ancient cliff dwellers used for ceremonies and as gathering places in inclement weather.) We also worked on several construction projects around the school, among them completion of the preschool's adventure playground, a project started years earlier, and finishing the smoking porch. We also engaged the kids in the design process through a project that required them to design and then construct a pasteboard scale model of a "rolling home," a personal residence that would fit in the bed of a pickup truck.

To give readers some sense of the trials and tribulations of orienting newcomers to this unusual school, we'll sit in on an F.A.C. that occurred at the end of Block One classes. F.A.C., or Friday Afternoon Club, was the staff's term for its periodic Friday-after-school-get-togethers-over-drinks, usually at one or another of Evergreen's little pubs. This F.A.C. was also a work session, a sort of post mortem that Bruce, Susie, and I conducted of Spaces and Places when we looked back on the just-completed experience and evaluated how effectively we'd oriented our 22 new students to the workings of the Open School.

CHAPTER 1

Saddle Up

On Friday afternoon, the first day of school for beginning students, Inge Pedersen enters the Open School for the first time.[1] There is no formal welcome. That experience occurred earlier in the day when the foyer was a zany panoply of high spirits and boisterous activity as arriving new students were greeted at the door. Veteran students were carrying placards and shouting names, tracking down new additions to their Advising groups whom they were to make a special effort to welcome into the school. The veterans had started their school year two days earlier with an overnight retreat at a church camp. After introductions, they would give each new student a tour of the building, embellishing points of interest along the way with anecdotes drawn from the lore of the Open School. The morning's effort to bring newcomers into the Open School community had been a success. But not for the late-arriving Inge. Thank God for Toby, she thinks. Toby May had been a friend for years. His strong will and energy had pulled her through more than one rough period in her life. Now he was literally dragging her into his school.

The building is nothing to brag about. It looks like a hand-me-down building. Maybe it's also a hand-me-down program? But maybe not. Everywhere, from the art and bumper stickers and posters on lockers to the life-size mural of a humpback whale with its great, blue-green eye peering enigmatically at her through the gym doors, Inge can see the imprint of students upon the school. And she knows how committed Toby is to it. She wouldn't be here now if it weren't for Toby. She'd still be at Adult High, Jeffco's continuation school for older and part-time students. But probably not for long. It wasn't working any better than a long, unbroken chain of prior attempts—some earnest, some half-hearted—to make school work. Inge's school career had started well enough—a hippie kid in a hippie school. But nothing much has worked right since. She'd always been an outsider and Adult High was turning out to be the same old bullshit: teachers trying to make students do stuff they didn't want to do and students playing games, getting by, doing as little as they possibly could.[2]

Inge had been on the Open School's waiting list for years. Her number had finally come up and she was accepted.[3] But as the new school year approached, Adult High looked like it would be less hassle and so she started the year there. Now she wasn't so sure. Here she was after only a couple of days of classes already cutting, coming up into the mountains to visit Toby. Toby for his part had seen enough of this crap from her. He wasn't taking no for an answer this time. He kept telling Inge, as he dragged her into Ruth Steele's office, that the Open School was the place for her. (Ruth succeeded Arnie as principal in 1986.)

Inge wanted no part of it. Once more she'd probably have to undergo a review of her mean past, a string of trying experiences in and out of schools, including her two months on the rolls of Lakewood High during which she hadn't attended a single class. Again she'd probably have to go over her heavy abuse of drugs that had led to her getting slammed into a residential treatment program for most of last year to dry out. Toby's letters and support had never been more critical than during her time at Rolling Meadows. An awfully pretty name for what amounted to a jail, Inge had thought.

Then there was the past year, a progression of part-time jobs—everything from flipping burgers at McDonalds to photographic work for a graphic artist—and the resumption in earnest of old habits. She'd done almost everything except heroin during those months, especially acid. Finally deciding enough was enough, Inge did what Rolling Meadows hadn't been able to do. She cleaned herself out. It hadn't been easy. Several times she almost gave in. Through all her struggles, Inge knew that the life she wanted required an education. Few things were clearer. If Toby had his way, the Open School would be her next stab at getting it.

Ruth's office is a surprise. It's quiet and homey with lots of books that look like they've actually been read, and personal things, maybe from trips she'd been on. Ruth is pleasant enough. Her black hair has flecks of grey. She's dressed casually in slacks and comfortable shoes and has a no-nonsense quality about her. The lady is not a bullshitter. The three of them take seats at a round table at one end of the office. After some small talk Toby's pretty certain Inge's not going to bolt and run and he excuses himself. Ruth turns the conversation to Inge's enrollment in the school. Happily Ruth doesn't drag out everything about her past, but she also isn't at all sure that the Open School is the place for Inge. Her quick flirtation with Adult High, Ruth points out, doesn't indicate much commitment to the school. Inge does her best to play the sincerity game but in fact she isn't at all sure what she wants—or needs.

Finally Ruth decides to let her give the school a try. She gives Inge directions to the Cooler, the little classroom in the tin building where Bill Johnson and I and our trail group already have begun preparations for the Wilderness Trip. The tin building's drabness makes the main building look almost palatial. The two buildings are separated by a wide asphalt sidewalk lined with big, unpruned spruce trees. It looks like it could be a really nice outdoor space but right now it's a no-man's land that people just hurry through, going somewhere else. Inge does too. The tin building, which is sheathed in galvanized steel, is a hodgepodge of rooms with temporary-looking walls that all seem to be in the wrong places. Its traffic pattern is indecipherable. Inge finally figures out where the Cooler is, takes a deep breath, and does her best to slip quietly through the open door into the small, overcrowded room. But a dozen pairs of eyes are all fixed on her. The feeling is familiar; she is already an outsider invading an established group. We even look like a group, all gathered around tables pushed together in tight confines. Inge immediately understands the room's name. Even on this sunny August afternoon, the room is freezing.

I manufacture a quick smile for this small, pretty girl. She has long, straight blonde hair. Her wide mouth and clear blue eyes are expressionless. Inge rightfully ignores my saccharine smile and responds instead to my quizzical expression. She answers the question before it is asked. "I'm Inge Pedersen," she announces. Throughout the day it's been an unembodied name on my roster of six advisees—a no-show. When Ruth handed me my roster at the beginning of the week, she mentioned that Inge was still questionable.[4] I'd given up on ever seeing the person who went with the name, but here she is.

We have just begun discussing our concerns about the Wilderness Trip. Each of us is relating what worries us about attempting it. The trip will be a new experience for most of us—4 days spent with a bunch of strangers, each carrying 40 to 80 pounds of gear up above 11,000 feet and back down. Eleven thousand feet—about the height of Mount Hood. Earlier in the week when the staff was planning the trip, the number had triggered a recollection of the incident a few years back in which several high school kids on a similar expedition had died in a freak snowstorm on the side of Mount Hood *below* that altitude. While the staff continued to discuss the trip, my mind had wandered into a consideration of the risks that the Open School takes as a matter of course.[5]

I have plenty of concerns to call on to model the sharing process for the kids. I try to measure how many of them I dare voice without scaring the hell out of the students. After all, I am supposed to be one of the leaders of this enterprise. So I talk about my Li'l Abners—the big, heavy workshoes I'll wear on the trip, even though they're hardly broken in—and I wonder about how my 47-year-old, out-of-shape body will perform, considering it is equipped with a set of lungs that have spent all but the last week of those years at 900 feet rather than at 9,000. I don't even joke about the recurring image of the kids carrying me out on a litter after the Big One has hit. And I don't let on that I even know that there is a Mount Hood.

After I finish, the kids start in, at first reluctantly and then gradually more freely. Several are heavy smokers concerned about their lung capacity. Most of them know they are out of shape. Sam Laumann was seriously injured in May when he rolled his car. This big, burly, urban kid quietly tells us about his brain surgery. He has a crewcut and is wearing a sleeveless Levi jacket, which reveals impressive tattoos on his under-muscled, milk-white arms. Sam confesses that he lives amid so much concrete and asphalt that even grass looks a little strange to him. He wants to go on the trip and knows it will be good for him, but he's not sure about the injury. As Sam continues I glance over at Bill Johnson. It is Bill who is really leading our trail group. I feel more like a green second lieutenant "leading" a platoon into battle for the first time, hoping that my seasoned top sergeant will get us all out alive. Bill says what I'm thinking: Sam needs to check it out with his doctor before he can go. CJ Ault doesn't have to voice his concern. The full cast on his broken left arm speaks for itself. We ask that he also get an okay from his doctor to participate in the trip.

Inge's turn comes. She has spent the time thinking about the opportunity the trip presents. She has always wanted to do Outward Bound, to really be challenged. In a way all of her substance abuse has been a form of risk taking, working on the high wire without a net. But she is unwilling to risk saying any of this to strangers. She rolls her pack of Camel filters over and over in her small hands, trying to decide *what* to say. Finally she talks about not wanting to leave her cat, which has just had a litter of kittens. Inge feels the need to be around to help the cat watch after them. I study her face for a hint of a smile. She's serious. I'm worried about dying on the side of an alien mountain and Inge's concerned about kittens.

Even though we haven't made it all the way around the group, Inge, needing a dose of nicotine and a change of scene, asks if the group can take a break. We seem to have shared about all the concerns we're willing to and, with some kids silently seconding Inge's motion by standing and stretching and fumbling for cigarettes and generally telling us by their actions that they've had enough, Bill and I say okay.

The 10-minute break turns into 20, an occurrence that is beginning to look like a pattern. These new kids are already running on the loose timetable that everyone refers to as Open School Time. We spend the remainder of the afternoon going over equipment lists, finalizing our meal menus, and making lists of food items to buy on Monday. Over the years, the school has amassed a large supply of camping and backpacking equipment. A portion of each year's budget is devoted to increasing, replacing, and repairing this inventory. Kids without their own equipment can draw on the school's. Two of our boys, Evan and Bert, who talk as though they are quite experienced in the outdoors, seem to have enough equipment for themselves and for the rest of us, too. They are ready to contribute everything from tents to backpacking stoves to large lightweight tarps. Bill is privately wary of their avowed expertise. He has seen the same picture too often, boastful kids who fall apart in the field.

I wonder about one of the two, Bert Lucas, mostly because of his age. At 14, he's younger than the rest of the group and at times acts younger still. Bert is a tuition-paying student from outside the district. Tuition is $2,300-a-year, and three or four students each year attend the school under these circumstances. After a disastrous junior high experience, Bert was given three choices by his divorced parents and their new spouses: go to Cherry Creek High, which looked like it would be more of the same; get shaped up at a military academy; or go to the Open School and see if a really different form of education would turn things around. Since he knows no one in the school, Bert is pressing, straining too hard to make friends too quickly, and his effort is proving counterproductive.

Compiling a food list is the next order of business. Gummy Bears and M&Ms get mentioned enough to become a running joke. Both Bill and Leslie Warren, our student assistant for the trip, keep swinging the group back to nutritious and especially lightweight foods. Finally, the group manages to build a credible menu for the 4 days, and a subcommittee converts it into a shopping list.

Leslie is a safeguard. There *are* limits to the risks even the Open School will take. The school has nicely buttressed the green rookie that I am, teaming me not only with Bill, a retired Air Force Colonel and former parent in the school and a veteran of many Wilderness Trips, but also with Leslie, one of the strongest student assistants available. A second-year student, she's a vivacious, lithe young woman with long sandy hair. She sits with her huaraches up on the edge of the table, her knees tucked up under her chin. Her long print skirt reveals just a bit of her unshaven, tanned legs. Leslie is hardened and bronzed from a month of Outward Bound in Steamboat Springs. Ruth had mentioned to me earlier that the experience would form the core of Leslie's Adventure Passage.[6] She periodically explodes in unbounded enthusiasm, so much so that I worry that it may eventually become a pain rather than an asset. Because she is so experienced, Leslie has a credibility with the group that I envy—a credibility with everyone except Sharon Kelsey, anyway. Sharon and Leslie's mutual disdain goes back to their Tanglewood days.

Sharon's smoldering anger and distrust are the perfect antithesis of Leslie's exuberance. I can't remember a comment Sharon has offered the group that was not a gripe or putdown. Her habit is to lash out with vicious language at anyone who seems the least bit critical of her. She may just be very frightened, but if so she hides it in a very convincing manner. Some doubt persists about whether she will go. She apparently has an asthmatic condition, and if she goes she may have to be brought out of the wilderness early on Friday morning for some sort of minor surgery. She holds back from the group and especially its three leaders to a disconcerting degree. We worry about the effect 4 days of this attitude, out in the middle of nowhere, will have on the group. But Sharon is only the most visible symbol of many problems. As the week ends, too many questions remain about our readiness for the week ahead.

MOST OF MONDAY MORNING is spent at the local Safeway. Even with the school's discount, our bill will come to about $230. Indeed, most of the $25 fee each of us pays for the trip goes for food, with the remainder covering the cost of buses that will get us to and from the Mount Evans Wilderness Area.[7] We're not the only trail group in the store. The school has unleashed dozens of high-spirited teenagers in this one supermarket. They roam the aisles, crashing carts into each other, occasionally taking the opportunity to put down the dumb food choices that another group has made (You bought how many pounds of Gummy Bears?) or wondering why *they* didn't think of taking popcorn. For the checkers and sackers, our invasion is an anticipated annual event, a welcome one-day diversion from the usual routine of shoppers wanting to know why the tomatoes are so bad or when their favorite toilet paper will be restocked. Like the first snowfall or a formation of geese heading north in the spring, the running of the Wilderness Trippers is an annual reassurance to the Evergreen com-

munity that there is an order to the universe.[8] We watch the checker
tally our haul, moving pile after pile of food past the register. After
awhile, she begins to look like she's doing a one-armed sidestroke
through our groceries. Everything is sacked and loaded into my car
and Leslie's cancerous old truck and we all head back to school.

Everyone has brought their packs to school, and the remainder of
the morning is spent figuring out how to equitably distribute the
mound of food on the tables. Each person's carrying capacity is determined by his or her body weight. Since I weigh more than twice what
Inge does, for example, I am expected to carry more than twice her
load. The system, however, is imperfect. The trip is designed to teach
cooperation and helpfulness, neither of which is very evident in our
group at this point. After everyone has taken what he or she considers
to be a fair share of the load, a significant number of particularly heavy
items—things like jars of peanut butter and spaghetti sauce and a bottle of maple syrup—remain, orphans abandoned in the expanse of Formica before us. No one will even look at them. After a time Bill takes
the lead in modeling a spirit of pitching in by adding some heavy items
to his already overburdened pack. I follow suit, thinking again about
the Big One. The awkward minutes that follow turn us into suckers.
No one else, not even Leslie, makes a move to emulate our sacrifice.
We end the morning on a down note as Bill comments to a stone-faced
group that we'll leave the remaining items behind if no one can carry
them, even if it means running out of food on the trail.

The afternoon is spent adjusting everyone's pack. The packs of a
couple of the smaller girls, Inge and Jane Solomon, are particular
problems. Their packs are too tall for their petite torsos. We do the
best we can to make them fit, but they may prove a problem on the
trail. Sharon's pack is more a day pack than a real backpack. Its small
size means she can carry almost no food. I consider her asthma and
wonder if the pack may be a blessing in disguise. We do manage to
find room for most of the food and then finish the day with some final
group building activities: trust falls, group knots, and other activities
designed to build trust and a sense of group. We will have to depend
on each other a great deal over the next 4 days and we each need to
learn that we can.

After the kids leave for the day, Bill and I put our feet up and
consider where we are. Bill's white hair and weathered features make
him look more grandfatherly than his mid-fifties age. He first knew
the school during its early years when he was an active parent watching his son, Keith, grow and benefit from the program. Bill was still a
colonel in the Air Force then, back in his home state after long stints

in London and Korea. With his retirement in 1979 after 24 years of service, he began looking for ways to productively fill his time. He applied for a 10-hour-a-week, $2.80-an-hour teacher's aide slot at the school. Though he was the only candidate for the job, the kids on the hiring committee, suspicious that his military background was evidence that a raving authoritarian lurked beneath his amiable exterior, put him through a grueling interview process before giving him the nod.[9] Bill has worked almost full-time in the school ever since. For years he worked toward achieving teacher certification so that he might eventually apply for a professional position, but having come to value the freedom his present arrangement offers him, he has cooled on that idea in recent years and now seems content to remain an aide.

I've known Bill, who completed a master's degree with me at Indiana, almost as long as I've known Arnie and Dag. Knowing what his answer will be, I ask him if he thinks we're ready. He's anything but confident. The main reason for the rush is that the wilderness area supports many interests besides backpacking. One of these is black powder hunting, guys sneaking around the woods with muzzle-loading rifles trying to bag an elk or deer in the tradition of Davey Crockett. The opening of black powder season has been moved up this year. We can't postpone the trip to the end of the short season because we would almost surely encounter snow. A later start also gives reluctant kids time to conjure up "legitimate" excuses to get out of the trip. To eliminate the risk of running into a near-sighted zealot who can't tell a teenager from a 12-point buck, the trip has been moved up a week from previous years. The problem with the change is the way in which it has shortened preparation time. Instead of a solid week of orientation to the school and preparation for the trip, we have had 2 days. We have traded one form of reasonable and prudent behavior—a standard phrase in the Open School's trip lexicon—for another. To avoid catching a 225-grain lead ball, we have shortchanged the careful, systematic planning and group building that typify the school's preparation for a trip. The short time has led Bill and me—I'm not sure if by circumstance or preference—to make most of the decisions for the group. As a result we have almost no experience in group decision making. Worse, we will go into the woods tomorrow hardly knowing each other.

WE REACH THE WILDERNESS AREA shortly before noon. Everybody has eaten sack lunches on the short bus trip here. Two groups, Jeff Bogard's and ours, will enter at this particular trail head and then quickly part ways, as Jeff's group takes one of the toughest routes available. Another

10 groups, each containing 10 or 12 new students led by one staff member and a student assistant or two, simultaneously launch their expeditions all over the wilderness area. Our trail will start as a gradual climb for a day and a half to the top of Rosalie Pass. Only then, as we head down the other side, will we encounter tough, steep conditions—on the way *down*. Again, the school is covering its bets on the green rookie.

Toby is a student assistant for Jeff's group; while group pictures are taken to document the outset of the trek, Inge spends a last few minutes kidding around with her best friend and getting in one last smoke before we start.

Finally it's time. Despite cautions to stay together, the exuberance of some of the kids, particularly Evan, Bert, and Inge, and the reluctance of others, especially Sharon, cause us to quickly spread out along the trail. Again we're not functioning as a group. Bill is trying to stay near the front and I elect to bring up the rear, doing my best to walk slower than Sharon, who is barely moving, punctuating every step with complaints about conditions and the trip in general. One statement—"I was fuckin' stupid to even come on this fuckin' trip"—pretty well captures the gist of her continuing soliloquy. As she inches up the trail, Sharon drags her water container, a puny little Cub Scout canteen, on the ground behind her. We had asked each student to carry at least a quart of water. Sharon's canteen may hold half that. I occasionally try to get her to enjoy the scenery and move a bit faster (all the while saying silent thanks for what the easy pace is doing for me and the Big One), but it's wasted effort.

The trail ambles gently upward following a stream. Often the path is wide enough for two or three to walk abreast, but occasionally we wind our way, single file, through boulder fields. Bill calls to the pace setters up ahead, suggesting that they find a spot for our first rest break. They are on their second cigarette by the time Sharon and I reach the glade by the stream where they have selected to stop. As kids drag on their smokes, we talk about staying closer together. Nobody suggests that Sharon move faster; we've all had enough of her angry retorts to criticism. Rather we talk about slowing people down to a "group pace."

Marty Robinson flops on the stream bank and plunges his long brown hair into the icy waters. Bert joins him and, while messing around the edge, manages to fall in above his knees. It's still early afternoon and warm, but Bill cautions the group about the way temperatures will drop—perhaps below freezing—after the sun goes down. Staying dry is a prime requisite to avoiding exposure and hypothermia.

I try to read their faces, looking for clues that they're listening. We encourage everyone to drink plenty of water to avoid dehydration, which can sneak up quickly at this altitude. Everyone drinks some water, but the kids all know that they'll have to start treating stream water with iodine when they use up their current supply. Too much rationing is going on in the hope of forestalling the inevitable. Sharon drinks some water, too—mine. Although her little canteen lies within reach, she asks for a sip of my water bottle, which is still open. Searching for an edge to begin building a friendship with her, I comply.

We set out again and after a time gradually begin to close our ranks to the point where we're all within sight of each other, everyone except Sharon and me. At a rest stop Bill and I privately discuss her slow pace. I suggest moving ahead of her, beginning to leave her behind, to see if the ploy will speed her up. Bill thinks it's a bad idea. He has seen kids simply quit and head back down the trail in such circumstances. We do trade places, though. He'll take a turn at tripping over Sharon's canteen.

Sam is also a concern. He isn't looking good and he's getting a headache. We've ascended less than a thousand feet, but it may be the beginning of altitude sickness, which, as I understand it, is caused by pressure differences inside and outside the skull. Because of Sam's recent surgery, Bill and I caution him not to be a hero. We are only a couple of hours into the trip and it will be no trouble for one of us to walk him out if he's got a problem.

The next rest stop comes quickly. Sam has plopped on a granite boulder in real distress, not only from pain but from having to give up on the trip. He isn't a quitter and his bitter disappointment is evident. The group talks over the situation. Sam will have to go out. Bill will take him, carrying Sam's pack for him, and will drive him home in the emergency vehicle we've left at the trail head for just such an occurrence. We apportion Sam's share of the food throughout the rest of the group, with too many again unwilling to share in the additional burden. Evan finally picks up most of what's left. Before departing with Sam, Bill hides his pack beside the trail for pick-up on his return.

Bill had recently scouted our trail and had come across a great spot for our first night's campsite. The problem is its distance, perhaps 4 miles up the trail. As fatigue sets in, our rest stops get longer and closer together. The bickering escalates. The kids begin asking when we will stop for the night. I'm doing a crummy job of sharing decision making with the group, but this doesn't seem the time to reform. I'm afraid that if I do, the kids' decision will be to stop right here, a particularly inhospitable stretch where the trail has separated from the stream. What has become my pet phrase to end each rest period, "Okay, let's saddle up," is becoming a major irritant for the group. But, like a pun so bad it induces a groan, I can't resist using it just because of the rise it produces in the group.

For the last three rest stops, I've been watching CJ struggle uncomplainingly with only one good arm to remount his pack when it's time to continue. I simulate the task with my own pack and find it so demanding that I can scarcely accomplish it. Inge is beginning to have pack problems, too: Too much of the weight she's carrying is riding on her hips, and they are being rubbed raw. Nevertheless, like CJ, she suffers her discomfort without much complaint. And so we are a diverse group in yet one more way, ranging from Sharon, carrying the lightest pack and doing the most bitching, to Evan, who is gradually becoming a pack horse, to CJ, who doesn't even comment about real duress.

With darkness approaching and the smell of rain in the air, it's clear we need to find a campsite soon. The trail finally rejoins the stream and we come upon a good spot, perhaps a mile short of our original destination. Stopping here has the added advantage of shortening Bill's return trip. A few drops of rain begin to fall, so we quickly make camp, gather wood, and get a fire going. Evan has brought his huge, bright blue tarp; it takes on real value as we stretch it high among the trees over a considerable portion of the campsite.

Bill is scheduled to cook the first night's dinner—a chicken stir fry that is his gift to the group, sort of. We can't change the schedule because the chicken is a perishable that won't last another day. We will have to wait—we don't know how long—for Bill's return. In the meantime the kids go crazy over the M&Ms and manage to drink up almost the entire week's supply of hot chocolate mix in about an hour. Someone—Terry Dodge, I think—has turned the campfire conversation to minority groups. The kids, each desperate to feel an integral part of this nascent group, take turns at a particularly vicious version of "Can You Top This?" in which just about every minority and subset of minority, including white trash, is vilified in what may be the most bigoted, racist conversation I have ever experienced. "Fuckin' niggers" and "greasy spics" and "goddamn Cubans" and "dirty Puerto Ricans" and "drunken Indians" and you name it each take their turn getting excoriated through the telling of some conflict or confrontation the kids or an acquaintance has had. It's really a feeding frenzy of sorts, feeding their need to feel better than at least some others and, more important, their need to belong. I oscillate between walking away from the group when I can't take anymore venom and returning to try to interject yet another observation about the particularly ugly brand of inhumanity they are displaying. Fleeing isn't helping me and my comments aren't affecting them. Finally the glut of bigotry ends. The conversation has worn itself out. Happily, Jews somehow have been neglected in the verbal carnage. With two Jews in the group, I'm not sure what would have happened to the rest of the trip if they hadn't been.

Inge suggests that some of us head back down the trail and collect Bill's pack so he won't have to carry it back himself. It sounds good to me if Leslie is one of the people to go. She's game, as is Evan, who apparently hasn't yet carried enough today. Inge has brought a cold with her on the trip, but despite a hacking cough that is painful to hear, she will join the expedition. We make sure they've got good flashlights and they take off with a couple of empty packs in tow in which to distribute Bill's load. In their absence the rest of us do what we can to begin preparations for dinner.

The trio returns in about an hour to the cheers of the group. They've been sharing Bill's load three ways and are duly impressed that he has been carrying such a burden alone. We barely have welcomed back the kids when Bill emerges out of the darkness into the warm glow of the fire. His return is cause for more celebration from the famished assembly.

An hour later we have finished off what we *know* must be the best meal any of the trail groups scattered throughout the wilderness will have on any night of the trip. After clean-up we gather around the campfire, gazing into the coals and enjoying each other's company. The kids reminisce about other campfires they've experienced with family or friends. Hunting and fishing trips and Girl Scout outings are recalled. The heat on our faces contrasts sharply with our freezing backsides. The temperature is dropping steadily. As it does, everyone begins adding layers of clothing. Some of the kids may not have brought enough heavy stuff with them.

Leslie suggests we play a game that involves a magic pot. Each of us in turn takes something from the imaginary pot that we need to make the trip go better for us and we put something in as our gift or wish for the group. It is indeed a magic pot. I watch, dumfounded, as the hatred and intolerance of the earlier diatribe is replaced by perhaps the most loving, caring conversation I have ever heard from a group of teenagers. Leslie offers her enthusiasm and asks for understanding from the group. A couple of the kids put love in the pot. Sharon asks for help in reducing her bitching. During the activity, Tony Simms, to the gasps of the smokers in the group, dashes his cigarettes in the fire, vowing that he has taken his last smoke. At an earlier age Tony's was a four-packs-a-day habit, so we know it will be no easy task for him to maintain his resolve.[10] He asks our help in doing so.

Terry, who was a prime instigator of the earlier orgy of bigotry, suggests a second exercise in which we each tell three truths and one lie about ourselves. The group then tries to guess which statement is the lie. The exercise is a chance for us to test how much we are each willing to risk being known to the group. We learn that a younger sister is a junkie and that Bill has flown at mach 2.4 and that various relatives have performed impressive or outlandish feats. Bert participates but continually plays in the fire, poking coals and creating fly ash that gets all over everybody. As the gentle rain resumes, we gradually begin turning in for the night. Sleeping arrangements are coed in the New World, the operant rule being that at least three students must share a tent. Knowing my bladder, I grab a spot by the opening of a four-person tent that five of us will share. My spot is next to Inge and her terrible cough. I have the feeling that before the week is out it will be one more thing the group will have in common. But right now as the lulling rain falls above our heads, what's most important is that we've made it through our first day together.

WE AWAKE TO THE SMELL of bacon frying. The sun has not yet reached the bottom of the valley and it's cold. All night, our warm, moist breath has been condensing on the frigid tent walls and anything in contact with them is now soggy. As people arise they stretch their wet belongings out on the driest places they can find, hoping things will dry at least a little before we pack and break camp. Inge hasn't brought many warm clothes and she's a comical sight, stumbling out of the tent in shorts over long johns. She's hardly out of the tent when she lights up a Camel. Our group is divided into several work parties, each with its responsibilities—cooking, clean-up, or gathering firewood—on a given day. Inge seems glad she's not on the cook crew this morning. Her cough didn't let her sleep very well and she's starting the day tired.

After a leisurely breakfast of bacon and eggs we sit around the fire, sipping coffee and the last of the week's ration of hot chocolate and then begin breaking camp. We talk through the plan for the day, which is to get up and over Rosalie Pass, work our way down the other side, and make camp in the next valley. I had walked the last miles of our trail the previous weekend with Roberta Page, another staff member, and found a great campsite beside a small pond. It's a long way, though, probably 5 miles, most of which is the steepest trail we will travel. I risk another "saddle up" and we are about to set out when one of the kids notices a backpacking stove still sitting in the middle of the clearing. No one admits to having responsibility for it. A now too familiar, awkward silence builds as we wait for the culprit to own up, but no one does. Evan, exasperated at the continuing delay, swoops it up and starts stamping up the trail, tying the stove onto the outside of his pack as he goes; there is no possibility of stowing it inside. The rest of us fall in behind his angry pace.

Inge and I end up walking side by side for awhile, talking. She wonders why someone would just leave the stove for the rest of us to carry. Trying to be philosophical and objective as 70 pounds begin to bite into my shoulders for another day, I talk about one purpose of the trip being to learn how to deal with adversity as a group. Her clear eyes probe me. "What's adversity?" she asks. I know little more about Inge than what she shared around the campfire the previous night, but I am nevertheless struck by the irony of a young woman who has experienced so much of it in her life not knowing the meaning of the word. "It means tough times, Inge, tough times." She nods knowingly as we trudge in tandem toward Rosalie Pass.

The group is settling into a routine. The morning goes uneventfully except that Bert again ends up in the stream during one of several times the trail crosses it. The narrow, barkless, and very slippery logs could have done in any of us, with our heavy packs, but somehow only Bert succumbs. A little before noon, we arrive at the place Bill originally had thought would make a good spot for the first night's campsite. It is situated on the edge of an alpine meadow where two streams converge. Mountain peaks rise up in several directions. Our planned meal—peanut butter and jelly on pita bread—does not match the scenery, though it may not matter since no one can find the peanut butter. We ask everybody to be sure they don't have it in their packs. CJ thinks Sam had it in his. Some people are so sure they *don't* have it that they won't even look through their packs, which pisses off other kids. We finally decide that Sam must still have it. So we all choke on dry bread and squeeze-bottle jelly, washing the concoction down with iodine water.

Despite the wry smile with which I deliver it, my "Let's saddle up!" is greeted by the now standard medley of groans and threats of bodily harm. We trudge through the meadow past low berry bushes and clumps of aspen, which are showing the first signs of their fall yellow. The last hints of patch after patch of withered wildflowers notify us that the area was even more spectacular a week or two earlier. The trail begins ascending to the pass in earnest. Everybody's doing lots of puffing in the rarified air, but the complaining has evaporated with the morning dew. Even Sharon is keeping up better, even though this is the toughest climbing of the trip. At one point, perhaps in a lapse, she comments about the great view. Sharon Kelsey has made her first positive comment as an Open School student. I fight back the urge to pounce with an, "Aha! I caught you being positive!" Should I risk reinforcing her change of heart, perhaps in the process making too big a deal of it, or just respond in kind? I settle for, "It is great, isn't it?"

The rest stops get shorter as the top of the pass becomes a concrete attainment rather than an abstract goal. The pass *has* to be just over the next rise, we keep saying. As we accomplish yet another rise, across the wide meadow, we can see approaching figures in the distance. Eventually we make out that they are Roger and Tammy, two members of Rick Posner's (Poz's) trail group, which is negotiating the same piece of wilderness as we but in the opposite direction. Roger and Tammy, who have run on ahead of their group, are twirling, arms outstretched a la Julie Andrews atop the Alps in *The Sound of Music*. It is a particularly fitting celebration of their first significant triumph as Open School students.

The meadow flattens out at the top of the pass. The last 3,000 majestic feet of Mount Evans, still bearing a bit of last winter's snows, rises to our right. Despite the altitude, our pace hastens. The kids are anxious to join up with Poz's group. Some trot on ahead to find the group lazing in the lush grass at the zenith of the pass, leaning against their packs, passing around bags of gorp. A small wooden sign beside the trail confirms our accomplishment: "Summit—11,200 ft." The sense of important achievement is very tangible, and we savor its delicious taste for a long time.

But conditions are changing. The kids in both groups, enjoying seeing some new faces, seem oblivious to the rumbles of distant thunder. Our high meadow, wide open and treeless, is the last place to be in a thunderstorm. I begin thinking about Mount Hood and look at Bill. He suggests we get our asses down off the mountain. There are no clouds directly overhead yet, but we are about as exposed as you can be to a lightning strike and will continue to be for the next hour's hiking. About all we could do to increase our current danger is hand out steel rods for everybody to thrust defiantly skyward. The kids are still lounging in the grass, trading anecdotes of the trek up the mountain. They don't want to move. Bill and I are considered turds for pressing them to leave. The thunder gets louder. The deepest blue sky I have ever seen is now dappled with mottled grey clouds threatening to consolidate into something serious.

Fearing bodily harm, I resist the urge to ask everybody to saddle up. Saying goodbye to Poz's group, we finally get the group moving down out of the pass. The trail works its way through an area that within the last few years was ravaged by fire. The burn area extends all the way down into the valley. We're moving fast now, losing altitude quickly down steep, narrow switchbacks, but it will be some time before we have any more cover than low brush and charcoal snags. The sky darkens and the first few drops of rain spatter our faces, but we're making good time. Once we reach the valley floor the trail flattens out and picks up a stream. Most crossing points are downed trees that function as foot bridges, for everybody but Bert anyway, but none seems to exist here. We search several yards in both directions, struggling through dense, high brush. Before Bill and I abandon our search for a crossing point and rejoin the group, the kids have made a decision: Crossing the stream will require a cooperative effort of handing packs across precarious footings and then moving people after them, trying hard not to get anyone dunked in the icy waters. Evan has positioned himself in midstream and is handing packs across, probably feeling more useful than he has the whole trip. Bill loudly orders him out. I know that what's provoking Bill is the memory of a scary experience several years ago with a boy suffering from hypothermia, but the kids don't know that. Evan's enthusiasm is deflated and he's angry. Some of the other kids visibly smolder. I fear we've botched it again. The kids have finally shown some initiative and we've squelched it. A steady rain is falling now and everybody's tired and angry. Bert, still wet from his last encounter with the stream, makes it this time. I quietly rejoice. But with a very cold night ahead of us we now have two guys wet up to their knees.

Another half hour, with rain falling lightly, brings us to the campsite I had found earlier. It's a great spot above a pond, the whole valley opening up before us, but the campsite is getting wetter by the minute. Some kids start erecting Evan's Barnum and Bailey tarp so we can get all our equipment under cover. Others begin gathering firewood before it gets too wet to burn. Bill and Bert get a small fire going. Through the flurry of activity Terry and Inge sit on a log, legs crossed, smoking and talking. A piece of the girls' conversation spills over into my part of camp as Inge says, "I'm not going to bust my ass for anyone." I can feel the back of my neck redden; we've all been working so hard to build a group and now Inge is trashing our efforts. I explode in a flush of anger. "Well, it's a good thing some are willing to bust their asses or your ass would be wet tonight." Inge's only response is a blank glare.

Neither she nor Terry does much during the half hour or so of scrambling required to establish camp.

Dinner will be spaghetti. The cook crew starts rounding up all the fixings from our various packs but can't find one of the jars of sauce. It apparently is yet one more item we failed to get out of Sam's pack. We're hungry enough to eat the spaghetti anyway.

In between light rain showers we erect the tents in the gathering darkness. The group—except for me, still sulking about my altercation with Inge—sits by the campfire on logs positioned just under the edge of the tarp, sheltered from the showers. I try to figure out why I'm still so upset. There are many reasons. Like the kids I'm beat. Inge, who has tried to tear the group apart with one comment, is now its queen bee. The kids have formed a tight circle and are giving back rubs to each other. Despite the plummeting temperatures, most have stripped down to T-shirts so the rubbing will be more effective. Bert and Evan are still drying out wet shoes by the fire. Evan is barefoot and oblivious to everything except the other kids, while I'm shivering despite five layers of clothing. Bert, again playing in the fire, is still wearing his wet socks. Once white, they're now as black as the charcoal dust that surrounds the fire pit.

Eventually, Leslie comes back and offers me a little advice: "Lighten up, Tom." I'm not sure I have it in me. I'm just not very interested in being a member of the group right now, but the weather is getting cold fast and occasionally I spend some time by the fire, warming myself. I end up moving away again, though, trying my best to escape teenagerdom for a few moments.

Later Inge comes over and apologizes. "I've really been in a shitty mood because of my cold," she says. I'm not ready to talk about it and I keep my thoughts to myself. Inge slammed the whole group with her earlier remark—we are all dumb asses for trying to help each other. I end up staying angry and not acknowledging the difficult step forward that she's taken.

Although the weather has cleared and we are now under a cloudless, starlit sky, the rain has complicated our plans in one important way. We had planned to do solos tonight. Solos have been a standard fixture of the Wilderness Trip for years. Students spend the night alone in contemplation or deep philosophic thought, so the theory goes. The kids are usually too green to solo on the first night of the trip and a group typically wants to spend the last night together, cementing its particular collection of individuals into a cohesive group. So tonight would be the ideal point in the trip for the experience—if the ground weren't so wet. Solos don't seem like a good idea under current conditions.

Bill leads us through a consideration of alternatives. Some past groups that haven't done solos have been razzed back at school, called chickens and wimps by kids who have weathered the experience. We have a relatively short, easy hike tomorrow, so we could get up early and at least do 4-hour, daytime solos before breaking camp. Some kids think we should be doing them tonight, but the ring of conviction is missing from their protests. The group decides to do short solos in the morning.

THE SOUND OF FIREWOOD being broken into usable pieces awakens the last of those still asleep, except for Inge. Although she still has her cough, she seems to be sleeping better. When she does get up she reaches first for her cigarettes. Warm sunshine is gradually bathing the entire valley. Even though it has not yet tracked across the valley floor to our campsite, just the anticipation of it heartens the group. Bert is fashioning a spear to go after some trout, ending any speculation about what today's water adventure will be. Terry gets some water on the fire for coffee and clean-up. Some of us take over the fire-building duty from Bill, who has been up for some time. His work team has cooking duty today, so he turns to mixing a big pot of pancake batter. The fire's so hot that the pancakes are sticking and getting pretty mangled during flipping. Bill gets mangled, too, as we let him know what we think of his cooking skills. But except for a couple of truly disgusting globs of half-cooked batter that get tossed to the camp robbers — the beautiful, indigo stellar's jays that hang around camp for just such handouts — everything gets eaten.

After spreading personal articles on bushes to dry in the sun, we all begin finding our spots for solos. Once we find a spot to our liking, we have Bill check it out. Safety is not much of a concern for a daylight solo, but we do want everybody to be out of sight of each other so that a modicum of solitude is maintained. Inge picks a spot on the sunny side of a granite boulder and spreads out her sleeping bag. Lighting up a Camel, she settles down to do some journal writing.

I pick a huge boulder with a flat, canted surface the size of a living room. The spot is tucked away in a grove of aspens perhaps 200 yards from camp. I spend about a half hour just enjoying the spot, gradually peeling off layer after layer of last night's clothing in the warming sun. I decide to write something about everybody in the group and, if the mood is right tonight around our last campfire, I'll read the passages to the group. So I begin. I write about Bert's young age and his problem of finding his place in the group; about Jane Solomon's intolerance of mud and grime and smelly open latrines; about Terry's ability to swing a conversation toward the heights or the depths; and about Sam's early departure and what we can do when we return to bring him back into what will then be a very tight-knit group. I've thought a lot about Sharon on the trip while dodging her canteen. Her paragraph comes easily.

Sharon almost didn't come. Because of her asthma, her father wasn't going to let her. She had to talk him into it, a really positive move for a young woman whose habit is to express the negative. I wonder what set of life experiences has hurt her so badly that she must resort to keeping all of us at arm's length? I have seen enough of the soft, caring young woman under that hard-bitten exterior to know that I like her. I have on occasion worked with students whom I suspected I liked more than they liked themselves. Sharon may be another. She is a gifted artist and maybe that's the toehold that I need, as her advisor, from which I can work. But most of all, Sharon needs to learn to trust.

Evan, another of my advisees, remains an enigma. I write about his desperate attempts to belong.

Evan has become one of our self-appointed pack horses, adding the burdens shirked by several others in the group to his own. He understandably resents the situation but that doesn't help build the group. We have both givers and takers here. Evan is a giver. He is also a competitive conversationalist who plays *Mine Is Bigger Than Yours* more than he needs to. I'd like to help him accept others' ideas and really attend to what they are saying and not just listen for openings in which he can try to top the current story.

And I write about Inge. I've thought a lot about her.

I suspect Inge holds, in her arsenal, the weapons to turn a whole class against its teacher. So far Inge and I have been like oil and water. I've got to figure out how to break through our mutual antagonism if I am to be an effective advisor for her. Right now I tend to view her as a spoiled princess who usually gets her way.

Our solos end and unsignaled we all gradually make our respective ways back to camp. We are uncharacteristically subdued, still rapt in unfinished thoughts carried back from our solitude. We have a quiet lunch, break camp, and hit the trail. We have only a few miles of downhill hiking to reach a position that will put us within easy striking distance of the trail head tomorrow. Because all groups are doing the same thing on all trails, we will be in the general vicinity of two other groups this last night. Although we spread our campsites out over a mile of trail, the kids' radar still tells them other teenagers are in the area. Shortly after making camp most of our group, without asking or telling Bill or me, simply takes off. On an evening when we had hoped to emphasize group building, the group has been fractured. Three kids—Sharon, Jane, and Bert—each an outsider in his or her own way, have been left behind with Bill and me. Even Leslie reminds us that, despite her extensive abilities, she is still just another kid. She has gone with the group.

The three who are left immediately begin trying to bond to each other. In some ways it works. Jane and Sharon decide to tent together tonight. In that special code that only teenagers know, they talk about how they have always had trouble fitting in, without really using those words. Jane's problem, as she sees it, is that she has always been too much the intellectual. Sharon talks about coming from a family of dummies. Bert joins the girls' fireside conversation, all the while rearranging the hot coals in 20 or 30 different ways. Finally having had enough of it he goes off to his tent at the far edge of the campsite to read. In my brief acquaintanceship with him, it is the third or fourth time I've seen him retreat from awkward social situations into books.

After an hour or so the rest of the group returns. Evan, as tight as a drum, announces that the kids want a group meeting. They have seen how another trail group—Roberta's—is functioning and they don't like the contrast. They have a list of grievances about how Bill and I have been conducting our group. Roberta's group, we are told with as much tact as Evan can muster, is functioning like a well-oiled democracy in which all decisions affecting the group are made by everyone and kids are making great strides toward empowerment. These very same newly empowered kids have done a great job of coaching our kids on what they should say to us: Bill and I haven't left enough to the group. We have been too directive and too demanding with all our saddle-up shit. They are tired of being bossed around. Evan is close to tears from the tension as he lays out the particulars. I search for the right response. Their departure in some ways has wrecked our last night together, but what is happening now seems productive. I'm still trying to frame a response when Bill begins talking about what a great move they've made, beginning to take responsibility for setting the direction of the group.

"It's exactly what the Wilderness Trip is all about," he says. They've displayed great growth, especially Evan, who has volunteered to play verbal point man.

Yeah, I think, *that's* what we ought to tell them. My overt response is more reserved, though, as I remind them that they've effectively cut five of us out of their group. "How are we going to repair that?" I ask. No one has an idea, but they have great faith in the healing powers of the campfire.

After a dinner of overcooked Top Ramen and instant cheesecake that is more soup than cake, we take up our places around the fire. We try to draw together but the fractures in the group are still evident. Some kids come and go. Sleeping locations have been rearranged so that we five outcasts are in separate tents. Everyone makes a valiant effort to rebuild but the cleavage is too deep and too little time remains to heal it. My journal entries that I'd hoped to share with the group remain my private thoughts. We gradually drift off to our sleeping bags, knowing that the climax we'd hoped to achieve hasn't happened—won't happen on this trip. The group is not a shambles. But I'd be much more satisfied with tonight if I didn't have the high standard of our first evening by which to judge our performance. Bill and I, now tenting together because the kids want the other tents to themselves, talk over the situation. He thinks the evening's gone well enough and that clearly some individuals—Evan, Sharon, and Inge, to name three—have made significant strides. We decide not to provide any direction tomorrow. We'll give the kids their head. They seem ready for it, we hope.

BILL AND I DO OUR BEST to not be the first ones up. Until now the kids have awakened to a camp that's already functioning. We want to break that pattern. Someone else will make the fire this morning. Someone else will suggest that the day's cook crew get breakfast started. When we do get up we grab a cup of coffee and sit. The kids look at us oddly but catch on quickly: Tom and Bill aren't going to initiate anything. We do make it clear, through our actions, that we're ready to follow instructions, to do our share to make things work. The kids finally get in gear.

After some instant oatmeal and another cup of coffee, Bill and I pack our tent and get our packs ready for the last leg to the trail head where the school buses will pick us up at noon. The kids make no move to follow our example. Rather, they laze around, joking and talking. Bill and I decide we'll let the kids break camp alone and travel the last mile or so of trail without us. We make plans to leave ahead of the group. Before leaving we go over the map with the kids, making sure that they can interpret contour lines and are oriented correctly to the sun, doing as much as we can to guide them without pointing and saying, "That's the direction you want to go." It would really be hard for them not to find their way out, but it would also be a logistical disaster if they somehow got headed back up the trail rather than down it. And then Bill and I take off. As abandonments go ours is awfully mild, but our uneasiness is a measure of what little confidence we have in the group.

After about an hour of easy hiking and conversation about how the week has gone, Bill and I reach the trail head. We sit and relax in the sun and wait. And wait. After a time some members of the other two groups finishing at this trail head begin appearing. Rod Jameson, Tom Rohrbach's student assistant, comes trotting down the trail carrying two packs—his and Tom's. Tom, it turns out, is back up the trail, *carrying* Mary Appleton, whose trick knee has gone out, piggyback. They've been carrying her for most of the four days. Rod drops his load and jogs back up the trail to help Tom. Roberta's group begins arriving as does the rest of Tom's, but still no sign of our crew. Roberta says they were showing no signs of breaking camp when she passed our campsite. It's now 11:30. Our uneasiness grows. Finally the first few of our kids appear up the trail. Bert's in the lead, running as fast as the heavy pack flopping all over his back will permit. The pans and stoves he's tied on the outside of it make an awful clatter that rudely shatters the serenity of the setting. He's a one-man band, bass drum booming and cymbals crashing, in a 100-yard dash.

One by one the rest appear. Bill and I had planned to take pictures of the kids as they each finished the trail, trying to document their individual achievements for posterity. But most of them are tearing past us as fast as they can. Some of the girls, whose hair has now gone 4 days without shampooing, will have none of the photo session. Like felons on the newscasts, they put sweaters over their heads or hold hands in front of their faces to hide their embarrassment. Among the last to appear is Leslie, strolling triumphantly down the trail with a proud smile on her ash-smudged face. Despite a 4-day coating of grime, she is the very embodiment of success. They are here, she seems to be saying, and Bill and I really had no reason to worry that they wouldn't be.

The buses arrive right on cue and everybody piles their gear and themselves on board. We are truly a mangy lot. I am braced for about an hour of war stories being traded among the three trail groups sharing the ride home, but the trip is quiet. Everyone's tired but the self-satisfaction in the assemblage is very tangible. We have accomplished a significant feat we really weren't sure we were up to. The contentment is written all over our faces. As the buses reach the school, all the veteran students come streaming out of the building to welcome us home. Several kids have organized a party for this evening and they're passing out invitation flyers to all the returning warriors. The GIs returning from World War II got a bigger reception, but we hardly notice the difference. We are not just being welcomed home; we are being welcomed into the school community. We have survived our initiation and now feel very much a part of the Open School.

CHAPTER 2

F.A.C.

I sit at the Langbergs' big fir table biding my time, trying not to kill off my martini before Bruce and Susie arrive for our little F.A.C.[1] At its last meeting the staff decided that the teaching team for each interest group should compile some key observations about how well this new approach to Beginnings had worked. After discussing the observations the staff will forward its recommendations for next year's Beginnings to the group known as "Futures." Futures is one of the Open School's unusual structures. Half class, half committee, it comprises both students and staff members. The group's task is to formulate proposals for altering the school's future academic program. Futures functions as a major committee of the school and everyone considers its work highly educational. Indeed, students can enroll in Futures just as they do in any class and therefore its size can vary greatly from one block to another. It is one of several means—Governance and Advising are others—through which kids in the school become mindful of the intent of a high school education. It leads them to talk differently than most teenagers do about school. Bert Horwood (1987), who closely observed the workings of the school in 1983, noted the phenomenon. "I was struck," he wrote, "in every student interview, by statements that could only be construed as philosophies of education." He described the students as being "aware of what the program stood for, how it worked and what they thought of it" (p. 65). Futures is guided by one core value: students should play a central role in setting a direction for the program.

I gaze absently into my glass and take another sip. What has been most notable for me about Beginnings? I'm not sure that this year's interest groups have been a more effective vehicle than the S.D.L. I've only heard about. Interest groups have brought kids from all Advising groups together in what are sometimes larger and probably more impersonal groups than those of S.D.L. Our group, though, was almost as small as S.D.L. classes were, but unlike S.D.L., we started off strangers to most of our 25 students. Bruce may have done a better job of connecting with many of them than Susie and I, in part because he encouraged many of his new advisees to enroll in Spaces and Places. He already knew these kids from the Wilderness Trip and that seemed to help. The topical nature of each interest group—whether it was the city or performing or, in our case, building things—probably distracted both staff members and students from S.D.L.'s historical mission, learning how to direct one's own learning.

But S.D.L., too, I've been told, often produced dissatisfying results. Some kids would leave the experience with too little notion of what it meant to take control of their own education. Because the effort to undo 9 years of learning about school in a few weeks often seems a losing battle—at least with some kids—Futures' search for the Holy Grail of an introduction to the Open School continues.

Our general plan for Spaces and Places had seemed workable. We started the 8 weeks very concretely, developing fundamental carpentry skills—hammering, nailing, sawing, and measuring—as we worked on two projects. As we built things, we had theorized, we would build a group. We worked on two projects, finishing the smoking porch and the preschool's adventure playground. Neither of these projects had quite made it to completion before the inspirational fires that launched them in previous years died out. Neither project was big enough to use more than a few of the students at once, so we divided up into work crews. At times we also flip-flopped inside groups (which began working on some of the more cerebral elements of the course) and outside groups (which worked on the projects).

The outside work went okay. The kids started with lots of standing around until they learned what needed to be done and gained enough confidence in their skills to begin whaling away with hammers. More than anything, Bruce wanted an activity in Beginnings that kids could jump into quickly and experience immediate success. These two projects, which involved building stairs and railings on the smoking porch and a suspension bridge and a climbing wall made of old tires on the play structure, accomplished that goal.

The inside work was a different story. Most of the new kids were quite adept in the finer points of passivity. Some of them had chosen the Open School because of unsuccessful academic experiences in other schools. Many of them had learned to cope with that lack of success by keeping a low profile in classrooms. That habit affected the proceedings of Spaces and Places. When Susie would encourage them to drop their inhibitions and plunge into some artistic activity, or Bruce would seek a higher level of commitment from them in planning the trip we were to take, or I would ask them to take pencil or mat knife in hand and begin executing some element of their individual designs for a rolling home, they would sit motionless, their hands hidden under work tables perhaps in an attempt to trick us into thinking they had disappeared along with their tongues. The students would stare at these three over-animated adults as though they were speaking an unfamiliar language. We in turn would stare back, probing for the source of the malady that had rendered them so helpless. Though Bruce and Susie had been through the experience in one way or another at the onset of previous years, the process still frustrated them. For a rookie like me the kids' learned helplessness was maddening. I came to understand Jeff's lament—voiced in one of our first staff meetings—that teaching at the Open School was like building a house. But no matter how much he had accomplished the year before, he had to resume the task each August by beginning again to lay the house's foundation.

Veteran students could sign up for interest groups if they wished, and the three who had elected Spaces and Places did their best to be models of productivity. They pitched in immediately when a staff member would ask the class to try some new activity. However, it seldom helped us engage the other students.

The problem came to a head in the middle of the block, as we tried to finalize plans for our 5-day trip to the four-corners area. We would spend a week at a private educational facility in Cortez, Colorado called Kelly Place. Kelly Place is a large tract of private land dotted with Anasazi ruins. The facility normally would charge a student who wished to spend a week there about $300. The fee pays for food and lodging and for instructors. Bruce had arranged for us to camp at Kelly Place and cook our own meals. And we would offset the cost of Kelly Place's instructors by providing the labor to complete several projects in progress at the facility. Much of the work—enclosing a pole barn and building a deck for a hot tub—would fit our emphasis on building. Only our agreement to help pick apples in Kelly Place's orchard seemed of dubious educational merit. In return for our services we would have the opportunity to renew an effort started and then abandoned years ago: the excavation and restoration of an Anasazi kiva. The whole arrangement made for a wonderful trip that would cost the kids $50 each, $25 of which they had already paid as an activity and materials fee that each Beginnings student was assessed.

But early in the block we had made a significant tactical error. At the beginning of the year, Rick Lopez had told us that we probably would not be able to get enough vans to take all of our kids to Cortez. We announced to the students that the trip would be optional, a risky course to take with students not yet committed to the school and therefore wary of trips. Normally, if a student takes a class that includes a trip, he or she commits to the trip or else takes some other class. Spaces and Places broke with that practice.

A couple of weeks into the block, Rick was able to find enough Jeffco vans for everybody to go. But our most passive, least empowered kids began coming up with all kinds of excuses not to go to Cortez. Kids who earlier were having trouble coming up with $25 suddenly had jobs they couldn't get released from. Kids who we suspected never did anything with their families suddenly had binding family obligations they couldn't ignore. Other kids had trick knees that were suddenly acting up. And, of course, we had told all of them that they didn't *have* to go. Had they known earlier—well—they probably could have successfully cleared their busy schedules or treated their trick knees with special care so that they would have been in good shape for the trip.

Spaces and Places, which had been striving to build a sense of group, had succeeded in creating two groups: the 15 more empowered kids who were making plans to travel to Cortez, and the 10 less empowered kids who were having difficulty connecting with the school. We would press for more involvement and they would stare at us, unmoved. That the kids were only doing what had come to be natural behavior for them in school made it no less maddening. But the contrast between these newcomers and our three veteran students was clear. With the new kids, one strongly sensed how well most kids learn to undermine the efforts of school to change them, how easily they take control of a learning setting by simply being passive.

Finally we decided we had to confront the problem directly. One afternoon we split the group. Bruce worked on trip planning in the art room with the Cortez group while Susie and I took the rest of the kids down the hall to Rancho Pavo, née the Turkey Farm. (The room's name was changed sometime following my first visit to the school after some of the kids repainted it; deciding that the room's improved ambience deserved a classier name, they elevated it to Rancho Pavo.) It would be our final, all-out attempt to salvage some of the kids for the trip. They sat quietly around a square of tables, carefully studying the scratched Formica as Susie and I encouraged and then cajoled and finally sermonized. Susie's frustration boiled over.

"The whole purpose of Beginnings is for you guys to latch onto the school and make a significant step toward becoming self-directed learners," she said. "Nothing we will do this block will foster that more than Cortez. It's a great opportunity and you guys are dropping the ball."

I watched the kids' faces, trying to assess what impact our diatribe was having on them. They remained passive. Their eyes had a dullness to them, as though they'd drawn shades over them against the glare of yet another hurtful school experience. Only Chris Morely fought back. He stood, saying, "This is bullshit. I'd like to go to Cortez, but I can't get off of work." And then he stormed out of the room.

Later Susie would explain to me how hard it is to do the first trip to a new place. "After the first trip, we have some veterans of it who are ready to sell other kids on the trip's merits. But that first time, it's just us—the staff—saying how great it will be and our endorsements are always a little suspect, especially with kids new to the school." But at that moment I searched for a way to fill the awkward silence in the room. "There's still time to make some useful gains out of Beginnings," I said, "but we've got to begin turning this around. We're frustrated because the trip will probably teach you what the school is all about better than anything else we'll do."

"Many of you were not terribly excited about doing the Wilderness Trip either," Susie added, "but I know that you're glad you had that experience. Cortez will be the same story."

"It's not just the trip," I said. "Many of you are not taking hold of your education in other aspects of Beginnings as well. I see very little happening with your rolling homes. It's as though you're waiting for us to tell you exactly what to do."

"We *can't* do that," Susie said, hammering our point home. "In the final analysis, it's *your* education, not ours."

MY THOUGHTS ARE INTERRUPTED by Susie's old BMW rumbling up the gravel drive. I greet her and her six-pack at the door. Susie, small and wiry, mostly teaches art and is a real whirlwind. She is one of the Open School's storytellers—one of its keepers of the culture.[2] Susie opens a long neck and puts the rest in the refrigerator.

"Sorry it took so long," she says. "Carol Wonko stopped by after school to tell me that a painting of hers has won an award in a show in Arvada. What a kid."

"She keeps surprising me," I reply.

Carol, a senior, is wonderfully talented yet doesn't quite know that she is. She's a beautiful girl who wears army fatigues and combat boots. She is one of Spaces and Places' three veteran students.

"I think she's going to be a Gregory All-Star," I announce. I get up to make another martini. "Over the years, I've amassed a mythical class—the Gregory All-Stars," I tell Susie. "A student must be very special to make the All-Stars. The group is the best of the hundreds—I guess thousands—of students I've taught through the years. The All-Stars include Molly Hillenberg, who, as an eighth-grader, mastered the Saint-Saens Clarinet Sonata that I played at my Graduating Recital at Ohio State, and Harley Warthen, an undergraduate honors student who reassured me that I was on the right track when I made my first tentative attempt to abandon grading in my classes at Indiana."

I tell Susie that I think of the All-Stars as always numbering 25, though I have never kicked anyone off the team as a new All-Star came along. "Usually, near the end of my experience with an All-Star," I explain, "I'll find a time to tell a student of her ascension and thank her for brightening my professional life."[3]

"Did you know that Carol and Craig and Don are making plans for a return trip to Cortez in the spring?" Susie asks me.

The trio represents our entire contingent of veterans in Spaces and Places. Carol and Don Troxell have been standouts. In some ways I have difficulty imagining that they were ever beginning students. I can't believe that the school has transfigured them so significantly in a year or two. I would have inferred that Carol never *was* a beginning student if Bruce hadn't told me that she couldn't bring herself to talk to other kids when she first entered the Open School. But even with her shyness she possessed a zest for learning; the 4-year-old's curiosity about the world was still very much alive in her. It didn't take Carol long to see the Open School as a big candy shop.

"They're talking about spending as much as a month there. They want to focus the trip on the art of the Anasazi," Susie continues, "pottery, maybe some basket-weaving, but mostly they want to finish excavating the kiva. I'm excited about it. I hope they can pull it together."

Susie was planning an art-focused trip to the Lightning Field near Cordes Junction, Arizona in the spring. The Lightning Field is a giant work of art, a remote mesa top full of collector rods that becomes a fantastic pyrotechnic display in a thunderstorm. Susie explains that she may scrap that trip in favor of a return to Cortez if the kids remain excited about it.

Bruce arrives. His plaid flannel shirt and red beard make him look like a mountain man. (He did most of his growing up in L.A.) He has the compact build of a linebacker and did play the position in high school. Bruce teaches biology, among other things, and enjoys working with his hands as much as with his mind. He adds his six-pack to Susie's in the fridge and we settle in around the table. Susie tells him we've been talking about Cortez. Despite rain and cool weather the trip had been more than we dared expect it to be. Several kids had even transformed the picking of apples into something of an aesthetic act. We'd made a good start on the kiva. Eventually it will be rebuilt as it existed a thousand years ago so that kids studying at Kelly Place will be able to see what these circular subterranean chambers were like. Nick Krueger, Kelly Place's owner, is a man full of great dreams. He hopes someday to have kids who come to Kelly Place discard contemporary life for a week and live as the Anasazi did.[4] An earlier excavation to reclaim the kiva had been covered with a sheet of black plastic, but over the intervening years much of the dirt piled around the rim of the kiva slumped back into the hole. Our task had been to re-excavate the site, filling bags with the dirt that had fallen back into the kiva, gradually working our way back down to the black plastic that marked the stratum where more careful digging would once again be required.

Even though we were digging disturbed soil, we kept finding artifacts—potsherds, animal bones that hinted at the Anasazi's diet (or maybe that of the last excavators, we'd joked), bits of blue stone, even a hand-worked piece of jasper that an ancient hand had hidden in a niche in the stone wall. Any shovelful of dirt might yield a new surprise. In return for our labor Nick paid Wendell Rhodes, an engineer who specializes in stabilizing ancient ruins, to supervise our work. As each kid came upon an item, we'd huddle around and Wendell would explain its significance to us. When Carol Wonko found a potsherd with a little hole neatly drilled along its broken edge, Wendell speculated that it was probably from a special pot that had ceremonial significance. Or it might have been a prized gift. When it broke, it was not discarded as most pots were, but rather was repaired by drilling holes along the break and lashing it back together with buckskin.

As Wendell talked, Carol turned the small triangle of fired gray clay over in her hands, examining its carefully executed design in black dye. Everything we found on the floor of the kiva was special just because of its age, but that shard was even more so because something of the importance that it held for its owner had crossed the centuries to us. Carol would have loved to keep it as a memento. Her skillful hands would have transformed it into a piece of jewelry that she would have treasured for a lifetime. But she would be stealing a piece of history. Her ethics were strong and, without protest, she gently added her find to the bag of accumulated artifacts.

BRUCE TAKES A LONG SWIG of his beer. "So what have we learned?" he asks. He makes the question sound like a challenge. I have strong feelings about what should change, but they are the opinions of a shell-shocked recruit who has just survived his first major battle. Even my remedies are drawn from the battlefield, as I think of the need for Beginnings to practice a sort of triage, separating kids into three groups: those who are clearly ready for the Open School's unusual brand of rigor, those who will likely make it if we can provide enough special attention in what I even think of as an Intensive Care Unit, and those who seem beyond our help. With such dire images running through my mind I'm reluctant to speak first. Finally Susie does.

"It's been a crazy block," she says. "We seem to get more and more unempowered kids each year. I don't know if this year sets a record but it's really hard to orient so many new kids to the school."

"We don't have enough control over the learning environment," Bruce adds. "That really becomes clear with a group of kids like we've had. Even in Beginnings, where we assume that most of the kids will be reluctant to engage the learning setting—won't even know *how* to engage it—we don't have enough control."

There are some kinds of control that the school will never have, control over a kid's past school experiences, control over what's happening at home. What remains the kids' big, only partially learned lesson of Beginnings is that they have the power not only to resist at the Open School as they have in other schools but to create a sensible learning environment for themselves, just as Carol, Craig, and Don are trying to do as they conceive a return trip to Cortez.

"I know we're all painfully aware that making the trip optional was a critical error," I say. "It divided the group in many ways—not just into goers and stayers."

Bruce takes us in a different direction. "I think we lost something important when we organized the kids around interest groups rather than keeping them with their advisors after the Wilderness Trip," he says.

Susie says, "We had to start all over again building some trust with the kids. It never happened with some of them."

Bruce writes it down. "The rolling homes project may have come too early in these kids' development," he says. "The assignment required order, planning, and a certain self-assurance. At this point our kids were satisfied with a van that contained a humongous stereo."

Susie and I nod agreement and Bruce writes it down.

"I still don't know why many of our kids *chose* Spaces and Places," Susie adds.

"My guess is we were picked by default by some kids who wanted no part of the physical rigors of the Adventure group or of making lots of trips down into Denver or of performing," I say. "It's not that they had a burning interest in building things; I suspect we looked—to some of them, anyway—like we'd be less of a hassle. I'm thinking particularly of those kids who didn't buy in to Cortez."

"The whole notion of interest groups falls apart if the kids can't find a group they're interested in," Susie concludes.

Bruce writes it down and, pausing momentarily, says, "Maybe we need to have a no-interest interest group for those kids." He writes that down, too.

As the afternoon wanes we add to our list of observations about Beginnings. It grows in length as the refrigerator empties. Few of our observations about this year's version of Beginnings are positive. We talk more of triage. Our F.A.C. feels more and more like a post mortem.

I decide there will be no better time to say what I've been thinking for weeks but have said only indirectly. "I think that there's a built-in paradox to Beginnings. It's an other-structured experience that's trying to teach kids how to begin structuring their own learning. We're always searching for the right combination of force and freedom. We never hit on it because we're trying to find the magic mix for a *group*. It's not a group issue; it's an individual issue. We need to hold the reins differently for each kid. With interest groups there is very little of what the school does best: helping one kid understand himself. There was almost no sense of each kid *as a learner* being the real subject matter of Spaces and Places, as I gather it has been in the past in S.D.L." I invoke the memory of S.D.L. as though I really know what I'm talking about. I don't. I only have a vague understanding of the many different approaches the staff has deployed over the years under that rubric.

"That's true in some ways," Bruce says, "but on a trip—like Cortez—the individual is more accessible to us than he is in a typical class."

Susie nods agreement. "That's definitely something our interest group had going for it," she says.

Outside the late October afternoon has become early evening. Susie glances at her watch and says that she needs to leave soon. We've about run out of gas anyway. We search for closure. I ask them what was positive about this version of Beginnings. Bruce is convinced the combination of the physical and the mental that has been a core thesis of the design of Spaces and Places is important. It's an idea he's been building on at least since the first Tallahassee Work Trip in 1986.[5] For Bruce, learning how to think and how to work are effective foils to each other. "That part of Beginnings has worked," he says.

Susie and I agree and Bruce writes it down.

"Some kids have made real progress," Susie says. "Think about what Andy and Howard were like at the beginning of the block. They—and some others—are visibly changed. Who's to say how much change has taken place in other kids that's still undetectable?"

Bruce doesn't write anything down this time. By some silent cue, we decide we're done. We rise from the table and stretch. As he opens the door to leave Bruce looks at Susie and me and says, "Well, we'll get 'em next block." I have the impression he has made the same statement at the end of other blocks. As first Bruce's and then Susie's tail lights disappear around the bend, my thoughts return to the kids. My mind's eye scans our group of 22 beginners, searching for signs of nascent Carol Wonkos within its ranks. It finds none—yet.

Getting Started on the Right Foot

I know of a few schools around the country, mostly private ones, that start their year with some sort of powerful, 'round-the-clock experience that removes their students from the physical and, more important, psychological confines of the school. The Wilderness Backpacking Trip is a particularly potent version of this sort of introductory bonding experience. No one—student, teacher, or visitor to the Open School—can come away from such a trial expecting it to be followed by an ordinary educational experience. Someone in the Old World reasonably might ask if the trip is really worth all the effort and duress; are the educational payoffs sufficient to warrant the scope of the endeavor? The Open School's staff, to a person, is convinced that it is.[1] The Wilderness Trip is so critical to success in the school that, in the dozen or more years that the trip has functioned, not one student has graduated from the school who has not participated in Beginnings, of which the trip is an integral element.[2]

During the few days leading up to the trip, various staff members had talked about the sort of learning that occurs on the Wilderness Trip.[3] They saw the trip as a powerful jump-start for the advising system that was so central to the school's program. Because new students typically made the trip with their advisors, they were able to cement a personal relationship that would take months to develop under typical school conditions. The trip also functioned as a sort of initiation rite for the school. Students who completed it had a sense of belonging to the school that was quite tangible. Bill Johnson mentioned the stereotypes that new students hold of adults, particularly teachers, and of school in general—where it occurs and what learning entails. Through the trip students learned that school is more than facts in textbooks and includes not only intellectual concerns but also personal and social ones. And, of course, the trip was great preparation for the major trips to all parts of North and Central America that were such an important element of the Open School's academic program. Students on the Wilderness Trip, including some who had never been away from home, learned firsthand the power of such experiences. The trip primed them for more trip taking. It was also a palpable risk. Risk taking, a topic we'll return to in Lesson IV, was so central to the philosophy of the school that students who learned, through the trip, that risk has its rewards had a leg up on successful completion of the program. In this sense, the trip was a confidence builder. Anytime a person accomplishes a task previously deemed unattainable, he or she has made a significant stride in personal growth.

Beginnings, the other central fixture in the Open School's welcoming regimen, was as frustrating for me as it is critical for the kids. The behaviors that students have learned as coping mechanisms in other schools stand out quite vividly when kids quite naturally attempt to employ them in the Open School's informal, self-directed context. Many of the new students behaved as though they could just wear a teacher away by choosing to not participate. Each individual's quiet act of resistance was reinforced by those of his or her fellow students. The resulting group lethargy was a formidable barrier to a teacher's efforts. In Beginnings, with its relative absence of the positive models that most veteran students present, the quiet resistance of individuals could accumulate into a critical mass. Sizer describes the phenomenon in *Horace's Compromise* (1984).

> In this sense, kids run school. Their apparent acquiescence to what their elders want them to do is always provisional. Their ability to undermine even the illusions of certain adult authority and of an expectation of deference was admirably if benignly displayed by the students. . . . [A] challenge can be made by students in any classroom when, for whatever reason, they collectively, quietly, but assuredly decide to say no. The fact that most go along with the system masks the nascent power that students hold. Few adults outside the teaching profession understand this. (p. 140)

I'm not sure if effective noncoercive means exist for combating this behavior in groups. It was through one-on-one dialogue, in the forum of Advising, that the Open School's staff probably accomplished most of its breakthroughs in combating this learned passivity. I wonder if big high schools, with their limited opportunities for one teacher and one student to "just talk," have *any* effective tools to apply to the problem.

Beginnings was also being taxed by subtle changes in the student body. The recent implementation of new — some say, arbitrary — graduation requirements trapped many kids in Jeffco's big high schools in no-win situations, in some cases suddenly adding years to their high school careers. Because of such shifts in society and in the absence of corresponding changes in educational practice, the Open School in 1987 was getting more tough-to-teach kids than well-adjusted, motivated ones.

It also was getting fewer students already attuned to open education than it once did. Philosophical shifts toward mainstream education by the elementary faculty at Tanglewood, the district's one remaining open education feeder school for the Open School, were having an impact. The Open School staff felt that the elementary faculty no longer strongly recommended that students continue in Tanglewood's junior high program. Only about half of the school's sixth-graders moved on to its seventh grade.[4] The resulting empty slots often were filled by kids having trouble in one of the district's 20 plus conventional junior highs. They came to the school having learned that they were crummy students, a self-image that may have been confirmed when they encountered a strange new philosophy of education. The influx altered the atmosphere of the junior high program, fulfilling the elementary teachers' prophesy that it was not the program for *their* kids.

Because of these problems, over half of the Open School's entering students at the time of the study were kids who had learned that schools in the Old World didn't work for them, but didn't know what would. They had strong, well-formed reasons for leaving the county's other schools but seldom had good reasons for coming to the Open School. They also had seldom been trusted to do the right thing in school and may even have learned that they were untrustworthy. Their disorientation when they entered a program as heavily based on trust as the Open School's was understandable. Because Jeffco, like most school districts, was not accustomed to advertising the unique qualities of individual schools within its boundaries, whatever entering students knew of the school had likely been learned from two relatively unreliable sources—Old World teachers and counselors who may or may not have had positive views of the school, or friends who attended it. The friends were often first-year students without a clear understanding of the school and its philosophy.

In 1987, 51% of the school's 238 students were new to the school. Attrition was high at the Open School because it was a demanding program that took on all comers. (While reliable numbers were not available, the lore of the school had it that over half of the school's entering students left the program before graduation.)[5] The school's highly individualized, self-directed program was unusual in that it was the *only* program available to students. The school had just conducted a self-study (Steele, 1987), which was then audited by an outside panel.

A major finding of the panel was that this was a single school trying to meet the needs of many different types of kids (Smith et al., 1987). After praising the school in a number of respects, the panel reported:

> It is obvious that some students have serious trouble in assuming the responsibility for independent, self-directed learning. Some of these enter the school totally unprepared to take responsibility for their own learning. (pp. 3–4)

The panel recommended the formation of several additional alternative schools within the school district, each with a distinct character and purpose.

Few of the school's early leavers appeared to be dropouts; rather, they moved out of the district or chose to return to a conventional high school or decided to pursue a G.E.D. (General Educational Development) certificate. Because students' reasons for leaving were often complex, cataloguing them and the students' destinations was difficult, but during the year of the study the school launched a systematic procedure to attempt the task.

The slots vacated by early leavers and graduates were filled each August with new students. Almost all beginning students go through a period of adjustment to the program as they try to make sense of this strange new place.[6] As Brian Fitzpatrick (Fitz), an Open School teacher put it, they confront the existential void. This trial was so regularly a part of a student's first experiences with the school that Rick Lopez joked that the school's mascot ought to be the flounder. Still handicapped by Old World thinking, students typically began their Open School career viewing the program as a comfortable, supportive place where they could do as they pleased. It often took even successful students months to become empowered enough to understand that *they* were responsible for providing direction to their education. Unfortunately some never built that conception; while they blithely moved down the path to becoming an attrition statistic, they naturally conveyed an erroneous view of the school to their friends back in the Old World.

The worry persisted that the school was gradually changing from one with a richly heterogeneous student body into one for "certain types of kids." The school used to expend considerable energy providing information to the district's students and their parents. In the early 1980s the kids and staff assembled an elaborate slide/tape presentation. Teams of students would visit every junior high in the district and tell the Open School story. But as the waiting list grew to extraordinary proportions, the energy and money (it cost $1,000 just to send letters to all Jeffco freshmen) expended on recruitment seemed less and less warranted. Unfortunately many on the burgeoning waiting list were there for the wrong reasons, referred to the school by professionals who had little understanding of what the school stood for.

THE CORTEZ TRIP, like the Wilderness Trip before it, was a major lesson in what students can learn from these experiences, a topic we'll return to in Lesson V. The contrasts between the beginners and two of our veteran students who had already mastered self-direction were instructive. The submerged payoffs from any of the school's trips, for even the least empowered kids, kept popping to the surface in unexpected places. But these residual benefits were especially evident in those kids who had learned how to use the school. I learned one more lesson in that regard several months after the trip, when I was having lunch with Carol Wonko in Munchie. She had just returned from the spring trip to Cortez, which she had in large measure arranged. I used the occasion to finally tell her something I'd never said on the first trip. "I was proud of the discipline you displayed in not keeping that potsherd that clearly meant so much to you," I said.

"I did a lot of reading over the winter term," she said, "getting ideas for my Global Awareness Passage. My Passage goals were to inform people about the destruction of artifacts and about the national treasure that we have there. Suddenly I realized that everybody was destroying them in one way or another, even the archaeologists. Even if you leave the artifacts buried, what is the point of leaving something in the ground when you don't have the information from it? I started to realize that maybe I was wrong. Maybe my Global Awareness Passage was wrong. And I decided that there are other levels of looking at things. And maybe it is not such a bad idea that everybody is fighting over these things. I started thinking that small, private collections are not so bad. How much, really, is a potsherd worth? Maybe it's not so bad—taking one or two—because there are thousands of them all over."

"The fact that they are now valued in so many ways by so many people is perhaps an indication of the way they continue to enrich human experience," I said. "Maybe much more so than they did originally."

"The fact is that the artifacts do enrich," Carol said. "Saying self-righteously that these things should be preserved is wrong. God did not lay down the rules that these things should be preserved. The only way they will be preserved is if we go out there and do it. And people can get in your way. But that's okay. Just because you have a hard time at it is no reason to give up."

"Did you take some potsherds this time, then?" I asked.

"No, I didn't," Carol said, her brow furrowed. And then her serious expression melted into a wide grin. She leaned toward me and, feigning a conspiratorial tone, she whispered, "Just a couple of stone tools."

THERE ARE REALLY TWO ISSUES blended into this section of the book: the issue of welcoming people into a community and the separate but related issue of orienting them to it. As I consider these pages I fear that they may suggest that only unusual schools need worry about the latter and only small, informal schools need attend to the former. Most big, formal schools create community in other ways; the unifying force of interscholastic sports is a prime one. (That the bleachers at many schools are now populated by more adults than students seems scarcely to have dampened school officials' zeal for athletics as a tie that binds.) But schools send messages to their students in small ways, too. I recall an elementary school in which the teachers, almost on a lark, decided to celebrate the opening of school by decorating the cafeteria with tablecloths and candlelight for the first lunch of the year. The quietude and civility that this simple act produced in the kids was little short of astounding to them. And the junior high that, I was told, ushered all of its students into the auditorium on opening day for a recitation of the standard penalties that would be meted out for an extensive list of offenses was surely communicating how it viewed young people. Even when it does nothing, a school sends messages to its newcomers about how welcome they are and how important they are to the school. It informs them of their role in the ongoing enterprise, even when the school's inaction implies that a new student has no important role in the school. Shouldn't a school consciously strive to act in ways that uplift individuals and foster a sense of community, rather than the opposite? What content that might be lost to the curriculum because of the time devoted to getting school started on the right foot could be so important that it should take precedence over that effort?

Lesson II

EMPOWERING STUDENTS

Empowerment is discussed widely in educational circles these days. It is a central element of many restructuring efforts. But most of this dialogue deals exclusively with the empowerment of *teachers*. Little of it deals with the empowerment of students; perhaps the concept is unimaginable in most of the schools we have created. One of many important lessons I learned in my year at the Open School, perhaps the most important, was what empowerment can mean in the lives of kids. Before my year at the Open School I thought that I understood the concept of empowerment; I used the word often before journeying to the New World. I would speak of it in solemn tones in speeches about the power of small high schools. I was quietly grateful that I had chosen a life's work—professoring—that offered me large doses of autonomy, which I then confused with empowerment. More than once I had walled off a piece of the university as my private empire, gained significant control over it, and thought I was empowered.

Many members of the Open School community, even some of its students, wouldn't have settled for so limited a realm of influence. Rather than building walls as I had, they were as likely to try to expand their influence by tearing down those built by others. A major mechanism through which students expanded their realms of influence were the six Passages that were required for graduation. Passages were a central element of the school's Walkabout curriculum. Walkabout, which was first proposed by Maurice Gibbons (1974), is based on the notion that modern Western society, unlike other, more "primitive" societies—the Australian Aborigines' with its Walkabout was Gibbons's model—contains too few rites of passage into adulthood. Young people seldom feel as though they have "arrived." At their best, Passages at the Open School functioned as an antidote to this societal malady. For example, I heard both staff members and kids refer to them as six steps to adulthood. Each Passage embodies its own challenge:

- The *Adventure* Passage is a quest, a personal and meaningful challenge, the pursuit of which requires courage, endurance, self-reliance, and intelligent decision making.
- The *Career Exploration* Passage is a broad investigation of a field of employment, including an in-depth study of at least one job within that field, with particular attention to possibilities for the future.
- The *Creativity* Passage requires students to develop a product that is an expression of their personal imagination, together with a detailed analysis of the process by which it was created.
- The *Global Awareness/Volunteer Service* Passage entails identifying an issue that has global impact and then studying how the student's own culture and at least one other culture deal with this issue.
- The *Logical Inquiry* Passage requires a student to conduct a systematic investigation.
- The *Practical Skills* Passage requires a student to develop proficiency in a skill or set of skills for which he or she was formerly dependent on others and that has the potential for life-long usefulness.

One indication of the close link between the Passage process and student empowerment was that students typically didn't begin Passage work immediately upon entry into the school. Indeed a widely shared goal among advisors was for their beginning advisees to have received approval for their first Passage proposal before the end of their first year in the school. Staff members sometimes spoke of a kid as "being ready" or "not being ready" for Passages. As the year progressed it became clear to me that a central determinant in these assessments was how empowered an individual student had become. To understand the mechanisms through which students were empowered in the school, we'll encounter in the closing pages of this section several students who were extending their influence on the world through their Passages.

Long before students contemplated Passage experiences at the Open School they had to learn some preliminary empowerment lessons. Most students struggled with these almost from their first day in the school. A fundamental way in which the school empowered its students was by giving them control of their education; it did so regardless of whether they were ready to exercise that control. We'll begin this section by watching some beginning students—my advisees—as they grappled during their first weeks in the school with the meaning of a high school education.

The structure of the school's academic program provides a useful context for understanding each student's task. The Open School's academic year was divided into five terms; the school called them blocks. The year both began and ended with two 8-week blocks, separated by a special 4-week block that occurred in January. Several long trips occurred during January Block, taking large numbers of kids and staff members away from the school. The program offered to those who stayed behind in January emphasized the arts.

In preparation for each block, students created their individual schedules, which had to be approved by their advisors. Block One registration occurred immediately after the Wilderness Trip. The registration process in all subsequent blocks was elongated into a 2-week schedule. Before the start of a new block staff members posted on the foyer wall one-page descriptions of the classes they would be offering during the coming block. The dynamics of free choice were evident in these offerings. The titles of courses, their descriptions, and their occasional eye-catching illustrations were designed to attract the indifferent shopper. The Old World worries that free educational marketplaces will propagate watered-down offerings. Although most of the advertisements for the Open School's offerings did convey the idea that classes would be enjoyable, few hinted that they would be easy. Some took the opposite tack, cautioning students of the challenges in store for them.

Because a significant portion of the staff's energy in Block One was absorbed by Beginnings—more than a day each week was devoted to it—offerings for that block were slimmer than they were during the rest of the year. Besides the four interest groups that constituted Beginnings, the staff posted 28 other offerings for Block One. Still, to proportionally match even this somewhat limited display of variety, a high school of 1,500 students would have to offer over 200 different courses. Each staff member typically offered two or three classes each block, each class meeting one to three times a week. The length of a particular class might be as short as an hour or as long as an entire school day. Usually a staff member offered at least one class that was a familiar academic offering: Geometry or Physics or Essay or Anarchy (Roberta Page's attention-getting title for her social studies class for Block One). One or two of a staff member's classes were more unusual, "high-interest" contributions, like Fitz's Peripatetic Poetry or Dan's Recording Studio or Mary Beth Teitelbaum's (MB's) Ornamental Headgear.

Staff members who had trips occurring in a particular block might offer one or two classes during that block that linked directly to the trip—a planning class almost always occurred prior to it and related, follow-up study occasionally followed the trip's completion. They might also offer a class unrelated to the trip and scheduled to end early or start late in the block. Such classes became useful options for those students who were going on the trip and might, therefore, have difficulty establishing a full schedule for the portion of the block while they were at the school.

The offerings that the staff posted on the foyer wall each block were augmented by descriptions of classes being offered by volunteers. For Block One these included classes like Elaine Spuzich's Writing Help and Otto Steigerwald's German class. Elaine was a former Open School parent who saw no reason to sever her ties with the school when her son graduated. Otto was a retired military officer who found teaching at the Open School a productive way to fill his idle hours.

Parents and other volunteer adults are involved in the program in a number of ways. They sometimes are members of trip staffs. Gary Halpom, a history professor at the University of Colorado, has played a major role in organizing the content that will overlay the Yellowstone History Trip. He will accompany his daughter Jamie on the trip, periodically pulling from his bag handouts that highlight the history of places along the group's itinerary. And I watched with some fascination as an unsuspecting piano tuner entered the building to perform his routine tasks, only to leave it asking if there was some way he might get involved in the program. (An apprentice showed up at his shop a few days later.)

Students also taught some classes—offerings like Junk Jewelry and The Blues—and their descriptions were also posted on the foyer wall.

Through a process of proposal and negotiation students and their advisors developed programs that both parties found acceptable. The 8-week plans that resulted were quite appropriately called Mutually Agreeable Programs, or MAPs for short. MAPs were single sheets of paper that laid out students' weekly schedules for a block: the classes they would take, the Passages on which they would work, and how other activities outside the school—internships, community experiences, and individual travel—would tie into their Individual Education Programs, or IEPs for short.

An IEP started as a loosely configured statement of a student's current developmental status regarding each of the Open School's 28 Graduation Expectations. These Expectations were, during the year of the study, an evolving innovation in the school. They covered three areas of effort—what the staff called domains. The *personal domain* included expectations such as meeting one's commitments to self and to others and being willing to take risks and accept challenges. The *social domain* encompassed expectations such as being able to constructively confront others and work effectively in small groups. The *intellectual domain* contained the familiar communication skills and the traditional content areas such as science and math, but it also included the cultivation of a sense of humor. New students were confronted with these myriad choices and with the task of analyzing their strengths and weaknesses and building the beginning stages of their IEP, even as they tried to understand the concept of an IEP.

We'll also learn in this section of the book, by listening in on the first of five extended discussions that I had with the staff during the course of the year, how the staff conceived the empowerment of students. This discussion concerned the sticky problem of how one translates the utopian ideal of giving students power over their lives into the real problem of how best to go about accomplishing that task.

CHAPTER 3

Giving Students Control of
Their Education

An Open School student begins the process of building an IEP by assessing his or her current competence in each of the Expectations. The process emphasizes strengths—what aspects of an Open School education the student has already mastered—rather than making long lists of deficits. New students are asked to develop their first attempt at an IEP during their first months in the school. Getting a new advisee just to understand the process is a major challenge for an advisor. A graduating senior talked about the critical role advisors play in this orientation. Without it, she said, "we would have a bunch a students running around, not knowing what to do, where to go. I know that I would be. My advisor helped me set up my timetable and get things done. Without that, I would just sit around" (Int. 3/88).

Of my six advisees, Marty Robinson is approaching the task of building an IEP most seriously. At my suggestion, he started his analysis with the domain most familiar to him in his past school experiences: the intellectual. He attempted to identify how far he had progressed in each of the domain's 16 Expectations. We then began discussing what the school expected of him in each of these areas before he could graduate.

The use of Graduation Expectations is a new approach that replaces a list of 49 competencies—what were called Pre-Walkabout skills—that each student used to have to achieve to graduate.[1] The competency approach had two clear drawbacks. Some kids began eschewing some experiences that both they and their advisors thought valuable for them, simply because the experiences didn't contribute to the completion of any of their unfulfilled competencies. Also, every so often a graduating senior completed all the competencies but still seemed—to the staff—an incomplete young adult. The staff thought of these students as "falling through the cracks" between the competencies. Rather than create yet more competencies—and, therefore, more cracks between them—the staff elected to develop more holistic guidelines. Over the year before I came to the school, the staff worked on creating a set of these guidelines for each of the Expectations. While the process was not complete, current drafts of each guideline were available to advisors. Each guideline was two or three pages long and contained a description of the desired outcomes, suggestions for different ways of achieving competence, and examples of competent performance on that Expectation.

Marty and I began going over these, identifying the things that he could already do. We talked about how he might amass the evidence he'd need to demonstrate that he was already competent in some ways, maybe as competent as a graduating senior needed to be. Then we looked at those things that he could not yet do and began listing some appropriate ways—taking classes or doing independent study or performing Passage work—through which he could first increase his awareness of an Expectation and then develop enough skill in that area to satisfy its requirements. As he continues the process, week after week, an important byproduct will be the new sense of purpose with which Marty will approach his pursuit of a high school education. The plan—the IEP—that results will periodically undergo informal revision as his interests change and new opportunities present themselves. What is important for now is that he has *a* direction, not that he has *the* direction.

BECAUSE BEGINNINGS ABSORBS a major portion of each new student's schedule for Block One, establishing MAPs with my six advisees was a relatively easy matter. Bert and Evan are in the Adventure Group. Terry is one of only a few girls in the school who are in that group. Inge and Sharon are in the interest group that is studying the city, and Marty is pursuing his interest in the electric bass in the Performance Group. Each of them is also taking two or three classes. Sharon is in a Skills Lab working on her math and is taking Drawing and Painting. Evan is in Bahamas Trip Planning, German, and Biology.

Advisors are asked to include some unscheduled time in each student's first MAP so that he or she is forced to grapple with the issue of productively using unstructured time. It's not hard to convince most kids that they should have some "free" time, but Rick Lopez has told me that there are a couple of new kids each year who do their best to make their first Open School MAP look like a *real* high school schedule, with every hour of the school week scheduled into some structured activity. They find themselves in the strange circumstance of having to lighten their schedules before their advisors will endorse their MAPs.

The weekly schedule into which the staff inserts course offerings contains several reserved time slots. Governance always meets first thing Monday morning. All of Friday morning is devoted to Advising. The staff usually spends the first half of Wednesday morning in its weekly staff meeting (classes offered then are taught by community volunteers or students), but the entire Wednesday schedule for Block One is devoted to interest groups. During Block One the staff meetings take place before school on Tuesdays and Thursdays. Lunch hours, too, contain scheduled activities. Each Passage area has two or three staff members who act as consultants. Consultants in three of the six Passage areas are available to discuss students' ideas for Passages at lunchtime on Mondays. The consultants for the other three areas are available on Tuesdays.

Other activities scheduled in the lunch hour include Budget—a shifting ad hoc assembly of staff members and students that meets around Marilyn's desk on Thursdays. Anyone needing funds for a trip or supplies for a Passage—what the school calls a Passage grant—must make his or her request to Budget. Friday noon is Staff Lunch, the one day of the week when the staff meets as a group rather than eating with the kids. Staff Lunch occasionally—and only reluctantly—includes a brief agenda; most days it is purely a social gathering.

Classes can meet in some of these reserved time blocks. Some classes, for example, that are exclusively for returning students are offered on Wednesdays of Block One, and Thursday lunch is identified as a time when Wilderness Trip groups can meet to complete their follow-up activities. But most classes are offered at times not devoted to these other activities. And two time slots—those for Governance and Advising—are inviolable.

MY EARLY ANTICIPATION—that Advising would be one area in which I could learn to swim in the shallow end of the pool—hasn't blossomed into reality. Like most predictions it was based on too little information. It is already eminently clear a few weeks into the school year that I really didn't know what I was getting into as an advisor. The warning signs were there from the start, but I ignored them. I remember Rick's long pause after I told him that I planned to maintain a half-time load *and* carry an Advising load. His concern didn't alarm me because I had a plan. I had decided very early that I would try to make up for my lack of experience and underdeveloped skill as an advisor by devoting more time to the task than could full-time staff members who carried two or three times my Advising load.

Advising at the Open School is an individualistic art form. Jeff

Bogard might meet with kids on an as needed basis, corralling a kid in the hallway for a 10-minute chat if he had something to talk about. I watched one of these short sessions with Ricky Hartgraves. Ricky was starting all his responses to Jeff's questions with a "Huh?" I took it as a habitual ploy through which Ricky gained time to think of an answer. Jeff's hypothesis became clear as I watched him perform an informal check of Ricky's hearing right there amid the hubbub of the foyer. Other advisors leave less to chance and spontaneity than Jeff does. MB pencils in half-hour appointments into her weekly schedule with each of her 18 advisees.

I, too, have scheduled these half-hour appointments with my kids. Of my six advisees only Marty has been showing up faithfully. The kids' avoidance skills—well-honed in years of functioning in big, anonymous schools—are proving superior to my puny entrapment skills. I'll see Sharon hanging out in the hall before school on Tuesday morning—our appointment day—and remind her that we are scheduled to meet at 11:30. I might even see her at 11:20—always with a couple of friends and doing her best to make me feel as though I'm intruding on yet another important conversation. Sharon, pointedly displaying her exasperation with me, will invariably assure me that she'll be there— right after she grabs a quick smoke. Out on the smoking porch someone will talk several kids, including Sharon, into having an early lunch down at the Pizza Hut and Sharon will blow off our appointment. Sharon is not the first student to view this unusual relationship she must build with an adult at the Open School as an invasion of her privacy. An older student, who craves more anonymity than the Open School allows, looked back on her early experiences with her first advisor.

> I didn't want her on my back. She used to really make me mad. I would tell her to just lay off of me. And she would say, "But we need to address this," and I would say, "No. Lay off of me." And I wouldn't talk to her for weeks. She was too confronting and she was too feminist for me, because I am not real gung ho [on most issues] like a lot of people at this school are. (Int. 3/88)

Bert will simply forget our appointments. He and a couple of the other less mature boys in the school have developed a strange sort of friendship that often has Bert as the odd man out. The others share his fascination with water. The three of them will play along the bank of the stream that runs past the school—Bert will occasionally get wet up to his knees. Or the boys will head up into the hills behind the school to mess around on the construction sites of new houses.

Evan will have some new crisis in his life—car trouble or a truck accident that has blocked all three lanes of Interstate 70 coming up to Evergreen from his home in Golden—that intrudes on our Advising time. His best excuse so far has been his account of driving several fellow students somewhere. One of the boys riding in his car gave a carload of Evergreen High boys the finger. The Evergreen High boys took umbrage at this display of disrespect and pursued Evan's car in what—to hear Evan describe it—became a high-speed chase through most of Denver's interstate highway system. It ended, according to Evan, only when the Evergreen High car ran out of gas. Mostly Evan would just rather be with his friends and will miss our meetings unless I tackle him in the hall.

Inge has major mood swings. On her good days she'll open up easily, talking about her past experiences and what she'd like to accomplish during her career at the Open School. She and I have had one very good session, sitting on a tiny bench in an alcove that functions as a cloakroom for the preschool. She talked at length about her past problems with school and her past heavy experimentation with drugs. We ended the session in a long hug, with me thanking her for sharing her story. Two days later she seemed to consciously ignore me as we passed in the hall.

Terry shows up regularly for our private sessions, but the strains of her and her mother's efforts to scrape out a living sometimes seem an added weight that she carries uncomplainingly through her school day. She is gradually building an agenda of things to learn. After she read my editing of a portion of her Wilderness Trip evaluation, she asked me to do more of it so that she might improve her writing through the process. She also is the first of my advisees to formulate an idea for a Passage; she will propose as her Adventure Passage to quit smoking.

With all the no-shows the 3 hours each week I've scheduled for Advising conferences are turning into double that time as I attempt to track kids down or corner them or call them or their parents at night or reschedule missed appointments. I have become a victim of my six kids' misplaced priorities. I have also become a victim of place. Few advisors have spaces that can be called private in which to talk to advisees. Ruth does, but it's adjacent to Marilyn and the circus maximus that continually surrounds her desk. Living in Ruth's office would be like having your home in the lobby of Grand Central Station.

Her office has two doors that can be closed, but she does so reluctantly, probably because of the tone of inaccessibility the action conveys to the kids. Jeff's office is in the camping equipment room off the gym. It was very private until he offered to share his 6- by 24-foot cloister, which also holds musty-smelling sleeping bags and leaky camp stoves, with Greg Lomme, a new staff member in a part-time aide position. Fitz, Dana Orin, and Gayle Civish, the school's part-time psychologist, share a small retreat above the girls' john. Whenever any one of the three requires confidentiality the other two fend for themselves elsewhere. One of Dana's advisees refers to her as the nomad advisor: "You never know where she is," he says (Int. 4/88). MB, tucked away behind the darkroom, may have more privacy than anybody else. It is her compensation for taking on one of the more distasteful chores of the school—managing the A-V equipment that is stored next door to her office.

My office is a desk tucked in a corner of Rancho Pavo. Because I am new and Rancho Pavo is one of the few classrooms that is neutral turf, I am reluctant to ask kids using the room, sometimes for a very legitimate purpose, to leave just so that I can meet with an advisee. So I try to find somewhere else for conferences. I must, anyway, at those times when a class is meeting in the room. An advisee and I will typically meet in the foyer and then try to find a quiet spot. When the weather was still warm, we could go outside. Now we are more likely to pick a corner of the hall. Its usual level of activity both masks our private conversation and occasionally distracts us from it.

I have good counseling skills at least with college students but I am finding it difficult just to get my advisees to talk. After several sessions in which they have given monosyllabic answers to my questions, our meetings have come to feel more like interrogations than discussions. They will look at me as if to say, "Okay, I'm here; now what do we do?" I keep reminding myself that the kids, like me, are new to the school. After 9 or more years of school situations in which adults controlled the agenda, they are only acting out of habit. Learning how to use an advisor is one of the beginning students' major tasks. Their success in the school ultimately depends on their ability to build a trusting relationship with at least one adult. A second-year student looked back on the beginning students' quandary.

> In a lot of ways, I'm scared for them because I know that last year, if certain things hadn't happened to me, I wouldn't have changed. The school could do so much for them if they would just take

advantage of it, if they would work with people and be more open and honest. It just doesn't happen all of the time. (Int. 4/88)

These are lessons that most of my six kids have yet to learn. As I wait for them to open up, the feeling grows that I am losing in my struggle to be more effective. I work less at corralling them when I'm uncertain a conference will be worth their time. Gradually our sessions have become less frequent. I feel as though I have too little leverage. I can see the kids sliding through, not responding conscientiously to what they know to be their obligations. Not only do I not know how to move the levers, I'm not even aware of what some of them are. On occasion I mention to Ruth a specific instance of Evan or Sharon or Inge stalling out. She casually says, "That's usually a sign that the kid doesn't belong here." I pass her observation on to the kid in question and his or her overdue work appears in a week. The kids may have a lot to learn about Advising but so do I.

ON FRIDAYS THE ENTIRE MORNING—almost 3 hours—is reserved for advisory group meetings. Advising is a forum in which more empowered students can help less empowered students take more control of their lives. The conduct of these meetings varies from advisor to advisor and each advisory group will vary its activities from week to week. Once every couple of months, for example, an advisory group will do something that is purely social: go skiing or bowling together or have a sleep-over, either at the school or at someone's house. More typically the group will meet in its regularly assigned place in the school. The group will usually work through a list of issues and announcements, the closest the Open School comes to the intrusive daily P.A. announcements of most schools.

The list is generated mostly from two sources. Leadership is one. Leadership is a class, taught on a rotating basis by many different staff members, that is taken by students who wish to lead the Monday morning sessions of Governance. The class also functions as an agenda committee for Governance and indirectly for Advising. The staff is the second source of announcements. It typically generates a list of several during each Wednesday morning staff meeting as it proceeds through its own agenda.

The list of announcements that Advising groups receive might include information that those students who in other schools would be termed freshmen (Bert is one of the school's very few) and juniors need to meet a Jeffco requirement by providing samples of their writing; such an announcement might mention that Judy Sherbert and Tom Rohrbach would hold a workshop the day before the test to simulate the actual test.[2] Or because of low student attendance advisors might be asked to reiterate that the last half of each staff meeting is open to students.

Occasionally Advising groups become small forums in which major issues in the school are discussed. One of these involved a formal list of the requirements for graduation. Like many practices of this informal school, a full list of the requirements had not been compiled recently. The staff did so and submitted it to Governance for reaffirmation. Governance in turn wanted to be certain that so important a topic received wide consideration and asked that each advisory group devote time to discussing the list and forwarding its written reactions to Governance. Many of the nine requirements—completion of the six Passages, for example—had become so deeply woven into the fabric of the school that they needed no debate. One, the requirement that every student work in Munchie at least eight times in his or her school career, was more controversial.

Because Ruth's and my advisory groups are both small, we meet together. An added advantage of the arrangement is that Ruth has several returning students while I have none. An important element of Advising is the old-timers telling the rookies how to deal with the school. That element has become especially important this year with the introduction of Triads. We haven't yet found a good name for these small support groups. "Triads" doesn't work well because the groups often have four or even five members. Ruth's and my kids had taken to calling the four-member groups that dominate our configuration "quadads." The term was gradually corrupted into "crawdads." This new name for our small groups, regardless of their size, seems to have stuck.

As the end of Block One nears, we have already fallen into a routine. We have established a schedule in which each crawdad in turn is asked to lead Advising. The crawdad is supposed to consult Ruth and me for agenda items. At times they do. The crawdad then plans some activity for the group for the remainder of the morning. A typical schedule will have the advisory group covering announcements, discussing or clarifying some of the items and then having some sort of small-group activity that can focus the work of the crawdads. These activities can range from kids helping each other develop their IEPs to exercises that ask them to identify some peak learning experiences they've had and then analyze them for those characteristics that made them so potent. It is also a time when kids can seek help from their peers. One student said:

> When I want something, my advisory group's there to help make it happen for me. They're really open. They're willing to sit for any length of time. They'll talk to me and they'll help me come up with ideas. They'll help me write out my Passage proposals or wrap-ups. They're just there for whatever I need them for. If I just need a shoulder to cry on or somebody to laugh with, they're there. And if I am having a problem on math or anything, they're there for me. (Int. 4/88)

After a mid-morning break our crawdads are on their own to complete the task that has been set up for them. Typically Ruth and I will ask the crawdads to return to her office a little before lunchtime to wrap up the morning. That element of our routine has begun to grate on the kids. They view it as a way for us to ensure that they stick around school for the whole morning.

"You don't trust us to use our time wisely," they tell us. "For example," they ask, "why can't a crawdad head down into Evergreen, have an early lunch together, and work on their activity as they eat?" They point to other advisory groups that are free to spend the last part of Friday mornings as they deem useful. In part they are right; we don't trust them to use their time wisely. But eventually we relent and loosen the reins, although a crawdad or two each week—even under the old plan—has blown off its assigned activity.

The kids would also like to reconstitute the crawdads, something Ruth and I had hoped would occur eventually. We had established the composition of the groups at the beginning of the year, with each having one or two veteran students and a couple of beginners. Considerable counterbalancing was required since some of the new students were better self-starters than some of the returning students. Now they will re-form into groups that maintain a mix of returning and beginning students, but also align more closely with the friendships that have developed in the first weeks of the school year.

BEGINNING STUDENTS HAVE yet one more task to complete by the end of Block One. They must select their permanent advisors. New students were arbitrarily assigned to temporary advisors to get the year started. Now each student must consciously choose an advisor. Almost all kids select the one with whom they have been working, but they must nonetheless formally make the selection. They make their decisions for varying reasons. A graduating senior said, "Some advisors are more taxing intellectually, and some are more taxing personally, and others are more taxing socially." Looking back on her school career, she thought she had chosen a permanent relationship with her temporary advisor mostly because she didn't want to hurt her advisor's feelings. She now saw it as "a bad reason to stay with your advisor" (Int. 3/88). She eventually did switch to an advisor she judged to be more intellectually demanding.

Another student talked about the varying demands of advisors. "Some of the advisors—from what I have heard—are just real easy about things. As for my advisor, I can't get anything past him. I can't slip by with him at all."

How did that make him feel?

"That doesn't bother me," he said, "because I need to do extra. I want to get all I can out of the school. I want to do a lot because some of the stuff is really easy for me" (Int. 4/88).

Advisors, too, have clear views of the different roles they play in the school. One thought that the "most powerful" function he performed for his advisees was being "a good model for them of how to handle crisis, to be there when they need me and to let them know that I really do care about them" (Int. 6/88). Another staff member talked about being

> considered one of the tougher advisors at the school, one of the more structured ones. Which is weird too, because I think the staff would consider me liberal on issues such as kids staying in school and the rights of the individual. But even some of the people [who hold other views] know that I am a tough advisor. I place a lot of demands on kids and I check up on them a lot. (Int. 5/88)

Kids sometimes switch advisors one or more times during their careers. Both the new and the old advisor must agree to the change, which is consummated in a formal meeting of the three individuals involved. A key criterion for okaying a change of advisors is that the switch is not just a way for a kid to escape a demanding relationship. Occasionally an advisor will reach the end of his or her rope with a particular advisee and will ask the kid to find someone else. In Open School parlance, the kid is "cut loose" or a support group meeting is convened to discuss the problem. If these interventions don't work and *every* staff member has come to feel that the kid's problem is deeper than an inability to work with one or even a few different advisors, the student will be asked to leave the school.

Because of his strongly held view that the Open School was a place where any kid could succeed, Arnie often chose to function as an "advisor of last resort" for these kids, taking them on as personal reclamation projects when no one else would. Arnie purposely didn't maintain a continuing group of advisees so that he could be the school's catcher in the rye. His departure from the school in 1986 had an impact on the future of these kids. Three staff members talked privately at that time of the need to continue the role of advisor of last resort.[3] They decided to jointly assume the role. But other advisors had not given up on these kids without some justification. Taking on these tough cases as additions to a regular Advising load can overwhelm an advisor. One advisor, looking back on the past year, considered the amount of energy she had expended without making visible progress with several kids. "If I'd expended it and ended up helping, that would have been fine," she said. "But I just had so many kids that I questioned my effectiveness. I just overloaded on needy kids. Now, I'm trying to keep a balanced group" (Int. 5/88).

Some kids may see these advisors as asylums. Some staff members see them as rescuers. But as a staff member explained, some of the perceived differences in Advising styles are mostly illusory. He described a colleague as "really confronting kids in terms of their behavior," but added, "I don't think kids perceive her that way until it happens" (Int. 5/88).

ALL OF MY KIDS have decided to stay with me—more I think out of a sense of continuity than of dedication. But they now number not six but five. Terry Dodge, who was quickly learning how to use the school, has moved out of the district and transferred to the Denver schools. Terry's 2 months in the school had to be converted into the Carnegie units that other schools use to mark progress toward graduation. The Wilderness Trip was converted into a quarter credit of P.E. and, when she completes a paper, she will also get a quarter credit of English. A final support group meeting is held for any kid leaving the school for any reason. Ruth and I held a quiet one for Terry. We talked about the successes she had experienced in her short stay in the school and suggested ways in which she might build on them in her future schooling. After a last hug, she was gone.

As my five remaining advisees settle into the year it becomes clear, even amid the continuing frustrations of Advising, that they are beginning to catch on. On an occasion or two, I have had clear evidence that individual advisees have developed some trust in me. But progress is slow, with major relapses occurring frequently. After a rough start,

Sharon has become a bright spot. Our relationship was so rocky for
the first few weeks that I had called her former advisor at Tanglewood,
hoping I could find an edge to break our impasse. I found his attempt
to encourage me discouraging; he thought I was making good progress
with Sharon if she was willing even to talk to me. Sharon views me as
a "traditional thinker," a term that she definitely uses as a pejorative.[4]
In just a few weeks, though, she has gone from my most worrisome
advisee to one who is beginning to risk trusting me. The first clear sign
of the change occurred when I finally got her to write her evaluation of
the Wilderness Trip. Trusting others had been difficult for Sharon from
the start. It was particularly evident on the Wilderness Trip. She had
become aware enough of the problem to write about it in her evaluation of the trip, revealing confidential information about herself that
clearly indicated a willingness to risk trusting me. Sharon has her
relapses but continues to improve. She smiles occasionally now, something that she never did at the beginning of the year.

For my five remaining advisees and me, the struggle to develop
productive relationships continues. My five kids are all stumbling in
one way or another but they are each making important strides in
other ways. Undoubtedly other advances are occurring that remain
invisible to me. They are doing okay. And so, I guess, am I.

CHAPTER 4

The First New World Seminar: Empowering the Unempowered

An event that turned out to be very important to me occurred at the beginning of the year during the second day of staff meetings before students returned to school. At one point during that day's ongoing discussion, the topic turned to the problem of transforming each new group of students, well-habituated in the fine art of getting by in a conventional school, into empowered, autonomous, self-directed learners. It is not an easy process. Rick Lopez, white-haired with hawkish good looks, had initiated this new direction to our ongoing discussion. Among other things Rick teaches some social studies classes. "If we're going to sit back and wait for kids to take control of this school," he said, "then we've got a long wait because they've only got 3 years and then we've got another whole new batch that isn't in control either. It's just a perpetual problem."

I used Rick's statement as an opportunity to interject a question that I'd pondered for years, one that any teacher confronts who prizes student freedom and struggles to improve students' efforts to use that freedom wisely. "What happens to a kid in this school who doesn't *try?*" I asked. I didn't know it at the time but this was the first of several discussions that would occur in which I would ask the staff to teach me about subjects that prove particularly sticky on this frontier of public education. Because of their high educative value for me, I eventually came, at first jokingly and then quite seriously, to call these sessions New World Seminars. This discussion became the first of these seminars.

DANA, WHO AS MUCH AS ANYONE on the staff accepts the challenge of working with the most injured of the Open School's students, responds first. "Interestingly enough, there have been a number of kids who have been here whom nobody has really thought of as trying. Sometimes they leave. Later when we check, we see that the very student we thought wasn't getting anything at all out of our program was indeed getting quite a significant amount. That's where the power of modeling comes in and that's where we transfer our own sense of self-esteem. Just giving kids the opportunity to observe staff members doing things that are productive and involving—just being happy—*is* viable educationally as far as I'm concerned. I do think that's absorbed by students. Whether or not they're at a point to actively work on it or not is immaterial. Even though you can't see it at the time, there are benefits down the road."

Dana's a very thin woman in her early forties with a bubbly enthusiasm. Her long, straight strawberry blonde hair is streaked from a summer's worth of sun, which has also brought out her freckles. Her deep, husky voice seems like it should belong to someone else. Her apparel—a broad-brimmed sun hat and a dress that looks a little like chiffon—is more costume than dress. It seems of another time and place, suggesting not work, but play and celebration. I wonder if in the 1970s Dana might not have been the archetypical flower child. I try my best to counter her remark. "But those kids might have had those same benefits floating on the street, too. Right?"

"Right," she responds. "There are people who are personally successful in the real world."

"Yes, but not with the same models," I say. "Some models are more appropriate than others."

Jeff joins the discussion. His long, unkempt hair is a running joke with the group. Jeff's appearance—bushy beard, well-worn Levis, and weathered hands—hides a formidable intellect and appreciation of the arts. "That, to me, is the benefit of an organization that focuses on trying to help people educationally," he says. "It can provide models it hopes people will pick up. There *are* models all over the street. While it's good to see them for comparison, for analysis, and to help you see why some are worthwhile, that's pretty random. You may learn a lot of science, especially on TV, but you're going to learn it in a very nonsequential and a very nonrelated fashion. You'll learn a lot of names and you'll learn that a trapdoor spider does this or that but you'll have no idea what situations it occurs in."

I interrupt. "That's an argument for a conventional school."

"No, it's an argument for guiding rather than allowing everything to be accidental. That's all it is. And if you don't have some intention, some place that you think is worth getting to, then why is there a school? We do have a place that's worth getting to. It has to do with training someone through experiences to be *able* to learn in the real world. And I don't think the real world has a lot of potential as a learning environment unless you learn to look for it (or haven't yet learned to ignore it). That's what we're doing."

"Can I learn here," I ask, "that I can just lie back and not do anything and still be safe?"

"For awhile," Dana answers.

Pat Sliemers echoes Dana's comment. Tall, with short blonde hair, Pat is a certified elementary teacher holding a noncertified position in the school. She coordinates the school's many community-based activities, including all the apprenticeships and volunteer work that the kids do in the Denver area. Committed at an earlier age to becoming a nun, Pat dropped out of preparation just months short of taking her vows. Years later she married Warren Sliemers, formerly her high school teacher and a priest. Pat and Warren's son, Aaron, is an Open School student. Pat adds, "But several kids each year get counseled out of the school, either permanently or for awhile. Some of our best successes are kids who had to leave because it had become either a waste of their time or a waste of our time. They were just hanging out. We say, 'It's not productive for anybody; it's not worthwhile for you to be here.' We ask them to leave for a month or a semester or a year, or maybe forever, and make *them* make a choice. Some kids are asked to leave for a semester and told, 'When you accomplish these kinds of things, you'll be welcomed back.' We even refer to such experiences as sabbaticals. When they come back they are raring to go.

"That doesn't happen with every kid, though, who happens to be hanging out," Pat continues. "We surely have kids who haven't caught on yet. We're *always* talking about that fine line. Do we hold them too long or do we not hold them long enough? It comes down to the advisor's discretion. We have a philosophy here that we all subscribe to that, as long as there is one person on the staff who wants to work with this kid, we will respect and support that. In most of the cases those turn out to be the right decisions. But we never know for sure; our individual levels of tolerance are all different."

Bruce talks about the pressure that wielding so much discretionary power places on advisors. He describes the place of professional ego in coping with the problem. "My self-esteem is wrapped up in these kids the same way yours is, Pat—in what kids do here and how they do it. I know Susie's is with art. The way I feel about myself is wrapped up in the way people perceive our school and the way I perceive the kids. That's unhealthy for me and I have to separate those issues."

Pat says, "That's the tightrope we walk in experiential ed. What can we do to help kids?"

Turning the question around, Ruth asks, "What can the *students* do to help? They need to do that on their own steam and in their own way and in their own time. We're each a resource for that; we're there to help when we can. They're teaching us—all the time—how to help them."

Attempting to reveal yet another layer of the problem, I take a stand. "My view is that we are a school and one of the things that separates us from lots of other very worthwhile social agencies is that this is a place where people learn. A very fundamental requirement of learning is that a person be willing to *try*, that he or she not be too damaged or frightened to at least be able to try. I'm concerned about the role that some alternative schools, especially those that deal almost solely with 'battered kids'—the label currently in vogue for them is 'students at risk'—are playing for those kids. I'm talking about kids who are dropouts or potential dropouts or who have been kicked around in the system. Schools that exist exclusively for these kids sometimes become places where the kids learn that they don't have to try. The school takes on the role of an intensive care unit, performing a very worthwhile social function that isn't being fulfilled anywhere else in the community with kids that may be lost if they aren't responded to at that time, in that way. But I have trouble calling those places schools."

Dana responds to my statement. "But there's a period of readiness to learn that's different for every student and if you do view the student as having been battered by the system, isn't there a period of healing that needs to take place before that person is ready to be empowered enough to take on his or her own educational program? That's what we deal with: How long is that period for each individual student? I view that as a testing period in which they're watching me to see if I'm going to reject them like a million other people have before me. When I don't, then perhaps they're ready to stop being defensive and begin to love to learn the way that I hope we model for them.

"I don't look at it as though they are intentionally not trying," she continues. "I look at it as a defensive posture they've adopted because it's all they've learned so far, and they've learned that so well that I take it as evidence that they can learn other things too, but it might take some time."

"I think you're very right, Dana, in identifying it as a trust issue," I say, "that they need to build some trust. It's very admirable to try to do that; it's got to be extremely difficult to make those judgments, to decide at what point a kid is just using the system."

"And you can make mistakes by *rescuing*, which is something I did for a long time here," Dana answers. "It was not in the students' best interests. I was in essence solving *their* problems and sending them the message that when they had a problem, someone else would solve it and take care of them. I'm practicing very hard not to do that but there's that fine line." Her eyes take on an added intensity as she continues. "I believe we save lives here. I've said it a thousand times. I see it all the time. Every year I see students turn a life-long pattern around and become successful, productive, happy, cooperative people."

Jeff, probably wanting to be sure that I don't view the staff as a bunch of coddlers, makes one last point: "While I think we all believe, with Dana, that there is a period of readiness that is very different for every individual, we still smash 'em right off the bat with the Wilderness Trip, which is a forced, required experience that they're not ready to take on themselves. Through it we show them that they *can* deal with difficult learning situations."

CHAPTER 5

Walkabout Day

The Open School devotes one Wednesday each month to the committee work that is an integral part of Walkabout. These Wednesdays, known as Walkabout days, begin at 10:30 right after staff meeting. All regularly scheduled classes are suspended for the remainder of the day so that staff members and students are freed to arrange the formal meetings that officially mark the beginning and end of each Passage.

Several days prior to each Walkabout day Ruth posts sign-up sheets — one for each of the six Passage areas — on the foyer wall. Students who are ready for a meeting then arrange a time with their advisor and their Passage consultant and reserve a half-hour block of time on the appropriate sign-up sheet.

Three types of meetings occur on Walkabout day. The first of these is the proposal meeting. After a student has discussed an idea for a Passage with his or her advisor, the student refines the idea with one of the staff members who consults in that Passage area. Together they tighten its logic. They develop a time line, establish a budget, and plan how to acquire the funds that will be required to execute the Passage. For a student who is combining Creativity and Practical Skills Passages on a project that has her first designing and then building a suite of bedroom furniture, for example, the task of figuring the cost of materials is straightforward. When a Passage entails international travel — a proposal, for instance, that combines Adventure and Global Awareness Passages in an extended stay in an Israeli kibbutz — finding the funds can be quite complicated. Money is often an obstacle, especially on Passages that involve travel. The school's long-standing philosophy is that kids should earn a portion — one-third is an often mentioned amount — of the costs of experiences like Passages and trips. Planning in such cases may begin months in advance not only to establish an itinerary but also to allow time for the student to earn the money the Passage requires. Students can sometimes arrange loans from the school. And Passages that represent improvements to the school are eligible for Passage grants. Matching grants for amounts of up to $250 are available for this purpose. The funds are drawn from the $82,000 gift that the Open School received from an anonymous donor in 1981. Advisors sometimes function as brokers, helping their kids see that impossible dreams can occasionally become realities.

Upon completion of a Passage experience the student writes a second paper that is part self-evaluation, part conclusions. The student describes what he or she has learned—about the topic but also about self—from the experience. Completion of this paper signals the student's eligibility to schedule the second meeting—the wrap-up meeting—for a subsequent Walkabout day.

The third meeting that occurs on Walkabout day is a variant of the wrap-up meeting: what the Open School terms a retroactive Passage. Occasionally, important life events—the sort that result in significant personal growth—occur in the natural course of a kid's life. Overcoming an addiction to alcohol or drugs, working extensively in a political campaign, or giving birth are such events. In judging the educational value of such experiences, the Open School places no time or location restrictions on them. The school does limit a student to two retroactive Passages. But if an experience—even one that occurred before a student's entry to the school—fits the requirements of a Passage and the student can document that it occurred as described, it can be used to fulfill a Passage requirement.

Sally Riechart is completing a retroactive Passage. She came to the school with a history of sexual abuse, first by an alcoholic stepfather and then by two brothers and her grandfather.

> I came into the school with really low self-esteem. I thought that I was shit and I didn't know exactly what to expect. I'd come to school and it would physically hurt to talk. I couldn't get it out and I would start crying. I would cry to get attention so I could talk and try to solve these problems. I got to the point where I could finally say things, but I still couldn't get my points across. (Int. 3/88)

Then, during a school trip, a resident of a ramshackle trailer park that adjoined the campground where the group was camping befriended Sally. They talked for awhile and he invited her to his trailer. Once there he made sexual advances toward her. Sally was able to escape and return to the safety of the group. In tears but struggling to compose herself, she told Dan McCrimmon, the trip leader, what had happened. Dan immediately called the school—standard practice any time a problem occurs on a trip—and then called the sheriff. The sheriff turned out to be a trained professional with a competent staff that included a female rape counselor, who helped Sally through the first hours of the incident's aftermath. Sally was once again faced with all her doubts about herself, but what had always been, before, a humiliation she suffered in private was this time the public knowledge of the trip group.

> It was really hard for me to be in the group after another of those situations and have to think about myself and still have to think about the growth [of the group.] There was no place to go and hide. I *had* to be with the group. And so I just shut up and I wouldn't talk. I felt sorry for myself. I even thought about killing myself again.

The group rallied around her and was not put off by her demands to be left alone. Dan took her aside and said, "I know how you feel. I know that it has got to be really hard to go through this and be angry and be sad and be hurt. But you still have to be a part of the group and they still love you. They want to see you through this." Sally risked opening up to the group. The experience made her realize, as she put it, "how much the group really did care and that it was okay to let them care. It was a true caring."[1]

The group's unrelenting support became a turning point. Upon her return to school, she began a year of therapy with a psychologist during which she finally dealt with the anger, with the pent-up frustration, and with her low self-esteem. Every Passage, and particularly Adventure Passages, must include an element of risk. No risk—no growth goes the thinking. Adventure Passages regularly involve physical risk but some—which the school terms internal Passages—involve significant psychological risk. In the staff's view, Sally's struggle toward self-knowledge entails that sort of risk and her therapy will form the core of her Adventure Passage.

WITH THE ADVENT THIS YEAR of Triads, students have acquired obligations beyond simply attending their own Passage meetings or those of their close friends. Triad members are now expected to attend all of the meetings of each member of their Triad. The purposes of the requirement are twofold. On the one hand, these Passage meetings are key events in an Open School student's career; Triads are support groups and there are few times when support of a fellow student is more important than at a Passage meeting. On the other hand, students—especially beginning students—can learn a great deal about the Passage process, about its demands and its standards, by attending the Passage meetings of others.

Advisors are enforcing this new requirement with varying levels of strictness. Bruce, the father of Triads, may be the most stringent. He views attendance as a fundamental responsibility that Triad members have to each other and will not allow a meeting involving one of his advisees to begin unless all Triad members are present. His uncompromising stand first became evident on October's Walkabout day. Students can graduate from the Open School at any time during the year. Most scramble to finish by the deadline for participation in the school's formal graduation ceremony in June, but a few each year complete their requirements at other times. Pam Tinsley, one of Bruce's advisees, is such a case. She returned to school this fall needing only to complete one Passage and finish writing her Transcripts. She wrote her wrap-up paper, the description and evaluation of her Logical Inquiry Passage, and scheduled her meeting. She'd developed the idea for her study while taking a graduate course in marine biology at an institute in Mobile, Alabama. Her Triad included two beginning students, Roger Mayer and Nancy Ruiz. Neither showed up for her Passage meeting. Bruce canceled it. Pam stood before Bruce in the foyer, fists clenched tightly at her sides. Tears streamed down her face. She told Bruce that she had done everything that was expected of her. She'd written her wrap-up. She'd arranged the meeting with Bruce, and with Kurt, her Passage consultant. And she'd informed Roger and Nancy of the meeting's time and place. It was unfair, she said, for her graduation to be delayed because Roger and Nancy had cut out. "Neither would have done anything but sit and listen at the meeting, anyway," she said.

"I understand your anger," Bruce said, "but you knew the rule and the reason for it. So did Nancy and Roger, and they're not here."

"This is a lot of crap," Pam said, as she turned on her heel to leave. "I'm going to change advisors."

In the end the two beginning students were properly chastened by the anguish their irresponsibility had caused. Pam kept Bruce as her advisor and rescheduled her wrap-up for the November Walkabout day. Roger and Nancy were in attendance this time. And Pam Tinsley ended her Open School career. Although she'd officially completed her high school obligation, Pam would take one last school trip in February to Tallahassee—with Bruce.

MY SCHEDULE FOR THIS WALKABOUT DAY is a light one. Kris Ondrik, one of Roberta Page's advisees, has invited me to attend the wrap-up of her Global Awareness Passage. Her topic is the growing problem of missing children. I'm the consultant on Stephanie Woodward's Logical Inquiry Passage; Stephanie's proposal meeting is scheduled for late afternoon. I make it a point to attend every Passage meeting of the members of Ruth's and my combined Advising groups, and one of Ruth's advisees, Maggie Galyan, is wrapping up her Creativity Passage late this afternoon. Maggie plans a career in art and I understand the product of her Passage is a sculpture.

Kris Ondrik's meeting is scheduled for 11:00. She gave me a copy of her wrap-up paper early in the week but I haven't yet read it. Six of us gather around a table in the science room—Jenny and Dave, who are members of Kris's Triad; Tom Rohrbach, her Global Awareness consultant; Josh Hollers, a close friend whom Kris has also invited; Kris; and me. We are awaiting Roberta's arrival; she had a 10:30 Passage meeting elsewhere and it is apparently running long. Kris is small, with short blonde hair. Her chatter is even more rapid than usual. A porkpie hat sits precariously on the back of her head. She looks nervous but confident. I try to scan her wrap-up paper while participating in the small talk going on around me. Kris has studied the reasons for the increasing abductions of small children, what happens to them, and what steps can be taken to reduce the problem.

Roberta rushes in at 11:05. Dumping her armload of books and folders on the table, she apologizes for her tardiness. She takes a moment to compose herself as she shuffles through her stack looking for Kris's folder. Roberta's 25, a Denverite who's lived all her life in Colorado. She played basketball in high school and graduated fifth in a class of over 500—yet another in what seems an unusually high number of Open School teachers who excelled in high school and college. (Tom is another.) Because we were housemates at the Langbergs' for a time, I've come to know Roberta well. She earned a sociology degree in 3 years at Colorado College, where she got both intellectually and personally involved in a range of social issues. College also taught her that her high school preparation had not included learning how to think. The revelation dismayed her and she began to look critically at her high school experience. In a way—years before she would stumble on it—Roberta was already searching for a place like the Open School. She had a brief encounter with law school, which taught her that the law was not a fast track to social justice, and then turned to teaching. She did most of her preparation to teach within the environs of the Open School and then landed a job in it. Roberta finds Kris's folder, brushes a lock of blonde hair back from her forehead, and asks Kris to tell us the story of her Passage.

"I wrote my Passage proposal last November," Kris begins. "It's been just about a year now. I already had an idea for a community service project that could help find a child who might come up missing. I wanted to set up a program of fingerprinting and videotaping children. A videotape of a missing child can be played on TV. People can hear the child's voice and observe mannerisms and personality. Even if the tape is several years old when they see it, there's a good chance that they'll recognize the child if they've been around him. And fingerprints never change. And so I planned to tape and fingerprint all the kids at Tanglewood. The tapes and fingerprints would be given to the parents for safekeeping."

"I know some of your plan didn't work out," Tom says. "Could you tell us what happened?"

"Well first, Tanglewood wanted me to put everything in writing. That took a couple of weeks. And then, after I did all that, they decided that the project was too controversial. The ego in me was outraged. Tanglewood—my old school—wasn't just rejecting my idea, they were putting me down. I was discouraged. Trying to fight through the problem was making me miserable. I dropped my Passage in April."

"But you really didn't drop it," Roberta says. "What did you do?"

"Well, I decided that I'd survey the parents," Kris continues. "If they were for the idea, Tanglewood could hardly refuse. But Tanglewood wouldn't even let me distribute the survey. Finally, I had to switch the service part of my Passage to just trying to inform people—mostly here at school—about the problem and what they can do to help. I did that at Governance a couple of weeks ago and I also put up a bulletin board about missing children outside Kurt's room."

Passages often are altered in the course of their execution. A recurring theme running through them is the learning that occurs as kids cope with the sort of setbacks that occur in real life. These are rarely taken—by the student or the staff—as failures. Our conversation turns, as conversations regularly do in Passage meetings, to the personal growth that has occurred during the experience.

"What have you learned about yourself from this?" Roberta asks. Kris reiterates what she's written in her wrap-up paper.

I have struggled with this Passage for over a year. I have found the main frustration and obstacles occur in the dependence on others to complete a Passage. I was not prepared for any rejection toward my idea and it set me back greatly when I first experienced it. I feel that I got through the obstacle by completing the Passage. I have a new enthusiasm for working with others now because I don't let my ego take over.[2]

Roberta asks the other students present if they have any questions for Kris.

"If you had to do it all over," Dave asks Kris, "would you again try to involve Tanglewood?"

"I probably wouldn't," Kris answers. Then, after pondering what she's said, she adds, "But while I might have had a smoother Passage that way, I wouldn't have learned some things—about myself and stuff like that. I don't think I'll take it so personally the next time someone blocks me like that."

Tom closes the meeting. He tells Kris that she's accomplished a great deal with this Passage. "Just because you weren't able to do the videotaping and fingerprinting doesn't mean that those weren't good ideas. Even good ideas don't always work out. I think you've got some clear thoughts about how you've changed. That tells me that this has been a good experience for you and it's probably one that'll have payoff as you work on your other Passages."

Kris beams as we pass a clean copy of her wrap-up paper around the table to be signed by each person present as testimony that she's successfully completed her Global Awareness Passage. She will place the signed copy in her personal dossier, the file that documents her accomplishments at the Open School. She will rely on that body of evidence when the time comes to make the case—as she writes her Transcripts—that she has indeed become a capable young adult.

AFTER LUNCH I SIT IN on a couple of other wrap-ups. Bob Lovins has studied AIDS for his Global Awareness Passage. His wrap-up paper describes how the social stigma of the disease's dominant modes of transmission—homosexual relationships and the sharing of drug needles—"has caused religion and medicine to turn their backs on the disease and its patients and treat the afflicted as pariahs and outcasts."[3] Over the objections of his family, which had feared that he would somehow contract AIDS, Bob performed volunteer work in the Denver Public Health Department's AIDS counseling and testing facility. As a part of his work there he observed testing for the virus and learned how to do the testing himself.

I also attend Beryl Dittemore's wrap-up of her Adventure Passage. Ruth had said it would be a good one. It is. Beryl, who is one of Jeff's advisees, has made seven trips into the outdoors—some with groups of people, some with close friends, and one alone. Two of the trips were Outward Bound experiences. Another was to Alaska. Her central quest through all of these experiences has been self-actualization. Beryl maintained a journal throughout the Passage. On her solo trip she backpacked up into the mountains. Her third night out, she wrote in her journal:

> I could get mauled by a black bear, get dehydrated, trip and break my leg, choke on my gorp and die. But I don't care. Big deal. If something happens I will know it is bad Karma and I will try to do better next time. Now I know why Jeffrey can see things so simply. It's this living with the earth stuff. I get it.

She continues:

> Why did Jeffrey marry Susie?
> Or why did Mom marry my dad?
> And why do I think of marriage when I'm setting up my tent?[4]

Beryl judges the set of experiences, especially the solo trip, as a great success. "I managed to bring my realizations home," she says. "I'm happy the people in my life believed I could do this as much as I did. For a brief time I felt like I belonged. I felt grounded."

WE CONVENE AT 2:30 FOR Stephanie Woodward's Logical Inquiry proposal meeting. We are really holding two proposal meetings simultaneously; Stephanie is also proposing her Global Awareness Passage in this meeting. She will be using one experience to meet the requirements of two Passages, a common practice in the school. Besides Stephanie our group includes Rick Lopez, Stephanie's advisor; Pat Sliemers, her Global Awareness consultant; and one member of her Triad — Josh Messmer. We meet in the office that Rick and Pat share. Stephanie and I have discussed the design of her study. She will interview a number of unusual Open School students, the school's most visibly idle — the ones I started the year thinking of as bummed-out kids. Bummed-out kids don't just trouble Stephanie, as they do many of us; they enrage her.

Rick and I have talked about Stephanie's study. She is well-prepared for it. She has been reading Abraham Maslow and Lawrence Kohlberg. She is one of three students I have hired and trained to interview other students, as part of my study of the school, so she's had a modicum of training as an interviewer. But there is a more important reason we see her study as a particularly good one for her. It's sometimes difficult to build much risk into some Logical Inquiry Passages. Students who are trying to adopt the scientist's aura of objectivity are not as easily touched during the Logical Inquiry Passage as they are in other Passages. But there is considerable risk for Stephanie in this Passage. Now a graduating senior, she has for most of 3 years been one of the most headstrong and opinionated members of the Open School community. She has made harsh statements—some in forums as public as Governance—about the behavior of the kids she is now proposing to try to understand.

Stephanie begins the meeting by describing the design of her study. I have always thought of her as self-confident but she now avoids our eyes. Instead she studies her proposal, which she clutches tightly in her moist hands. We have few concerns about the study so I ask her the big question. "Can you really be open-minded about these kids?"

"There's no way to know for sure," she says, finally looking at me directly. "It may sound self-righteous but right now I have trouble even understanding how people can have opinions differing from mine on important issues."

"Do you mean that you think the only valid view is the one you hold?" Rick asks.

"Yeah, sort of," she answers.

"What will it do to you, do you think, if you find you have to change your mind about these kids?" Pat asks her.

"I don't know," she says. Her serious expression slowly melts into a mischievous grin. "Do you think it will be bad for me?"

We approve her proposal. Because we are reviewing proposals for two Passages, the meeting is running long. I'm already late for my next commitment—Maggie Galyan's wrap-up. As the group moves to Stephanie's Global Awareness proposal—what she intends to do with the information she collects—I quietly excuse myself.

MAGGIE'S MEETING IS NEXT DOOR in Ruth's office. I slip quietly into the room. Maggie's painted sculpture—a cowboy, lariat in hand—sits on the round table in the middle of the group. The cowboy—almost 3 feet high—stands in repose, his weight resting on one hip. Despite the satiny quality of the muted colors in which he's painted, Maggie's cowboy has a glitzy feel, almost as though the piping on his western shirt should be neon. The smooth form before me is executed in papier-maché, what I have always thought of as a crude medium of the elementary school classroom. Maggie's Career Exploration Passage—apprenticing herself to a local sculptor—is linked to this Passage. The sculptor has not only taught her the ins and outs of making art one's livelihood but has also taught her his favorite medium. The piece before us is evidence of how well Maggie has learned to use it.

The school day comes to an end. A number of students leave the building with new direction. A few others have attended a meeting in which the germ of an idea for one of their own Passages has been planted. Still others leave, basking in an aura of accomplishment; they have met yet one more of the challenges of an Open School education, taken one more step toward adulthood.

School as a Place of Empowerment

At the policy level at least the Open School was not a school for some particular kind of kid. Indeed the school's wild heterogeneity gave it a special potency and made it unusual among the thousands of public alternative schools, most of which establish their raison d'être around a particular clientele that they serve. The principle that this was a school that took on *all* comers was deeply imbedded in its culture. Indeed the staff clung tenaciously to the concept in the face of outsiders' recommendations that the school practice some selectivity. A major finding of the already-mentioned panel of outside evaluators that audited the school's self-study (Steele, 1987) was that this was a single school trying to meet the needs of many different types of kids (Smith et al., 1987).

The school's stand caused misconceptions. Its commitment to serving all kids made it easy to mistakenly identify it—as so many public alternative high schools are—as what I call a Statue-of-Liberty school (give me your tired, your poor, your huddled masses yearning to breathe free). The school was not a place, as so often seems the case with public alternative schools, where the district banished its dis-kids (the disadvantaged, disruptive, disoriented, disgruntled, disenfranchised, discontented, disagreeable, or discombobulated). The Jeffco school district, unlike many others, did not impose barriers to the transfer of students to the school. As a result each dis-kid was matched by another who came to the school for positive reasons because he or she had looked at the program and found it appealing.

For most of the staff, working with that portion of the Open School's student body that entered the school very unempowered was one of the job's frustrations. Perversely, it also created the conditions for one of the job's great rewards. The transformations that occurred in those most unempowered—what in the seminar I termed the school's battered kids—were sometimes swift. Arnie once talked about it.

> You can see the kids change in three days. There has to be something about the kids that enables them to respond so quickly. We can't be doing

92

that much in so short a time. I think it is mostly that we allow the kids to be themselves. Some schools start with a kid by figuring out what he or she doesn't know, what I call a deficit model. We try to do the opposite; we try to help them see what they are already good at. It's a critical difference. (Gregory & Smith, 1987, pp. 103–104)

Watching those transformations occur—watching the unempowered become empowered—whether it took 3 days or 3 years, and knowing that one played some part in bringing them about was just one of the many professional rewards of teaching at the Open School. Still, learning that lesson with my own advisees was a draining experience. Establishing a trusting relationship with a strange adult in a strange school is seldom easy for a beginning student, as one second-year student explained:

It was real slow, just because of a lot of the things that I was going through. I never talked to anybody. I had a real problem with talking. My advisor didn't push me to talk but he was there if I needed to. And I started taking advantage of that more and more. He showed me that he cared and he was really friendly but not to the point where you just wanted to shut up. It's not a fake caring and understanding like I see from a lot of teachers at a regular school where there are so many students. (Int. 4/88)

Once a sound relationship is established between an advisor and a student, the school's power to transform a kid—or more accurately to empower a kid to transform herself or himself—begins to work. The student can get on with the task of becoming a young adult.

My advisor is very supportive of me. He doesn't put me down when I share ideas with him. He helps me elaborate on them. And if they are not potential Passages, then he helps them to become part of my life anyway. He doesn't say, "Well that's really neat," and then blows you off. He cares about my education. He wants me to take classes and stuff that are going to be an advantage for me. And he is fun. I can trust him. Trust is real important. I could not have a relationship with an advisor if I didn't trust him. (Int. 4/88)

The Open School's Advising system and its personalized academic program were so interrelated that it was difficult to envision either functioning effectively in the absence of the other. The extensive amount of time—3 hours on Friday morning and the untold hours of individual conferences that staff members held each week—that were devoted to Advising often prompted visitors from the Old World to ask if it could possibly be worth it; wouldn't much of the time that the Open School spent building relationships be better expended in delivering content to students? It almost certainly would not. Nor is it in most schools. A recent national study, for example, concluded that the most frequently voiced concerns of teachers, administrators, parents, and students centered on issues of "discipline, motivation, lack of respect, teacher apathy and lack of parental involvement—all relationship issues" (Strother, 1990, p. 159; see also Comer, 1989). The lack of learning we see in our schools is due not so much to an absence of content as to students who are simply refusing to receive the content that is being so arbitrarily delivered. With growing numbers of kids today, what will be learned must be negotiated. Advising was the forum in which that negotiation occurred at the Open School. The time lost to content as kids learned about themselves and came to understand why an experience would be beneficial to them was often regained when finally, in the quest for content, they became active agents rather than passive resisters. The aimlessness of many beginning students was counterbalanced by the relentless drive of graduating seniors, some of whom structured their last months in the school so tightly that they carried appointment books.

But knowledge of these transformations did little to help me feel competent as an advisor of beginning students. I was deeply dissatisfied with the slow pace at which my relationships with my advisees were developing. My self-repudiation softened only when I happened to compare what I knew of these kids—after only a few weeks—with what I had known of the kids with whom I had worked in some cases for 5 years back in the 1960s. For the first time I realized that in many ways I already knew Sharon and Evan and Bert, Marty and Terry, and even Inge better than I had ever known all but a handful of the kids that I'd taught in the 1960s. Why was I so satisfied then and so dissatisfied at the Open School? I decided it was not so much a change that had occurred in me in the intervening years. Rather, at the Open School I was in a context in which the expectations for familiarity, for strong relationships between students and teachers, were dramatically higher than they'd been in the large, anonymous high school in which I had taught 20 years earlier.

THE SEMINAR, TOO, HAD AN IMPACT on my understanding of a school as a place to empower students. After the discussion I spent some time thinking about what had transpired and about the kind of school the

Open School was. Many of the school's students, perhaps as many as half, might have been termed battered kids. They came to the Open School after experiencing some degree of failure or at least frustration in one of Jeffco's conventional schools. Those schools had done an effective job of teaching the kids that it was they, not their schools, who had messed up. For those students the move to the Open School may have been an escape or an appeal to a court of last resort.

They were products of high schools and junior highs that were designed to fit the needs of their great grandparents. Both they and the society in which they live have changed dramatically during the intervening generations. Secondary schools have regularly updated and fine-tuned their programs in response to these ever-changing conditions, but the fundamental premises upon which they were founded remain largely intact. In these respects our children have outgrown our schools. In 1972 James Coleman described the shifts that occurred in society in the century-and-a-half since the schooling model that we still employ was devised. Early-nineteenth-century agrarian America was, for the young, action rich but information poor. Children often functioned as responsible adults by age 12. *Telling* children about a world they could not know through any other means was a necessary activity. A boy in the 1870s in rural Illinois could sit awestruck, "open-mouthed and incredulous" as his teacher mentioned in passing that he had been on a train that traveled 60 miles an hour. Our 180-degree transformation into an information-rich, action-poor society has not been matched by a commensurate change in our schools.

> The school of the future must focus on those activities that in the past have largely been accomplished outside school: first, productive action with responsibilities that affect the welfare of others, to develop the child's ability to function as a responsible and productive adult; and second, the development of strategies for making use of the information richness and the information processing capabilities of the environment.
>
> The activities that have been central to the school's functioning, such as expansion of students' factual knowledge and cognitive skills, must come to play an ancillary role. It is not clear just what the shape of future schools will be, but they must not have as their primary goal the teaching of children. Anomalous as this principle may seem, it is the key to successful educational institutions of the future. The failure to recognize this principle is a major source of malaise in present schools. (Coleman, 1972, p. 75)

More recently, Coleman (1987) described the growing dysfunction of schools regarding a second founding premise. When the high school was created, he points out, a very different concept of authority existed between the old and the young. Authority then was much more inextricably linked to financial dependence. As long as a child lived at home he or she was expected to mind the head of the household. Accordingly, the schools that were created for the youngsters of that era expected them to *mind*.

Gradually over the past few decades that fundamental relationship between the older and the younger generations has changed. In most families in the United States today, Coleman believes, a fundamental shift in the relationship occurs around the age of 14, sometimes much earlier. As today's children mature, minding adults begins to be replaced by a form of negotiation. But our young people still attend schools based on the idea that adolescents will mind. Most of our secondary schools are far too large to be able to operate on a negotiation model even if they chose to try. Negotiation does occur in schools but it is far more likely to occur on the scale of the classroom, where teachers, beleaguered by students who won't mind, have resorted to tacit social contracts. I once heard a researcher who was working on a national study of high schools say, "There are schools in this country where teachers will tell you that the most important technological innovation in use in the schools today is not the television or the computer, but the Sony Walkman" (Hout, 1983, cited in Gregory & Smith, 1987, p. 62). "This innocent piece of technology allows students, forced by law to be in school, to remove themselves psychologically from an unworkable situation. In turn, teachers can look over their quiet, docile classes and pretend that they are teaching" (p. 62). These social contracts or pacts that are more and more often forged in classrooms are far more difficult to develop at the school level because of the degree to which they violate a fundament of the institution: Kids are expected to *mind* adults. A school designed at a time when adolescents were treated as children has great difficulty today treating them as adults.

Advising was one of the primary forums in which the Open School treated its students as adults. Walkabout was another. Each Passage wrap-up was in its way a public celebration of tangible achievement. Open School students were engaged in an education that had no grading, that emphasized self-evaluation, and that had the appearance of having few externally imposed standards. Yet several students had described the school as one of the toughest high schools in the state. They pointed to Walkabout as evidence supporting their assessment.

[The Open School] demands not only the traditional academic expectations that other schools have, but we also have the six

Passages to adulthood, which are equally important here. The school requires a lot of self-motivation and self-discipline. You have to just do it all by yourself. Nobody's sitting here saying, "You have to do this and then you have to do this." You just have to do it right off. And you are doing everything for yourself rather than regurgitating stuff for other people. So I do feel like its harder here to graduate. (Int. 4/88)

Because of the high degree of control that students exercised during Walkabout over the course of their education, no segment of the Open School's highly individualized program presented a more varied picture. That variety created problems. Early in its inception at the school, for example, Walkabout inspired a competitive mood in the school's high flyers. Passages took on an uncomfortable materialism, with students vying to be the one who would travel to the most distant, most exotic land, stay for the longest duration, or suffer the severest deprivation while there. Happily for the staff that mood has abated with time.

Students controlled the content of Walkabout. The staff's role was to gauge whether an experience that a student proposed represented a challenge—for that student. Even if one ignored the extremes of the Open School's student body—the gifted and special ed kids who made up about 20% of the school's population—the range of experiences that met the criterion of being personally challenging was very wide. Staff members probably did occasionally misgauge a student's reach. A graduating senior confessed that she had blown off her first two Passages. "That's terrible to admit, but yeah, two of my Passages are a total joke" (Int. 3/88).

While the kids were aware of the range of difficulty that existed in Passage experiences, they seemed much less aware of the range of abilities that existed in the student body. One of the most gratifying byproducts of the Open School's individualized program was the manner in which it led students to think of each fellow student as just another regular kid. While the staff, functioning within the legal protections afforded the handicapped (statutes that require certain kids to receive certain services), occasionally in private discussions, referred to "staffed" kids, I cannot recall even once in my year in the school encountering an instance of a student implying that some students in the school were less able than the rest. When students heard that an "easy" Passage had been approved, they didn't seem to consider that it might be an appropriate experience for a student of limited ability. They were more likely to see a regular kid being let off easy by a soft advisor or Passage consultant. A student talked about being bothered by easy "Passages that the other kids are doing, baking a cake or something. That's what some of the advisors let them do" (Int. 4/88). If the laws of Colorado—promulgated in response to the group instruction that dominates other schools—did not mandate the labeling, sorting, and special treatment of some students, I'm not at all certain that even the staff would be able to spot most of them in the Open School's individualized context. I know that I was surprised in several instances to learn that some apparently quite capable kid was receiving special ed services. Empowerment may be a key factor operating here. We admire people who have gained a measure of control over their difficult circumstances; they have, in our eyes, accomplished something important. And they are by definition "capable."

The amount of control that students exercised over content manifested itself in other ways. An unusual characteristic of the school, for example, was that it had no extracurriculum. None of the clubs and activities that fill the afternoon and evening hours of students in other schools existed at the Open School. There was no National Honor Society; no Thespians; no band, orchestra, or choir. The closest the school came during my year in it to having an interscholastic athletic team was in basketball.[1] The Open School's team, coached by Rick Lopez, played a one-game schedule. This situation has a simple explanation: There is no such thing as an extracurriculum when all knowledge and experience fall within the curriculum. Transformations such as this alarm some critics of the public schools. Mortimer Adler, who is probably the foremost living champion of a classical education, once condemned the Open Schools of another era—the schools of the Progressive Education movement. In 1939 he wrote that they were "throwing the curriculum out of the school and putting in extra-curricular activities in its stead. [They are] supplementing the curriculum of the school with claptrap" (Tenenbaum, 1951, p. 240). What would appall Adler about the Open School impressed Bert Horwood (1987), who studied the school in 1983. After observing the school for several months he discussed the phenomenon.

> The fundamental issue here is what counts as curriculum, what counts as learning. In the Walkabout program there is no mention of extracurricular activities. The concept is foreign to the underlying value system driving the school. Everything counts. All learning is creditable, whether made over coffee in Munchie, or by sweating a calculus problem in class. Knowledge of literature is as important as knowledge of wilderness. The crucial matter is the development of general competence including the ability to continue learning throughout life. (pp. 90–91)

Walkabout took the seniors who graduated during my year in the school to several foreign countries, including Germany, Sweden, England, Spain, Mexico, and Saudi Arabia, for periods as long as a year. Individuals spent between 1 and 6 weeks in places such as Big Bend National Park and the Everglades. They stayed for extended periods in New York, New Orleans, and San Francisco. Besides the expected paintings, sculpture, and photography, the products of their Creativity Passages included a Victorian gown, a biography, a screenplay, a restored piano, and an electric generator for a rural home. Their Global Awareness Passages explored topics such as Northern Ireland, nuclear energy, teen suicide, Islam, and the decline of the grizzly bear, and included activities such as winterizing the homes of the needy and working with physically abused children. Careers in photography, acting, social work, teaching, writing, the military, and psychology were explored. The graduates conducted research studies on animal behavior, on the reasons for the then recent increase in Colorado's minimum drinking age, on effective ways of preserving wildlife, on the relationship of diet and nutrition, and on the eating habits of fish. Several students lived on their own to satisfy their Practical Skills Passage requirement. One student learned bookkeeping for a family business, and another learned how to rebuild an automobile engine.

And through all these experiences the students of the Open School learned who they were and what they were capable of accomplishing. They became empowered. A second-year student assessed the impact that Passages had already had on her development.

> You can see it in people's lives. I am not the same person I was when I came here. Those six steps to adulthood aren't a joke. I have become so much more mature, so much more alert. I mean, it's really different. (Int. 4/88)

Each wrap-up meeting was a milestone, an opportunity for a young person to pause along life's path, look back, and gauge the difficulty of the terrain just traveled. Each successful venture prepared a student to approach the next leg of the journey with heightened confidence. Did these young people enter the world more ready than the average high school graduate to meet the day-to-day vagaries of adulthood? The staff clearly thought so. More important, the kids thought so.

I OBSERVED OTHER EXAMPLES of the school's ability to empower kids; one in particular stands out. In a staff meeting in early October, Judy

Sherbert, her voice sounding like a sigh, announced that Don Troxell, one of her advisees, would be leaving the school. Don was one of our three veteran students in Beginnings. Judy was on the verge of tears. She paused to compose herself. Judy, in her early forties, was a teacher's aide in the school the year before my stay, and the Hiring Committee—comprising both staff and students—had offered her an appointment to a certified position this year.

Each year a few Open School kids who reside outside the district enter the school through some form of deception. For example, Margie Thayer claimed residence with her natural father, then divorced from her remarried mother, because he still lived in Jefferson County. Don had been engaging in such a deception. His home was outside the district, in Clear Creek. He paid tuition to attend the school the previous year but was now claiming residence with an aunt who lived in the county. She had become his legal guardian to permit him to attend the school free of charge. The Jeffco bureaucracy had finally figured out that Don was still living with his family in Clear Creek and that the guardianship was a ruse to avoid tuition. He would either have to leave the school or resume paying tuition, an expense his family could no longer afford.

As Judy shared the news, my thoughts turned to Don's quiet enthusiasm on the Cortez Trip. His interest in archaeology predated his entry to the school. Cortez had been an important event in his life and he was working hard to renew the experience by planning a return trip in the spring. He, Carol, and Craig had begun lining up interested students. They'd even contacted Wendell Rhodes, who'd committed himself to supervising their work. Wendell had been quite taken by the kids. Their industry had surprised him and he'd appreciated working with a group of young people who brought to the task not only enthusiasm but a sensitivity to the fragility of the kiva site. A few of them, like Don, also brought enough knowledge of the Anasazi to be able to ask intelligent questions about what they were about. The kids' ethics in dealing with artifacts seemed to surprise Wendell, too. He told the trio that he would be there when they returned, even if it meant dropping whatever he'd be working on at the time.[2] It looked as though Susie was going to complete another piece of the plan by becoming the staff member the students needed to "lead" the trip. Now for Don those dreams had been dashed.

Judy talked about the progress Don made in the little over a year that he was at the Open School. "When I think of how much he's changed since even last winter, I . . . ." Her voice trailed off in the stillness of the meeting room. Pat Sliemers reached over and gave Judy a hug and rubbed her back. "Everything was going so well for him."

A few days later I bumped into Don in Munchie. I took a seat across the table from him. We exchanged greetings over the clatter of pots and pans as the day's work crew cleaned up after lunch. Don was wearing the plaid flannel shirt and Levis that were his standard school outfit. I told him I was sorry to hear about his leaving the school and asked him what he was going to do.[3]

"I've always had trouble with the cliques in other schools," he responded. "Even when you're a member of one of the groups — say, the Jock group — the Jocks in one grade don't even get along with the Jocks in another grade."

"Doesn't the Open School have cliques?" I asked.

"They're small," Don said, "very small. They're really just groups of friends." He commented that there was no sense that they ostracized others. He'd often been on the outside looking in, in other schools. The Open School had been different. He'd sensed that from his first day in the school when many returning students and most of the staff members had made a point of introducing themselves to him.

Don seemed to have accepted his situation. He showed no anger at being forced to leave the school. It was almost as though he'd expected the guardianship ploy to fail. He told me his plans.

"I'm not going back to Clear Creek," he said. "I'm trying to work out a plan to finish high school through home schooling."

Growing numbers of families, dismayed by the single brand of education that is available in most public school districts, are choosing to educate their children at home. Parents of all stripes are exercising the option, but home schooling's image seems unduly flavored by its extremes: parents on the far left — ex-hippies and Vietnam-era radicals — or parents on the far right — religious fundamentalists and survivalists. Some states make it very easy for parents to set up a home school. Others fight against the idea. Colorado was fairly permissive in its dealings with home schoolers. Most home schooling occurs with young children, but at least one child from Utah who was educated entirely at home has entered Harvard.

Brushing back his light brown bangs, Don said, "If I can work out a home schooling arrangement, maybe I can still have something resembling an Open School education." He paused, perhaps thinking about the task ahead. I wondered if he, like I, was considering all the pieces of the school — the friendships, the interchanges with the staff, the psychic support — that would be missing from the education he would build for himself. I was thinking about asking him about these issues when his face brightened.

"Maybe I can figure out a way to still do the Cortez trip in the spring," he said. "Maybe I could just meet up with the other kids down there."

Lesson III

COMMUNITY

One of the great advantages of small, informal schools is their potential to create strong, supportive communities. Over the years, as I've watched small alternative high schools function as communities, I've been struck by their power to influence positively the behavior of socially conscious adolescents. On occasion I have also had the opportunity to contrast these social settings with the sometimes dysfunctional forms of community that develop in very large schools as adolescents attempt, subconsciously, to create workable communities inside them and instead create cliques.[1] Like other small, informal schools, the Open School contained no subgroups that might be called cliques. Small "friendship groups" of five or ten students were omnipresent, but I sensed none of the animosity between such groups that I have seen in large high schools.

The small scale of the Open School was almost certainly a factor that shaped its social climate, but the staff and students also worked to build community in many ways. For example, the school had two opening days. One of these, as we have already seen, was the day when beginning students first entered the school. But the school opened its doors to veteran students two days earlier. They immediately began rebuilding the community by going on an overnight retreat at a church camp some 30 miles from the school. In a sense, they and the staff used the retreat as a way to re-establish the school *before* they had to deal with the added complications that would arise with the introduction into the school community of over 150 newcomers who had little sense of what the school was about. One event of the retreat—a spontaneous litany of tributes to the school offered up by students and staff members in an all-school meeting—exemplified how community building was integrated into the school's program.

Conceiving high school as preparation for life is almost a cliché. We are justified in viewing such pronouncements cynically; they seldom are more than mere reifications. Preparation for life in most schools remains covering content and passing tests. Even events of great import may have little visible impact on the routine of most schools. An event of this kind—the tragic death of a student—occurred early in my year at the school. The response of the school community to this tragedy was anything but routine; for a week the entire school engaged not in learning history or algebra, but in a process of grieving and healing. Helping young people cope with death became *the* curriculum, as the school said goodbye to Toby May.

The Open School's academic program was more highly personalized than that of any other school that I have experienced. Individual students were regularly engaged in very individual pursuits. The program was also much more externalized than that of any other school that I have experienced. Students' individual pursuits regularly took them out of the building and the town, often took them out of the state, and sometimes took them out of the country. As I watched the school function as a community, this tension between individual pursuits and the goals of community became of interest to me and eventually I made it the topic of a New World Seminar. That discussion is presented as a part of the development of this lesson.

CHAPTER 6

Tributes

The rains return in earnest during dinner. Afterward everybody darts here and there, dodging puddles, attending to personal matters during the short break before the all-school meeting (really, the all-*returning*-student meeting), which will take place in the church camp's sanctuary—a big A-frame structure dominated by a huge stone fireplace and hearth. We take our places, ignoring a couple of rolling racks of folding chairs; everybody simply plops down on the red-carpeted floor. Probably because the wall makes a good backrest, most everybody picks a spot on the large room's perimeter, which creates an awkward arrangement for running a meeting: We are seated in what amounts to a huge rectangle, perhaps 40 feet by 80 feet in size. But running the meeting is the kids' responsibility. Gradually a few students and staff members begin to fill in the middle of the large room, primarily because all the good spots along the wall are full.

Keith Leander, a student dressed in punk rocker gear—a black leather jacket with lots of silver studs, and what a student seated nearby tells me is a liberty-spike (as in Statue of Liberty) mohawk—leads the meeting. One item becomes, for me, the highlight of the whole retreat. Ruth suggests that it is useful for us to periodically remind ourselves why the Open School has become so important a part of our individual lives. After some silence the antiphon begins as one and then another student or staff member voices his or her valued trait of the program.

"The freedom." "Being able to design your own curriculum." "The ability to have a friendship." "We can work together on things." "We can cling together constantly." "Not being in a position where you have to compete with your friends." "The acceptance of people."

"The teachers," a student says, to which Pat Sliemers responds, "The students." "Everyone's a teacher and a student."

"The warmth of people." "Back rubs," is offered by a student currently receiving one. "Trips." "Trust." "The way it helps you to become an individual." "The way it helps you to become whole." "The way it involves parents." "Trips, trips, trips!" "That I can ask questions and not be made to feel stupid." "Smiles and hugs." "The different types of people." "Being able to see the whole universe." "The sense of family." "The good food and books." "Advising." "The evaluation system." "Being able to talk about stuff." "The support system." "IEPs." "Apprenticeships." "Being able to leave the classroom."

Joy Jensen offers, "Being able to leave your stuff around and have it still be there when you come back." The parenthetical, "Most of the time anyway," that she adds as an afterthought draws chuckles from the group.

"Classes," a boy says. His contribution is followed by a long silence. Ruth then closes off the activity and Keith moves us on to other business.

CHAPTER 7

Toby May

"Shotgun!" Inge shouts as she bolts past Toby, knocking his derby cock-eyed as she leaps down her front stoop, covering several steps at once.[1] This little contest for the right front seat—where the guard with the shotgun would ride a stagecoach—has been going on between them for months. With her surprise head start, Inge easily reaches the Communist Destroyer ahead of Toby, as she almost always does. Toby's first impulse is to pursue, but once it's clear the seat is Inge's he stops and collects himself. Carefully readjusting his derby and lifting his nose ever so slightly, Toby makes a dignified descent, commenting haughtily as he gets in the back seat on the childishness of such games.

There are more interesting things to think about than seating arrangements. Toby has planned a little adventure for the group. Well, if not much of an adventure, it is a way to spend what is looking to be a pretty dead Friday evening. Six good friends are on their way to Central City, one of Colorado's many old mining towns turned tourist traps. Toby had started organizing their little junket earlier in the afternoon at school. He is interested in producing a video about vampires—part of his long-standing interest in the occult—and he needs to find a house that looks like a castle to use as a filming location.[2] Toby has heard that Central City has several likely candidates, big Victorian mansions built by the gold barons of another era. Once he'd talked Ritch Hahn into driving, getting the rest of the group together was easy.

Toby's brash, outgoing manner will play a key role in his production plans; once a location is identified, he will simply knock on the door and ask to use the place for a couple of hours. Toby's ability to execute so brazen a maneuver in an endearing manner had gotten him through many doors, both figurative and real. Since junior high school it's helped him land a string of acting jobs, experiences that have taught him how to bluff his way through awkward situations. It's also caused him to create a few. If the behavior of anyone at the Open School merits the appellation "outrageous," Toby's does. A formidable reputation for unpredictable behavior accompanied his move from

Tanglewood. Toby did nothing on the Wilderness Trip last year to tarnish it when he mooned Susie Bogard. Her unabashed, "So what? I've seen a million of 'em," had effectively cemented an advisor/advisee relationship between them that remained close but often frustrating. Susie understood—perhaps better than he—his reluctance to grab hold of his dreams, his fear of disappointing first himself and then others. Susie would confront him when he hadn't followed through on something. He'd be chagrined and she'd cast about for some way to support his sagging self-esteem, all the while cajoling him to sustain his commitments. Toby's response was often evasive; he would tease and flirt to avoid being serious. He was also seen by many on the staff as a loose cannon. Some had taken to holding their breath whenever he started to speak at Governance, braced for whatever scandalous pronouncement this little imp of a kid was about to utter in front of the day's collection of visitors from the Old World.[3]

Inge is the last of the six to be picked up. Already in the car besides Ritch are Roger Chambers, Natasha Stewart—Tasha to her friends—and Inge's current romantic interest, Jeremy Hill. Toby's feigned disinterest as he returns to the Destroyer fools no one. He receives a round of "bullshits" for his effort and gets ridden unmercifully for again losing the shotgun. By 5:30 they are winding their way up Route 6 through Clear Creek Canyon. No one quite remembers how Ritch's hulk of a '64 Buick got the label "Communist Destroyer." The car is what might be described as a totalitarian grey but the name probably stuck because the damn thing is so big it needs to be docked more than parked. The Destroyer's crew is in high spirits. As they pass through each of the canyon's several tunnels, the kids stick their heads out the windows and yell nonsense phrases just to hear the impressive boom they create against each tunnel's unyielding walls.

As they cruise into Central City, Tasha spots an ice cream parlor and suggests they start by fortifying themselves for the work ahead. The others think it's a good idea and Ritch eases the Communist Destroyer into a nearby berth. The sign on the parlor door reads "Back in 5 Minutes." Jeremy suggests they get a cup of coffee while they wait and they find a spot a few doors down the street.

Over coffee they begin planning the video. Roger will play the vampire. Several of the others will be dinner guests at the dining room scene Toby hopes to shoot in the yet-to-be-found castle. They share ideas on where they can get costumes, evening clothes mostly, and where to obtain the props they'll need; finding candelabras may be a problem. One idea leads to another as the whole group becomes infected with Toby's enthusiasm for the project. The coffee is strong, the company good. Checking the time Roger observes that it's been over an hour since they sat down. They pay their bill and head back to the ice cream parlor where the Back-in-5-Minutes sign is still hanging on the door. It gets cussed at some as Tasha gives the door a half-hearted kick, but ice cream doesn't seem like such a good idea anymore. The sun's down and there's already a chill in the mountain air. There's hardly enough daylight left to even begin a search for a shooting location so the group decides to head home. "Shotgun!" Toby shouts as he dashes for the Communist Destroyer. For once he's beaten Inge to the punch. She reconciles herself to the back seat where she can stretch out across Jeremy's lap and take a nap on the way home. Inge demonstrates that she, too, can play the game within their game, claiming that the back seat and Jeremy's lap is where she wanted to be anyway. Nevertheless her "You won this time only because my heart wasn't in it," brings jeers from the group. Inge's a little irritated. She tries to act nonchalant but the Destroyer's creaking back door won't cooperate. It takes several slams, each increasingly more angry, for Inge to finally get it to stay shut. Each attempt produces another ripple of giggles through the group.

Now in darkness the Destroyer heads back down the winding canyon highway. The car is warm and quiet. The drone of the Destroyer's well-worn exhaust system has a lulling effect on the group. The lights of each passing car flash across satisfied, sleepy faces. It's been a good evening together even if they never got started looking for Toby's castle. Toby especially is feeling good. The school year has gotten off to a great start for him. Being Jeff's assistant on the Wilderness Trip had worked out beautifully. Toby had ended the week feeling nothing but success. To top the week off he returned home to find a phone message awaiting him from the Denver Center Theater. A producer wanted him to audition for the role of a young Truman Capote in an upcoming production. Toby's not sure he's right for the part. He's small enough for the role but his voice may be too deep. He'd almost passed up the audition but when he told Susie about the call, she'd said that she thought he'd be perfect for it. He always hated to disappoint her. Finally Susie's persistent cajoling convinced him to arrange to read for the part. If only the rest of the year can be like these 3 weeks, Toby thinks.

A FEW MILES AWAY in Golden, Randy Ledbetter, a construction worker down on his luck, pushes his stool away from the bar at Tony's.[4] Randy spends a couple of hours at Tony's most Friday afternoons. It's a convenient place to cash his paycheck and drink a few beers, putting the week behind him and getting primed for the weekend. Standing, Randy gives himself a minute to adjust to this new position by taking time to check his pockets, looking first for a match to light up a cigarette and then to make sure he's got his money with him. He finally finds the money in the pocket of his flannel shirt and walks out to his Toyota pickup. He fumbles through pockets again, looking for his keys, and notices they are still in the ignition. Randy fires up the engine and begins the winding drive home, up through Clear Creek Canyon.

THE COMMUNIST DESTROYER CONTINUES to hum along. There's quite a bit of traffic. On a dark, serpentine road like this it's often hard to figure out if an approaching car is in its own lane or yours. Then, too, cars often creep over the center line only to correct their paths well before meeting oncoming traffic. Roger and Toby continue to talk quietly about the video as the Destroyer drones on. Roger is getting drowsy and he says, "I think I'll take a nap."

Toby says, "Sure, go ahead," and then he adds, "I love you, Roger." Toby never hesitates to tell friends that he loves them. Life is too short not to express important feelings, even if some people might think it's unmasculine.[5]

Roger, his eyelids heavy with sleep responds, "I love you, too, Toby."

As Toby turns to face front, Tasha says, "Oh, shit!" The headlights ahead *are* headed right at them. Randy Ledbetter, his reflexes dulled by the many beers at Tony's, has cut off the inside of the curve they are both in and he is not correcting his path. The road, gouged as it is out of the canyon's wall, offers little room for escape. With the creek meandering 20 or 30 feet below on the Destroyer's right and the steep canyon wall beginning just off the opposite edge of the highway to the left, Ritch points the Destroyer at the only opening available—the lane of the highway vacated by the headlights ahead. The maneuver is too little, too late. There isn't even time to scream as the right headlights of the Destroyer and the Toyota meet head-on.

After interminable seconds, the car comes to rest along the canyon wall and pointed back up the highway. The Destroyer predates seat belts. Ritch struggles out of the car. Leaning groggily over the front fender, he begins to feel his injuries. His lip hurts really bad. His nose is broken. He soon is joined by Roger who is limping badly. The two stand dazed in the eerie headlights of the traffic already stopping to lend assistance. Jeremy, too, has managed to extricate himself from the wreckage. The Toyota truck sits in the middle of the road. It has been spun completely around by the force of the collision. Ledbetter, hunched over and clutching his stomach, approaches the three boys. "God, you guys really look fucked up," he says. Jeremy, who's 6'5", decides to let this smartass know what he thinks of his prognosis, but as he takes a step forward he collapses in pain. Ritch, whose head has hit both the steering wheel and windshield, falls to his knees and then slumps to the ground. Bystanders begin lending him what assistance they can. Ritch looks to be in the worst shape of the three. His face is covered with blood. Still dazed, Roger slides slowly down the side of the Destroyer into a sitting position on the ground.

SOME TIME LATER, Ritch regains consciousness. He is shaking uncontrollably. Bystanders have moved the three boys over to the side of the road and have covered them with blankets; the boys are lying directly on the damp, cold ground and are shivering. Randy Ledbetter thinks it's time to try to lighten the setting. He jokes that *he's* hot; maybe he ought to lend the kids his jacket. The bystanders also are doing what they can for Tasha, Inge, and Toby, all still in the car. Clearly they should not be moved for fear of harming them further. Tasha's right leg has been driven through the floorboards. It is shattered. She is conscious but in shock, her face badly lacerated. Inge is in what's left of the back seat, partially in it and partially in the trunk. She is unconscious.

Toby has taken the full force of the collision. He's been thrown through the windshield and is unconscious, half in the car, half out. He has massive head injuries and a severely lacerated abdomen. Someone has notified the police, and emergency vehicles begin arriving, splashing garish hues of blue, white, yellow, and red across the crumpled car.

SUSIE LEARNS OF TOBY'S DEATH just before midnight; Linda May calls her from the hospital and tells her what has happened. Linda seems to be in control; she apologizes for calling so late and says, "I don't know why I'm calling, except that I know you loved him." Susie asks her what she can do to help, wondering at the same time, though, what she really *can* do; Jeff is away on a hunting trip and she is alone with their two small children. After the phone call she sits in bed—she was asleep when the call came—looking at her trembling hands and thinking the thoughts one does when someone close dies before his time. Toby had possessed tremendous potential. He tried to run away from it, from anyone's expectations but his own. Five-year-old Todd is in the big bed beside Susie and Leah is sleeping in the crib nearby. She makes sure they're covered and watches them both breathe. She is suddenly aware of those members of the Open School community who are not near at hand. She thinks about packing everybody into the car and driving up to North Park where Jeff is hunting with Rick, Bruce, and Kurt on a trip that has become something of an annual fall pilgrimage. Should she call Ruth? What could Ruth do if she did? Isn't the morning soon enough?

The phone rings again. It's Mary Pedersen calling to clarify what's happened. The two girls are in intensive care in two separate hospitals. The ambulance medics do a good job of sending victims to the area hospital best equipped to handle particular injuries, and Tasha's leg was clearly going to require special attention. Inge has a concussion and back injuries and has yet to regain consciousness. Tasha's leg is in terrible shape. She is already in surgery. The other three boys will be held at least overnight, Jeremy probably longer. His crotch was torn open by the force of the collision. Ritch has a severe concussion and a broken nose. Roger has an injured leg and the expected bruises, but looks to be okay otherwise. Susie asks how Linda is doing. As well as can be expected, Mary says. Neither woman mentions Toby.

After hanging up Susie considers calling Pat Sliemers, who lives nearby. But what could Pat do? She'd listen with compassion and then ask if she could come over. What could she do here that Susie can't handle herself? Finally at 1:00 Susie does call Ruth. She retells the story. Ruth's calm voice, always a source of stability in the frenetic existence that is the Open School, asks if she can come up. Susie thinks about the 20-mile drive up into the mountains in the middle of the night. Ruth's offer is wonderful but Susie declines.

Susie begins pacing, padding barefoot over the house's cold floors. She thinks about all the experiences she had with Toby and the confidences he'd shared, including his heavy experimentation with drugs and his identification with Alex, the antihero of *A Clockwork Orange*, which had led to his wearing the derby. Susie thinks about the many conversations she had with Linda, who was struggling to raise an independent-minded son alone. Their life together was often one of uneasy roommates rather than of mother and son.[6] Neither wanted control to be a part of their relationship. The way Toby had set a direction to his life and his willingness to accept responsibility were sound. His judgment, while always well-thought out, sometimes drove Linda a little crazy. It was at those times that they would fight, screaming and swearing at each other. Toby would tell Linda that they fought because they were so alike. She would deny it, all the while knowing he was right. Periodically during her pacing, Susie looks in on the kids, gazing at them in their deep sleep. And after hours of thought she finally falls asleep.

SATURDAY IS SPENT ON THE PHONE. Calls go back and forth between staff members or with kids. The Open School community, always close, begins to draw itself even more tightly together. Keith Leander, the biggest, toughest kid in the school, calls Susie. He's sobbing. She searches for the words that will console him, knowing there are none.

Sunday evening the staff gathers at Ruth's home. Details of the funeral are still undetermined but the whole school will likely be invited to attend. Since Monday morning always starts with Governance, the story of the accident can be told to the students then. Most of the kids already know the story. It looks like Roger and perhaps Ritch will be in school to explain what happened. The staff decides that after Governance, advisory groups will meet to give kids an appropriate forum in which to express their feelings and to give the staff an opportunity to begin helping kids deal with them. From phone conversations with kids, the staff already knows there is much anger directed at Randy Ledbetter, who has been arrested on several charges related to the accident. Ruth is getting copies of a book, *How to Survive the Loss of a Love* (Colsgrove, Bloomfield, & McWilliams, 1976), for the staff to use as a resource in helping kids through the grieving process. The accident, occurring as it has near the beginning of the year, has turned the Open School into two schools: There are all the returning students and a few of the new ones who knew and loved Toby, and then there are the other kids, for whom he has been little more than the brash kid in the derby hat. No one knows quite how to deal with the understandably different reactions these two groups will have. The staff decides that until the funeral classes will meet at the discretion of the teacher. Some classes, like Beginnings, which is populated almost exclusively by new students, probably will meet, while others may not. As the meeting breaks up no one is looking forward to the week ahead, a week that will overflow with anger and remorse and grieving.

THE HALLS BEGIN FILLING earlier than usual on Monday morning. The entering students are very quiet. Small groups of kids cling to each other. There are tears. Some students are already seeking out their advisors. Some staff members float, looking for especially distraught students who may need to talk. Some kids have made a point of finding friends who were close to Toby, just to be with them.

Governance usually meets in the library, which can hold about half of the Open School community. When something of importance to the whole school occurs, the meeting is moved to the only space that can hold everybody—the gym. With its overly live acoustics, the gym is a terrible place to hold a meeting, especially one in which quiet, heartfelt communication will occur. But it's the best the school can do. The kids assemble, sitting here and there in small groups on the hardwood floor. Most are on time, certifying the meeting's importance.

Barbara Ward, the student scheduled to conduct today's meeting, makes some opening remarks and then gives Ruth the floor. Ruth starts by announcing what everyone already knows. "There has been a terrible accident involving six of our students. Toby May is dead." While the formal announcement offers nothing new, it somehow lends reality to the incredible events of Friday night. They did happen. Ruth reviews the condition of each of the five surviving students. Jeremy may be out of the hospital in time for the funeral. Tasha has already undergone 6 hours of surgery, the first of many sessions that will be required to repair her leg. The doctors now think they may be able to save it. Inge has regained consciousness periodically but has total amnesia. Mostly she sleeps. Questions about visiting the hospitalized students are answered. Even though Inge is in intensive care, they're allowing visitors in the hope that some face or comment will break through her amnesia.

Ritch and Roger, who leans heavily on a cane, are present. Through his bandages, Ritch tells the story of the accident in flat tones that belie the enormity of what's happened. The acoustics in the gym and the injuries to his mouth make him barely intelligible. Only the group's stony silence enables the message to come through.

Then it's time for questions about the accident and about Randy Ledbetter. Though he, too, is hospitalized with possible internal injuries, he is under arrest with a very high bail. The accident is only the latest in a long list of misdeeds: assault, selling drugs, and an extensive driving record that includes seven speeding violations. Preliminary charges filed against him include criminally negligent homicide, vehicular assault, driving while impaired, driving without insurance, and driving on the wrong side of the road.[7] The anger boils to the surface. Many of the kids want their pound of flesh; will Ledbetter get off with a slap on the wrist or will he get what he deserves? Others are concerned that newspaper articles by omission have allowed the impression that the students were probably also drinking. Pat Sliemers will call the papers to be sure that misconception is rectified in follow-up articles.

The group turns to ways in which it can transform this terrible event into something positive. The students talk about starting a local chapter of SADD, Students Against Drunk Driving, as a memorial to Toby. Russ Molby and several others plan to organize a march against drunk driving.[8]

Then the funeral is discussed. Linda May wants the kids very involved and she wants it to be the kind of funeral that Toby would have wanted. Toby and Linda often had long talks, and one of them had been about the kind of funeral each would like to have.[9] Toby wanted a secular ceremony that his friends and loved ones would attend, dressed as he had known them, in comfortable attire. They would share stories and memories of their times together. There would be no mourning. For Toby death was a form of graduation. Toby wanted a party—a rousing Irish wake—with dancing and drinking.

He will be buried in a crude pine casket, the very sort that he had been planning to buy to use as a bed. The funeral director has a number of ideas about involving everyone in the burial process, to help the students let go. The casket will be brought to the art room tomorrow and students will be encouraged to decorate it, to personalize it for Toby. The family asks only that drawings and messages appearing on the outside of the casket be in good taste. Other personal messages can be drawn and painted on the inside of the casket. Toby had been fascinated by ancient Egypt and the group decides that Egyptian tomb drawings and hieroglyphs will be a fitting theme for the outside of the casket.

As Governance concludes, Tommy Reeves and Jim Fortune, who experienced how previous schools they attended dealt with the death of a student, stop Ruth to make an observation about what has just transpired. They say that their previous schools didn't seem to be able to do much more with the situation than make an announcement over the P.A. and ask everyone to observe a moment of silence. One of the schools had a memorial service in the form of an assembly. The boys are aware that the dialogue they've just experienced is something very different, something much more personal. They don't use the word but they seem to have sensed a therapeutic quality to the proceedings. They just wanted to thank Ruth for the way in which the issue was handled.[10] Ruth reminds them that she really hasn't had much more to do with what's taken place than they have. It is the Open School community that made Governance whatever it was today.

THAT EVENING I AM ONE of perhaps a dozen people who visit Inge. We are quietly ushered in, one at a time, and asked to keep our stays short. I think I'm prepared for what I'll see but I'm not. I had expected lots of cuts and bruises. I see none, but Inge must have 20 tubes and wires connected to her body and she now looks even smaller and more fragile than usual. Her arms are tied to the bed rails so that her writhings of discomfort won't dislodge the tubes. Heavily drugged to numb her pain, Inge lapses in and out of a fitful sleep, sometimes dozing off even in the middle of a delirious utterance.

I'm her advisor but I feel I hardly know her. We've had several talks but only one was about her rather than about the procedural matters of getting her year off to a good start. She knows even less about me but the mind works in strange ways. For some reason, I am recognized. Inge, who doesn't even know her mother, knows me, the first break in her amnesia. The quirk of circumstance makes me feel strangely special.

THE CRUDE PINE BOX arrives Tuesday noon. The wood is full of knots and checks. The handles are rough hemp pushed through holes drilled in the sides of the box and stopped with knots. The casket is placed on a long, high worktable in the art room. The power it has over us is palpable. The stark presence of these few boards unceremoniously screwed together in the double trapezoidal shape—so familiar, not from real life but from movies and cartoons—is jarring. Some stare at it for long periods, trying to absorb its myriad meanings; others choose to avoid the art room completely while the casket is present in the school.

The imprinting begins. Kids have been digging books on Egypt out of the library, finding hieroglyphs and depictions of gods that communicate appropriate thoughts about Toby and the particular brand of unbounded freedom he represented to so many. Jim Sanders is copying a hieroglyph about being true to yourself on the inside of the lid, facing where Toby will lie. Carol Wonko, one of the school's most gifted artists, does several paintings of gods. Others choose to paint icons from contemporary life; Carl Simpson copies the logo from a Dr. Pepper can, Toby's favorite drink, inside the box. On one side of the casket Susie Bogard musters all her craft as an artist to copy an icon of the winged goddess, Isis, who guides the dead on their journey to the afterlife. As people work hour after hour at their task, the conversation often returns to Toby, about how much he would like some message now being added to the emerging work of art. At other times someone will tell a story about some crazy thing he had done. Several students work right up to the 4:30 deadline when the casket is taken away.

THE MEMORIAL SERVICES TAKE PLACE at 11:00 on Wednesday at the grave site a few miles from school. A bus has been provided for those who need transportation. Oscar Warden, Toby's regular bus driver, has requested to be the driver. The mourners gather at a chapel on top of a low rise overlooking the small cemetery, which is on the edge of a sunbathed meadow. The peaks of the front range of the Rockies are visible in the northwest. Toby's casket has been placed in an antique horse-drawn hearse with beveled glass sides. The hearse, drawn by the kids rather than a horse, leads the cortege of 300 family members and friends slowly down the hill to the grave site.

The casket, still open, is positioned over the grave and the assembly gathers around it. Some people have brought folding chairs; others sit on the freshly mown grass, still damp with morning dew, or else stand on the perimeter. Some purposely take up positions that ensure that they will not be able to see into the open casket. Our dress varies widely, from somber, dark suits and dresses to typical school dress to wild outfits that loudly proclaim the event a celebration of sorts. Dan McCrimmon, for example, has worn the brightly patched and embroidered jeans of his professional folksinging days. Some boys—who are not Open School students and are dressed as cowboys—stand in a loose group on a rise some distance away. Only their detachment from the group with its panoply of different costumes makes them look out of place. How had they fit into Toby's life?

The simple ceremony begins. Warren Sliemers, Pat's husband and a former Catholic priest, presides. He starts by telling the story of Friday evening and of the accident. Then those present are invited to offer their own eulogies. For most of the next hour individuals have their say. Several adults—family members or parents of Toby's friends—talk of the lightness he brought into their lives. Mary Pedersen remembers fondly how he always called her Mom. But mostly the words come from the kids. Libby Guilford, Toby's girlfriend, speaks first. Throughout the ceremony she sits on the ground next to the casket, holding Toby's hand, looking just a bit theatrical in her genuine grief. Many talk of Toby's craziness and how they will miss his continual questioning of conventionality. Others talk of how they will miss his love of life—how he needed to taste and touch and smell and feel and *be*. There is now a hole in their lives that used to be filled by his energy.[11] Some finish by placing some memento or a flower in the casket. Of the staff members, only Susie speaks, not wanting to but feeling that at least one of them should. She talks of Toby as a bright shining comet who flew into all our lives for a brief time. He had lived life with an intensity that made one wonder if he would burn up at any moment. We couldn't help being changed by his presence.

The written program for the ceremony contains the writings of several people, including Toby. Just weeks earlier, Libby had written a piece to him, eerie in its prescience, that included the lines

> If somebody splits off in a different direction, even though our physical bodies will no longer be close, there will always be a cord, made of memories, connecting our hearts.

Linda May wrote a poem in 1974 about a 4-year-old Toby that ended

> I remember that the trees were budding with spring and he with a child's curiosity carried him to a low hanging limb.
> And he—with all the brightness of the sun—found so much delight in the simple pleasure of a lady bug. He went too close and it flew away.
> He ran to me crying and I held him in my arms and told him that all of nature should be free.
> He seemed to understand. He was quiet for a moment. Then, he put his small, chubby arms around my neck and squeezed a happy squeeze. And I remember that he said, "I love you mommy," and he went off to play again.

One of the pieces, a poem entitled *Destruction and Rebirth*, was written by Toby. It ends with the lines

> I am a wonderful human being
> I can do anything
> I will not accept negativity from anyone
> I deserve Happiness and Positive things
> My spirit can now soar to the heights of joy
> My higher self has joined once again with my lower self
> And with this unity I am whole and complete
> I can now Rejoice with Happiness I am one
> Life love peace
> I am reborn everyday
> Becoming more Powerful and Positive with each Rebirth
> The chains of Negativity are lifted
> I AM FREE!

The time comes to close the casket. One of the kids starts up a boom box. The strains of Pink Floyd's *The Wall*, Toby's favorite album, waft over the sunny meadow.

> We don't need no education;
> We don't need no thought control.

Libby removes Toby's derby—it will be her keepsake—and the lid is placed on the casket. Several hammers and a can of 12-penny nails appear. Any mourner who wishes is invited to participate in nailing the box shut. Many—mostly boys—do. Each blow of the hammers resounds as emphatically as a gunshot off the nearby hills, proclaiming the finality of what we are about.

> No dark sarcasm in the classroom;
> Teacher, leave them kids alone.

A herd of bison, grazing not 50 yards away, pauses briefly in its daily routine to gaze at our curious assembly.

> Hey! Teacher! Leave them kids alone.
> All in all, it's just another brick in the wall.

The boys who have been appointed pallbearers lower Toby and his pine box into the grave; the funeral director is down in the dark hole making the final adjustments and removing the ropes. The assembly opens a path so that a tractor carrying the vault can make its way to the grave. The vault, one of the few reminders that this is a twentieth-century burial, is lowered and positioned. Anyone who wishes may use one of several long-handled shovels provided to help close the grave. Some choose to contribute a symbolic shovel or handful of earth to the task. Others shovel for a minute or two. The final act in a string of final acts is the planting on the grave of a broadleaf cottonwood tree whose broad limbs someday will shade the entire area.

To the strains of *The Wall* people begin to say their goodbyes and thank yous and depart. The embraces are long, full of consoling words offered through quiet tears. There also are smiles and here and there a little laughter. It has been an extraordinary experience, this saying goodbye to Toby. We have witnessed a mixture of ritual and informality, of sorrow and joy, of futility and promise.

CHAPTER 8

The Second New World Seminar: The Individual and the Community

The Open School has a much stronger sense of community than any big high school can develop; it is also superior to almost all of the very small high schools that I've studied. But this school's efforts to build community are tempered by its highly individualized program, which tends to create an opposition to the school's sense of being a total group. As a result, community feels different in this school than it does in other small, informal schools I have visited. Because of this difference, I knew that a discussion of issues related to community would be a natural topic for a seminar.[1] After the impromptu experience of the first seminar, I prepared a written statement that introduced the topic of each subsequent seminar, and distributed it to the staff a few days prior to the meeting at which that topic would be discussed.

> Probably all workplaces experience a tension between the needs of individuals and the needs of their work community. Schools are no exception. The Open School struggles with this issue more than most schools, and through its highly individualized and externalized program it has succeeded admirably in honoring the needs of the individual. Nor does the school shirk its responsibilities to the community. Governance, for those students who attend it regularly; Advising, especially with the addition of Triads; and the group building that is integral to trips are all clear evidence of the Open School's commitment to community. But the conflict—perhaps competition is a more accurate word—between individual and community interests is also strongly evident.
>
> For example, many older students, especially seniors, scrambling to complete their individual academic programs in time to graduate, often avoid and sometimes even resent communal

obligations. Some respond to exhortations to get involved and to exploit their natural positions as leaders of the school by saying, "I've paid my dues to the community; it's time to satisfy my own needs."

The behavior of individual students is a second example. It sometimes has an adverse effect on community (when it creates a negative image of the school with the general public, for example). My unconfirmed sense of the school's stance on such problems is that only when the condemnation of inappropriate behavior is widespread (in other words, approaching a consensus), does the matter become a concern of the community. As a result, the honoring of individual rights continually seems to erode community in many subtle ways.

The manner in which admittance policies also honor the individual is a third example. The school's commitment to a first come, first served admittance is laudable, but when it results in entering classes heavily populated with kids who have run out of options and who are choosing the school as a sort of court of last resort rather than for its strong program, community is jeopardized. The program maintains its standards, allowing those students who can't meet its demands to fall away. But the high attrition rate results in yet larger entering classes (if the school is to maintain its current staffing level). The annual influx of large numbers of new students unfamiliar with the Open School's program has a predictably adverse effect on the school's sense of community.

The handling of the recent—and I take it rare—incident of a theft in the art room is a fourth example. The theft of a volunteer teacher's wallet was discussed within the community, but seemed to be treated as a problem of an unknown, perhaps sick, individual.[2] Some staff members viewed our seeming unwillingness to grapple more purposively with the issue as symptomatic of a wider problem. I'm not sure how they would characterize the problem but it might be viewed as a reluctance on our part to deal with sticky issues of community.

Until this year, most of my information about the Open School has been hearsay, what you or others have told me or what I have read about the school. My sense from that information, though, is that the community was more self-policing in the past than it is now. Was my previous impression erroneous, or has community eroded somewhat in this respect? If it has, to what degree do you think it may be an issue of scale; are we too

big? Or is it a problem of too many new students this year; to
pose the question another way, can community interests compete
effectively with individual interests when over half of the student
body has had no experience with the community? My sense is
that the staff in general is not satisfied with the current sense of
community. If that is true, what do you each think we should be
doing to improve the situation?

Pat leans forward over her coffee cup and starts the discussion.
"One thing that's going to help is the set of graduation requirements
that we've just reconfirmed—as a community," she says. "They're going
to help us, as advisors, establish much more clearly our expectations
of individuals' responsibilities to the community. Contributing to
Munchie's operation and to governing the school will now be more a
part of people's IEPs than they may have been in the past."

"Your sense is that more needs to be done on the community side
of the equation?" I ask.

She nods. "Yes."

Dana looks around to see if anyone else is ready to jump in and
then says, "The highest level of self-actualization is the giving back
part. So it takes some time to get there." She straightens in her chair.
"Because of the individual work we do with our students—the IEP,
individual counseling, and building self-esteem—you can expect our
students after a period of time to begin sensing some individual ownership of the school and to begin 'giving back' to the community. Individual work is the foundation for that, for being able to get to the point
where a generosity of spirit begins to take over. *Then* they cannot
only take but also give." She leans back again. "Of course, that doesn't
respond to your question about seniors." She seems to be wondering
out loud as she says, "If what I've said is true, then why do we see
seniors pulling back and not giving as much?"

I fill Dana's ensuing pause. "Do you think my observation about
seniors is accurate?"

She ponders the question a moment, leaning her head to one side.
"Yeah, I do," she says. "Clarifying some graduation requirements that
deal with community should help, as Pat has pointed out. Students'
awareness early on that they have to accomplish a certain critical
mass of obligations to the community may help them have less frantic
senior years. Now they suddenly realize they still have to do lots of
things, some of which are community issues." Dana picks up her coffee
cup but has another thought before she can take a sip. "My Advising
group is largely first-year students. Because they've been reviewing

every word of the requirements, they're much better informed than the class before them. It may help them be much better leaders when they're seniors."

Ruth seconds Dana's comment. "My Advising group really liked Kurt's idea of making the end-of-the-year evaluation an interim or temporary Transcript," she says. (Kurt had made the suggestion in an earlier staff meeting.) "They want to avoid the struggle to finish Transcripts that they see the seniors having right now. The seniors in the group also see it as a quite helpful step."

"And it relates to this discussion," I ask, "in that you see seniors, less burdened by the effort to finish their individual programs, being able to give more to the community?"

"Yes," Ruth answers. The sun streaming in the high windows behind her head makes it difficult to read her expression. "I don't think of the disengagement we sometimes see from seniors as necessarily indicative of a withdrawal from community. A lot of seniors who are not doing something in *this* community are doing Global Awareness Passage work out in the larger community. So it doesn't necessarily follow that because they're not doing much here they don't know how to contribute to a community. I believe that's one thing our graduates do well. They *can* give back; they can be thriving, contributing members of the community."

"It's interesting," I respond, "that you've taken the community side of the issue and turned it into an individual one again. The potential of the individual comes out of the experience with the community. But I'm also interested in the extent to which there is a sense of community in the school. There's a power to the sense of community within this staff that can be quite useful, and I'm wondering to what extent you all feel comfortable with the sense of community that has developed in the school?"

A long silence ensues. I scan the faces around the square of tables. Some look tired but no one seems disinterested. Ruth finally breaks the silence. "I'd like to respond to one of your statements in the last paragraph of the written statement: 'My sense is that the community was more self-policing in the past than it is now.' I do think that this year has been difficult because of the large number of new students. (You make that point, too, in your written statement.) But I also feel that in some ways we have more of a sense of community than we have had in the past. One of the things that always happens here is that kids—and sometimes staff—will say that the school is not like it used to be. That's true; it never is. One of the initial reactions that entering students have is that the school's a very warm, caring community of people who are very close to each other. Then, as they get into it more deeply and have to struggle with how they're a part of that, it seems less warm and caring for awhile. Usually by the time they graduate they're feeling that again. But there are ups and downs to it, and depending on who you talk to among staff members or the students, you'll hear different perceptions of what the sense of community is around here."

Dana, who's on the other side of the room, nods. "The sense of safety that's lost when they get pushed out into the real world is terrific," she says.

Poz takes us in a new direction: "I'm not sure how many of *us* have a real sense of community." He looks around the group for a reaction; none is evident. "Maybe I should just speak personally. I don't think that I had experienced a real sense of community until I came here." Poz, the school's special ed teacher, is a Milwaukeean who was a campus radical at Wisconsin in the mid-1970s.[3] He moved to Evergreen after graduation and held a variety of odd jobs, including driving a school bus for handicapped kids. The experience taught him that he was really good with them and that he felt great doing it. He scrapped his plans to study law, earned a teaching certificate, and got a job in the Jeffco schools. After completing the coursework for a doctorate at Denver University in 1983, he ended up at the Open School. "After all," he continues, "we are constantly battling against the values in this county. The individual is considered king here. I think building a sense of community is a very developmental process. I don't think writing down graduation expectations can automatically create a sense of community. In fact, it might just work the opposite way. I think we have the structure in place to build community but I'm not so sure it works all the time. I think, personally, that I've graduated quite a few kids who didn't have a sense of belonging, who hadn't made contributions to the community that I found satisfying.[4] I look at my own involvement with community and I see how long it's taken me to feel part of a group, and it gives me a different view of the kids."

"Does it follow then," I ask, "that you don't feel there are purposeful steps the staff can take—in concert with the students—to increase the sense of community?"

"That can be done. It *is* being done."

"Can you give me some examples?"

"Well, just the structure of what we do with kids," Poz says. "Starting off with an individual advisor, going to the Triads, building to a small group, going from a small group to classes, and trip groups. Then there's Governance, which allows kids to feel part of a much larger group, which is probably the last step on that continuum. So, I think we do it; it just doesn't always work very well."

"So you see the hierarchy of groups of different scales that the school's created as facilitating community," I say. "It helps kids find their niches where . . . "

"Yes," Poz answers. "It all boils down to the individual kids and how they respond to that structure, but we're battling against kids who have very little sense of family. They're products of 'the new American family.'"

"We have kids with *no* sense of family," Gayle Civish interjects.

"Yes," Poz says.

I try to make my point. "That's, in part, why I view a sense of community within a high school as becoming so critical. Increasingly in our society, kids are not getting it anywhere else."

"I understand why it's important," Poz responds, showing just a hint of irritation with my preachment, "I'm just saying that a lot of times we're starting from scratch."

Bill Johnson joins the conversation. "You're looking at a school that is constantly changing. The issues you identify in your opening statement are dealt with anew every year here. I remember the period before we installed Walkabout. There may have been a closer community then but we probably didn't have the quality of graduates then that we have now. We're undergoing a lot of evolution. Graduating seniors are under a very real pressure to get those last Passages finished, to complete their Transcripts, and to tie up dozens of loose ends before they leave. Because of the demands we now place on individuals, community probably does suffer."

"I see it as cyclical," Rick adds. "Within each year, the stresses on the community and the individual are tremendous. At the beginning of the year, as we've mentioned, we bring in a whole bunch of new people. It doesn't really matter how many new bodies there are; it could be 120 or 150. The process of entering this unusual place is so challenging to the individual that community *has* to suffer. Also many of those individuals are kids who have not successfully affiliated with one of the many groups that provide a sense of community in the big schools they've come from. We immediately ask them to do some things, like the Wilderness Trip, that are totally unusual. I'm always much more comfortable here in the spring than I am in the fall. Partly it's because our numbers are a little smaller in the spring, but also the new kids have gotten more comfortable with our expectations for community. There are lots of ways for kids to hook into community here. It can be as simple as committing to one class; you don't have to lead Governance to do it. That's why trips work so well. We *force* the collection of individuals on a trip to be a community until there's an end product and they've reached some closure."

"A trip group is a *real* community," Pat adds.

"I think we do have a community here," Rick continues, "but we have it in so many strange ways and sometimes it's hard to see it."

"And at so many different levels," Poz adds.

"One thing that's not always visible," Dana says, "is the help we get from students in doing that. Yesterday I had a conference with a new student. The topic was several older students who like to get high. She had talked to them about the inappropriateness of doing it during school hours. She felt she got a great response from them. When I asked her why she felt it wasn't okay to do drugs here her answer was, 'Because we could lose our family here; we could lose the school; we could lose the community.' This was a *new* student. When you can spend quiet hours with students, learning how they feel about the school, you discover that the strong sense of community they hold is impressive. Students help build community here in ways that we don't even see."

Ruth brings up the beginning-of-the-year retreat for veteran students. It really is an annual exercise in rebuilding community after a long summer apart, she points out. "I'd hate to start the school year without some event that brings everyone together and bonds people into a community before we have an influx of new participants."

Dana raises a clenched fist. Her "Right on, Ruth!" breaks up the group.

Rick, alluding to the current debate within the staff and in Futures[5] about whether there even ought to be a retreat next year, causes yet more laughter when he terms Ruth's contribution "a paid political announcement."

Ruth is red-faced. Over the din, she retorts, "Well, it seemed to fit, so I thought I'd slip it in."

As order is gradually restored, Annie Hazzard, one of our current crop of student teachers, asks a question. "New students have the Wilderness Trip to begin that bonding. What happens throughout the year to recreate that climate? If the school is becoming a kind of court of last resort for many entering kids, is there enough follow-up to that initial potent experience?"

Ruth, who's been with the school since its second year, responds. "Our advisory system is so strong now compared with what it used to be. Back in the olden days, there were no groups. We had no time to meet. It was just catch-as-catch-can. Advising was purely an individual matter. It took us several years to establish Advising groups as a norm and an expectation. It works so well now, with students regularly meeting in Advising groups, building relationships that last throughout their high school careers, that it's difficult to imagine that we ever operated differently. The initial bonding that occurs on the Wilderness Trip is carried on through the closeness of the advisory group and its constant weekly contact."

"We've done some all-school things, too, that contribute to that," Gayle offers.

Pat says, "There are some all-school activities that have worked very well in the past that we haven't been able to repeat this year, like the Caulkathon.[6] We could do a better job of finding activities that bring the *whole* school together."

Ruth acknowledges Pat's point. "All-school events are really important but they're also really hard to do. It's hard for any of us to put that much energy into coordinating an all-school event on top of everything else that we each do."

"I may be changing the topic a bit," Gayle says, "but I feel as though building a sense of belonging precedes building a sense of community. Many of the things we've talked about build self-esteem, which helps kids feel important enough to begin to contribute to community. Some of that may be happening on the Wilderness Trip as sort of a side effect. I'm uncomfortable treating belonging and community as though they were the same. Maybe if we could separate the two, it would help us build a process around what we're doing that's helpful and might better indicate what we might try in the future."

"I suspect you're right," I say, "and there may be yet another important element: a sense of ownership, the degree to which a student—or a staff member—sees this as his or her school. Let me try to focus that idea by introducing the policing issue into this conversation." I pause a moment to organize my thoughts. "My sense is that a great deal of the setting of a standard for behavior around here comes from the staff, not from the students. Once or twice this year I've heard students say, 'We don't do that kind of thing here,' but I've not heard it a lot. Perhaps I expected to hear it more than I have. For me, such acts are hallmarks of a strong community. In that sort of community, the staff doesn't have to act as cops and control situations a lot. The kids do a lot of it themselves."

"More self-policing goes on than we may think," Dana says. "The kids are pretty sensitive to the problem of correcting fellow students in front of the staff or even in front of other kids," she says. "I see it happen a lot individually. I hear about it happening more than I see it, but I have seen it directly in my Shakespeare class recently. There might be 40 kids in there and when somebody wants to read, another student will quiet the group if it's noisy. I rarely have to intervene. It's clearly understood that we share responsibility for maintaining a good level of consideration. That's why I love teaching here; I don't *have* to be a cop."

"I think it's real hard to play that role," Gayle points out. "I walk by the door out to the smoking porch all the time and in cold weather the kids often leave it open to warm themselves a little while they're outside smoking. It's hard for me, as an adult who's considerably more empowered than any of the kids, to continually confront kids about it. We need to acknowledge in a community of this size how difficult that is to do. If it is happening at all among the kids, it's a sign of how caring the community is."

"You've raised the issue of scale, so let me ask the question," I say. "Is the school too big to have a strong sense of community?"

"I sense it affects the staff as the school becomes bigger," Gayle says. "It's harder for us to reach consensus and work on projects together. I think we've always felt that smaller would be better but we didn't have a number in mind. But we know when it *feels* too big."

No one has a clear answer to what size that is. The discussion moves to the issue of the size of Advising groups and how it affects an advisor's work both with the group and with individual students in it. Ruth eventually returns the discussion briefly to the issue of scale as it affects the staff.

"I struggle with the size of the school as it relates to the number of staff members," she says. "For me, when the size of the staff gets over 18, it gets hard. We seldom have had fewer than 20 attending a staff meeting this year. I think it's a part of our frustration: We're trying to operate as if we're a much smaller group. The processes we use are much more appropriate for a smaller group and, as a result, we don't reach consensus or we don't make decisions or we don't move ahead. That's directly related to the number of people who are trying to express themselves and work together. That to me is a lot more important than the number of kids in the school, unless it results in advisory groups that get to be too large."

With that comment the seminar ends.

Community as an Organizing Principle for a School

Lesson I considered how the Open School says hello to people. Clearly that facet of the school's sense of community recurs in this lesson. The retreat for returning students at which the litany of tributes to the school occurred so spontaneously and so easily was an exercise in renewing old ties. I began the retreat with the expectation that we engaged in it in order to complete certain tasks, that we went away to the church camp to get some things done; I didn't understand until it was almost over—even long after the quite extraordinary few minutes of praise for the school and for how it brought people together—that the primary purpose of the retreat was the revitalization of a community that had lain dormant for the summer.

The way the school said goodbye to Toby May was an example of a strong community functioning at its best. It spoke volumes about this school community's commonly held values and priorities. But to paint the school's grieving for Toby as only a community issue is to diminish its importance. The funeral was an extraordinary event. Each generation increasingly seems to sanitize death. Just as Walt Disney has purged the blood and gore from ancient European fairy tales—and with them, much of the cultural and therapeutic value of these stories—we have made our contact with death less scary, less personal. The era when a pine box like Toby's lay in state on the dining room table is gone. We live in an age in which mourners are asked to leave the grave site before the coffin is lowered into the ground so that they are not reminded of the finality of burial. If they wish, mourners can even pretend that there isn't a deep, cold hole under the fake grass carpet, beneath that bright and shiny box. The reality of Toby's funeral was a crushing contrast to these contemporary experiences. No detail of it could be labeled impersonal. Those in attendance probably came as close as one can to confronting the many meanings of death. Because we were not shielded from them, those in attendance may be a little more alive than they were before the ceremony, a little more human. The Open School, the kind of community it is and what it stands for, and a courageous Linda May were responsible for what transpired in that sunny alpine meadow. Because the school's central concern was not so much covering a curriculum as helping individual kids develop into healthy, capable adults, it could make the mourning of Toby the school's primary mission for most of a week.

Because of the unusual nature of the school's program, I had much more difficulty gauging the health of the community at the Open School than I do at most schools. Most of the usual benchmarks I employ to assess community didn't fit the school very well. The Open School's academic year comprised largely a continual series of student forays, most to points within the contiguous 48 states but some all over the world. As a result, the building was as much a staging area as it was a gathering place. Even students staying closer to home often had approved programs that took them away from campus for a day or more each week, doing apprenticeships or performing community service work. Seniors who were especially involved in Passage work often became very scarce around the school. Two or three major trips occurring simultaneously might take as much as a quarter of the student body and the staff away from school at a single time, leaving the building feeling very empty. How does one define a productive community in this context? Is it the degree to which everyone else supports an individual's personal quest? If so the Open School was a thriving community. Is it how easily and deeply people engage each other when they are at school? Bonding of this sort happened quite easily in the school; I recall, for example, that Celia Morrison, freshly returned from 6 months of study and travel in Mexico, seemed in danger of being hugged to death when she first re-entered the school. The Open School doesn't have quite the same kind of community that other small, public alternative high schools have, I think, because its program is not very similar to those other schools. Nevertheless its strengths as a community became increasingly evident to me as my time in the school increased.

The size of the Open School is for me a related issue. During the seminar Gayle talked about gauging the impact of size by asking oneself if the school felt too big. The answer to that question is inextricably linked to one's conception of community. In my travels I have visited a school in Pennsylvania that felt that 200 students would be too big, a school in Oregon that felt that 85 would be, and a school in Indiana that felt that 35 was as big as it could get. Each of these schools had a different idea of community. That even the Open School's 238 students seems absurdly small in comparison to the typical American high school is a measure of how very different these comparatively new, very small schools are from those more familiar institutions. One can't even talk of community in big schools in the way that one can in a school like the Open School. One can't talk of the individual in them in the same way either.

The Open School's size has crept upward over the years in part as a way to retain yet another terrific teacher who had entered the school as an intern or student teacher or as a one-year replacement for a staff member on leave. (The school's unusual program has functioned as a real magnet in this regard.) Given the enrollment pressure exerted on a school whose waiting list at the time of my stay increased by about one student every school day, expanding the student body by the 20 or so students that would make the school eligible for an additional teacher had become an occasional practice.[1] In this way the school has grown gradually—and painlessly—over the years. But at the time of my stay, many on the staff had begun to sense that size was becoming a factor, and though the parade through the school of excellent teaching prospects continued unabated, there was a growing reluctance to pay the price of increasing the school's size in order to keep any of them.[2]

For me the seminar's closing topic of staff size was a fitting end to a discussion of community. After studying the social climate of about 100 schools—both big and small ones (Gregory & Smith, 1983; Smith & Gregory, 1982; Smith, Gregory, & Pugh, 1981)—in over 20 states, my friend Jerry Smith and I came to the conclusion that the critical factor in school size is not the number of students, though it certainly becomes important as the number of students exceeds that which most of the staff can know by name; anonymity works against everything for which a school strives. But the size of the *staff* of a school, as the flow of this seminar suggested, is another story.

The number of teachers in a school becomes critical before the number of students does.

All the teachers in a school need to feel that they play an important role in setting its course. Therefore, the number of teachers in a school needs to be reduced to the point where all teachers can sit down and plan the course of the school *as a group*. Much of the group dynamics research sets the maximum size of such work groups at about 12, and even this number is considered an upper limit. (Gregory & Smith, 1987, p. 63, emphasis in original)

This notion of the size of a staff being critical to goals of community was vividly validated in a visit several years ago to a small alternative high school in Wyoming.

> A staff of 21 [!] delivers a three-track curriculum to 175 students. A high degree of specialization exists. Besides a principal, assistant principal, and a full-time counselor, the school has two art teachers, two business teachers, a reading specialist, and a vocational education teacher. The comprehensive [high school] model is so faithfully installed that even the factions of teachers that typically exist in large high schools are present. Professionalism is defined by some teachers as doing their specialty with students and then sending them on to someone else. A prior principal, who sought to soften this compartmentalization of the curriculum (and of the child), was drummed out of the school by one faction of teachers. The current principal treads softly to avoid the same fate.
>
> The school has a low teacher–student ratio, but the strongest bond between teachers and administrators seems to be the wary truce they share. The students, who attend the school by free choice, seem satisfied though decidedly unexcited about its program; the climate compares quite favorably with what they had experienced in the community's large high schools. (p. 63)

Too many teachers with too little skill in dealing with each other was a deadly combination in that Wyoming school. The Open School may have had too many staff members, too, but the staff certainly was not unskilled in group dynamics. I found the smoothness with which it functioned, despite its size, remarkable. In a sense the school's dedication to the idea of inclusion—an important principle of community— was responsible for the large aggregation at staff meetings. The certified teachers in the school numbered only 15, a fairly workable size. But because everybody—teachers, secretaries, teacher aides, student teachers, and volunteers like me—was treated as an equal, the attendance at a staff meeting was more likely to approach 25. The Open School honored, empowered, and supported the individual better than any school I know. That it did so while also maintaining so healthy a community strikes me as laudable.

Lesson IV

BREAKING BOUNDARIES AND TAKING RISKS

I was struck from my first hours at the Open School with the unusual manner—unusual for a public high school at any rate—in which the Open School dealt with risk. During the first 2 days of staff meetings, the staff displayed a trusting reliance in the good judgment of teenagers that I found downright scary. Particularly to the uninitiated such as I, distinguishing whether such trust was a display of bravery or of foolhardiness was difficult. As staff members began the year, sharing their plans to mount extraordinary, even dangerous activities with students, I began to feel a little as though I had run away to join the circus and had suddenly found myself working the high trapeze. Our troop had not yet performed its first stunt but the easy confidence I saw displayed on the faces of my fellow aerialists as they struck triumphant poses for the cheering throng below suggested that there must be some sort of net down there to catch us should a critical handhold slip. If it was there, though, it was so far below us that it was out of sight.

Coming to understand the staff's and, to almost as great an extent, the students' clear vision of the important role that risk plays in human growth was a major lesson for me. That most schools run away from risk, equate it with liability, and immediately devalue any enterprise that places students in insecure settings is a measure of how different the Open School's program is from most public high schools. I think the culture of schools has attuned most professionals to respond to even relatively innocent new ideas reflexively, immediately building a list of reasons why the new idea won't work. On more than one occasion I found myself "falling behind" the staff as it encountered a new idea, because I had stopped to begin building that list while the staff had pushed on to a consideration of how to realize the idea. The power that is unleashed in a school that seldom asks why it *shouldn't* do something is formidable.

In this section of the book I'll relate some incidents that occurred during my year in the school that demonstrate how this school viewed risk, prepared students for it, and responded to the consequences when something, as it inevitably will, went wrong. We'll spend a night with Bruce Andrews on the Wilderness Trip, a night when much went wrong and Bruce struggled to locate Cindy McPhearson, who had become separated from their trail group and was lost in near-freezing temperatures.

Regarding the breaking of boundaries, we'll attend another seminar, one in which staff members discussed their different and in some ways conflicting views of the school's propensity to minimize the limits and boundaries it defines for its students. The school had few formal rules. The kids liked to say that it had only three, what everyone called the Three Noes: no drinking, no drugs, and no sex as a part of any school-related activity. The school did have other rules, of course—no skateboarding on the front steps and no playing of music in the hallways, to name just two. The Three Noes carried the distinction, however, of being the only rules that adults had unilaterally imposed on the school. All other rules were promulgated by Governance and were perhaps seen by the kids as being part of the natural order of things rather than as arbitrary strictures. The seminar was in part a discussion of the place of rules in a school. These are the ruminations of trail blazers, mapping new terrain as they expand the frontiers of schooling.

CHAPTER 9

Lost on a Dark Mountain

On the second afternoon of the Wilderness Backpacking Trip, Bruce Andrews's trail group is heading up through Truesdale Pass.[1] They're hiking through sleet. Despite all the systematic trip planning that can be jammed into 2 days, few of the kids are well-prepared for what the Wilderness Trip will require of them. It represents a form of adversity that few have encountered in their young lives. That's the point of doing it. As a student several years earlier put it, the trip and the Beginnings course that follows it function as a boot camp for the school (Sweeney, 1983).

Many of Bruce's kids fit the familiar profile of today's adolescent who has lived his or her entire life in an electronic push-button society in which needs are quickly and effortlessly satisfied and in which a young person seldom has been asked to accept responsibility for the welfare of others. Even kids from chaotic homes who have learned to cope with very demanding situations can fit the profile. Bruce has coined a particularly picturesque term for kids who have known little else but a life of ease and minimal accountability; he calls them urban weenies.[2]

This year's crop of weenies is particularly inexperienced in the wild. As the second day's trek comes to an end that inexperience is again evident. Most of the trails follow mountain streams, a backpacker's only source of drinking and cooking water. Because the planned destination for the night is a site away from water, Bruce asked before diverging from the stream earlier if everybody's water bottles were full. Everyone nodded yes. Only now, after making camp and beginning preparations for dinner, does he learn that the group has almost no water; each weenie has relied on the others to act responsibly. What little confidence Bruce had in the kids is quickly evaporating. The worsening weather conditions compound his concerns about this particular group. Despite many cautions to come prepared and vivid descriptions of the conditions they might encounter, few of the kids are dressed warmly enough for bad weather.[3] Bruce thinks to himself that they could use some luck.

Minutes later they get some. As the group proceeds with the evening chores, conditions start to brighten. Since the weather has improved, Bruce decides to go ahead with solos, in which the kids separate and spend the night alone in the wilderness. Ideally a decision like this is made by the group, but Bruce can't imagine this particular bunch of weenies choosing duress. Before making dinner the students will stake out their individual solo spots within earshot of the base camp. Each student heads out in a different direction, finding a secluded spot out of sight of everyone else; arranges her or his sleeping bag and gear; and then has Bruce check the site's acceptability. The whole procedure takes only a few minutes.

Fifteen minutes later, everybody has checked back into camp and been checked out by Bruce. Everyone except Cindy McPhearson. Something is delaying her.

After another 5 minutes, Bruce begins blowing a whistle just in case she is headed off in the wrong direction. Minutes pass. Bruce decides it's time to look for her. He heads out in the direction in which she was last seen, calling her name. No answer. It's getting dark fast. Bruce's mind races through all the ways in which the group hasn't been prepared adequately. Not every kid is carrying matches and a whistle. He remembers that he hasn't taught them to hug a tree, to stop moving the minute they realize they're lost. Two days' preparation hasn't been nearly enough for this group.

He heads back through the gathering darkness to camp, where the weenies are sitting around the fire, smoking and waiting to be told what to do. Bruce organizes search parties of three. The map is consulted and each party is given a sector of the surrounding area to cover. The groups fan out, panning flashlights, yelling, and blowing whistles. Everyone reports back in a half hour. No sign of Cindy. She can't have wandered so far so fast that she can't have heard the racket the group is making. The map is consulted again. The search parties will repeat the process. To Bruce's consternation all six remaining girls balk. Out of fear or fatigue or an alarming lack of regard for an endangered comrade, they won't go back out into the damp, cold darkness. Instead Bruce asks the girls to gather a big pile of firewood while the boys search the area again. Again the search parties are unsuccessful. They return to find that the girls have collected a few twigs and are again sitting around the fire. Bruce, trying to remember when he has been more exasperated, rages at them for their incompetence and indifference. Even this outburst of emotion doesn't stir them. They sit, staring blankly at the fire, fiddling with their smokes.

Bruce tries to figure out what to do next. "How warmly was Cindy dressed?" he asks the group. Together they determine that she has no hat and wet hair. She's wearing Levis, sneakers, and cotton socks. She has her sleeping bag with her, but if she's lost her way coming *back* to camp, she and it may be hopelessly separated. Her poncho is in camp but she probably is wearing her fleece-lined jacket over a tank top. The temperature feels like it is already in the low 40s. Hypothermia is a possibility if they don't find her soon. Bruce decides it's time to get some expert help. He asks Josh Eckert, one of the more reliable students, to prepare to hike out for help with him. Two of them will go in case one sprains an ankle or worse hurrying along the dark trail. The other can still get out in a hurry to call for help. Mark Angellis, Bruce's student assistant, will stay behind with the kids. The group is instructed to stand watches, keep the fire roaring, and periodically blow a whistle and yell and then listen quietly. In no circumstances are they to go out of sight of the fire. Bruce guesses that, moving quickly, he and Josh can reach the emergency vehicle positioned at their trail head by midnight.

Bruce and Josh gather some basic equipment—water, emergency phone numbers, a first-aid kit, and extra flashlight batteries—and make tracks. In places the trail is a stroll in the park but occasionally it becomes a rough, boulder-strewn cut in the side of a steep slope that would tax one's agility even in ideal conditions. While scurrying through a stretch of broken granite Bruce drops the flashlight. The bulb, one piece of equipment for which they have no backup, breaks. They'll have to make the last miles of their hurried passage in moonlight. After an hour or two Bruce wonders what the temperature has dropped to. He and Josh are so warmed by their exertion that they have no reliable way of telling. They also have descended over a thousand feet to somewhat warmer conditions.

They reach the trail head a little before midnight. The key to the emergency vehicle should be hidden in the front bumper. It isn't there. Bruce and Josh grope frantically for it in the darkness. They try the rear bumper, the wheel wells. Sometimes the key is taped to the top of a tire. No luck. They begin crawling in the darkness, feeling the wet ground all around the van in case the key has fallen from its hiding place. Now is when they really need the flashlight. Precious minutes pass. Finally Bruce finds the key lodged in an inconspicuous place—in the front bumper where it's supposed to be. The van's diesel engine protests the cold, damp conditions briefly and then catches.

The nearest phone is at the Ranger Station, but Bruce is uncertain that he will be able to raise someone there. Evergreen, where access to a phone is a surety, is only a few minutes farther away. He chooses the sure thing. Procedures for handling emergencies have been covered thoroughly in the staff's planning sessions. The call to Mountain Rescue is placed at about 12:30; a search effort will be mobilized immediately. Then Bruce calls Rick Lopez. Rick, one of the two teachers left behind at school with all the veteran students, is acting as primary contact. Rick reminds Bruce that Ruth, who's been out with another trail group, has hiked out early to attend a meeting. Bruce calls her and repeats the story. Ruth asks if Cindy's parents have been called. "Not yet," he says.

The call to Cindy's parents is the hardest. As the phone rings, Bruce searches for just the right words to start the conversation. How do you tell parents that their daughter, whom they've entrusted in your care, is now lost or worse in the dark on the side of a mountain? Jim McPhearson answers the phone and Bruce forces out the first words. Cindy is lost. The rest of the story comes easier. Jim and Alice, who has gotten on an extension, take the news better than Bruce could have hoped. He mentions how good Mountain Rescue is and the fact that the temperature seems to be holding. He hopes all this reassurance sounds more convincing to the McPhearsons than it does to him. After answering their questions Bruce gives the McPhearsons directions to the location, short of the trail head, where Mountain Rescue will be establishing its command post.

Leaving Josh in Evergreen, Bruce heads for that spot. Mountain Rescue has its command post in operation by 1:30 and has eight men in the field by 3:00. Seven hours after she disappeared, the organized search for Cynthia Elaine McPhearson has started. Bruce stays at the command post to help guide the search. Hours pass. Seven more men join the search as the eastern peaks show the first hints of the approaching day. The McPhearsons, huddled together under a blanket for warmth, are calm but understandably distraught. The temperature continues to hold. Finally, Bruce's best guess—that Cindy has probably come down the mountain, following the stream—proves to be correct. At 6:15, shortly after first light, the CB squawks out the news. She's been found wandering in a wet marsh in the bottom of a ravine about two and a half miles from camp. She's okay.

Mountain Rescue lifts her out by helicopter to the command post where, wrapped in blankets and drinking hot broth, she recounts events to Bruce and her parents. She had found her solo spot and was heading back to camp when she noticed Jerry Canfield, another group member, on a parallel course heading in the opposite direction. For a reason she doesn't understand, Cindy decided that he must be heading *back* to camp and that she had somehow gotten turned around. Without asking him where he was going, she turned and headed in Jerry's direction—*away* from camp. She'd gone a long distance before realizing that she was lost. In the gathering darkness without a flashlight, she might as well have been a hundred miles away. She quickly found the stream and stayed with it. Its roar had drowned out all the group's yelling and whistling to her.

After ensuring that he's done all that he can for the reunited Mc-Phearsons, Bruce hikes back in to rejoin the group. The 12 hours of exertion and tension now weigh heavily on him. As he trudges back up the mountain in the brightening day, he begins to feel all the effects of the past 24 sleepless hours. It seems to take forever to get back to camp. The kids already know of Cindy's rescue. A member of the search team had been in camp when word came over his walkie-talkie. Bruce studies the group for signs of emotion. Few are evident. The kids, especially the girls, are strangely subdued but their faces reveal the guilt of last night's miserable performance.

CHAPTER 10

The Third New World Seminar: Limits and Boundaries

Several weeks into the year, the regular Wednesday morning staff meeting ends early, just the chance I need to squeeze in another seminar.[1] I had again prepared a written statement, laying out several facets of the topic in a way that I hoped would stimulate a lively discussion.

I'm interested in how the Open School views and uses limits. It may be a misleading appearance, but the school seems to impose few limits on students, the Three Noes being an obvious exception. Let me frame the issue by relating four personal experiences.

The first experience occurred several years ago in an interview with a teacher in a conventional high school (Gregory & Smith, 1987). He said, "I may be old-fashioned, but I think kids need direction. They need to be somewhere accountable for some reason. They need someone to tell them" (p. 42).

The second occurred here, at the Open School at the returning students' retreat. Between 2:00 and 4:00 A.M. I spent a lot of time thinking about the merits of curfews and why the Open School's culture eschewed even a reasonable limit (like 1:00 or 2:00 A.M.). Going into it, I thought the main purpose of the retreat was to conduct important business. I now understand that socializing and renewing ties were also important goals. But by allowing students the option of not sleeping Wednesday night, the school seemed to be saying, to me anyway, that Thursday's agenda really wasn't that important.

The third experience also occurred at the retreat, when one of the Three Noes was about to be violated in the room next to mine.[2] It reminded me that some kids will test even liberal limits. The problem with violating the Open School's only clear limits is that the consequences are quite traumatic—being asked to leave the school, for example.

140

The fourth experience was hearing Susie relate an incident from when she was a high schooler. She was invited to a college weekend at a distant campus by a fraternity "man." Her mother wouldn't let her go and Susie was pissed. She pulled out all the stops, laying the whole guilt trip on her mother: You don't trust me. Are you always going to treat me like a child? But secretly Susie was grateful that her mother barred her from an experience that she wasn't sure that she was ready to handle. The Open School does not seem to bar students from such experiences.

All this discourse leads to two questions. If human nature dictates that we must try the grass on the other side of the fence, wouldn't it be useful to pull the fence in a bit, or, more accurately, build a second fence inside the first, so that transgressions have less traumatic consequences? How does the staff view the role of limits and boundaries in the rearing of adolescents?

After an uncomfortably long silence, Kurt comments about the enormity of the topic. Kurt is a former graduate student of mine who joined the Open School staff in 1984 to teach math. He's tall and dark with a beard and long hair, both carefully trimmed. His even gaze is interrupted by an occasional blink to moisten his contacts. More silence. I begin to wonder if a carefully constructed opening statement is a good idea. Maybe it stifles what is really a casual discussion? But the silence seems a good one. I can almost hear the wheels turning as everybody thinks. Finally MB expresses her concern about the lack of regard students were displaying at the retreat by being noisy into the wee hours of the morning. For her, being considerate of others has always been a clear boundary at the Open School. While I'm not sure she's viewing the topic as I am, I'm nevertheless grateful that someone is finally talking.

MB searches for an explanation for behavior that she sees as atypical of the kids. "Maybe they just didn't know you were up there. The idea is well-entrenched here that you can't just do whatever you want to do whenever you want to do it." Looking to the rest of the staff for confirmation, she asks, "Isn't that underlying notion pervasive?"

Susie says, "It is. I think we're sometimes reluctant to confront people when it needs to be reinforced, so there's some slippage between our rhetoric and our actions. We do expect tired kids on Thursday, Tom, but that doesn't invalidate the agenda. Unfortunately you were sleeping in a main gathering area. It was a different scene in the cabins where revelers were confronted by students as well as staff members."

Dana says, "I trust that every advisor has very clear limits and boundaries with their advisory group and their individual advisees. If that isn't true, I would be surprised. While other staff may not know what mine are, I trust that they know that I have them. For example, a fundamental one for me is honesty. I won't continue to work with an advisee who can't be honest with me. I would guess that each of us has a set of such considerations that forms the core of his or her relationships with advisees."

Kurt agrees, to a degree. "Many unwritten limits and boundaries for the students do exist here, within us as advisors. Some of my students may go to class, not because of its intrinsic value, but because they think they're going to get in real trouble with me if they don't." Kurt is also concerned about our consistency across advisors. Inconsistency communicates the wrong message to the students in a lot of ways. "What I'm after became clear to me the other day when I got my first traffic ticket in years. The officer didn't impose the consequences based on his own judgment like we do here. He didn't say, 'Well, I think today I'll take away your license.' Rather it was, 'Here's what you did; these are the consequences; here's your ticket; have a nice day.' It made me really angry but there was no one to be angry at. I couldn't be angry with the officer; he was only doing what he was supposed to do, enforcing consequences that were already in place. I think that the absence of well-defined consequences at the Open School allows students to place, inappropriately, the responsibility for some of their mistakes on us rather than on themselves. I think we need to have some consequences in place that we just enforce, rather than each of us acting on what may appear to the students to be personal fiats."

"But doesn't that create the problem," Dana asks, "of listening to a voice outside your own head? When we establish a set of consequences, students in turn don't have to internalize the rightness or the wrongness of their actions. It becomes, 'Well, Kurt said . . . ' or 'The school said . . . and they must be right.' If I'm a student in such circumstances, I always need to be in a structured situation where someone else will tell me what's right because I presumably don't have enough good judgment to act on my own standards."

"Not at all," says Kurt. "I think it allows them the freedom to make whatever choices they still choose to make, but they do so understanding exactly what the consequences of their actions will be. That's the way the real world operates. I don't have to stop for a stop sign if I don't want to. It's still my choice but the consequences for that action are clear and consistent."

Gayle pushes her coffee cup away from her and asks, "Why *do* you stop at stop signs?"

"Because I don't want to get into trouble," Kurt answers, "because it's unsafe not to, and because it's not an issue over which I'd want to expend a lot of rebellious energy."

Gayle pursues her point. "I think that a lot of students come here *not* doing things because they *do* have externalized limits placed on them that they don't accept. We in turn have to deal with their reluctance to commit to anything that results from those unyielding settings. Anne Wilson-Schaef's (1986) book on codependence describes us as an addictive society in which institutions like churches and schools continually reinforce our addiction to rules and boundaries. What I understand us to be about is helping kids internalize their own limits and boundaries. One important way they do that is through relationships with us in which they learn what our limits and boundaries are."

"I can never remember," Dana adds, "learning a lesson because I was punished—and I know, Kurt, that you're not trying to say that the consequences of inappropriate actions are necessarily punishment—but *natural* consequences are much more emphatic at times. When I've let myself or other people down, it's been much more memorable than when someone has said, 'You're absolved from guilt because you're not mature enough yet.' When the latter has happened, it's been much easier for me *not* to internalize the event. It has much more impact when someone says, 'You look at what's happened; what's the meaning of it for *you*? You deal with it.'"

Gayle reinforces Dana's point. "We are critical models in that regard. We all have different values, which dictate how far we each will go, and so do people out there in the real world. But what we don't teach our kids—what Kurt is speaking to—is that the Open School is not the real world. The real world does not accept people operating on the basis of their own boundaries. It expects people to yield to externalized, legislated standards. Because of that lack of development of internalized standards, especially in the critical period of adolescence, our kids—really all high school kids—are especially vulnerable to getting hooked on externalized standards."

I look for clarification. "Is Schaef saying that schools are addicted to rules?"

"No, students become addicted through the school's rules," Gayle says. "Schools and similar institutions teach that you are not there to discover who you are; you are there to learn how to operate in a world filled with external rules and regulations. As a result you may not develop a core identity. Schools may even punish people who try to do that. Helping kids develop a core identity is what this school is about: teaching students to become who they are. We each pursue that goal differently. I for one tend to encourage kids to test limits. That doesn't mean they don't need guidance. I think we all feel they do. But we have different conceptions of the nature and quantity of that guidance.

"I agree with you, Tom," Gayle continues, "that we sometimes set kids up to fail by not giving them enough guidance, that we sometimes expect them to have internal boundaries when, in fact, upon entering the Open School they may not have developed beyond a 5-year-old in some ethical contexts. But rather than imposing yet more external boundaries on them, we need to work harder to help them develop internalized ones."

"And isn't it true," Dana adds, "that people in the real world have different limits, just as each advisor here has? Different institutions have different limits. Different counties have different laws. We're consistent with the real world in that regard. I do think our community is built on respect and mutual appreciation, as MB said."

Kurt for the most part agrees with Dana's view. "But within the flexibility of establishing internal boundaries, there has to be an overlaying structure in which that happens. I agree that most people probably heed stop signs because they want to and because they see it as a sensible rule, but there is also a structure for those who don't heed them. We have laws to inhibit those folks who don't have those internal boundaries from messing up the rest of us. Would you agree with that, Gayle?"

"Sure, that's a developmental necessity."

"So there is a need for a structure within which we operate. I don't think we have that here. We can still be really flexible and help kids develop their internal boundaries, but without any consequences other than the ultimate one of being booted out of the school, I think our current boundaries become ineffective. We don't help kids who don't have internal limits to understand that, even if they aren't developing them, there will still be something that they have to deal with along the road to self-governance. Does that make sense?"

"That makes sense," Gayle answers. "But I think it *is* a developmental issue. That's why I don't like lots of rules. I think most of us come here not having developed internal standards, at least not to a high level. We help newcomers—kids *and* adults—to do that. I'm not sure that generalized rules are helpful in that developmental process. That's the value of flexibility. That's what I think we all try to do. I acknowledge that we, including myself, make a lot of mistakes."

Kurt interrupts, "I want flexibility but with a bottom line and some consistency. I need that."

"Do you believe that only a minimum amount of restrictions should be in place?" Gayle asks.

"Yes. But we really haven't enforced those restrictions that we do have. We make many exceptions for individual students. I'd like us to have some real limits here, some consequences and some real boundaries beyond which we will not go. For me, abusive behavior would be one beyond which we should not budge. Looking the other way in the face of physical abuse is something that I will never support. I think we need some real clear limits there."

Dana asks, "Don't you think we have them?"

"No. I really don't think we do," Kurt answers. Referring to a recent fight between a boy and girl that was so rare an occurrence in the school that it was referred to simply as "The Fight," Kurt says, "I think what happened was a clear demonstration that we don't have them, that we won't be consistent from one kid to another.[3] I agree with Tom that we have three clear rules and beyond that we have almost nothing to guide us. We need to have some other mechanisms in place that can be appropriately applied to individual cases. The current situation puts pressure on us as advisors to be continually making rules for each individual kid. That puts an unreasonable burden on us and allows the students to interpret the consequences they do experience as being imposed by an individual, not a social system. As a result they don't have to focus their anger on themselves; they can focus it on one of us. I'm not sure that's a good message to give them."

I try to tie together the conversation's several loose ends. "Kurt, I hear you calling for a set of rules we don't have now, something more intermediate . . . "

"Some kind of procedure, I think, is what I'm talking about more than a fixed set of rules," he says. "Something that would help us deal more consistently with kids who are having similar problems. We need a mechanism that encourages accountability beyond the advisor/ advisee relationship, something beyond the fact that I'll be mad at them if they don't act appropriately."

"On a related point, Gayle, I hear you saying that most kids who come here are not developmentally ready for the lack of constraints in the school," I say.

"I don't think that anyone coming here for the first time—including the staff—is developmentally ready to deal with the realities of self-directed learning." The quiet laughter in the group suggests considerable agreement. "Clearly, I have learned a whole lot about myself here, including my limits. Everyone here gives you lots of feedback and support to help you through that process, but I'm not sure, after 4 years here, that I'm ready yet. Our goal is an ideal that none of us may ever reach. What we do is take kids where they are and do what we can to help them grow. I like that.

"Clearly, some people would be more successful by some generally accepted criteria in settings more structured than the Open School's," she continues, "criteria that I'm not sure we would agree with. So how do *we* define success? I'm not ready to define it simply in terms of graduation because I think we are highly successful with most kids who don't graduate. I also want to resist attempts to screen entering students just so we'll look more successful to outsiders."

"Would you also resist the development of a more familiar mechanism or structure for entering students," I ask, "something that could operate as a sort of halfway house at the Open School for unempowered kids who are not ready for the demands of governing themselves?"

"That's what Beginnings is," Gayle answers. "It's designed to help kids through that transition."

Susie joins the conversation. "The structure that Kurt is asking for needs to be enabling. We often think of structures as being restrictive. Maybe we need to help each other more, just as Kurt is saying. Some sort of intermediate mechanism might be helpful."

"I think we already do that as advisors," Pat counters. "We can be as structured as any place ever can be. I'm very structured with Karen and Maggie [two advisees currently in deep trouble] right now. They have limits that are very clearly defined . . . "

"By *you*," Susie interjects.

"By me."

"But that's the problem that Kurt's talking about," Susie says.

"But my advisees don't all need the exact same thing," Pat answers. "My group, right now, is mostly new students and most of them are functioning quite well. They're not perfect; they haven't 'arrived.' But they're attending classes, meeting their commitments, trying to go to Governance, and generally meeting my expectations. Karen and Maggie weren't living up to those expectations so I told them, 'You can't stay in this school unless some things improve. This is how things are going to change: You are *required* to go to Governance. You are *required* to go to all of your classes. And you are *required* to go to Advising. At the end of the block, we may renegotiate this arrangement.' But for now, they're on a strict contract, a strict probation. My view is that they weren't ready to make choices for themselves. They needed me to have strict limits set for them to enable them to function right now. I think they're beginning to experience a little success now and to feel better about themselves, and I can envision soon being able to loosen their current constraints."

I try to build a general principle around what has been said. "Then the model that operates here is one that is imposed after a student fails."

Several say, "No." Dana explains their answer. "It's based on knowing an individual advisee very well and tailoring the program to fit that kid's needs. That process can begin long before failure is experienced."

"Sometimes we make mistakes and kids fail," Gayle adds, "but we all learn from those experiences."

Pat elaborates. "I think the *students* are the bottom line. They're responding to *their* expectations, not mine. But as their advisor I help them to discover what their current expectations are and what the consequences of them are."

"You're talking about standards. Where are we drawing those from?" Kurt asks. "What's the basis of the expectations they're choosing to hold? That's where it gets muddy. I don't think we have a common set of expectations students can look to as a standard. There is no bottom line. I don't think there's a bottom at all. It's like walking on a river bed; it's real squishy and you never quite find the bottom and it's constantly changing."

"I think we have expectations," MB points out. "When students enter we say, 'Go to Advising and Governance and meet all the commitments of your mutually agreeable program.'"

"And what happens when they don't?" Kurt asks.

"Then it depends on the individual kid. My first question is why; what happened? And then we go from there."

"Then there's no accountability here that's consistent across the board," Kurt says. "It's only an agreement between me and my advisees and so the only messages they're getting that are consistent are those that I'm giving them. There's no consistency across the school and so it's as confusing as hell for them to figure out which of our many models to follow. We place high value on modeling, but we're operating with 20 or 25 different models."

Dan McCrimmon joins the debate. Dan, bearded, with thinning brown hair, is seated next to me. He kicked around the country for over a decade as a professional folksinger and even calls himself a "recovering performer." He still sings Friday and Saturday nights, dressed in frontier garb in a local restaurant of similar motif. "That isn't what I'm getting from my advisees," he says, "whether they're successful or unsuccessful. Both our students and their parents comment favorably about our consistency. My kids all know where the limits are. That they choose to test them at times is a separate issue."

"We have a process in which kids play an integral role in setting standards," MB adds. "That process operates on trips, in classes, and in Advising. It's not a set of standards that I set up and they all have to follow or I'm going to intervene. Instead I try really hard not to be the one who's always leading. I seem least effective in Advising when I fall into that mode. Not leading worked really well on the New York trip last year and I think Bruce and I are going to try it again for Tallahassee. I also expect students to play a role in setting the direction of our classes. When they do, the whole class begins to make much more sense to them."

Kurt, looking exasperated, tries one last time. "I guess I'm interested in some process in between having students just 'think about it' and having to kick them out. I'm thinking about the Western Civ class where many kids didn't do final term papers.[4] Little has happened to them, despite their inaction, and I wonder what they've learned from that? Has that experience affected how much they're following through on assignments this block? If you can demonstrate to me that the kids that didn't do those papers learned from that experience and now are functioning at a different level, then I'm ready to buy what you're saying, Dana, but that's *not* what I see happening. The next time they have an assignment like that, are they going to respond to it more appropriately?"

Dana, perhaps deciding that the current debate won't be reconciled, chooses not to rise to Kurt's challenge. Instead she looks around the group and then says, "There are a lot of people who haven't said anything here. I hate to see a few of us monopolize the discussion."

Pat tries for some closure. "There's a tendency for teachers to want to work with kids who already have all the skills. But what is teaching? Why are we all here? If all the kids walked into the school having all their internal yeses and noes in place, then what would our job be? Our job is to bring them along, to work with them. Working with different kids in different ways is what it's all about. That's why we want the Open School to be a school that takes on *any* kid who wants to come here."

That seemed as good a place as any to end this seminar.

I WASN'T PARTICULARLY SATISFIED with the way the seminar had proceeded. Too many people had said nothing. Later I probed for reasons. Ruth felt some views on the staff were not presented though she didn't know why. Joy was put off by the tone of my opening comments; she took them negatively, felt defensive, and simply didn't want to respond while she felt that way. Bruce, reacting to the monopolization that Dana had sensed, simply withdrew. I suspect others felt considerable ambivalence about the topic, valuing the flexibility and autonomy that several had described, but sharing Kurt's frustration with the burden of responsibility that freedom places on each of them.

Kurt's question about Western Civ—"The next time they have an assignment like that, are they going to respond to it more appropriately?"—was an important one that never got answered. Rick Lopez, who taught the Western Civ class, thinks he unfortunately gave the kids permission *not* to do the paper "unless they thought writing a paper would be a useful learning experience" for them.

The incident came up again in a discussion with Arnie. He wondered how we can expect any other behavior from kids whose whole experience with term paper assignments is that they are only that— assignments—vehicles for teachers to check to see if kids are "doing the work" rather than opportunities for clarifying and synthesizing ideas. In other words, opportunities for learning. Preparing kids to view the experience in a new light is critical.[5]

Jeff pinpointed a problem I may have with every seminar. While each represents a new discussion for me, the staff has wrestled with all these issues numerous times over the years. I have to keep remembering that each person here, like me, has had to make the journey here from the Old World. Most, as Gayle pointed out, are still trying to complete it. Under all their seeming security with what they're about and their obvious facility in the ways of the New World, staff members' questioning never stops. They all periodically confront the crazy paradox of *knowing* that this school is a valid response to today's society, while simultaneously questioning whether one or another facet of how they keep school is the right way to do it. When you're as far out on the frontier as this school is, you do a lot of improvising. There are no formulas, no experts. There are very few guideposts pointing the way, except the fundamental precepts of what it means to be human.

Perhaps a better word for all the questioning that goes on at the Open School is *invention*.

Expanding the Envelope

All schools ask the question of any unusual activity, "What if something goes wrong?" Most schools allow the fear of the unexpected to deter them from ever attempting the trips that the Open School undertakes so matter-of-factly. Their first thought, to put it indelicately, is to cover their asses. The sort of bias for action, as Peters and Waterman (1982) would term it, that exists in the Open School is probably best exemplified in an anecdote that Arnie related to me in one of my early visits to the school. It was about a school trip to Helena, Montana.[1]

Jeff had read in the paper that a solar eclipse was going to occur in a few weeks. It would be about 50 years before another total eclipse would be visible anywhere in the continental United States. The total eclipse would be visible only along a narrow path across North America. Helena was Evergreen's closest point on that path. Jeff and Arnie talked about turning it into a trip. "We should do it!" Arnie said. Several other staff members got excited about the prospects and got a large group of kids interested in viewing the eclipse, and together they quickly organized the trip. The group built the special equipment it would need to view the eclipse safely and four vans headed for Helena, a town with two high schools of its own. The response of those two schools to this once-in-a-lifetime event is instructive. According to Arnie, they viewed it as a liability issue: Their kids might burn their retinas. One high school sent the students home early, before the eclipse started; if they were going to burn their retinas it would be on their own time. The other school purportedly herded all its students into the auditorium and showed them movies during the critical period.

Anyone who has spent time in public schools knows that there were numerous reasons for *not* going to Helena. One that struck me immediately when I heard Arnie's story was the possibility of an overcast sky ruining the observations. I asked Arnie what they would have done if it had been cloudy in Helena. A silly grin formed on his face. His bias for action was so strong that my question hadn't occurred to him. Such a stance may be a prerequisite for a staff whose day-to-day decisions are not on matters such as which textbook to adopt or whether sophomores should be allowed to attend the prom, but on whether to take a group of kids to Alaska or Central America.

Because it is so closely linked with growth, risk is a central theme of the Open School. The Jeffco administration clearly places great trust in the risk management capabilities of the Open School staff. It is not unfounded. For example, one of the last steps in the preparation for each trip is what has come to be called the "Reasonable and Prudent Meeting." It gets its name from operational rules that have become ingrained in the fabric of the school and are a part of its ethos: Learning is a risky business; one must risk a little to learn a lot; but no adult has any business subjecting kids to risks that cannot be justified as reasonable. Furthermore, these risky activities should include safeguards and backups that are prudent. In the Reasonable and Prudent Meeting, Ruth—guided by a formal checklist—performs a long, thorough interrogation of the trip staff. The tone of the meeting is not unlike the preflight check that commercial pilots must perform. The items take form as questions from Ruth: Parental sign-offs for everyone? Health insurance and special medical treatment information for each student? Does the trip staff include at least one person with a current first-aid certificate? Are an itinerary and daily phone contacts on file in the office? Have you talked to all parents, either at the information meeting or individually?[2] Does every family have a copy of the itinerary?[3]

Each trip is a carefully planned activity that must be approved by the central administration. While many trips each year involve considerable risk, not one trip over the years—not even a trip in 1984 to the Middle East with its persistent potential for violent acts—has been vetoed by the district as being too dangerous. One trip—to Nicaragua in 1986—would have been the acid test of the district's trust in the Open School staff. The trip was developed by four graduating seniors. Although their hope was that graduation would not bar them from making the trip themselves, the four boys had designed the trip primarily for others—a wonderful graduation present to the school. Their very thorough planning included a mid-summer trip to Washington, DC, accompanied by Bill Johnson to seek permission for the trip from the State Department and the Nicaraguan Embassy. The trip was planned to occur the next fall, but Nicaragua began heating up again and the trip's two staff leaders, Bill and Fitz, decided the venture was indeed too risky and let it die quietly.

THE STAFF DIDN'T MAKE STRONG DISTINCTIONS between the constraints that the bureaucracy did try to place on the program and those of time, space, and money. Limits most school people would consider reasonable, maybe even proper, were regularly transcended. The circumvention was rarely subversive. Arnie once described the different ways that administrators and teachers deal with bureaucratic constraints. For me his statement exemplifies the school's propensity to expand the envelope of acceptability.

"There are three ways to respond to inappropriate or arbitrary rules," he began. "Some people follow the rules whatever they are. They never overstep them without first getting permission." The problem with their actions is that the arbitrary nature of the system never changes.

"Other people become subversives," he continued. "They take risks; they ignore and bend rules to promote kids' learning. Some administrators even give permission for this behavior, saying, 'Go ahead and do it, but just don't let me know about it.'" Kids and teachers can do some worthwhile but taboo things within this approach, but the arbitrary nature of the bureaucracy again goes unchallenged.

"A third group of people does what must be done to deliver a good education to kids," Arnie said in closing. "These people will break or bend a rule when they're confident of the merits of their position, but then they do something unusual. They tell their superiors what they've done—and why—so that a dialogue is initiated within the system that may result in change."[4]

The Open School makes a practice of using this last approach. In doing so it sometimes alters the limits and boundaries that are placed on all Jeffco's schools. Is it too much to hope that they may also have an effect on schools beyond the district's boundaries?

Lesson V

EXPERIENTIAL LEARNING

The Open School conceived of itself as a base camp from which to launch individual and group expeditions into the real world as much as it did as a school. The school's extended trips were one of its most dramatic features. Taking a group of teenagers thousands of miles from home, sometimes for several weeks at a time, is not for the faint of heart. The liability risks alone regularly dissuade most schools from attempting such ventures. Why did the Open School do it? I think because the students and staff had learned that these ventures were rife with learning possibilities, a lesson that they learned through experience. In this section we'll briefly join two trips in an attempt to understand firsthand how such ventures might justify the time and effort they require. And the money. Every trip had its expenses, and before we disembark I should address how a school of ordinary means accomplished what seem to be extraordinarily expensive forays.

The nine-passenger vans that the school used for almost all trips were provided by Jeffco and half of the mileage costs were borne by the school. Jeffco provided the school with $12,000 for this purpose during the year I spent there.[1] Where did this money come from? Very small high schools like the Open School are thought to be expensive operations. The research, however, suggests that they are not more expensive than their bigger brethren. Indeed big high schools have many expenses—football coaches, athletic directors, choir and band directors, and security guards, to name a few—that the Open School didn't have. The Open School was one small school that had figured this out and was able to negotiate with the central administration to have some of those funds—which most public alternative schools *never* see—made available to it. So one way to view the school's trips is that they represent a trade-off. The money to subsidize trips exists in any public school; other schools just choose to spend it on things like interscholastic athletics. Or their anonymous, alienating environments create problems that have expensive solutions, like security

153

guards and the repair costs of vandalism, which sap resources from instruction. Rather than an interscholastic sports program and people who prepare lunch each day, the Open School took its students on extended trips throughout North and Central America.

Lodging on trips is most often provided by camping. The Navajo Work Trip, one of the trips that will be described in this section, was something of an exception; most nights we slept on the floors of Chapter Houses, the town halls of the reservation. Because most food is bought in bulk at a discount, the costs of most trips are kept low enough that parents occasionally claimed it was more expensive to keep their kid in groceries and pocket money at home than it was to send him or her off to some exotic place for several weeks. For example, transportation, food, and lodging for our 2 weeks on the Navajo Reservation, a trip of 2,500 miles, cost each of us, students and staff members alike, $110. The budget included $15 for each of us to buy some Navajo jewelry at a trading post before we headed home.

I participated in two other trips during my year in the school.[2] Our week of assisting in the excavation of an Anasazi kiva as a part of our Beginnings class in October cost each of us $50. I also spent two weeks with a Spanish class in Mazatlan, Mexico in January. (A portion of that trip is related in Chapter 16.) Mazatlan was second in expense to the Bahamas Trip, which cost each of its participants $425. Our Mazatlan budget included our round-trip airfare to Mazatlan, our language-school tuition, and $35 spending money. The trip fee included $15 for a gift for our host family—we each lived in a Mexican home— and money to put on a Fiesta as a way of saying thank you to our host families. The fee also included a $100 contribution from each of us to a scholarship fund that would subsidize the costs of several of the Mexican host kids to visit the Open School later that spring. With the school's mileage subsidy, those two rich and personally rewarding weeks *inside* the Mexican culture cost each of us $400.

But $400, or even $110, can be an astronomical sum for a kid from a poor family. Clearly, a school that engages in ventures such as these must have a mechanism that ensures that these kids are not left out. The Open School was committed to seeing that no kid missed out on a trip because she or he couldn't afford it. For example, trip loans were provided out of a small account that contained about $1,000.[3] It had been accumulated over the years from donations to the school and from interest that accrued from several other school accounts. Kids could borrow up to $250 for an expensive trip to supplement the money they'd been able to earn on their own. But the Navajo Work Trip, to be described here, occurred at a time when the loan fund was in dire straits, with an unusually high number of unpaid loans. The staff had recently reaffirmed the policy that no student would be allowed to borrow more money until he or she had paid off earlier debts.

The policy had placed Matt Bowers of our trip group in a bind. Matt came from a poor family. I first learned of his circumstances in early January, while making small talk with him in the hall. I'd asked him if he'd had a good Christmas. He hadn't. The only gift he'd gotten was from a neighbor. Matt already had an outstanding loan from the Yellowstone History Trip, which had occurred earlier in the year. When the long-standing policy became public knowledge, he announced in a trip planning meeting that he was going to have to drop out. The trip staff had talked about Matt just as it had about most of the kids in the group. We'd discussed what a quiet kid he was, new to the school and still having some trouble making his place in it, and how he had seemed to be making a real commitment to the trip. So, as Matt made his announcement, it didn't surprise me to read concern in other staff members' faces.

But the kids in our trip group also were aware of Matt's commitment to the group and would have none of his dropping-out talk. The group began considering alternatives. Many trip groups engage in a variety of money-raising projects. The funds they earn are thought of as group money. The group decides how it will be spent, whether it's used to reduce the price tag for the trip or to pig-out on pizza on one of the last nights on the road. After a short discussion, the kids voted to use a portion of the group money that they had earned through bake sales, garage sales, car washes, and the Kiss-a-Llama Contest to pay Matt's way. Most of the time, Matt presented himself as a pretty tough kid, the strong silent type. But he didn't let the glaze of tears that filled his eyes as he learned of the group's largess embarrass him. He said a long sincere thank you, vowed to do some extra chores on the trip to repay each of us for our generosity, and then found a reason to leave the room.

SOME READERS MAY ALSO WONDER how the Open School gets its teachers to go on these demanding trips. We'll return repeatedly in this account to the idea of schools that work for teachers. Staff members "did" these trips because they were exciting learning experiences *for them*. Jeff Bogard described it as going to places that were magical for him that also held the prospect of being magical for the kids.[4] Family circumstances had a great effect on how many trips each staff member took. Jeff and Susie used to be big trippers, for example, taking kids as far away as the Yucatan peninsula for as long as 7 weeks to study the

Mayan culture, but with two little ones at home, neither had taken a
major trip in years. Dana Orin was in a similar situation. She had a
3-year-old son and hadn't been on many trips in the years immediately
preceding my stay in the school. But Jeffco required that every trip
staff include a certified teacher who was employed by the district,
something that the Dinosaur Trip described in this section of the book
was lacking. The trip was short enough, though, that Dana could do it,
taking little Michael along.

Young lives are sometimes changed by the unexpected events that
can occur on a trip. One may well have occurred on this short trip to
Grand Junction, Colorado. We'll join the trip as the group searches for
a long-lost dinosaur dig and watch Dan Corrigan, a young man already
intensely interested in fossils, have an experience that may well have
changed the course of his life.

But first we'll join the Navajo Work Trip, 4 days into its adventure,
as it prepares to descend into Canyon del Muerto—to plant fruit trees.
The impetus for this service trip is rooted in history. The major canyons of the reservation are terribly important places to the Navajo;
they truly are magical places that in some ways are the very heart of
the Navajo Nation. In the 1800s Canyon de Chelly contained an orchard of over 5,000 peach trees. In 1863, when the federal government
decided to relocate the Navajo to Fort Sumter, they retreated, as they
had for hundreds of years whenever under attack, into the canyons.
The army contingent, led by Colonel Kit Carson, tried several ploys to
dislodge them but the canyons were natural fortresses. In the end Carson starved the Navajo out. He and his men killed all their livestock,
burned their crops, and cut down and burned the peach trees. The
third consecutive Navajo Work Trip, described here, was part of the
school's continuing effort to undo what Carson and the U.S. Army had
done to the Navajo a century earlier, by planting thousands of donated
fruit trees, not just in the canyons but all over the reservation.

CHAPTER 11

Walking in Beauty
(Some of the Time Anyway)

We park the vans near the rim of the still unseen canyon. Canyon del Muerto, the Canyon of the Dead, gets its name from two historic events. One was the discovery of Mummy Cave, which contained the mummified remains of many Anasazi. The find was an extraordinary archaeological event, not only because of the remains' high state of preservation, but also because of its contrast with the scant skeletal record of the Ancient Ones that exists elsewhere. The lack of remains of a people that numbered in the tens of thousands is so much a mystery that they are sometimes said to have vanished. The second event occurred at what has come to be called Massacre Cave, where in 1805 more than a hundred Navajo women, children, and elderly men had been hiding from invading Spanish soldiers. The group was discovered and, one by one, systematically shot in their hiding place turned tomb. The Spaniards then crushed the skulls of the dead and dying with their rifle butts (Locke, 1986).

Our group of 30 includes 16 Open School students, 9 eighth- and ninth-graders from Tanglewood, and five adults. We don our packs and strike out single file on what seems to be the trail. We hike for minutes, gradually growing accustomed to the heavy loads on our backs, heading toward the canyon rim. Excitement builds in the group. The veterans of past Navajo Work Trips anticipate that our few days in the canyons will be the highlight of their trip. The kids scan the scene ahead but the high brush obscures any sign of the canyon. Then as we round a rock pinnacle, stretched out 800 feet below us and framed for miles into the distance by red and purple sheer sandstone walls is the green floor of the canyon. We feel as though we're entering another world. I am bringing up the rear, looking down at our assemblage strung out for a hundred yards on switchback after switchback. The grandeur of the setting has transformed our ragtag band into a stately procession. We move down the trail. As we each round a boulder the size of a small house, we're confronted with yet another magnificent view. The towering walls are now more above than below us. Small purple flowers, brilliant in the mid-day sun, dot the scrub around us. A jack rabbit bolts from the safety of a nearby bush.

Once we reach the canyon floor, Frank Nez's aunt's land, where we have been invited to camp, is perhaps a half mile farther into the canyon. Some Navajos have hogans in the canyon but these hogans are only part-time homes used during the spring and autumn. Because of the canyon's extreme depth, the low winter sun never reaches the canyon floor to melt the snow, and the canyons become impassable until spring. The Navajo spend the winter on the canyon rim. The canyons are also insufferably hot during the summer, a time when the Navajo move up into the mountains. Frank's aunt has no hogan, only a small outbuilding and a privy. We pick a large cottonwood tree as our campsite. An old, rusting harrow sits nearby.

Our heaviest equipment and the fruit trees we will plant are coming into the canyon in Vincent Kinlacheeny's pickup truck. There are no roads; trucks enter the canyon through its mouth, using the stream bed as a thoroughfare. Because the route is mostly quicksand, the journey has its perils. If a truck gets stuck and the driver has to leave it for more than a few hours, it will slowly disappear beneath the sands unless it settles on top of an earlier victim. So many trucks have been lost in this manner over the years that the Navajos joke that Canyon de Chelly should really be named Canyon de Chevy. The main strategy for avoiding this automotive disappearing act is to drive like hell. The trip in by truck is consequently an exciting, wet event in which the truck is constantly enshrouded in a wall of spray. Bert Lucas, perhaps sensing an opportunity to get wet in the line of duty, has volunteered to accompany the equipment into the canyon. It and a very wet, very happy Bert arrive shortly after we do.

THE NEXT DAY IS FULL of planting fruit trees on farms in the area. Joe Yazzi, a sheepherder with canyon land near our campsite, already has quite an orchard going. It includes some trees that the first Navajo Work Trip planted 2 years earlier. They are in bloom. The veterans who were on that trip are elated and Bill Johnson, who has led all three of these trips, almost busts out of his T-shirt with pride. These trees are the first tangible evidence that the efforts of these trips are literally bearing fruit. Joe shares water from his spring with us and we are happy to plant some more trees as compensation. He is over 90 years old, looks 60, and rides a horse like a 30-year-old. Since the Spaniards introduced the horse to this region, the Navajo have enjoyed the reputation of being consummate horsemen, and Joe's skill in the saddle is evidence that this reputation is well-earned. After the planting, we stand in a tight circle around Joe, resting on our shovels. He shares a little of what life in the canyon is like. Joe's speech is a mixture of English and Navajo, and Buddy, a cousin of Vincent's who is acting as our Navajo escort, translates for us. Joe's small house is perhaps 50 yards away. It's a rude structure, about 12 feet square, with walls of tightly bound sapling trunks. The dwelling seems almost transparent. Its flat roof extends out from its front to form a veranda almost as big as the house. Joe's wife sits silhouetted against the bright sunlight with her hands in her lap in the veranda's deep shade, looking off into the distance. Her clothes are billowy and her hair is drawn tightly back into a bun. The scene has a dignity and wholeness that make it little different than it might have been 200 years ago.

Joe tells the kids that a sheep will sometimes find her way up the canyon wall to a spot from which she can't extract herself. Sometimes the herder can't reach the spot and he will shoot her off the canyon wall to reclaim what he can of his investment. At other times, the herder will make the perilous climb to retrieve the marooned animal. The kids listen in rapt silence as Joe tells the story of when, as a young man, he went high up the sheer cliff face after a sheep. He lost his footing and fell. He tells us that he survived the fall by tearing open his large shirt and holding it against the wind as a makeshift parachute. It's an incredible tale but we believe it nonetheless.

As I stand at the edge of the group watching the kids soak up Joe and gazing at his wife in the distance, I consider the many things these kids are learning as they measure themselves against unimagined conditions in a previously unexperienced environment. Their visible respect for Joe—who has thrived for 90 years in a life that they hope to survive for 2 weeks—approaches veneration. The Navajo have a title of respect—Hosteen—for their elders. The kids don't know the word but their actions nevertheless convey their feelings for Hosteen Joe Yazzi.

Late in the day, Jim Zeller and I return to Joe's spring to replenish the group's drinking water. Our walk of close to a mile through lengthening shadows and the stillness of evening occurs mostly in a silence that is broken only by the soft clatter of our plastic water jugs. Jim's a quiet kid, the sort who never causes problems and always does his job. He has handsome dark features. We sit by the spring on our haunches, waiting for the pencil thin flow of water to fill each of the many jugs. The spring, located at the back of a narrow draw off the main canyon, is now cloaked in darkness as the last of the sunlight works its way up the far cliff face. While we wait, we talk.

Jim points to a small stone formation high on the cliff wall and asks, "What's that?"

"It's an Anasazi granary," I say. I go on to describe how the Ancient Ones would wall off niches in the cliff face with stone, sealing their grain in them against the elements and rodents. "It was one way that they stored the food supply they would need to get through the winter. That advance in their technology helped them to stay put long enough to build their remarkable cliff dwellings. It enabled them to maintain a population greater than the one that now inhabits this whole region. That wall is probably a thousand years old."

The story is finished before I realize that I have just taught a very compact little lesson. Unlike almost all of the thousands of lessons I have taught, I sense that this one may be remembered for a lifetime. I savor the moment. As Jim and I crouch, mesmerized by the steady stream of water filling another battered jug, I think about thanking him for asking me about the granary. But I'd have to go into a protracted explanation of why I was doing so, and I rather hope his thoughts are off somewhere else, with the Anasazi. I avoid looking at him in the fear that a glance may break the spell. Instead I gaze silently at the last sliver of sunlight on the canyon rim high above us, enjoying the coolness of the spring on my sunburned face. The peaceful quiet of the darkening canyon is broken only by the evening call of a songbird and by the steadily rising pitch of the water as another jug is filled.

WE TAKE SOMETHING OF A SHORT mid-trip break at the Navajo Community College in Tsaile. It's a chance to do laundry and for the kids to use the college's library and museum to research the individual learning projects that each is doing as a part of the trip. During the stay we make a side trip to Window Rock, the capital of the Navajo Nation. Our visit includes a brief audience with Peter MacDonald, the tribal chairman. The days following our stay at the college settle into a routine of planting visits to various Chapter Houses across the reservation. The towns include Teec Nos Pos and Nazlini, Many Farms and Rock Point. Each of the small towns we visit has its significant events within a now familiar pattern that has us arriving at a Chapter House parking lot jammed with Navajos, waiting in their pickup trucks. We grab 5-gallon buckets and shovels and break into groups of two and three. While some Navajos are there only to pick up the two trees they have been allocated, more are ready to take advantage of our offer to plant the trees for them. Each family collects its trees and waits for a planting team to become available. When one does, it hops in the back of the family's pickup and makes the often lengthy journey to the family's home. After considering the most favorable location for the trees, we dig holes, plant the trees, and water them. For the Navajo, a planting like this has its spiritual element and each of us in his or her own way tries to honor the importance of this life-renewing event. Some of the kids actually say a prayer for each tree as they finish planting it. The always shy children of the family watch the planting activity from afar, hiding behind a billowy skirt whenever we look in their direction. It becomes a game of peekaboo and gradually they warm to us. The last stage of each visit is the offer of a cool drink and sometimes fry bread, hot from the skillet. Whatever conversation we may have with the family often occurs as we finish our fry bread. As these individual experiences accumulate, each kid gradually builds a picture of reservation life that few Anglos ever see.

Two locales become notable exceptions to this general routine. In many ways they represent for me the low and high points of the trip. Sweetwater is the low. We arrive late in the morning, but to an empty parking lot and a locked Chapter House. It's not a new experience; no one ever did show up on the Sunday afternoon we spent at Teec Nos Pos. Bill had speculated only half in jest that the Navajos may have found it hard to believe a group of Anglos would really show up for work on a Sunday. Sweetwater is so isolated that it has no phones. Communication with the outside world is accomplished by radio. The town consists of a trading post, the Chapter House, and a well from which we presume the area gets its name. No one seems to know what's going on. And so we sit in the burning afternoon sun and wait. Some kids walk over to the trading post and pay its outrageous prices for Cokes and Ding Dongs. And then they walk back. Some explore the area. Some head back to the trading post. Bert finds a sandy spot in the parking lot and begins building sand castles, alone. His immaturity makes him something of an outsider, and this is a comfortable way for him to withdraw from the group, which doesn't always make an effort to include him. Bert has developed a number of ways to remove himself. Reading is one. On the trip to Window Rock I watched him finish a sci-fi novel and then reread it completely on the way back to Tsaile, just to avoid, I think, dealing with the other kids.

The hours pass. Jean Maryboy is out driving the roads trying to figure out what's going on. Jean, a young Navajo woman, is coordinating much of our trip from the Navajo side, continually replenishing our supply of trees, for example. A college-educated single parent of three kids, she embodies a combination of polished Anglo skills and Navajo savvy. We couldn't be in better hands.

The kids are slowly going mad in the heat. The Dumb Friends

League, the self-ascribed appellation for a tight group of seven boys and one Tanglewood girl that shares one of the vans, becomes a marauding band of raiders making sporadic attacks on the kids in the other vans, abducting a new woman for their "tribe," or commandeering a coveted cassette tape. The other kids, of course, retaliate. The sorties from van to van escalate. So does the language. Plenty of kids are calling other kids motherfuckers and sluts and homos. The language is crude but lacks a mean edge. It's mostly innocent fun, the sort with which Golding begins *Lord of the Flies.*

Finally, after 3 hours of this aggressive mayhem, the Navajos begin showing up and we fall back into our planting routine. The bitter memories of the afternoon fade with some hard labor, followed by a good dinner, which we prepare in the Chapter House kitchen. In the evening, Willie Smallman, a local jewelry maker, transforms raw turquoise and silver into a beautiful ring before an audience of about 20 of the kids that tightly encircles his work table. Willie is no lecturer, but the kids ask one question after another. He fields each as he works. The kids even learn of the exploitative economy of the jewelry business. After he pays for his materials, Willie will clear about $5 for his 2 hours of work in crafting a ring that will eventually sell for $35 in Santa Fe or Albuquerque.

THE HIGH POINT OF THE TRIP for many of us is Cove. We are coming into the small community from Red Valley and the weather has turned foul. The last 8 miles of the trip are on dirt roads and the steady rains have turned them into a quagmire. The only way to keep moving in the rust-red slurry is to not slow down. So we follow Jean, careening through rim-deep mud at 30 or 40 miles an hour. We are a spectacular sight; red clay's flying everywhere. It's so thick that, despite the steady rain, the windshield wipers can barely keep up with it. Occasionally the ruts ahead indicate that the locals have judged the best route to be off the road, and we blindly follow their lead, first lurching down into the drainage swale at the roadside and then up out of it into the low brush, only to repeat the precarious maneuver to return to the road a short distance later.

We make it to Cove. The Navajo refer to rains as being male or female. Male rains include the pyrotechnics of thunder and lightning. Female rains are steady, soaking. This is a female rain, but she is one persistent female. The miserable weather has not dampened the turnout, and the whole town seems to be at the Chapter House. The explanation for the unusual response is that Cove is Jean's home chapter, and she's made sure that we will be treated with more hospitality here than anywhere else on the reservation. Local pride is at stake.

The roads are such a disaster that the locals fear that were we to follow our usual routine and send planting teams out into the hinterlands, some might not make it back. So we only distribute the trees to families. But we feel the least we can do is provide a demonstration of how to plant them. So, despite the steady rain, we all throw on our ponchos and wade into the mud and begin planting trees around the Chapter House so that the Navajos will understand the process. Our holes fill with water as fast as we dig them. We don't expect the trees to be planted in a downpour so the demonstration includes instructions on watering, which the Navajos find pretty funny.

Once the trees are distributed, we remove as many layers of mud as we can and enter the Chapter House. It's a new building—contemporary architecture—with circular windows here and there. Wonderful aromas greet us. The Cove women are preparing dinner: Navajo tacos, mutton stew, and all the trimmings. The rain also has saved the kids from what some had anticipated would be the most difficult trial of the trip, a sheep butchering ceremony. Jean had arranged the ritual— normally reserved for the return of a long-departed family member— in our honor. But the rains have washed it out. One of the Navajo men says, straight-faced, that the sheep is stuck in the mud. Some of the girls who have for weeks been trying to figure out how they could politely wiggle out of the event are openly grateful for the change in plans, as is a silent boy or two.

Gradually we all make it through the two available showers. Being clean has become the ultimate luxury of the trip and we each take our turn reveling in the simple pleasures of soap and hot water, trying to ignore the protests of those still in line that we are taking too long. Then we stuff ourselves with good food. A Cove man carries in a VCR and some movie tapes—very macho, shoot 'em up fare—so that the kids will have some entertainment for the evening. The women will have none of our offers to help clean up the kitchen. We are their guests. No sooner is dinner out of the way than they begin making popcorn. What's a movie without popcorn? We are clearly being pampered but we take it bravely, politely stuffing away the popcorn where there is no room for it.

Normally the last task in our morning routine before departing for the next town is cleaning the Chapter House, but that schedule clearly isn't going to work here. The Navajos have started cleaning up all the mud that we've tracked in and there is no way to dissuade them from the chore, so we all join in so that at least they won't have to do the entire job. During the evening we break into many small groups at tables around the big meeting room. Some kids watch movies. Others play games or talk. And then, one by one, we crawl into our sleeping bags, as satisfied with our day as we will be on this trip. The Navajo have a poetic phrase for the special state of grace we have brushed against today. They say you are walking in beauty.

About 3:00 A.M., I make a trip to the john. My route takes me past the Chapter House office. The light is on. Through the large window, I can see Johnny Arviso, a Cove man, at the desk. He's drawing. I stick my head in. "What's keeping you up so late?" I ask.

"Working on a picture," he says.

I enter and peer over his shoulder. It's a pictogram. I learn that when Johnny wasn't running up and down the football field at Oklahoma State, he was studying art. "It reminds me of your sand paintings," I say.

He explains the picture's components. It portrays many symbols of life and friendship and of the relationship that the Open School has built with the Navajo over the past 3 years through its tree planting. Johnny plans to give the picture to the kids in the morning, a final gift in a 24-hour orgy of giving. He will be up most of the night to meet his self-imposed deadline.

The Cove women are back early in the morning, well before most of us have stirred in our sleeping bags. They begin breakfast. We are again politely told to stay out of the kitchen while they prepare a huge batch of fry bread. After breakfast and a final clean-up, Johnny presents his picture. The kids are thrilled. They will in turn present it to the whole school at our Governance presentation. Every trip group has a responsibility to bring a part of the trip back to school so that other students may benefit from the experience, at least vicariously. This sharing typically takes the form of a loosely planned presentation in which the whole trip group takes part. It will usually include a slide show, maybe some music or artifacts, and always many lively anecdotes. Through such presentations younger students in the school learn of the value of trips. After hearing our presentation some kids may decide that next year's Navajo Work Trip is one they want to take. We say goodbye and, as we have so many times before, load our packs into the vans and depart for the next town.

ON THE DAY AFTER WE RETURN from the Navajo Reservation and before we start our trip processing—the 4-day group evaluation of how well each of us has performed as a contributing member of the group—one of our final chores is to clean the vans and the equipment truck. A half dozen kids join Bill and me as we drive the vehicles to the do-it-yourself carwash near the school. Bert quickly volunteers to man the high-pressure hose and the rest of us fill buckets with soapy water. The high-pressure spray's difficult to control and occasionally Bert dowses one of us. These accidents gradually take on a purposeful pattern. We retaliate, throwing sponges at one another or cracking wet towels across bent-over behinds.

"Danae and Sheila should be here," Margie Thayer says, recalling their water fight in the stream bed in the bottom of Canyon del Muerto. Danae and Sheila are back at school, helping put away the camping equipment. "I haven't been this wet since the truck ride into the canyons," Bert says. The reminiscing continues as we work and play. We remember the grace of Joe Yazzi in the saddle as he rounded up his sheep, and the parking lot at Sweetwater and the people of Cove. Soon we've washed away the last of Cove's red clay. It will not be so easily removed from our memories.

CHAPTER 12

A Discovery in Dinosaur Land

The small group of seven students and two staff members—the Old Bones, New Ideas class—is trudging through broken brush searching for fossils near the dinosaur-rich area of Grand Junction, Colorado. The class is Judith Miller-Smith's idea. Judith is a graduate intern from the University of Colorado. Married, with two kids, she is a former geologist who abandoned a high-paying management position in the petroleum industry to retread herself as a teacher. She is assisted on the trip by Dana Orin, a regular member of the Open School staff. The Grand Junction trip is the class' culminating activity. The search for fossils continues. As she moves through the low brush, Jenny Demsky's been gazing at the ridge line in the distance. "This is it!" she shouts to the others. "It's *got* to be in this general area." The group agrees.[1]

The *it* is a lost paleontological dig. They'd seen that ridge before, in a huge blow-up of a very old photograph back at the Dinosaur Valley Museum. It showed a long-dead paleontologist, a real-life Indiana Jones in rolled-up shirt sleeves and battered fedora, beginning work on a dig of a big Camarosaur. Tim Weiss, the museum's curator who's leading this fossil hunt, had told the group the story of the lost dig. Money had run out shortly after the photograph was taken and work was abandoned. Though the site was known to be in the area, its precise location remained a mystery. As Tim's story unfolded, everyone had gazed up at the photo, studying the scene, recording clues to the site's location. Tim had mentioned, maybe a bit too casually, that rediscovering it would be quite a find.

This trek through the rough landscape with Tim is something of a lame replacement for what had been the planned activity for the group—working on an actual dig. That became impossible when paperwork from the Bureau of Land Management okaying the work was late in arriving. Surely Tim had studied the photograph back at the museum for clues just as the kids had, but if he had, he wasn't letting on. If anything was to be found, it was going to be the kids' discovery.

Tim acknowledges, "Yeah, Jenny, you might be right. This *may* be the place."

The group spreads out in a line with Tim leading the way and begins a sweep of the area, looking for fossils or signs of the old dig. The kids find lots of fossilized fragments of dinosaur bones—gem bones they're called, because of jewelry makers' unpopular practice of destroying prehistory by cutting and polishing the agatized material for use in their wares. Dan Corrigan, who's scanning the ground near Judith, suddenly stops short.

"Judith, isn't that a bone?"

Only a small rounded shape looking nothing like a bone is visible. Tim, in fact, has just covered the same ground; surely his trained eye would have spotted anything important. But Judith also knows Dan to be a formidable fossil finder. He's spent his 2 years at the Open School devouring every geological experience the school offered. His prowess in finding fossils on the Utah Geology Trip earlier in the year had led that group to dub him Doctor Dan.

Judith and Dan call Tim to the spot. Some careful scraping reveals that Doctor Dan has indeed done it again. Handing Dan his dentist's tools, Tim employs an old paleontological adage: "You killed it, you clean it."

Dan spends several minutes kneeling over his bone, excavating it with care. He occasionally pauses to brush his shoulder-length hair back from his face. The excitement grows in the group huddled above him. The kids offer first encouragement, then advice, and finally caution as the work proceeds. Dan works with great care. Finally, the bone is freed, and amid the cheers of the group Tim holds it high above his head in a gesture of triumph. After turning it over and over in the mid-day light, he proclaims the find a "specimen bone," complete enough that the museum staff will likely be able to identify, from this single bone, the type of dinosaur from which it came. Only time will tell whether the group has indeed found the lost Camarosaur site in the photo, but it's still an important event. Tim carefully packs the fossil and marks the site for future investigation. Everyone again congratulates Dan for his accomplishment and the sweep resumes.

Dan and Judith are again walking side by side. After thinking for a time about what has just transpired, Judith whispers, "Dan, how do you feel?"

Dan's reply is barely audible. "Judith, I *really* feel good inside."

Learning *in* the World

I thought before my year at the Open School that I understood and had a high commitment to the principles of experiential learning. But I'd intellectualized the concept. My year in the school gave me a much more personal understanding of—and commitment to—the power of direct experience. Fittingly, that transformation was stimulated—as it was regularly for the kids and staff members of the Open School—by direct experience. The supporting evidence is inescapable: Too many of the potent learning experiences that I saw kids have during the year occurred outside the confines of the school building to allow me to discount them. These were not interesting augmentations to the regular program; for many kids, they were the very core of their personal, social, and intellectual development. The events that prompted these transformations were as unpredictable as they were significant. One doesn't plan an encounter with a Joe Yazzi.

In the immediacy of the moment, the learning that one can observe directly during a trip is often pretty general. But I also recall on the Navajo Work Trip a memorable conversation in the darkness of the van during the 20-mile trip back to our campsite in Chinle, after we had attended a powwow in Tsaile. As we drove, the kids replayed parts of the evening that they had just shared with several hundred Native Americans from all over the western United States. The kids related particularly interesting tidbits of information that they had picked up from one person or another during the evening. Liz had struck up a conversation with a young Navajo woman, a dance contestant, who wore a beautiful buckskin dress ornamented with understated beadwork. In a gym full of striking regalia, its simple elegance had stood out for several of us. The woman had told Liz that the dress was worth $6,000. Randy had learned that a beadworker always puts one imperfection in her work, one bead out of place that ensures that perfect symmetry is avoided. Others had learned the distinctions between plain northern dancing and fancy northern dancing. I don't think I could have devised a test to determine what had been learned that evening, but clearly, much had. The evening's curriculum had included firsthand information about a proud people with ancient roots, about the rewards of not being afraid to try something new (joining in the dancing), and about how people who seem very different from us can be approachable and giving.

But what is learned on a trip is not always so immediately evident. It may be months or years later when the full significance of an event on a trip—what Eliot Wigginton (1975) calls the teachable moment— becomes clear. Older students talked of being "turned around" on a trip. Donna Helms described the personal growth she experienced on a trip:

> Through trips I have been able to find myself, find who I really am. And I've just gotten to know *me*. Trips have been, for me, a very, very positive thing. I mean I have grown in ways that I couldn't have even here [at school] or at home or anywhere. Its just a sense of doing something for yourself. I was struggling— really—with God and on my trip to the Bahamas I came back and I wasn't anymore. I had found my concept of God. (Int. 4/88)

Shortly before my departure at the end of the school year, I attempted a simpleminded quantification of the school's commitment to direct experience. I dug through the records and tallied up the people involved and the miles traveled on the year's trips. And I attempted to catalogue the sights that the kids had seen. Nineteen trips were taken by groups ranging in size from five to 25 students, each group accompanied by two to five adults. (The Wilderness Backpacking Trip was a special case that involved about 145 students and a dozen adults.) The trips ranged as far west as California, as far east as the Bahamas, as far north as the Boundary Waters of Minnesota, and as far south as Mazatlan on the Pacific coast of Mexico. All told, an aggregate of almost 400 students and staff members traveled over 43,000 miles, a total of over 600,000 person/miles.

In January, 15 students sailed across the Gulf Stream to the Bahamas with Dan, Poz, and Greg Lomme. Another 15 lived in Chicago with Roberta and Judy in a drafty, roach-infested, 18-story tenement in a neighborhood that claimed the city's highest homeless rate. The Bahamas trip laid the groundwork for a future service project—building bookshelves in an impoverished Bahamian school. The Chicago group spent its days speaking with community people and performing community service.

Early in the year, Roberta, Kurt, and a parent who was a professor of history took 12 kids on a history tour of the northern plains. The itinerary included several days in Yellowstone. Greg and Roberta took seven kids on the Winter Ecology Trip over the continental divide at Brown's Pass, where they spent one of their four nights in a snow cave. Rick and Bruce led 15 students, mostly graduating seniors, on a canoe trip through the Boundary Waters of Minnesota; Joy, assisted by Ruth's son, Andy, and by Fitz, led a group of six students to the Esalen Institute in California. The Boundary Waters Trip included an extended solo experience, with each kid on a separate island; some kids fasted for the 3 days of the solo. Esalen included group encounter experiences that remained the confidential domain of the trip's participants.

Where does the staff find the energy to mount all these trips? As much as possible, they require the kids to do the legwork; it's part of the learning that occurs on every Open School trip. Every trip has a planning group comprising the students and adults who will form the trip group. Planning a major trip typically takes 6 or 8 weeks. The group meets regularly, often two or three times a week. The activity is scheduled into the weekly school calendar just as any class would be. Almost everybody thinks of the activity as a class. Because the Navajo Work Trip was among the year's most complicated ventures, it had one of the most involved planning efforts. Bill Johnson was the trip leader, a role he'd played from the very first Navajo Work Trip. He really began planning the trip the year before, as the previous Navajo Work Trip was ending. Because of the trip's unusual logistical problems—procuring 2,000 or 3,000 bare-rooted apple and peach trees and raising the $6,000 or $7,000 needed to pay for them—the first Navajo planning group began meeting at the beginning of the school year. The trip had another unusual feature that complicated planning: Nine of our 25 student slots were filled by eighth- and ninth-graders from Tanglewood. The two schools were 25 miles apart, so getting everyone together regularly for meetings wasn't easy.

The planning effort for any trip accomplishes many goals. It allows a collection of individuals the time that it needs to become a group. Everybody learns to work together, with each person pulling his or her fair share of the load. To prepare for the Navajo Work Trip, for example, our trip group broke down into a variety of committees. Keith Leander headed up the Equipment Committee, which made sure all our tents, camping gear, and planting tools were in order. The Food Committee, headed by Danae Reichling, planned our daily menus for the 2 weeks we would be on the road, got them approved by the group, and then organized the grocery list. Another group, headed by Nancy Smithson, worked out the details of the itinerary. We would be out of reach by phone for several days of the trip, but whenever possible we had the name and number of a contact person whom parents or the school could call in case of an emergency. All the details of the trip, including the few times we would be able to take showers, were laid out in a five-page document. Committees were also formed to deal with finances (Russ Molby controlled the dispersal of all monies—several thousand dollars—on the trip) and for fund raising, trees, vans, and public relations. We even had a committee whose early task was to see that we became a smoothly functioning group.

The older, more experienced students were expected to take the lead in all this effort. In general they were very aware of their leadership responsibilities in the planning process. One student described the developmental process of starting out as a new student at the school as "just sort of going on trips," but as he gained more experience, he gradually began taking on his share of the "running and planning of a trip to the point where we older students more or less run it" (Int. 4/88).

Through all the months of effort, individuals had time psychologically to buy in to the trip. Each of the Open School's 19 trips during the year shared this characteristic. Those kids who didn't develop sufficient ownership of a trip began falling away as they learned that it wasn't important enough to them to make the commitment and the pressure grew to either participate fully or drop out. So it was with the Navajo Work Trip; we started out in January as a complement of over 30 kids and six or seven adults, but the final trip complement was 25 kids and five adults.

All the concomitant cooperation of the planning process has an impact. Students sometimes talked of first learning to work with people on a trip. Lief was one.

> It showed me ways to work out problems with people and some problems that I had with myself and how I relate to other people, especially the processing on the trip that I really valued. (Int. 3/88)

The processing that Lief was describing is the group assessment that constitutes each trip group's final activity. Processing took many forms. It might have included a group evaluation of the entire trip, but more often it took the form of the group giving each individual, student and staff member alike, extensive feedback on how he or she had performed on the trip. The Navajo group was so large that our processing took over 12 hours, distributed over 4 days. Processing typically occurred on school time; it *was* a learning experience as the group assessed how each individual had performed as a member of the group.

This sort of evaluation is a skill that must be learned, and the more experienced trippers tended to do it much better than the neophytes. As we worked our way through the group, we had our share of "you're a rad' guy" and "I had a real good time," especially from the less experienced students. But we also had many more specific insights.[1]

For example, Dylan had undergone a visible metamorphosis on the trip. He started his segment of the processing, as we sat in a circle on the floor of Judy Sherbert's living room, by talking about how shy he was and how he had hoped to learn to socialize better on the trip. The kids offered a number of comments about how important he'd been to people and how much they had enjoyed his sense of humor; people began remembering the little things that he'd done, how he'd been the one guy who played basketball with some Navajo boys for 3 hours at one of our stopovers—even though he was a crummy basketball player. We thanked him for doing so many little unsung jobs—like straightening up the load in the equipment truck—that made everybody else's existence much easier. Dylan had exemplified the spirit of pitching in on the trip. Judy Sherbert remembered standing outside the Chapter House in the pouring rain at Cove talking to him. With water dripping off his nose, he'd confided to her that he was worried about returning to school and lapsing into old habits with old friends. After telling the story, Judy reminded him, as the group nodded agreement, that he now had a support group—all of us—who would be happy to help him if he had any difficulties maintaining the gains he'd made.

Tears flowed occasionally as we worked our way through the group, not because the feedback was negative, but because it was uplifting. Judy mentioned to Sheila McCulloch that, though Sheila was a second-year student, Judy really hadn't had an opportunity to get to know her before the trip. Judy admired her courage in attempting the trip so soon after knee surgery and appreciated her upbeat demeanor. Her ability to lift the rest of us when we were down by being optimistic or saying something funny was an important asset. It made Judy wonder how she had missed knowing Sheila during her time in the school and how happy Judy was that they knew each other now. Some of us joked about the before-and-after photos that we had taken of Sheila's hands. Two weeks of hard labor had transformed the elegant, crimson manicure with which she had started the trip into broken stubs and snags. No one asked her of which picture she was most proud. We knew her answer.

Danae's words for Sheila were personal and glowing. She remembered the outrageous water fight in the canyons that ended with both of them sitting, waist deep, in the middle of the stream laughing at their predicament. They had become close friends on the trip.

Eventually we worked our way completely through the group in this manner. An overwhelming amount of information had been shared. I wondered if the kids were able to digest more of their share of it than I. When we finished processing the last kid, the Navajo Work Trip officially came to an end. All that remained was the writing of self-evaluations of the trip. For an experience to become an official part of a student's record at the Open School, she or he must write a self-evaluation of the experience, which is shared with trip leaders and with his or her advisor, each of whom writes a reaction to what the student has written. As was the case with other parts of the program, older students displayed much more skill in constructing useful and revealing evaluations than new kids did. The older students' written exchanges with the staff sometimes displayed an unexpected maturity. But even the young kids could provide perceptive analyses of their growth. Bert Lucas's self-evaluation was only one and a half pages long, but despite its fractured prose, it revealed much. Bert wrote about the highlights of the trip for him: sleeping in a hogan and planting trees in Canyon de Chelly. But he also wrote of his habit of withdrawing.

> To deal with my frustrations I usually withdrew, and dealt with my problems inside, and that is not healthy, but usually people give a very hard time and then I feel like I can't talk to any body and that will be hard to change.[2]

The three staff members on the trip—Bill, Judy, and I—each, in turn, wrote reactions to each student's evaluation. We also tried to correct some of the writing problems, all the while being careful not to appear to be treating the writing as an essay assignment rather than the very personal expression that each was. Bill wrote to Bert that there were times when he was concerned about Bert's apparent withdrawal from the group. "As you begin joining in during processing and at other times, you have important things to contribute; don't be afraid of it." Judy wrote that she saw some real growth on Bert's part during the trip.

> Often you allow your "peers" to get to you (you almost seem to enjoy it) and then you pout. Often you deliberately leave yourself on the outside in what seems like a justification on your part to

not like people. I saw you working on this in the van on the trip
home.

She went on to talk about how important it was that Bert was now
aware of this problem because it enabled him to consciously work on
it. Because I was his advisor, Bert and I had already talked at length
about the trip. In my written reaction, I cautioned him to be careful
that in his efforts to build himself up in a group he *not* fall into the
counterproductive tactic of tearing others down.

How does a staff build the commitment to overcome the dozens
of reasons for *not* taking kids on trips? It does it gradually—through
experience. Commitment is built as one sees the transformations that
occur in individual kids on trips. My own understanding of the importance of trips in the lives of the Open School's students is encapsulated
in how the Tallahassee Work Trip, which occurred in late February,
changed Josey Fink. The central activity of this annual biology-
oriented trip was the construction of another animal habitat at the
Tallahassee Junior Museum. Josey was a first-year student and was as
shy and withdrawn as I can imagine any young woman being. During
the first half of the school year I had scarcely heard her speak outside
of an occasional "Hi" that she would squeak in response to my greeting
as I'd pass her in the hall. She wore her hair forward and lowered her
head, seemingly to avoid eye contact. I presumed that her behavior
was neither new nor easily changed.

Perhaps because it wasn't a single transformational event, an
epiphany hitting her like a bolt of lightning, Josey couldn't pinpoint
what happened in Tallahassee to change her.[3] But she returned a different kid, standing straight, smiling, looking people straight in the eye,
and *talking.* The trip group even asked her to be one of its chief spokes-
people at its presentation about the trip at Governance.

When I asked Bruce Andrews, who had co-led the trip, what
caused the transformation, he described an erosive process that works
on many kids on trips. To Bruce it was a familiar pattern, a gradual
wearing away of old habits that either don't work or are no longer
necessary. He said that the 3-day van trip to Tallahassee—"3 days in a
steel box," as he put it—is a form of boot camp. "Experiencing a sense
of wonder is a part of it," he told me, "the feeling that the kids are a
part of the ecosystem—of something bigger than themselves." Most
trips are to places that staff members have found to be interesting,
even captivating. They often have the same effect on the kids. The
personal growth that occurs on a trip is caused by a succession of

simple acts: "Eating the beans *you* picked or realizing that *you* moved a canoe 30 miles today," was how Jeff described it. "Kids learn that they have power to do at least simple things."[4]

Like most everybody at the Open School, Josey returned from her trip understanding the power and utility of trips and sharing a commitment to seeing them continue. That commitment has prompted the Open School community to engineer the more formal academic program of course offerings in ways that minimize the disruption that trips cause. "So many of the limitations in life are self-imposed," Jeff pointed out. "On trips, the kids learn to eliminate all these perceived impediments." Because of the Tallahassee Work Trip, Josey learned that there was another way for her to be and that it felt good. These overnight transformations are seldom permanent. Whatever forces are causing a kid to behave as she did are still there, waiting for her, when she returns. But a seed for change has been planted. Bruce, who was Josey's advisor, wouldn't let her forget Tallahassee. He'd occasionally remind her that she had a potent model—herself on that trip—to draw on whenever she might dare to make the change more permanent. And each subsequent trip that Josey took would, in its own way, reinforce that feeling.

Lesson VI

STANDARDS

The pages of this book are filled with references, some direct but many others indirect, to the ways in which standards, both academic and behavioral, were communicated and maintained within the Open School. For example, Chapter 10, the seminar on limits and boundaries, was primarily a commentary on the degree to which individual staff members feel that standards must be internal to each student. The degree to which the school accomplished this goal was inferable in Chapter 5 in the description of several Passage experiences that students had proposed or executed. Through the school's governance structure, students, too, played integral roles in establishing the school's standards, roles that become clearer in this section of the book.

In a way, the highly personalized nature of the school's program complicates a discussion of standards. The *person* that each kid is becoming was inextricably linked in the staff's thinking to the *student* that each is becoming. That holistic linking was most apparent in the staff's weekly discussions of individual students. Each week, five students — the fabulous five — were picked at random from the school's rolls to become the focus of attention of the entire staff. The first portion of the 2½-hour meeting — usually 45 minutes to an hour — was devoted to discussions led by the advisors of these five kids. While the remainder of the staff meeting was open to students, the fabulous five and the agenda item that always followed it — other student concerns — were confidential discussions that occurred in executive session.

The Open School had several unusual space problems. One was the student lounge. The school had designated a corner classroom as a lounge but it was so inhospitable a space — dark, cold, and noisy, with a major route to the tin building running right through its diagonal — that the students' avoidance of it was understandable. The kids relaxed elsewhere, usually on the smoking porch or in the eddies of the corridors. We'll examine the way that standards were enforced in the school

177

by watching it grapple with the sticky problem of how to deal with a hall lounge that was created rather spontaneously by a small group of students. Over several weeks the antics of the inhabitants of the lounge gradually became a concern of a widening segment of the school community. How the school dealt with the problem is instructive of how it balanced individual and community concerns and how these were communicated throughout the school community.

The staff's standards were continually communicated through its discussions, and consequently we'll sit in on two more New World Seminars in this section. The first of these examines the culture of classrooms at the Open School. Some characteristics of classes at the school were byproducts of the school's highly externalized program, but the unusual level of freedom in the school reveals some issues that probably also pertain, in subtle ways, to classrooms in most high schools today.

Discipline, at least the connotations that the term carries in most high schools, isn't a very useful concept in discussing student behavior in the Open School. Most readers probably have trouble envisioning a school environment in which fights are such a rarity that the one that occurred during my year in the school could simply be referred to as The Fight. Readers probably also have difficulty understanding the nature of rule breaking in a school that has very few rules. Over the years, I have been able to learn much about the impact of the control issues that are endemic to big high schools by observing the almost total absence of such issues in very small public alternative high schools, even when these schools are heavily populated with students with histories of "disruption" in their prior schools.[1] It is this sort of marked contrast that has prompted me to analogize my year in the school to an exploration of a New World. We'll join the Spanish Language Trip in Mazatlan, on the Pacific coast of Mexico, as the group deals with a disciplinary crisis. While in Mazatlan, students and staff lived in the homes of Mexican host families. The students studied Spanish each morning in a foreign-language school, but afternoons and evenings offered opportunities to experience the many facets of the culture of Mexico.

Trips to Mexico have had a long heritage in the Open School. They had always been rich experiences, filled with both intense personal learning and fresh cross-cultural understandings, and because of their evident power to change kids, trips of various kinds to Mexico had become annual forays of the school. But Mexico's relaxed drinking laws for teenagers were often too great a temptation for the school's students. It became an issue on the Mazatlan Trip when several students were suspected of having violated one of the school's Three Noes: the prohibition against drinking alcohol during any school-related activity. The situation was one of the clearest examples of what most observers would term a discipline problem that I encountered during my year in the school. We'll watch Fitz grapple with the greys of what, on the face of it, would seem to be a black and white issue.

The last seminar to be presented also deals with standards, including those of a changing society, as the staff discusses how the school's students have changed over the past 20 years. The discussion focuses on the manner in which current Open School students respond to externally imposed demands, but it takes an unexpected turn to the topic of how parents have changed over the years and how the school works with them in the raising of their children.

We'll conclude this final lesson with a description of how the school closes the academic year, the school's unusual graduation ceremony. One way to understand the school's standards is to learn what happens to its graduates. A program such as the Open School's may strike outsiders as exciting and challenging but also as an unacceptably high gamble that may close doors for its students. And so we'll look at what happened to the 30 students who graduated from the school during the year of the study.

CHAPTER 13

The Fabulous Five

Some staff members are still entering the large room in the tin building as Judy Sherbert calls us to order. It's just past 8:00 A.M. Staff members lead all regular meetings of the staff and Judy is leading all the staff meetings during March. Most of the group of 20 or so has settled in around the large square of tables. Some are still wearing coats or down vests; it's a cold, sunny morning. Fitz and Dana split the dregs of the coffee pot between their two cups and start another pot. Judy announces that Ruth is attending a district-wide meeting and will be late to ours, if she makes it at all. Judy moves us to the fabulous five.[1]

Judy asks Pat Sliemers to talk about Rachel Earl. Pat pauses a moment to compose her thoughts. She sips her coffee and begins. "I'm concerned about Rachel right now. Her attendance is bad, for one thing. Her life is full of ups and downs because of her family situation. She's taken on the responsibility of caring for her family and particularly for her mother. In one way, that's very noble, but in another, it prevents Rachel from having a life of her own. Her mother has not been working. She has arthritic knees. Won't go to the doctor. She supposedly can't get out of bed. When she can't, Rachel stays home to take care of her and to take care of Becky, her little sister. The family has money problems. Rachel won a TV in a giveaway at Walgreen's a couple of weeks ago. She was excited because they'd be able to sell it to pay the rent.

"Rachel's angry with me right now," Pat continues, "because I've been pressing her about her attendance. Joy will attest to that." Joy, who's witnessed a recent confrontation between Pat and Rachel, nods. "Rachel can fix Becky's lunch in the morning and then come to school and the family can get along without her. But it makes Rachel angry to hear me say that.

"She's been working on a Passage proposal," Pat tells us. "She'll get busy and make good progress on her work and then something will happen at home that sets her back and then she has to start all over again. That cycle has occurred several times now. I was disappointed in her Creativity wrap-up. It was on the creative and expository writing

181

she has done for various contests. It was one of the worst-written papers I've ever seen. Susie was the Passage consultant." Looking at Susie, Pat says, "I really appreciated your follow-up and your comments on it.

"So, Rachel is not in a good place right now," Pat continues. "And I don't know what she needs. I want to be sympathetic but not too sympathetic. I'd just like all of you to be aware of this so you can take it into account in her classes and in her Passage work. I appreciate all of your comments to Rachel and your feedback, and I appreciate your being honest with her. That's what she needs right now: real honest feedback." Pat looks across the room at Rick Lopez, who kids Rachel about being Pat's shadow, always hanging around the office that she and Rick share. "Rachel needs to hear stuff like that," Pat says.

"Why don't you just make the stuff at home a Passage," Rick suggests. "Let her stay home and keep house. Tell her to stay home; raise the kid; raise her mom; do it. Don't come to school for about 3 months."

"That'll cure her," Susie says.

"It probably won't cure her," Joy says. "It will just enmesh her even more in the role of being a mother and her mother being a child."

"I'm also afraid," Judy says, "that even though she has a lot of things to do at home, she tends to sit a lot . . ."

". . . and read Harlequin novels," Pat says.

"She reads and sits," Judy continues, "and she doesn't exercise. I think she eats a lot. She'd lost some weight but now she's really gained it back."

"Boy, that family situation is something else," Susie says while rising to refill her cup.

"But you're not going to change this family's structure unless you intervene—in the family," Rick says. "That may mean a home visit, sitting down with her mother and telling her, 'You can't let your daughter do this anymore.'"

"A direct intervention," Jeff agrees.

"Gayle or someone should make a visit," Rick says. Gayle is the school's part-time psychologist.

"I don't think Pat should be in that position," Joy says. "I think it should be someone else, someone like Gayle. The other thing her mom does with a fair amount of regularity—whenever Rachel gets things under control and is happy—is to threaten to move the whole family back to Virginia."

Dan emits a low whistle.

"Her mom will create a crisis in the absence of others, so that Rachel can't be fully happy or comfortable here at school," Joy adds. "That's happened numerous times since she's been here."

"Does Rachel know that all families are not like hers?" Rick asks. His question brings chuckles from some of us. "Seriously, she may well think that all families are like hers, that all kids have to stay home and make lunch for their kid sisters."

Picking up on an earlier point, Pat says that Rachel has submitted an Adventure Passage proposal to lose weight. "That's a real good step for her," Pat says. "It's nothing she wants to discuss around the other kids, though."

"Her Adventure is all tied up with her family," Rick says. "She's a housewife, watching the soaps and eating herself to death."

Rick's comment is followed by silence. Pat gazes absently into her cup. The staff hasn't solved any of Rachel's problems; these conversations seldom do. But the group has shared some information that may help each staff member work more effectively with her.

"Does anybody have anything else to say about Rachel?" Judy asks.

"She's doing real well in Psychology," Dana says. "She volunteered to read an extra book—on child development."

The group moves on to the next student, Mike Weybright. Dana tells us that Mike, who's in his first year in the school, switched to her as advisor from Fitz about 3 weeks ago.

"I thought it was just last week," Fitz says, raising his eyebrows. He shakes his head. "The advisor's always the last to know."

Dana describes Mike's overriding social concerns. "He says this is the first school he's ever been in where he has friends. His whole universe, right now, revolves around pleasing his friends. And around his car. His car is his biggest handicap." She describes the several financial and legal scrapes that Mike's been in this year. "Money's always a major concern of his. He talks about not having enough to take trips, even though his parents say that shouldn't be a concern. He hasn't been on a trip yet."

"He's planning to go on the Utah Geology Trip," Kurt says.

"I'm glad to hear that," Dana says. "He hadn't told me."

Three voices chant in rough unison, "The advisor's always the last to know." Dana ignores them. "I think a trip will be very good for him," she says. "He's very bright but academics are a low priority for him right now."

"He seems so young," Pat says. "He seems like a little boy to me in many respects."

"He craves praise and attention," Judy says. "We need to let him know that we like him."

"He wants friends to the point of desperation," Fitz adds.

"And yet he doesn't treat the friends he has very well," Dana says.

"Really," Judy says, looking as though another tumbler has just clicked into place in her efforts to unlock the mysteries of Mike.

"He stands them up," Dana says. Her comment is followed by silence.

"Anything else on Mike?" Judy asks. When no one offers more she moves us to the next student. Dan talks about Linda Humphrey.

"She's doing okay," he begins. "She has some pretty severe ups and downs, the sort a lot of adolescents have." He describes her awareness of herself, how she takes care of people, especially the downtrodden. "She doesn't really know how to be a kid, to be one of the gang," Dan says, "because she always feels she has to be so responsible and so in charge. She understands that." Dan describes Linda's family circumstances, a very young mother and a father who's doing graduate work in physics at Boulder.

"Her father's really hard to talk to," Jeff says. "He's right about everything. Bruce and I don't know any biology. Linda's never learned anything in this school."

"He feels that a part of Linda is not being developed in this school," Dan adds, "the logical and the sequential. He does value the other things the school is doing for Linda, though."

Eventually Judy moves us on to the next student, Alan Chambers, one of Roberta's advisees.

"He is just so multi-talented, so bright," Roberta begins. "He's a gem. He wants to hold people at arm's length, but he's very charming about it. That gets him through a lot of situations, but he relies on his charm far too much. He and I are having this very gentle battle where I'm trying to get him to be a part of things. But he's really evasive and resistant. We may have a real knock-down, drag-out fight before the end of the year over some of those issues and maybe he'll change."

"He's had a difficult year," MB adds, referring to Alan's major abdominal surgery in November.

"Yes, he has," Roberta agrees, "but he also uses that as an excuse."

"Is this the time to pull together a support group for him," Dana asks, "so the group could help him focus on what he wants for himself and how he's going to get it? How he can get it here, at school? Get him thinking about next year? It wouldn't be good for him to have another year in which he's as loosely connected to the school as he's been—not only this year but last year, too."

"Judy suggested the same sort of thing," Roberta says, nodding. "Alan's a wonderful writer. He just finished some really interesting poetry. It surprised me. He's got great potential, but I need to figure out how to get him to learn some self-discipline."

The group discusses how Alan is doing in various classes. The theme of a talented individual who doesn't know how to apply himself is replayed several times in the conversation. MB observes that a major change occurred in Alan when he developed a relationship with Peggy Ammon.

"He really applied himself in class until then," MB says, "but then she just became the whole focus of his life."

"That's another indication that maybe we need to get him refocused back on his plans for the future," Rick says. Several others nod agreement.

Marilyn Wittebort walks in, not in jeans or even a skirt, but in a jade green dress and high-heels.

Dana gasps, "Oh my goodness," and the group deteriorates into whistles and jibes.

Unabashed, Marilyn says, "I thought we had a dress code."

"Yeah," Rick says, "you have to be. Dressed, that is." Rick occasionally lobs wisecracks into conversations as though they were grenades. They explode, igniting the whole staff, which responds in kind. Staff members even have a name for this incendiary mischief; they call it sky-rocketing. After more cackles, Judy moves us on to the last member of this week's fabulous five, Dan Shedd, a graduating senior. Dan is Judy's advisee.

"I don't know what I would have done without Dan," Judy says. He's pulled me through these first 2 years. *He's* been a wonderful advisor for *me*. I never really knew the other Dan that some of you dealt with before I came to the school. I've only known the one that had already gotten his act together. The one thing that still bothers me about him is his inability to deal with pressure and stress. They paralyze him, which is where he is right now with graduation deadlines closing in on him.

"I've asked him to cut back on his job," she continues. "He works 40 hours a week. He won't do it. He feels a lot of responsibility to his job. He has three Passages all wrapped up and ready to go to his committees. And he's half finished with his Transcript. So he's going to make it. I just can't say enough good things about him." With both palms she firmly flattens her stack of papers. "I'm going to miss him."

Pat mentions the metamorphosis that Dan has undergone. "He spent two years just having a really good time with his friends."

MB says, "Thank God for him on the Wilderness Trip." MB is dressed all in lavender, right down to her high-top Converse sneakers. She makes no claims to being a rugged outdoorswoman, and Dan was indispensable as her student assistant on the Wilderness Trip.

"He's always been interested in the outdoors and in psychology," Judy says. "He hopes to work out a career that combines those two loves."

"I have a great resource for him," Dana says. "I know someone who designed a whole program for himself in that vein."

"Great," Judy says. "I'll talk to you about it."

Judy moves to the next agenda item. "Are there any other student concerns?" Susie mentions that Carol Wonko has won yet another first prize in an art show. No one else has anything, and Judy says, "Why don't we take our break, then?" The mid-meeting break often occurs as students are arriving at school and beginning to pursue their morning routines. The timing gives staff members a chance to look up a student at the beginning of the day should they need to. "Let's keep it short," Judy counsels us. "We've got a lot to cover today." We smile knowingly. The break, like almost everything about the school, operates on Open School Time.

CHAPTER 14

The Hall Lounge

At the beginning of the year, an impromptu lounge took firm hold of a small tract of Open School hallway. Several kids became steady squatters on a 5- by 15-foot area just outside Kurt's room. A glass firewall—the sort with chicken wire embedded in it—and a row of bright orange lockers decorated with bumper stickers and photographs defined two walls of the Hall Lounge. Only the demands of passing traffic and access to Kurt's classroom held in check the space's remaining two boundaries.

The membership of the Hall Lounge shifted continually. Inge would occasionally cuddle with someone there, among the large pile of oversized pillows that the group had amassed. And I think Bert wanted dearly to be accepted by these older kids. He would hang out on the perimeter of the lounge, usually wearing his army issue raincoat. He'd be fiddling with something, maybe bouncing a ball off a nearby wall and catching it in his lacrosse stick, waiting for his presence to be acknowledged in some way. Whatever its makeup, the group always seemed to include Neuman Copenhaver and Daren TeSelle. As the Hall Lounge grew in the consciousness of those in daily contact with it, Neuman's and Daren's steady presence made many think they were the ringleaders of this largely innocent undertaking. The group committed only one official transgression: the occasional playing of a small boom box in not-so-quiet defiance of Governance's long-standing rule prohibiting the playing of music in the halls. The whole matter was sufficiently harmless that, for a week or two, no staff member or student felt strongly enough about the situation to take issue with it. But almost every staff member and a number of students were, at some level, disconcerted by the Hall Lounge as it was used more and more to excess. From Monday morning through Friday afternoon, Neuman and Daren never seemed to be anywhere but in their lounge.

Finally, several weeks into the school year, the Hall Lounge became a topic in Governance. The debate took on the classic dimensions of the rights of the individual counterpoised against those of the community. Some kids pointed out that the lounge group pretty regularly violated the school's prohibition against playing music in the hall. General discontent with the situation was expressed and specific complaints were raised.

"We have people running around the hall dressed in costumes," an angry senior said, "people who aren't doing anything, people who just sit there or crawl all over their girlfriends or boyfriends. It's just not good. We get prospective students and their parents as visitors to this school! I would never send my kid here after seeing you guys."[1]

The discussion led Governance to ask the guys to cool it. They did, for a while, but the situation gradually disintegrated into its familiar pattern and the Hall Lounge's most bothersome qualities irritated those who confronted it on a daily basis. Rick Lopez tired of ushering visitors past kids sprawled among the Hall Lounge's impressive collection of pillows. Kurt, whose door opened right onto the Hall Lounge, tired of asking the guys to turn off their music. I tired of looking at kids wearing knee-length Apache moccasins or kids sometimes not wearing shirts, kids sitting cross-legged on the floor, applying stage makeup to each other's faces in homage to Kiss. Passing through the Hall Lounge, stepping around and among the bizarrely decorated limbs that were thrust into what was left of the passageway, became a disquieting experience. We complainers were not very effective in voicing our consternation, perhaps because it was hard to frame the complaints in a way that did not also impugn the standards of two advisors—Daren's and Neuman's. Then, too, what were we complaining about? Those of us most bothered by the Hall Lounge understood, intellectually anyway, that much of the problem was our reactions to it. That acknowledgment restrained the level of protest. Beyond the gross amount of idleness being blatantly displayed by the boys and their shifting coterie of hangers-on, and the bizarre tableaus one occasionally encountered, no harm was being done. And so the situation drifted along. Except for the occasional sarcastic observation about the group's latest exploit that someone—Rick or me or, less frequently, Kurt—would drop into the middle of a staff meeting, it was a dilemma without dialogue. The situation would remain a thorn until Poz and Joy saw it as a problem.

One staff member railed to me about the "visual pollution" of the Hall Lounge. The school was being asked to serve too many kinds of kids. He appropriated a phrase of Jeff's to summarize the Open School's predicament: "The 'urban guerilla' has invaded the school," he said, "and I think I know why. It's because parents don't have anywhere else to put them. We are *the* alternative in Jeffco" (Int. 2/88). The Hall

Lounge—a hotbed of social experimentation—was not a situation to which one could easily acclimate. Just when I'd adjust to some recently introduced ritual, a yet higher level of craziness would be achieved. "What if?" was an often asked question in the group. It would lead Ryan Hunsucker, a sometime member of the group, to come to school one day—and only one day—dressed in a faded chenille bathrobe and slippers to see how people would relate to him. The bathrobe was a warm-up for the day he dressed in drag. The group was—as someone pointed out in a staff meeting—majoring in weirdness.

Neuman, in particular, aroused concerns in some staff members. He had apparently been "quite a regular kid when he came here," a staff member told me. Another staff member had told him that Neuman had taken one of her classes early in his Open School career. Neuman "attended class all the time; he did his work," I was told. But Neuman apparently "wanted a name" in the school and he achieved it through his bizarre behavior. "The school may not have caused his idiosyncracies," the staff member told me, "but the school hasn't helped him avoid developing them" (Int. 11/87).

After a few weeks, the problem of the Hall Lounge finally came to a head. From my desk in Rancho Pavo I overheard Linda, the preschool teacher, out in the hall scolding the group. I peered out the door through the chicken wire and saw Linda, who's about 5 feet tall, standing over these big guys who were sitting cross-legged on the floor. Neuman had colorful scarves tied around his bare biceps. Daren was wearing his floor-length duster and derby hat. They were looking up, wide-eyed, at Linda as she sternly explained that her 4-year-old girls had to pass through the boys' lounge act to get to the john. "Look, you guys," she said, "my girls are afraid to come by here and one of them has just wet her pants." The guys, sat there, waist-deep in pillows, looking as innocent and as respectful of Linda as their black eye makeup would allow. "Now enough's enough."

The incident got back to Poz and it prompted him to call a lunchtime meeting of the Hall Lounge's prime culprits and complainers. We met in the Cooler. As we waited for the last of the group to arrive I thought about my many interchanges with Neuman and Daren and Ryan. I'd said things to the guys—a request that they keep at least a 3-foot aisle for passers-by or an oblique reference to the no-music-in-the-hall rule—almost on a daily basis. But as we began to talk, I realized that for the first time I was going to *discuss* the matter with the students, to listen to their views. It had never occurred to me, amid all the craziness, that rational discourse was a possibility.

As the meeting started, it became clear that Poz *had* talked about the lounge, at least with Daren, his advisee. Poz asked the guys to explain their situation. They described some of the unsupportive physical conditions in the school. Everyone agreed that the regular lounge was inhospitable. Where else were they to go? What harm were they doing? I acknowledged that if they'd been doing any real harm, they probably would have been asked to disband weeks earlier.

"The problem is a bit more subtle than whether or not you're violating any rules," Rick said. He described his embarrassment in exposing visitors to so condensed a dose of the Open School's chronic public relations problem: idleness. "It's a crummy first impression to give those who are trying to learn about the school," he said.

"The school exists for us students," Ryan Hunsucker countered, "not for visitors."

Kurt talked about feeling besieged in his own classroom. The guys understood his situation. There *was* a problem when too many kids used the Hall Lounge at once.

"But it wouldn't be getting such heavy use if the school had a decent lounge," Neuman pointed out.

In the end, the guys agreed to reduce the size of their storehouse of pillows; to try to limit the amount of time they were on public display, especially on visitors' day; and to no longer play music, even softly. I offered to help them develop a workable design for rehabilitating the regular lounge space. The project might develop into Creativity or Practical Skills Passages for some of them.[2] In about half an hour, the ill feelings were aired and most of the differences were resolved.

The Hall Lounge continued to exist in one form or another throughout the year. But the discussion had served an important purpose; the *problem* of the Hall Lounge died quietly that day in the Cooler, when some students and staff members finally got around to talking things through.

CHAPTER 15

The Fourth New World Seminar: The Culture of Classrooms

The value of the New World Seminars had very quickly become evident to me. The staff, in response, had been kind enough to try to fit them into its heavy Wednesday morning agenda. Once my edited typescripts of earlier seminars began circulating for approval within the group, something gratifying happened. The staff began to see value in them, too. Having the discussions was okay, but *reading* them became, for some reason, educative. After the circulation of an early typescript, a postponed seminar, which was first scheduled to occur in December, suddenly became a high priority for the next staff meeting.

I had again prepared a formal statement for the discussion. The topic this time was the classroom.

> *Over drinks at the end of Block One classes, Bruce lamented that the staff doesn't have enough control over the learning environment. By that, I took him to mean that classes at the Open School are sometimes frustrating and ineffectual exercises, certainly in contrast to other elements of the school's academic program.*[1]
>
> *Examples of the Open School's classroom culture are fairly evident. For example, I have repeatedly witnessed, in my classes and others, the following conditions:*
>
> *Many students don't bring a pencil and paper to class. A few don't seem to have writing materials at school. Homework assignments are given infrequently, as they are in more and more high schools, and staff members have confessed to me that when they do give assignments they really don't expect them to be completed by most students. Perhaps because of the many legitimate unscheduled activities that occur each day, a lot of tardiness seems to be tolerated. Perhaps because of the flexibility of*

attendance that trips and independent study require, absences for other reasons seem to be tolerated. And staff members feel they can interrupt a class almost any time to confer quietly with a student.

Despite a strong aversion to each of these conditions, I have, in my short time here, personally committed or allowed students to commit every one of these transgressions. That situation leads me to suspect that a very strong set of cultural expectations is manipulating us—both staff members and students. I recently heard Greg Lomme, for example, talk about the need to reduce the demands of his new class, The Brain. He was talking to two motivated seniors who are taking the class.[2] They protested his proposed change. For them, a familiar pattern was recurring: Another meaty classroom experience at the Open School was being watered down.

As I see it, the academic program at the Open School comprises five major elements: Advising; trips; Passages; other independent work, particularly internships; and classes. Classes seem least effective to me. The expectations of the school seem to be that students should not engage in trips, Passages, or other independent work until they have demonstrated a readiness to accept the responsibilities that each entails, but that everyone is ready for the classroom. But over half of our students seem to be indicating, by their behavior, that they are not ready for the classroom, that they've learned poor classroom habits in the schools they attended before coming to the Open School. We seem to be reinforcing those habits rather than working to extinguish them.

Staff members here understand that they can each set their own standards. But isn't the school handicapping the potency of the classroom and of a very talented group of teachers by not establishing minimal expectations for a student's responsibility in all classrooms? Given that the Open School does so many wonderful things programmatically, with apparent ease—things that most big high schools would never even consider doing—why has it allowed the classroom portion of its academic program to evolve as it has? Why do we have such high expectations for students in other aspects of the academic program, but not in the classroom? Besides their educative function, do we use classes as holding tanks for kids who haven't progressed as self-directed learners? What is the staff's view of the function of classes in the Open School's academic program?

Although the staff had first read the statement weeks earlier, the discussion again begins with an uncomfortably long silence as everybody thinks about how best to start. The snaps and pops of a radiator springing to life fill the void. The tables, as always, have been arranged in a large square so that everyone can be seen and heard. Jeff finally breaks the ice.

"The problem centers on the conflict between our expectations as teachers and our protectionism as advisors. I think we sabotage each other inadvertently. As teachers, we each expect our students to meet certain minimal expectations. On the other hand, as advisors, each of us has a set of priorities that supersedes the classroom. Advisors deal with *all* the dimensions of these human beings we call advisees. That act is a tacit admission that classes are secondary in importance."

More silence fills the room. Ruth finally ends it. She is bothered by some of the language of my opening statement. She believes that the school *does* establish minimal expectations. "The problem is what happens when they aren't met," she says. "I think our expectations are beyond minimal at times."

I try to clarify my view. "What I was trying to say is that the *school* does not set minimal expectations, that such standards are left to individual teachers."

Ruth straightens in her chair. She can't even agree with that. Her voice has an uncustomary edge to it as she says, "Quite a bit is left to individual teachers, but we've had discussions in the past on just these issues—how we establish our individual expectations and support each other in that. Expectations are not just established by teachers in isolation, either."

"There *are* ways, then," I ask, "that the school communicates to the whole student body that students are expected, for example, to bring paper and pencil to class or they're expected to meet certain attendance obligations?"

"I believe," Rick Lopez responds, "that we communicate those things pretty clearly."

"Saying it in classes," Ruth elaborates. "Saying it in Advising. Saying it in Beginnings."

Jeff, in an apparent allusion to the widely felt notion that important elements of the school's orientation for new students were lost in the changes made to Beginnings this year, says, "I've said it a lot more in the past than I did this year."

"But you had the opportunity," Ruth reminds him. Again looking at me, she says, "We usually really emphasize it there." After a pause, she adds, "Another place I see it happening is in Passage meetings where students are told, 'You need paper and pencil; you need to be taking notes.' I hear it said a lot of different places and in a lot of different situations."

My paper and pencil example is proving an unfortunate device. Everyone's words are delivered in flat tones, but I sense I've made some people defensive, something that is hard to do with what I view as a very open group.

Jeff attempts to save the discussion. "A constant dilemma for me is what I call the entertainment culture." Looking at Poz, he says, "I *know* that your film class is an intellectually demanding class, but if there's a movie to see or a trip to go on, well, it's half in the bag right there. When the students know that some valued reward is going to come out of a class, their participation is a hell of a lot better. The entertainment factor is important."

Poz, whose film list includes such sophisticated movies as Antonioni's *Blow-up* and Fellini's *La Strada*, says, "But these movies are not very entertaining."[3]

The group erupts in laughter. Jeff tries to recapture the discussion's serious tone. "I'm not saying that's what your plan was, but there's still something they want to get."

Poz jams the stem back onto his unlit pipe. "I think a part of the reward for them is getting my immediate response to their written reactions to each film," he says. "Those reactions are their required 'tickets of admission' to each subsequent film."

Dan has not had a similar success in his Essay classes. Susie wonders if the difference is that, in Essay, the kids have got to pull the stimulus out of themselves. "It's easier to *react* to a film than to create something from scratch." She raises the issue of consequences in an uncoercive environment. "Last Friday, some kids did not finish their clay pots, even though they knew that their pots would dry out too much over a 3-day weekend to be workable. What are the consequences for them if they *don't* complete a pot?"

Her question is rhetorical, but several people can't resist offering an answer: "Then they don't have a pot."

Susie turns her volume up a notch. "And how does that feel? Their perception is that there are no consequences for their inaction. Those occur down the line, at Transcript time. I had the same situation with Margie Furgueson." Margie is one of Susie's advisees who is working on her final Transcript. "Margie said, 'There are no requirements here,'" Susie continues. "I brought up the Western Civ situation, when so many kids didn't write a final paper.[4] I asked her what happened to her. Well, she didn't write the final paper. I asked if she was putting that class in her Transcript. She said, 'No.' 'Well, how does that feel?' I asked. 'Well,' she said, 'I really liked the class but it wasn't all that important.' Margie functioned the same way in The Brain. The immediate sting for a substandard performance isn't there. It feels like we don't have enough clout, and they know it."

Rick, who taught the Western Civ class, reveals a new facet of the issue. "When I came here, I was under the impression that I had to teach differently. But no one taught me how to be an Open School teacher. I still face the dilemma of how to teach here, of what my expectations of the kids and of myself should be. Some of my best classes have been situations where I've let *them* do it. But I still don't have a clue how to teach a class here that isn't a trick class and make it work. It seems like magic. Sometimes it works and sometimes it doesn't. I really don't want to kid bash, but if you have a high-quality kid in an academic group, it makes a big difference. The Vietnam and South Africa classes were the two most successful classes I've taught here. I didn't do a thing differently, but those classes took off. But I don't know how to do that in the absence of those kinds of kids.

"I didn't know how much," he continues, "I might enjoy giving an F to a kid until I came to a school that didn't give grades. I never gave one in anger in those other schools. There was none of the heavy emotion I feel here. Our system of MAPs should mean that none of your advisees is in my class unless he or she wants to be there. It's not a requirement. Their presence implies that they want to do the work; they're buying in. But my experience, in the last few years, suggests that that's not true, that they're there just because they haven't got the creativity to develop their own learning settings. They end up in classes they really don't want to take and then they blow them off." Stabbing the table with his index finger, Rick says, "I want to deliver a consequence next year."

I try to build on Rick's need for consequences. "One of the things I've come to realize is that the sort of coercion that's a part of traditional settings—like mine at Indiana—is fairly subtle. We've all been immersed in the traditions of schooling for so many years that we're desensitized to them. There *is* a lot of coercion in the historical setting in which the idea of classes developed. And I've noticed here how difficult it is for me to figure out a way to get kids to do the tough stuff that may be required to get to real learning in the absence of that coercion. In some ways, I end up being subtly coercive where I haven't had to be in other contexts, where the coercion was imbedded in the setting."

Rick raises another problem of classroom teaching at the Open School. "A class, here, contains the whole range of abilities. There's no sequencing of our classes—that I'm aware of—so there's no taking a group of knowledgeable kids and running with them in an advanced history class. And able kids, in turn, have trouble avoiding the bullshit that happens in a nonadvanced class."

"But all teachers in all schools have that problem," I point out.

"Except that we don't have the consequences that most schools have," Rick responds.

Poz rejoins the debate. "I think you have control over class enrollment here, if you want it. You can create a course description that lists certain requirements and asks for certain kinds of kids. You can make students aware that they shouldn't take the class unless they have some background on the topic. You don't usually have that flexibility in conventional schools."

Ruth tries to understand Rick's view. "I guess you're saying that if you're not given permission to set requirements, then doing so is not okay? That the culture here expects you to teach everybody in every class?" She agrees with Poz that the opportunity not to do that is available.

Jeff says that one of his frustrations from 16 years of teaching in both conventional schools and here is trying to do science when kids don't have the tools they need to get to the concepts he's trying to teach. "I have trouble getting them to the Aha's! that are the rewards of science," he says. "Math is one of those tools. So are reading and writing and being able to ask questions. What's frustrating about the classroom is the time I spend, even as a secondary teacher, teaching those tools. All the curriculum guides for high school science presume that the kids already have those tools and that my job is to just lead them from one roseate bead to another. That's not the way it is in any school I've ever been in."

Susie agrees. "I feel a real resistance to learning the skill. The practice required is hard. Annie and I are struggling with that problem now." (Annie is Susie's student teacher.) "We're trying to come up with every rationale we can to sell the kids on learning *how*, which in turn will allow them to develop a real product. The kids drag their feet in the face of that sort of discipline."

Jeff continues. "I don't spend much time teaching the things I enjoy myself: being creative, having the opportunity to deeply probe topics. So I burn out and then my attitude is reflected in the class. Or I just give up and say, 'Fuck it; I'm tired.' Then, after a time, I pull myself out of it. I start over with another class or try to resurrect a current class, hoping that my energy becomes contagious. I know I take on varying degrees of responsibility for the success of my class, depending on how I feel."

"I think it boils down to the age-old argument of process versus content," Kurt adds, "except process, here, is more broadly defined. We're making the skills that you just mentioned, Jeff, a part of that process and, as a result, we don't get the content. I agree with you that things are out of balance here. When I walk into a class for the first time, I immediately sense what that balance is going to be."

"Whether it's going to fly or not," Pat interjects as she nods agreement.

Kurt continues. "Sometimes my first impression is wrong, but I think we need to recognize the unusual dynamics of classes here and try to understand their effect on both process and content. That's what I tried to do last block in my classes—to evaluate both content and process—so that I didn't have to feel that the class was contingent only upon content. If a student only made gains in process, it could still have been a successful class for him, even if I didn't think it warranted being reported on his Transcript. For example, Ray Clossin made great strides in Geometry last block, but he didn't finish the class and he didn't complete the final assessment. I wrote exactly that in his final evaluation. I mentioned he had learned a lot, grew a lot, but he hadn't met the expectations of the class, and, therefore, I didn't recommend that he be allowed to use the class in his final Transcript or for transferring credit to another school. He saw my comments when he came back from Australia and his eyes got real big. He was experiencing immediate accountability for what he'd done in the class. We spent 20 minutes discussing my assessment. His response was, 'Yeah, I guess that's true. I want to do this class again and learn the content next time.' I think we need to build more immediate consequences into the program, give clear feedback about acceptable performance in each class, and establish more intermediate milestones, like yearly Transcripts. If we do, kids will know where they stand. And we, in turn, can fairly assess their progress here when they transfer to other schools."

Kurt gets up, retrieves the coffee pot, and refills several of our cups.

Judy pushes aside her stack of papers. "I had a student transfer to Evergreen High last year," she says, "and an evaluation she'd written for a class she'd taken was missing from her file. It hadn't been returned by the teacher. We have to take our responsibilities in responding to evaluations more seriously—as a staff.[5] I'm annoyed when a student takes the time to write a good evaluation and the teacher's only response is, 'Good job; it was great to have you in the class.' I understand why, the next time, that kid doesn't bother to write an evaluation. We have an opportunity to be honest and say something meaningful to that kid. When Kurt wrote that Ray could not use Geometry in his Transcript, it was meaningful to him. He was devastated. It was probably one of the most meaningful evaluations that one of my kids has ever received."

Tom Rohrbach joins the conversation. "I want to comment on your statement, Tom, about classes being holding tanks for students. For one student, I'm glad if he shows up that day. For another, I'm glad if he shows up with paper and pencil. For another, I'm glad if he did the assignment this time since he didn't do the last one."

"You're saying there are no norms," I say, "that we have expectations for individuals rather than norms."

"In a lot of schools, norms are uniform for the institution," Tom responds. "Here, they are based on the class and a particular teacher and style."

I press the issue. "I'm saying that there are certain minimal expectations that I can't imagine not being applied to everybody."

Tom and I are seated on the same side of the square of tables. He leans forward to see me better. "Expectations that are school-wide?" he asks.

"Yes," I say. I lean forward, too. "There are some that ought to be embedded deeply in the culture, rather than things you keep reteaching in each new class."

"We try that periodically," Tom acknowledges, "and we always come back to the need to be able to make individual exceptions. It's a value inherent in the philosophy of the school."

Bill doesn't completely share Tom's view. "Since I've been here, I thought coming to class with paper and pencil was a norm. New students come into the school thinking that freedom means being able to do anything they want to do. It takes most kids a year, sometimes 2 years, to learn that, here, freedom means responsibility. That's who we're working with. They're always testing freedom."

Pat joins in. "One of the things we can do is improve our communication with each other about classes. When Susie let me know that Steve Drotar had shown up late to pottery class twice, I could follow up with him immediately. I think our responsibility, as advisors, is to make sure that the student follows through with his or her MAP, which means getting to class. Then I sort of let go and it's up to the teacher of the class to take it from there. My responsibility as an advisor is to make sure they're there and on time, but I don't think we're very good—most of the time—about communicating that to each other and giving each other the help we need. That's the advantage of being a small school. We can follow up with each other's kids immediately. So both Susie *and* I got on Steve right away. I don't know if that will change his behavior, but we've done what we can to improve the situation.

She continues, "One of the things I've been particularly frustrated with is *our* attendance and tardiness. I know we've dealt with it before as a staff, but I'm particularly aware of it now that I'm working with Leadership.[6] I see how hard the kids are working to get Governance started on time. Everybody in the school is walking in at any old damn time. I go around the school saying, 'Governance is starting; Governance is starting,' and people—staff members and students— look at me like I'm absolutely out of my mind because I'm reminding them to get in there. Advising is a similar situation. If Advising starts at 9:15 and half of the student body is out in the hallway, we have a problem. I think those are things we can cure pretty easily."

"So what's the cure?" Dan asks. "I go around doing the same thing, reminding people."

Pat sips her coffee. "I don't think we're communicating with each other," she says. "If I have a problem with a student not showing up, and I inform his advisor that he hasn't come, I expect the advisor to talk to the student. As an advisor, I hope that teachers will let me know when there's a problem with one of my kids. I think that's where we're falling short. That's why I'm saying that the solution is easy. We're a small school and we should be able to do that."

There seems to be no good moment to end the discussion. We've exhausted the time allotted to this seminar. I look around the room. Some people have slumped back in their chairs. They've had enough talk of the problems of the classroom. I bring the seminar to a close.

AFTERWARD, I THOUGHT ABOUT what had transpired. I wasn't at all satisfied with the course the discussion had taken. The early defensiveness concerned me. It may be that my chosen role in the seminar process—that of vocal skeptic, even cross-examiner—encourages defensiveness. Ruth's initial response to my written statement stuck in my mind as I reconsidered my role. Being principal of a school that has shattered so many of schooling's conventions has to be, at times, a strain. She is the major buffer between the staff's wild ideas and grand plans and the formidable bureaucracy that is the Jefferson County public schools. She is seen by all those school people out there—people with whom we never have to deal—as the instructional leader of the school. At the same time, she is also trying to support my effort to tell the story of the Open School—including describing its warts—in a very public forum. She is a brave woman leading an unusually brave school, and she should be permitted a little defensiveness.

I also wondered if the topic—that scholastic sanctum of sanctums: the classroom—contributed to the unusual dynamic of the discussion. I had the opportunity to raise that speculation with Poz later in the day. He didn't think the classroom was that much a sanctum at the Open School, but that the Advising system was. The two elements of the program are closely linked and—as the discussion illustrated—in some conflict with each other. Poz wondered if that might account for the manner in which the discussion proceeded.

I also didn't think I'd done a good job of framing my written statement for this seminar. This one, more than the others, had been too much a catharsis for me, a way for me to vent some frustrations I was feeling back in November, trying to make classes in the New World work for me. Although I revised the statement several times before distributing it, I never completely expunged it of its initial bile.

Over the next few days, several staff members raised the topic of the seminar. Bill commented that, while the problems of the classroom certainly were not new that year, it was especially critical to communicate expectations more formally that year, when over 50% of the student body was new to the school. "We can't be casual about the task in those circumstances," he said.

Dana, feeling she had talked too much in the previous seminar, had remained silent in this one. Afterward, she talked about feeling she was a traditional teacher in an alternative school. "You *can* have good classes here," she said, "even lectures, but you have to prepare well." Her presentations in her Shakespeare and psychology classes sometimes take on the elements of performance, as good teaching often does. When I shared her view with two other staff members, they raised the point Jeff had made during the seminar—though they made it clear they didn't intend it as a criticism of Dana's teaching. They felt that a class full of today's kids, raised on a diet of TV and Walkmans, can go well as long as you keep it entertaining. But it begins to fall apart when you begin demanding product from them. Dana had, unknowingly, provided a rebuttal to their point by sharing a couple of anecdotes about how blasé teenagers who had contracted her enthusiasm for Shakespeare suddenly began reading and writing in ways they thought themselves incapable of. I am, however, suspicious of anecdotes about individual students' triumphs; too many factors unrelated to the actual classroom experience can affect a student's performance.

Over the years, including this one, there *have* been some truly remarkable classes at the Open School, classes not tied to trips or movies or, as Rick might put it, tricks. One practice that has fallen away since Arnie's departure is the offering of honors classes. Several teachers, especially Arnie, used to team up to offer these classes. Kids of all abilities were welcome, but they entered with the clear understanding that they were expected to work hard. One honors class studied the conditions that led to the Vietnam War. Each kid read several books from the reading list provided and was expected to become the class expert on one of them, representing the book's position in class discussions. Another class on the American novel had everybody reading the same three books, each drawn from a different decade: Salinger's *Catcher in the Rye*, Greenberg's *I Never Promised You a Rose Garden*, and Nichols's *The Milagro Beanfield War*. The class dissected each book, trying to figure out the ways in which each reflected the society in which it was written.

The high achievement of kids in these classes probably was, in part, a response to Arnie's intellectual authority and the weight of his personality.[7] But not even these classes always went smoothly. A staff member who co-taught some of them told me that there were occasions when a class session was angrily canceled because homework hadn't been done.

On a Sunday morning over breakfast, I discussed the seminar with Arnie. He made an observation about how classes work at the Open School. He estimated that about one-third of a kid's education at the Open School occurred in the classroom—probably not too different from many other schools. The Open School differs from those other schools, though, in the ways it acknowledges the worth of other learning experiences. Arnie grabbed my paper napkin from among the remains of lox and bagels and drew a little two-by-two cell diagram. The diagram summarized all the places that learning occurs for teenagers (see Figure 15.1). "The Open School honors the importance of all four contexts," he said. "Most schools only honor one." In that atmosphere, classroom learning doesn't lose its importance, but it does take on a very different perspective.

A frustration that many rookies at the Open School may experience centers on this point. A couple of weeks after the seminar, Rick Lopez and I talked about Arnie's belief that classes are a minor part of

FIGURE 15.1 Arnie's Sketch

	In School	Out of School
Planned Experiences	Classes, curriculum, etc. (The only cell most schools consider "legitimate")	Extra-curriculum, family vacations, watching TV, etc.
Unplanned Experiences	Fighting, socializing, conversations in the restroom, etc.	Family and personal problems, buying a car, etc.

a kid's education. Rick noted the problem that reality poses for the staff. Because much of a student's education at the school is relatively invisible to the staff, it takes time for a newcomer to learn where to look to see it occurring. It also isn't very soothing to the ego of a teacher, fresh from the Old World, to learn that the most potent experiences that kids are having in the school are not being stimulated by good teaching, at least as it is traditionally conceived. Classroom learning at the Open School competes not only with TV, Walkmans, and teenage socializing; it also competes with exciting trips, individual Passage work, and the lessons about self that occur in Advising. These program elements, not classes, are the heart and soul of the Open School's academic program.

CHAPTER 16

Incident in Mazatlan

The Mazatlan Trip is a wonderful way for kids to be immersed in a different culture. While they attended a language school together each morning, they were on their own, with only the supervision of their host families, throughout the rest of the day. For some, especially the girls, the level of attention and concern they received from their Mexican "parents" could be overwhelming. Gayle Hunckler's Mexican mother rode to school each day with her on the city bus and escorted her into the central patio of the school, where she formally turned responsibility for looking after Gayle over to Fitz. At noon, she'd be back, ready to resume her en-loco-parentis role for the next 20 hours. For Gayle, who had enjoyed a high degree of autonomy since her junior high years, the tight supervision was stifling. Because of the sexual norms of the culture, many of the boys, in contrast, enjoyed great freedom in Mazatlan, even more than they experienced at home.

Word reached Fitz that some of the boys were not using their freedom wisely. He received a secondhand report from Carlos, the director of the school, that some of the boys might have been drinking. After Fitz heard a second, similar rumor, he called a meeting one morning after language school.

WE CONGREGATE IN A SMALL LECTURE ROOM. Its high seat-steps create a tiered floor. It has just been carpeted and carpet remnants are still strewn around the room's perimeter. The fragrant smell of new fiber and rubber hangs in the humid air. The 11 of us—the nine students and Fitz and I—gather on the lower steps. Fitz is a black-haired Irishman who grew up in the Bronx. He's been with the school since 1982, when he was lured over to the Open School from neighboring Evergreen High. The move, which the staff describes as an abduction, is part of the lore of the school: Several staff members purportedly carried his desk from one school to the other to signal how much they wanted him. Fitz contracted polio when he was a kid from swimming in New York City's polluted waters and walks with a slight limp. Picking a sport that didn't rely on two legs of equal length, he molded himself into a world-class kayaker who just missed making the 1980 Olympic team. He has a playful streak that is not at all apparent now as he relates what he's been hearing. He ends his opening comments by asking what the students have to say for themselves. A couple of the boys—the ones we most suspect of drinking—quickly deny any wrongdoing.

Without mentioning names, Fitz gets more specific about what he's heard. The group studies the new carpet. The silence is filled only by the quiet whirring of the ceiling fans above us. Finally, Marty Robinson allows that he has been drinking. Marty's revelation is a surprise to us. The rumors had been about others. He's my advisee and I try to digest the strange mixture of pride and anguish that is welling up in me, pride for his honest act and anguish for his abominably poor judgment. Eventually two more boys—Nick Lovette and Dave Whitaker—own up, but Fred Walker, who has a history of drinking problems and has become something of a natural leader of the group, remains silent. Because he's not a first-time offender at the Open School, the consequences for Fred, if he *has* been drinking, will be dire, perhaps including expulsion from the school. Fitz looks directly at Fred. The fans whir on.

"I know you think I'm in on it," he pleads, "but I have *not* been drinking."

Finally, Fitz dismisses the group, being careful as he does to praise the three guys for their honesty. The kids, knowing the school's rules as well as we, want to know what's going to happen to the boys. Fitz asks that everybody return to the school that evening to talk through what we'll do about the situation.

After the kids are gone, Fitz and I take stock of our predicament. All we have to go on are rumors. You don't send kids home on rumors. But three guys are on the verge of being sent home early for being honest, while Fred, the one we suspect is the ringleader, will stay in Mazatlan, enjoying the tropical sun and sea breezes, maybe even continuing to drink. We're about to not only punish honesty, but reward deception. Fitz's guess, or at least his hope from past experience, is that much communication will be going on among the kids during the afternoon and that the group will put heavy pressure on Fred to confess.

WHEN WE RECONVENE THAT EVENING, the effects of that pressure on Fred are evident and after difficult minutes, he finally folds under it.

"I was drinking, too," he says.

Trust is the overriding issue on Open School trips. The trip staff has to be able to trust the kids. Fitz explains to the boys that we're proud of them for being honest and that, because of the long discussion we've just been through, our trust in them is stronger now than it was, even at the beginning of the trip. Whatever can be learned from the experience probably has been; Fitz acknowledges that nothing much will be gained by sending the four boys home early, but he also cautions the kids that the boys' going or staying isn't our decision to make. One of the Three Noes has been violated, and not only this trip but all school trips have been put in some jeopardy. Fitz will call the school in the morning, explain to Ruth what has happened, and advocate that the four guys be allowed to stay.

The ordeal of the process we've been through has made us more a group than we've been at any time during the trip. The release of tension evokes tears in some, nervous laughter in others. Everybody begins hugging each other, saying thank yous, and offering support, especially to the four boys.

EARLY THE NEXT MORNING, I meet Fitz at the language school. As we sit in Carlos's cramped office, Fitz describes the wringer he's been through since we parted the previous evening. Word had gotten around the Mexican host families that four of "their sons" might be sent home. They can't understand why Fitz would punish the boys' honesty. Fitz isn't a very capable advocate of his position since he agrees with the Mexican parents' view of the situation.

Marty's Mexican mother and her daughter join us in the office. Mama displays her anger and frustration in Spanish, while the daughter, a lawyer, coolly presents her case in dispassionate English. Seeking at least one Mexican ally, Fitz turns to Carlos, a long-time friend of the school, trying to make him understand. For Carlos, rewarding the boys' honesty is the clear choice over punishing them for drinking. His strong sentiment shows through his Latin manners as he tells Fitz, "You can explain your position to me for a week, amigo, and I will *still* not understand it."

Fitz wonders if we can talk Ruth into our view of the situation. Before placing the call to the school, he rehearses the conversation to come, with me playing the role of Ruth. He can't make his arguments stick convincingly. As he waits for the ringing phone on the other end of the connection to be answered, he predicts that they aren't going to wash. Finally, Ruth is on the line. Fitz talks loudly to be heard over the bad connection. I can easily construct her half of the conversation: Fitz explains that trust is not an issue for us. The confessional has been a cleansing experience and we're confident that important learning has occurred. The account will be sounding all too familiar to Ruth, who has been through a similar experience herself on a previous trip to Mexico. Her strong conviction that she and her husband, Bill, made the wrong decision on the last Mexico Work Trip in allowing the guilty kids to remain on that trip works against Fitz now.

"Are you confident that the boys violated one of the Three Noes?" Ruth will be asking Fitz, to which he replies "Yes, but only because of their honesty. We . . . " Ruth will be interrupting, "Then it's a closed case. There's no other recourse but to send them home immediately. The School Board's policy is clear and unequivocal." The conversation goes on for several more minutes but Fitz's tone of resignation indicates that it's really over. Ruth has disarmed Fitz even more effectively than I had in our dry run.

Because they have created a condition in which the welfare of the school and its always contingent license to take trips to wonderful places like Mazatlan have to take priority over their own growth and welfare, four boys are sent home on the next plane. Four youngsters have made a mistake and then done their best to rectify it by risking honesty. And a school that normally encourages kids to take such risks in order to grow—rewards them for doing so—is left with no recourse but to punish their risk taking this time.

Strangely, despite the awkward circumstances of their forced departure, the boys experience a triumph of sorts. The outpouring of love from their host families, their Mexican parents' fervent exhortations that they return to Mazatlan when they can, and the strong support the boys have felt from our group for their actions, all have an impact. All four board the plane expressing the feeling that the Mazatlan experience has been an important event for them and voicing strong intentions to their Mexican families to soon return.

CHAPTER 17

The Fifth New World Seminar: Responding to Demands

The year was quickly coming to an end. The agendas of staff meetings were so packed that it was becoming difficult to squeeze in one more seminar. Finally the staff simply made the time during the last staff meeting of the year. I had, as usual, written an introduction to the issue for this seminar—how the students respond to demands—which had been in the staff's hands for the several weeks in which we had been trying to find time to discuss it.

This topic, how the Open School's students respond to externally imposed demands, has been of interest to me from the beginning of the year. I quickly became aware of major differences in the way the students I worked with 20 years ago responded to demands and the way kids I've worked with here—mostly first-year students—do. The kids I worked with in the 1960s seemed to respond much more positively to a range of demands—from cajoling to challenges to verbal prods to (even) pressure tactics—that are clearly counterproductive with our kids. While I'm not interested in trying to defend the dubious ethics of some of the ploys I used back then, they did share one positive quality. They spurred kids on to levels of performance that they had previously thought unreachable.

But the kids I was working with then may have been different from our kids. My students of 20 years ago had chosen to be part of a demanding situation. Indeed, a few would withdraw each year because they found the demands too great. The Open School's kids also choose to be here, but they may be making their choices on very different criteria than my students back then did. They may be choosing a way of life. At least some may come here to get away from the pressures of Jeffco's big high schools. A first-year student, for example, told me he had come here to get away from the drug usage in one of the big high schools [Int. 5/88]. He and his parents had concluded that there was less of a drug problem at the Open School.

I asked him if he thought their assessment was right, that in fact this atmosphere is more conducive to not using drugs than his former high school's.

"Yeah," he responded, "because I don't have pressures here like there."

"What kind of pressures?" I asked.

"The teachers, the rules they have. It was just so confusing there. It seemed like there was a lot of pressure and stress."

"And the staff here doesn't put pressure on you?" I asked.

"They don't really put pressure on me," he said. "They can talk things through, and you can get things arranged without having a total hassle."

I searched for some clarification. "You have an environment here based on negotiation?"

"Yeah."

Many of you have been teaching for close to 20 years. Do you think teenagers have changed in that time in the way that they respond to demands? Or does the Open School attract in part a particular subset of today's teenagers, students who are being driven away from big high schools by the pressures these big schools create? And, if that's true, what problems (and opportunities) does that condition create for you as teachers? How has it affected the program over the years?

The item on the agenda just prior to the seminar was Ned Richardson, one of our volunteer teachers, saying goodbye to the staff. Ned had talked about the frustrations of trying to put on a play this year that never came off. I decide to fill the usual silence at the beginning of the seminar with a reference to Ned's experience. "I think I'd been here only a few days when I first became aware of what I'll call a phenomenon. When I challenged some individuals to really extend themselves, they seemed to 'fold up' under that mild pressure. It was a marked contrast to my teaching experience of 20 years ago. I've seen a few additional examples of that response all through the year. Maybe Ned's experience in putting the play on is another. In part it may be due to a reluctance to subordinate oneself to the good of the group. Subordination occurs on trips quite a bit but maybe less so in other places."

Kids are arriving for school and bits of their conversations float through the thin walls of the tin building. They are almost intelligible in the silence of the room.

MB picks up on my query about who comes to the Open School. "The external audit identified four populations of kids that we serve.[1] What we're discussing here probably is a factor in each of those four groups, but there could also be an identifiable group of kids who choose our school only because of that." She pauses to frame her words. "Our expectations may be a factor. When Ned was talking, I was thinking about the videos we've done over the years. We've never had one go uncompleted. I don't know what the difference is. It may have been that we all had the expectation that it would be completed and that we'd all do what we needed to do to accomplish that. Sort of threatening them, telling them—only a *little* hysterically—to either get in there and put those plastic bags on their heads or they're *out*."

The group breaks up to MB's reference to what I am informed was a particularly traumatic video production from another year. "It was the shooting of the *After-School, Underwaterless Ballet Club*," Dana explains to me. "Mary Beth lost it when one student wouldn't put the bathing cap on."

" . . . and hadn't done anything else either!" MB exclaims.

After some order is restored, Rick says, "For me, it's an issue of control. I think kids may come here to take control of their lives. The school sounds so unbelievably good to them and certainly to their parents. If you sit in on any of the initial orientation discussions with parents, you strongly sense that. So the kids are getting parental support for what they're doing at school maybe for the first time in their lives. But it's really difficult to change 9 to 11 years of requests, requirements, and expectations. So they're constantly falling back on old habits, old ways of taking control of their lives, which is to say in so many words, 'Screw you; I'm not going to do that.' And then it becomes the problem of molding that by responding, 'Well, just do what you need to do but you need to take risks.'"

Fitz gets up and moves to a corner of the room to stretch the kinks out of his back. As he bends deeply first to the left and then to the right he listens attentively to the discussion.

Rick continues, "We're most effective when we reach that point, pushing kids in some ways beyond their comfort levels. I understand why they balk then, because those are the tough demands. In lots of ways they're really mini-Passages on the way to the monster risk of stepping into adulthood. I don't have a clue to how expectations fit into that except for the Boundary Waters Trip,[2] where we had real competition for limited spots. Trips *are* our best opportunity to stimulate risk taking. But that's no different from any other high school. When kids in any school find something they really want to do, a sports team or whatever, they'll go through hell to be a part of it."

Ruth, hearkening back to my question about how students have changed over the years, sees it as a change in society, which the kids are simply reflecting. "Society *is* different than it was 20 years ago. Most of those differences have to do with values. It appears to me that our students now are more concerned about money, more driven by a need to feel comfortable and have fun, less willing to look at global issues as if they could do something about them than students were 20 years ago. We still have those student activists whom we can guide toward a high sense of empowerment, but I don't find it generally running through the student body the way I did in the early years of the school. Those societal changes make it difficult for some of us whose values are different from the mainstream to deal with kids who have other values."

Dan says, "It's not so much that the kids' values are changing but that the kids are having trouble grasping what the values are. That makes it hard for any adult who has strong values to deal with today's kids. The first thing we do is ask the kids to assess themselves. That's a pretty heavy assignment."

"All our big questions are value-laden," Rick adds. "We know that."

The morning sun is warming up the room and Dan slips his sweater off. "I see some of my current students reacting to that in a very strange way," he says, "as if to say, 'What is this?' They've not been asked to look at their values." He returns to MB's observation about getting projects finished. Looking at her, he says, "Until last year every time I've attempted to do sound recording we finished it." The recording studio, where sound recording is done, is the core of an unusual music curriculum that builds on music's oral traditions by having kids compose, perform, and record their own music.[3] "Last year," Dan continues, "we didn't. They just refused to do it. It's happened again in some small ways this year."

Fitz finishes his stretching and opens a window before sitting down.

Bruce says, "I remember that one thing different about the early years of the school was the number of externally imposed demands that the students made on each other. The introduction of Walkabout may have changed that. We are a more individually oriented program now, with kids more concerned about their own education and less concerned about the community. The first example I've seen recently of students imposing their expectations on their fellow students is in

Triads.[4] They have resurrected on a much smaller scale some of that early feeling of mutual accountability that used to infuse the school. It isn't the same as the all-school meetings students used to call regularly to confront some burning issue but it's a start. Within the advisory group, students are now being confronted, by other students, about not meeting their responsibilities.

"I don't think," Bruce continues, "being responsible to another person is being modeled by the kids' parents very often. So when we hit the kids with Triads and they see, perhaps for the first time, how their actions are affecting somebody negatively, we're doing something that's filling a critical vacuum in the upbringing of most of our kids. We *should* impose demands on one another. That's what this school is about."

I follow up on what I think is an interesting point. "You think that more and more the kids' *parents* are not responding to demanding situations?"

"Yeah. And they in turn don't make demands on their kids."

"They call us," Dana adds, "asking us to impose demands on their children. I can't tell you how many advisees I have whose parents simply expect me to do what was traditionally the parents' work. It's amazing; it's frightening," she says, arching her eyebrows, "the sort of things they want me to confront their kids with."

"There are also different types of externally imposed demands," Bruce says. "I look at the greenhouse, for instance, which has had no energy devoted to it since Alicia and a couple of those folks left. Nurturing something is an externally imposed demand that many kids have, a *positive* one. When I first read what you'd written for the opening statement for the seminar, Tom, I was thinking about negative demands—You *will* do this!—but there are a lot of positive ways kids can have demands placed on them that help them grow, and they don't get that at home."

"It's not modeled," Susie adds. "They don't get opportunities to experience it."

"It's clear," Dan says, "that secondary schools are being asked to take on more and more of the function of the family. A lot of folks deny that's happening. They still want schools to stay within the domain of the three Rs and not get into socializing functions. But we're being asked to do more and more of that."

Pat makes another point about parenting. "Warren and I feel that among our kids' friends we are the only parents setting limits and making demands on our kids. I'm talking about commonsense kinds of things like not staying up all night watching TV and then trying to go to school the next day. Or not receiving phone calls that interrupt our lives after a certain hour. It seems like we are the only parents doing that."

The unbridled din of a rock group warming up in the recording studio over in the main building signals the start of the school day.

"We are not only in the business of parenting kids here," Rick observes, "but often teaching or helping parents to *parent*. That seems to be more of a task for us now than I can remember in the 7 years I've been here. In a way, that's nice. The parents are trying to be more consistent with what we're doing. When that happens we become allies. One of the things we need to learn to do better as advisors is to deal with parents in more helpful ways so we are true allies, not adversaries, in the process of working with their kids."

"I remember that back in the early days of the school," Ruth recalls, "Dick Yamaguchi used to observe that our kids were information rich and experience poor.[5] I think that still applies. Our kids are overloaded with information from the media but deficient in experience. Because they are deficient in experience they lack the confidence in themselves that they can do anything. That affects their willingness to take risks and try things they're not comfortable with.

Ruth continues. "There's a second point that relates to this idea: A personal struggle that I suspect is shared by others is that I want to be somewhere between permissive and authoritative. I don't feel that either of those positions is good for human beings. Yet finding that place where I have individual relationships with students in which I can make realistic demands, not *of* them but *with* them, perhaps inspiring them to see what they're capable of. Having high expectations for them is important to me, but more important is getting them to have high expectations for themselves. I know I'm resistant to people telling me what I should be thinking and what I should be doing and I'm therefore very sensitive to doing that with other people, especially adolescents who are more sensitive to being bossed around than I am. I had that same struggle as a parent trying to facilitate my own children's growth—how to have high expectations, how to not be too permissive or too controlling. While we probably all struggle with that dilemma the kids may be even more concerned about it than we are."

Dana's, "Well put!" exemplifies the group's general endorsement of Ruth's position and the manner in which she has stated it.

"I recently interviewed one of the students in my Wilderness Trip trail group," I say, "which was one of the places where I first encountered this phenomenon. He was quite open about our relationship on the trip. He said, 'The problem was, you wanted to get something done and we didn't want to do anything.' He said it was that simple" (Int. 5/88). I look across the group at Bruce who is sipping his coffee. "I've watched you, Bruce, in several situations over the course of the year and it strikes me that you're able to get kids to respond to demanding situations. I'm talking about more than just the Boundary Waters Trip. I can remember you saying amid the disorganization of the Cortez Trip, 'This is *not* the way I do a trip. You ought to see me do a trip. I do trips damn well.' But you do some things with classes, too, that get kids to raise their levels of expectation for themselves."

"I think it's because most of the things I do are experience rich," Bruce responds, perhaps picking up on Ruth's point. "It's active stuff."

"Some of our students are extremely experience rich in one little area, like drugs," Dan adds. "They can curl my hair when they talk about some of that stuff. And then they take that narrow area and they apply it to their entire life, assuming at some level that they're widely experienced and they don't need to do some of these things: 'I don't need to do that. I know all about it.' Just because they can waste you with their experience in one segment of their lives."

"That's an important clarification of the point I was making," Ruth says. "What Dan's describing is prevalent."

We've hardly dealt with some aspects of the issue but MB, who is leading this staff meeting, announces reluctantly that we've used up the time we have for the discussion, and the last New World Seminar ends.

BECAUSE WE ENDED SO ABRUPTLY, I expect that several individuals might have follow-up conversations with me on the topic. But perhaps because of the distractions of closing off the year, only two staff members approach me. Dana is one. I'd made a mental note during the seminar to ask her to share some examples of what she meant by parents asking the staff to impose demands on their children that they won't impose themselves. She offers one without my asking. She relates a call from a father who was angry because his daughter, one of Dana's advisees, had stolen some of his dope. He wanted Dana to confront her about it.

Fitz, whose record of never having offered a comment in a seminar has held through this last one, talks to me, too; he isn't as certain as Ruth that students have changed much over the years. The kind of student I taught 20 years ago is still around, he thinks; he could find several here in the Open School. "There is this monolith called society," he continues, "that's changing and as it does, it drags both the angelic and the diabolic students with it. A transition is occurring but the kids' vacillations aren't any more than the larger society's." Fitz thinks the type of student that the Open School attracts is a stronger variable in what I've experienced than time is. The Open School has a wide spectrum of students but it isn't a very representative one. "We do have a somewhat biased sample of kids if for no other reason than their being courageous enough to try alternatives."

I ask him if he thought the parents at Evergreen High, where he last taught, were pretty much the same as the parents we have.

"No," he responds emphatically. "The parents here are far more reluctant to 'get in line.' They have found alternative lifestyles. They're not, as a group, as much in the mainstream. We have our exceptions — doctors, professionals, and so on — but I think I've also heard that almost 70% of the kids who graduate from the Jefferson County schools are not living with both natural parents. So the kids are probably getting less nurturing, as Ruth mentioned. The narcissism that's infected our society in the last 10 years is a factor."

The extent to which this seminar focused on parents was surprising to me. I turn to a favorite topic of mine, especially with Fitz, who had a very positive teaching experience in an alternative program within Evergreen High before moving to the Open School and who doesn't share my conviction that big high schools have become obsolete institutions. I do my best to repress a grin as I raise the issue again with Fitz. "What do you think will happen to big high schools if this parenting trend continues?"

He chuckles at my attempt, once again, to set him up but is kind enough not to point out the unfairness of my question. "First of all, big high schools prepare students perfectly for our society," he says. "Like the society, they're impersonal." After a pause he turns serious. "I don't know how to answer that. Who's going to be in control? Who's going to be Secretary of Education? Who's going to get the funds? What's going to be the next fad that's going to sweep through education? One futurist is saying that the time for the education agenda is now because in 7 years the baby boomers are going to be wanting health care, not education. This educational revolution that we're waiting for has to happen quickly. We need a Mao or a Che Guevera to get it going."

CHAPTER 18

Moving On

The graduation ceremony takes place on a Saturday morning in late May. Like everything about the Open School, it is an informal affair, held late on a sunny morning in an alpine meadow—Marilyn Wittebort calls it the cow pasture—a few miles from the school. A grove of fir and pine trees forms a backdrop for the 30 celebrants, who take their seats in ones and twos, in the shade of the trees. Friends and family and staff members sit on folding chairs in the bright sunlight. There are no academic gowns, no procession to *Pomp and Circumstance*. The girls are wearing pretty summer dresses; most of the boys wear coats and ties.

Two graduating seniors, Stephanie Woodward and Ray Clossin, emcee the affair. Ray is wearing his kilt. The program is a progression of readings and music. Joanne Greenberg, author of *I Never Promised You a Rose Garden* and former Open School parent, reads a short autobiographical piece. She stands washed in sunlight before the group. Big sunglasses and the microphone hide much of her face. Her message is that—for most of these graduating teenagers—life will get better as they get older.

"There are things I have now that I didn't have then," she reads. "One of them is arthritis. Then last week at a party I spat a back molar into my hand like a cocktail olive pit and put it into my pocket.

"But another thing I have," Joanne continues, "is the presence around me of grown children and nieces and nephews to whom I relate in a way of special loving intimacy that I never thought to have. My friendships are deeper and more honest than they were at 18 or 30 or 40."

Then almost as an aside, she says, "This seems to sound like a commercial for Wrinkle City. It isn't. It's only the most optimistic message I could bring you without telling any lies. I'm not saying that age brings wisdom. I've a suspicion that twits are born already perfect, like geniuses, and that a fool is a fool forever. I am saying that most of you will become more comfortable and experienced in your world. And you don't have to grieve for childhood then.

"One more thing," Joanne concludes. "The less you trivialize the motives of other people the quicker you'll get to the good parts, and doing that, you might even hit the joy by 25 or 30."

Ray Clossin follows Joanne with an air on his bagpipes and then several parents, in turn, speak to the assembled group. Mary Ann Woodward—Stephanie's mother—reads a short statement, the composing of which, she tells us, required a whole box of tissues. It is a tearful thank you to the staff "for the spirit and quality of my daughter's 'wholly' learning." She thanks Rick Lopez, Stephanie's advisor, "for recognizing and calling forth the best that is in my daughter and invoking her gifts." It is one of many tributes to advisors, most of them delivered by grateful students, that will be offered during the ceremony.

John Buskirk, another graduating senior, reads some poetry, and Arnie has returned to address the group. He speaks of the need for passionate engagement, reading excerpts from Camus.

Beryl Dittemore reads "out loud for a spell" a pastiche of entries from the journals she's kept throughout her Open School career: "That aloof advisor," she reads, referring to Jeff, "he liked Indians, too. He teased my passion until I was planting fruit trees in a desert canyon for the Dineh and talking with the Lakota at the cemetery at Wounded Knee.[1] I was given time not to be selfish. I suddenly realized—7 years after her death—that I missed my mom. I met a great horned owl who could read my mind and whose stare acted like a mirror when I least expected it.

"In Alaska," she continues, "I followed the eagles and a howling wolf. I reeked of contentment and mourned the gaping hole it left a month afterwards. And before it was too late, I learned the Fish Gut Shuffle. I left behind some spirits in Pipestone."

A flock of Canada Geese flies over, heading north for the summer. They seem to have been choreographed into the ceremony.

"And I am grateful for my lightning," Beryl continues. "Lightning struck my obsession with words. I know I move in extremes; I know I take the risk to learn. Walk into the wind and your eyes will water. (I read that in a book somewhere.)" She ends with an insider's reference, invoking the word that has come to capture the spirit that overtakes some trip groups when all is right with the world. Beryl hails, "May Ernie be with you!" to the cheering, howling group.

I, too, have been invited to speak. I read some pieces of this gradually forming book. Earlier in the morning, before the wisdom and eloquence of first Joanne and then Beryl, they seemed more fit for public airing than they do now.

After a song by Dan McCrimmon Ruth speaks to the group. She summarizes the Passages achieved by this group of seniors, the places they have traveled, the products they have created, the services they have performed for others. "These are their accomplishments," she closes. "We who have worked with them and loved them say goodbye with a mixture of pride and sadness." Ruth shares the words of Krishnamurti.

> Without an integrated understanding of life our individual and collective problems will only deepen and extend. The purpose of education is not to produce mere scholars, technicians, and job hunters, but integrated men and women who are free of fear. For only between such human beings can there be enduring peace. (Fields et al., 1984, p. 30)

"These students are such human beings," she says. "They're ready to move into adulthood confident that they have the skills and ability to be freely involved in creating a world in which there is enduring peace." And then Ruth presents the Class of 1988 to the assembled group.

One by one the 30 graduates come forward to be presented their diplomas by individuals whom they have nominated—parents and advisors, grandfathers and best friends. Each of these designees personalizes the moment, sharing an intimacy from his or her experience with the graduate. Each granting of a diploma ends in a hug, some involving whole families.

The ceremony ends with the entire assembly singing the Beatles' song, *A Little Help from My Friends*. And then gradually we leave the meadow.

ON THE LAST DAY OF SCHOOL, a week after the graduation ceremony, copies of an anonymous note are placed in each staff member's mailbox.

To the Staff of the Open School:
It is time for me to move on now but I want you to know how much you mean to me.
You gave me time to experience what I needed. You gave me support when I wanted to stretch my limits. You held my hand through the painful times. You gave me an ever so gentle push when I didn't want to go. You made me stand up to my feats and gave me the courage to tackle my problems. When I least wanted

to work you had patience and bit your lip. When others would have given up on me you smiled and said, "That's okay."

You changed my life and I have a smile now. A smile that will forever shine. My pride in myself as well as my work is a result of your caring.

Thank you! I love you all.

Standards for Individuals

Those who conceptualize standards as general rules that everyone must meet would have some difficulty understanding how standards functioned at the Open School. A concern for *individuals* flavors all the school's discussions of achievement and compliance. Teenagers today seem to have many more pressures than I remember their parents having at this age. They certainly have different ones: the pressure to have sex at a younger age, complicated by the growing threat of sexually transmitted disease; the pressures of the drug scene; the problem of finding enough money to do the things they're supposed to want to do. As the pressures have changed, the kids' parents have not magically become more skilled in helping their kids deal with these things. And so the burden has increasingly fallen on teachers. Unfortunately, most teachers work in high schools that expect them to handle these problems in 4-minute conferences—the passing periods between classes—while they wrap up one lesson and prepare for another. Should teachers be cynical about society's expectations? Should kids think it ludicrous to bring up a personal problem amid the hurry? You bet.

The Open School's structure allowed—even encouraged—kids' private problems to become the stuff of learning. The school did so by providing time for adults and kids to talk. And the staff members held firmly to practices that enabled them to keep the personal lives of their students clearly in focus. The fabulous five was a vivid example of this resolve. Not once in my year in the school—no matter how trying the circumstances—did I see a Wednesday morning meeting start with anything but the fabulous five. The staff's conviction on this point was severely tested in October, when the Jeffco School Board announced that the Open School was on the list of possible program cuts necessitated by the latest budgetary crunch. The announcement generated a mood of crisis within the staff. If ever a staff meeting would forego these lengthy discussions of the lives of kids, I thought, it would be the next one, a meeting that would be dominated by a discussion of strategies to beat back the assault. But even that meeting began with the fabulous five. In this way staff members continually reminded themselves what was most important about the school and why they became teachers: They were there for the kids. The Open School was for years so small that every student could be the focus of one of these discussions each year. In 1987 that was no longer the case. Still, during my year in the school about 175 of the school's 238 students were each, for about 10 minutes, the focus of attention of the entire staff.

Standards were often communicated contextually to individual students through the school's elaborate Advising system. In that vein it's difficult to understand standards at the Open School without some understanding of the advisor/advisee relationship. In a way, I think, the Hall Lounge flourished because of a central tenet of the school's Advising system. It is clear in several of the preceding chapters that the Open School didn't view the establishment of lists of universal rules as a particularly effective way to solve problems. Matters of conduct and deportment were left to individual discretion much more than they are in most schools. Definitions of satisfactory progress were the professional judgments of advisors, the people who knew their advisees better than anyone else in the school. Advisors' decisions were occasionally questioned by other staff members but in my experience never overruled. But staff relationships were often in a tacit state of tension because of the range of philosophies held by individuals. A staff member told me:

> One of the things that we do is say to each other, "I trust you as an advisor." Frankly, there isn't anybody on the staff that I *don't* trust as an advisor but I think we use that as a mask. If we keep saying, "I trust you," we don't have to come down philosophically anywhere. (Int. 11/87)

But the staff also acknowledged the value of having several very different approaches to Advising available to kids. A staff member said:

> I think one of the strengths of the program is that kids get a chance to choose an advisor who is best suited to work with them individually. And if we were all the same that wouldn't be true. But I do think we get into trouble when, as advisors, we don't have a bottom line for what we'll tolerate from students. I think that gets us into trouble. The common expectation here is that every student has a mutually agreeable program and that he or she follows it. It's obvious that that doesn't always happen. (Int. 6/88)

When a student overstepped the bounds of propriety, it became not a public disciplinary matter in which he or she was banished to the principal's office, but a topic dealt with in the privacy of Advising. Individual advisors talked through issues with their advisees, determined *why* they were doing whatever it was they were doing, and, if necessary, obtained their advisees' personal assurances that the situation would change. If the matter involved a difference between two kids, both advisors might meet with the students to talk through the impasse and forge a reconciliation.

The linchpin that held the whole delicate apparatus together was the advisor's judgment. Not much happened until the advisor recognized that a problem existed. The Hall Lounge exemplified this condition. By accident or by design, Neuman and Daren had placed their lounge as far from Poz and Joy, their two advisors, as was physically possible. Poz's and Joy's home bases were on the other side of the school, out in the tin building. Because neither advisor had cause to pass the Hall Lounge probably more than once a week, Poz and Joy were likely among the last in the school to even know of its existence. Both were also probably more comfortable with the *appearance* of idleness than many other staff members. More important, they knew Neuman and Daren and what their needs were far better than the rest of us.

The manner in which the school tailored its program to the needs of each student was not always well-received. A graduating senior wondered if Advising's power to focus on the personal dimensions of a student's life was always for the good.

> You come in here and, if your advisor notices that you are not eating lunch, he is going to say, "Why aren't you eating lunch?" Sometimes I don't want to hear it. It intensifies my problem, actually. If I went to Evergreen High I think that I would be less nurturing of my problems. I would be more apt to let them go. (Int. 3/88)

Students often compared their relationships with staff members at the Open School with their relationships with teachers in their former Jeffco schools. Their remarks, almost always in praise of the Open School staff, present a different picture of advisors. "They are more caring and more willing to be in touch with the students than the teachers at Evergreen High are. You can feel that," was how one student put it (Int. 3/88).

The dominance of Advising in the school's academic program also became evident in the seminar on the culture of classrooms. Tom

Rohrbach said it clearly and several others implied it: There was a very tangible resistance—not by all staff members, but probably by a majority—to committing the school community to school-wide norms of conduct. Staff members shared a trepidation that formal rules and expectations would become procrustean constraints somewhere down the road, that sometime in the future an arbitrarily established rule would unduly confine an individual staff member, working to find the best solution to a problem with an individual kid in a particular circumstance. That wariness transcended the classroom. It was deeply imbedded in the culture of this school. The external audit (Smith et al., 1987) of the Open School's self-study (Steele, 1987) identified it as a weakness of the program. It was one of the few weaknesses the audit team identified in its strong commendation of the program. The team wrote:

> There is some confusion on the part of staff and students due to the lack of written guidelines for policies, procedures, expectations, processes, rules, and records. Time is lost by both students and staff because some simple guides have not been clearly recorded and maintained. (p. 5)

Most staff members would rather have paid the price of continually having to re-establish their own standards with each new class than risk having their responsiveness to individual problems limited by long lists of procedures and rules.

In some respects classroom learning worked about the same at the Open School as in other schools, except that it included no sense of involuntary confinement. That single distinction, however, is significant. Involuntary confinement breeds a hostility that encourages kids to act out. Some teachers in other schools counter the problem by forging tacit treaties with their students.[1] They are survival mechanisms: You don't hassle me and I won't hassle you. Open School kids could simply leave a class that they found meaningless. They also, unfortunately, could leave a class that might result in significant growth for them, just because it was too demanding or required an unfamiliar measure of self-discipline.

Those who would force students to attend classes to solve this problem should talk to Elizabeth, a friend of mine. Elizabeth is a gifted writer with most of a Ph.D. under her belt. Fifteen years my junior, she was also my teacher—though not in a classroom, I should add. She and I were talking about Columbus and the New World one day when she confessed that there were all sorts of rudimentary facts that she didn't know—how Indians came to be called Indians, for example. She had missed it all in school. Required to sit in classroom after classroom of—for her—meaningless content, she withdrew. Some kids withdraw by daydreaming; some, working within the boundaries of tacit classroom treaties, plug themselves into Walkmans and withdraw into music; some draw pictures or doodle; the bold sleep or get high. Elizabeth read. She would place a book on her lap and surreptitiously escape into its pages. Compulsory attendance forces the presence of a body but not of a mind.

That the culture of the Open School tended not to expect much classroom product (in contrast to the school's high expectations and the impressive performance of kids in other elements of the program) has the ring of validity to me. High output *in classroom settings* may have been seen as an anomaly by the staff. A classroom experience I had in December supports this view. During Block Two I taught Architectural Design, a class that started well with a dozen students— all boys—signed up. The enrollment quickly shrank to seven as issues of teaching style, personality, content, and expectations were clarified. A few weeks into the term the class first floundered, with little work being done outside of class, and then blossomed in the eleventh hour. The class was to culminate in a design review, with two professional architects serving as guest critics. The night before the review we had a voluntary all-night work session, what architects call a charette. Charettes are energizing experiences characterized by a feverish level of productivity overlaid with a giddiness induced by too little sleep and too much caffeine. They acquire a special flavor in the context of the classroom. Individual students who have worked side by side for months, struggling with their own solutions to the same design problem, discover that they share a camaraderie as they push to finish the drawings and models—the public product of untold hours of private creative activity and introspection—before the review deadline.

Six of the seven boys took part in our charette, which started at the close of school on the day before the review was to occur. An effect similar to what I had seen occur in architecture school occurred for us. The boys worked all night, ginning out work slowly at first and then much more rapidly. The first of our sleeping bags wasn't unfolded until after dawn the next day. Three boys worked right up to the 2:00 starting time of the review. We made the review a public event, holding it in the foyer, with everyone's final drawings affixed to large freestanding tack boards. Each boy made a brief oral presentation, explaining the concept of his design to our panel of architects, who would then critique the design.

The school community was impressed. The boys had produced

some very good sketches and schematics of interesting if underdeveloped designs that would improve selected places in and around the school. The quality and quantity of products that the kids had developed apparently transcended the boundary of what at least some staff members thought could be accomplished in an Open School class. Perhaps the staff was just trying to support a struggling rookie who had finally gotten something right, but the praise seemed to go beyond that. Susie, for example, thought the review was an important event in the history of the school.

There is another way to frame the problem of the classroom that is neither particularly original nor implausible: The classroom displays the symptoms of a dying institution. A national study (Sedlak et al., 1986) found that, at any given time, about two-thirds of the students sitting in high school classrooms are—to use the study's word—disengaged. Time appears to be working against the classroom. The classroom made inestimable sense in the society in which it was created— a pre-Gutenberg world thirsting for scarce knowledge. The classroom was a privileged place. But conditions have changed. The medieval classroom has been engulfed by the information age. Knowledge is no longer a scarce commodity. It bombards us in dozens of ways, all more palatable than the classroom. Can we abandon a concept so central to our notion of school, even the Open School's notion of school? At some point a sensible person must wonder if the diminishing rate of payoff continues to justify the increasing struggle. A veteran staff member told me that she wasn't at all sure that "putting a lot of extra energy into the classroom is [any longer] worth the effort" (Int. 2/88).

Staff members at the Open School who came to that realization had some choices. They were able to refocus their energies in more productive areas. They might redouble their efforts in Advising, or they might build into new trips the knowledge and skills they knew kids needed, or they might volunteer to take on some of the administrative tasks that helped to keep the school running smoothly. They were empowered to rectify an untenable situation. The same circumstance occurring in a typical big high school, manned by relatively powerless teachers, creates despair. Teachers there who can no longer make the classroom a vital environment have two choices: They can get out of the profession, a difficult, even unrealistic option for those well-advanced in their careers; or they may choose to follow their students' lead and psychologically disengage from the setting. They circle a retirement date on their calendars and put in their time, just as the kids do. An alarming number of teachers today are taking one or the other of these two avenues.

The problem of the classroom is not the Open School's. It is not Elizabeth's, nor is it the problem of the kids like her who are in school today. It is society's problem, maybe because society can't let go of an outdated notion of what school is. The Open School didn't have a solution but it appeared to be closer to one than most schools are, only because it had moved more learning out of classrooms than most schools have. It is both ironic and telling that the single element of the Open School's program that visitors from the Old World would probably find most reassuring, most like the schools they knew—the school's long list of class offerings—was the element that the staff found most troublesome.

A SCHOOL'S STANDARDS also manifest themselves in the ways in which they exact student compliance to an established, formal code of behavior. The Open School had its Three Noes. The penalties for breaking one of these rules were invariably severe. Sending kids home early for disciplinary reasons as we had to on the Mazatlan Trip occurred from time to time. The form that parents signed giving their child permission to take a trip even included a paragraph in which they agreed to pay the costs of these sometimes necessary early departures. That the evidence confirming these serious transgressions often took the form of a confession coaxed from a student by a staff member who had gained knowledge of the student's actions was not unusual. Indeed, the lore of the school was that the staff *always* finds out. Such is the nature of an informal environment in which staff members tended to be seen as trusted allies by many kids, kids who were also aware that the stakes were too high to allow behavior that endangered the unusual levels of freedom that the school had earned through the years. Standards were applied flexibly to individuals in the school, but in circumstances that endangered the community, they became as hard and unmoving as granite.

Standards must be defensible in the larger society and that task is complicated when the society is in a state of change. The seminar on responding to demands highlighted this relationship. To understand today's kids we must understand the families in which they are growing up. For myriad reasons, the relationships between parents and their children are changing. James Coleman's (1987) ideas—already discussed in the First New World Seminar—about how most families today no longer *impose* demands on children of high school age are also pertinent here. Today's adolescents must be reasoned with rather than simply ordered about. I wonder how many of the runaways we now have are kids caught in an impasse on this issue, kids expecting a negotiating relationship with parents that is similar to those of their peers but having instead parents who hold to an authoritarian relationship. Some families, of course, reflect these societal changes more than others and it may be that some families came to the Open School because it was seen as an environment more compatible with these new conditions than conventional high schools, conceived in another era for a different kind of teenager, could be. The day may have already arrived, at least at the Open School, where the idea of an adult imposing demands on a kid could be viewed as a Neanderthal notion. Few of the students would accept the imposition.

ONE OF THE IDEAS I HAD FORMED before my stay at the Open School was that it was a school for teachers, a place where they could really *teach.* That idea was confirmed repeatedly by staff members who volunteered that they wouldn't still be teaching if the Open School didn't exist. One thing that hadn't occurred to me, though, was the degree to which this school was also a sanctuary for parents. I met many during my year in the school who were caring, perceptive, unusually effective communicators with their children; I envied the skills they displayed in support group meetings and the private graduation ceremonies that each family holds. But I also met others who lacked these skills. Perhaps they lacked effective parental models when they were growing up or the skills they did possess were inadequate to the truly formidable task of rearing an adolescent in a society that places adult pressures on kids before they can cope with them.

One might view the Open School as a school that had developed mechanisms to replace an eroding parentage. But it may be more accurate to view it as Rick did, as a place where teachers and parents could be much more effective allies in the challenging work of rearing adolescents. The school's Advising system *required* that each student develop a trusting relationship with one adult. The school accommodated to individual kids in remarkably different ways, making its inflexibility in this one regard both understandable and notable. Ultimately, kids had to be able to trust in order to in turn be trusted. The freedom of the Open School's program became quicksilver without trust. A major tragedy of some kids entering the school was that their lives had been so deficient in trusting relationships that they couldn't learn how to respond positively to this requirement, or at least couldn't learn quickly enough to survive. I would guess with considerable confidence that most first-year students who left the school did so because they were unable to meet this fundamental obligation of participation in the Open School community. And perhaps the major philosophical contention within the staff—the issue that raised frustration, hurt, and even anger to the point where there was a tacit agreement to avoid discussing it—centered on how much time new students should be given to learn this fundamental lesson.[2]

THE FINAL SEMINAR ALSO CONFIRMED some basic convictions I had formed about the future of schooling. Clearly, the complexity and ambiguity of the task are increasing, perhaps rapidly, with time. Schools that cannot adapt to the sea changes that are occurring are doomed to founder. The inflexibility of big high schools is the embodiment of their undoing. On my second day in the school, at the onset of what would be the first New World Seminar, I had asked the staff what it did with a kid who didn't try. After a year in the school, I view that question as simplistic. It's relatively easy to tell when a kid isn't trying in algebra or English. For some schools that's the only important question. The Open School complicates the picture when it accepts the personal domain as legitimate learning. How does the staff know when a kid isn't trying hard enough to become an effective human being? The intractability of the question may be illustrated by examining the cases of my own advisees, or at least the five that remained at the school when my year there ended. (Terry left after only a few months, when she moved out of the school district.) Two years after entering the school, only two of my original advisees were still attending it.

In his second year, Evan continued his struggle to sort things out, a process that the school typically supports quite well. Because he was an intelligent kid he never stumbled academically. Indeed, if and when academic pursuits become vital to him, he may well accomplish impressive feats. But the lesson that some of us learn naturally—that there is something vital and important about us that exists in the absence of our friends—was not learned by Evan during his tenure in the Open School. He had a series of brushes with the law—most of them related to his driving, or his need to impress his friends, or both. These problems ultimately spilled over into the school and Evan was asked to leave. Eventually a second conviction for driving while impaired resulted in a jail term.

Sharon's course of study during my year in the school had centered on learning to trust. She'd made visible strides toward that goal in her first year. She no longer lashed out verbally when she felt threatened. She came back from the Tallahassee Work Trip in the middle of that year transformed, at least for a week or two. But she still struggled to free herself from the defensiveness, particularly with adults, that dominated her being. Only when she settled these issues would she be able to confront the tougher lesson, how to meet adults as equals on that psychological playing field that exists between them and her. She needed to learn to risk helping another human being with the same compassion that she reserved for animals, the one class of living beings that had never betrayed her. As time passed Sharon increasingly made good use of what the school had to offer and in that sense became a success story.

Marty's relationship with his parents remained an enigma to me throughout my year of contact with him. Its public manifestations were loving and caring. Marty, who was not a self-centered kid, knew that his periodic poor judgment frustrated and disappointed his mother and father. Their relationship hit something of a nadir when Fitz and I sent him home early from the Mazatlan Trip for drinking. Marty was still enrolled in the school a year after my departure. He was pursuing a most individualistic path, living on his own in Florida, playing bass guitar in a rock group, and working on his Passages there. Because Marty is fundamentally such a kind and honest person, I am optimistic about his future.

Bert was a complex kid who hadn't learned to apply his own structure to the natural world but had learned all too well how to resist the attempts of others to provide a structure for him. He was an able practitioner of what is known in the education trade as passive–aggressive behavior. I found it strange that upon my departure he picked Bruce, who had little patience for the aimless, as his next advisor. During the first months of his second year in the school Bert continued to float without purpose until he had exhausted all his options with Bruce, who finally "cut him loose"; no one else on the staff chose to become Bert's advocate, and he was asked to leave the school. For Bert, so immature for even his young age, the Open School may have been too much too soon. But the school may also have been, for Bert, too little too late.

And of course there is Inge. She switched from me as her advisor in December, choosing Dana. The change occurred shortly after she recovered from the physical injuries of the auto accident. I'm not sure she had recovered from its psychological damage in the year that I knew her. Inge stayed with Dana a few months and then switched advisors again, this time to Dan. When I asked Dana why the second change occurred she was uncharacteristically mute. The only circumstance in which I've seen her so guarded in her comments about a kid was when she thought ethics demanded it. A year after I left the school, Dan described Inge as being so independent-minded that he was not sure any adult could influence her. About a year after the accident Inge received a cash settlement—over $10,000—from Randy Ledbetter's insurance company. She spent most of it on a car and then started taking friends out to dinner, blowing the entire settlement in a few weeks. Some time later she moved out on her own, sharing a house—what Dana called a "party house"—with several friends. Her attendance at school became erratic, eventually prompting Dan to write to her, stating that he could see no way in which the school was aiding her development and that he was taking steps to disenroll her. Inge eventually took a part-time job and again pursued completion of her high school education through a program in one of Denver's community colleges, hoping to establish sound enough academic credentials to still pursue a college education and her persistent dream: to become a "fat-cat biologist." Always a bundle of contradictions, Inge, an animal lover, suddenly decided to move to Brooklyn. Several of the animals she had kept and loved died of thirst and starvation before they were found, abandoned in her Denver residence.[3]

Two years after these six bundles of complexity entered the school and confronted its seemingly quite reasonable standards, four of my six advisees—for reasons as complex and varied as they were—had moved on, contributing to the statistic that less than half of those who enter the school graduate from it. Repeatedly through my year in the school I'd asked myself if these kids were typical—either of the Open School's student body or of the larger domain of teenagers out there in the Old World. At mid-year my doubts about my ability to achieve breakthroughs with my advisees came to a head. In assigning advisees Rick Lopez had not loaded me up with problem kids. Indeed, as I looked around the school I saw advisors struggling with much more serious cases than any of my kids. I needed a reality check. I scheduled a meeting with Ruth, who knew my advisees almost as well as I. Was I the reason my kids were making so little visible progress?

"No," Ruth said, as we sat talking in her office. "You've got some tough-to-reach kids." She had a few suggestions but mostly she reassured me that it just takes time for the kids to change. And she made the point that *we* don't change them. Mostly they change themselves. We help them when and where we can.

My gnawing fear is that my six kids were more typical than I'm willing to concede, not only of the Open School's self-selected population but of most of the teenagers out there in all those impersonal big schools. As Arnie once told me, most kids have these same growing pains. What is different about the Open School is that it legitimizes these struggles. It says that it's okay for them to dominate a kid's consciousness, at least for a while. Has the school acted wrongly in labeling these all-consuming ruminations as legitimate learning? I think not. Indeed, I'm fairly certain that ignoring them is dysfunctional for most kids.

Students move on from high school in many different ways for many reasons. My four departed advisees were part of a larger picture. During the year, 45 students—about 19% of the student body—left the school without graduating. Fifteen of these—6%—seemed to be truly dropping out, at least for the moment. Seventeen other students transferred back to their home high schools; they or their parents may have found the Open School's structure too different from what they were used to, or a particularly long commute may have become intolerable. Seven students, including Terry, my first departing advisee, moved out of the school district. Four students decided to pursue other routes to a high school diploma, including the G.E.D. One of these was Don Troxell. His attempt to attend the school as a district resident thwarted, Don and his parents turned to home schooling. Toby May completes the accounting of those who left the school during my year in it.[4] The staff would view only a few of these students as people with whom it had failed. Gayle Civish said it succinctly during the Third New World Seminar:

> I'm not ready to define [success] simply in terms of graduation because I think we are highly successful with most kids who don't graduate. I also want to resist attempts to screen entering students just so we'll look more successful to outsiders.

BUT, CLEARLY, THE SUCCESSES of the school are most readily apparent in its graduates. A staff member once told Bert Horwood:

> We expect a fairly high level of ability to make commitments, to organize time and materials and to follow through with things. To be responsible and accountable. I think we have high expectations about those things but we're frequently disappointed. But for students that make it, that get through and manage to complete the Walkabout program and graduate, I am just amazed at what wonderful people they are, and at how skilled and mature they are. (1987, p. 66)

A year after graduation the Open School's 30 graduates of the class of 1988 were pursuing 30 very different paths. Twenty-three—over 75% of the class—were pursuing some form of higher education. Ten were studying at state universities and small colleges in Colorado: places like the University of Colorado at Boulder, Metro State College in Denver, Colorado Mountain College in Leadville, and Fort Lewis College in Durango. Seven other students were attending colleges with nontraditional programs—colleges such as Antioch, Evergreen State, World College West, Hampshire College, and Colorado College. Sherrill Dugan was studying drama at the American Academy of the Performing Arts in New York City. Pam Tinsley was pursuing her interest in Marine Biology at Texas A & M. John Stafford was studying massage therapy in Boulder, and Ellie Romig was studying fashion design in San Francisco.

That some students continued the travel to which they were introduced through the Open School's many trips was, from past experience, predictable. International travel was a certainty for three of the school's graduates, all international exchange students who returned to their homes in Mexico, Finland, and Italy. Jean-Claude Bernadino took the long route home to Italy, through the British Isles, Scandinavia, and eastern Europe. Upon his return he played baseball in the Italian League. Maggee Galyan had used several Passages to prepare herself for life in Saudi Arabia where she was moving with her family, and Chris Katowski used his Science Institute scholarship to travel to Israel. Marty Pottorf was one of only two graduates to get married in their first year out of school. His wedding ceremony took place at China's Great Wall.

A few graduates immediately began working, holding jobs such as telephone operator, concrete worker, clerk at a Seven-Eleven, and manager of a Domino's pizzeria. Tracy Ferrence was making muffs, hats, and mittens out of rabbit fur. Ann Kidwell was raising greyhounds in Evergreen. Jim Henderson went into business with his father, making auto accessories. Max Stoner became a teacher's aide at the school to pay his way through Red Rocks Community College near Morrison.

Four graduates entered the armed services. Russ Conklin joined the Coast Guard and was stationed in Alaska. Jim Leeper was driving a tank at Fort Dix.

Rod Jameson, who—as Jeff phrased it—became addicted to being dependable and being depended on, took a different path, joining the Divine Light, a religious community in Loveland.

I ONCE ASKED a veteran staff member to make an assessment of the general skill attainment of the school's graduates.

Their main strength, across the board, is their ability to express themselves verbally, their spoken language. They're also strong in solving problems that have to do with relationships and human interaction. I feel really good about their ability to plan and set goals and make things happen for themselves. Through the Passage process, they practice those skills repeatedly and they become quite proficient in them. I feel good about the writing of most of them but it's not 100 percent. I wonder about the level of their competency in math. But then I ask myself if it matters as long as they can do what they need to do. I think our graduates have some real strengths. Their Transcripts are inspiring; I get goosebumps reading them. Their accomplishments display significant learning; they're clearly becoming responsible adults. (Int. 11/87)

A graduating senior corroborated this staff member's concern about math. "It would be nice to create a balance here," he said, "where we still have the things that we have now but also have access to more facts like math. We need math a lot. Everything else you can kind of learn on your own by accident, just because of the Passage areas. But I think we need some more academic type programs here" (Int. 3/88).

A second-year student made it clear, though, that one needs to look beyond mere skills to understand the importance of the school in some kids' lives.

The school *is* my life. I wouldn't be who I am today if it weren't for the school and I would never want to be who I was before I came here. This school has helped me to change and to grow, in ways I used to only dream about: If I could just be like that person, I used to think, I wouldn't have to do this, I wouldn't have to impress this person or that person. And today I don't. Today I can be me and be proud of that. The school has helped me tremendously. It's really a miracle. I can't even imagine what I would be today if I wasn't in this school. (Int. 4/88)

Another graduating senior contrasted her first year with her last as she described the all too typical struggle to learn to use freedom productively. "My first year, I studied In-the-Hall-with-Your-Boyfriend 101. I had to be spoon-fed. Now, I've done more in the month of January than I have in the last 3 years, just because I now know how to [use the school]" (Int. 1/88).

Yet another graduating senior talked of the need to press oneself. "The school is not demanding; *I* am," she said. "The school gives you the openness to try everything and find your place within it and in life, where you want to be. But you can do it or *not* do it; you buy into it or your don't. I set up my program, here, so that my advisor didn't pressure me; I pressured myself" (Int. 3/88).

THE PRUDENT MAY LOOK at the Open School experience, see great value in it, and still avoid it in the fear that, by being so different from the conventional, the school closes doors to the conventional world of colleges and universities. Whatever else it may be, we view the high school as a place *not* to reduce one's options. The concern is at least 60 years old. Even then the high school was constrained by the entrance requirements of the colleges that received—at that time—a small minority of its graduates. In 1930 some 200 educators and parents convened to explore the problem (Aiken, 1942). The group concluded that "the high school in the United States should be a demonstration, in all phases of its activity, of the kind of life in which we as a people believe" (p. 31).

The group formed a commission, which in turn initiated a study group that enlisted the participation of 30 high schools. Some of the schools were among the nation's most progressive. To enable these schools to experiment freely with very different conceptions of a high school education, the group asked the colleges of the country to waive their standard entrance requirements of Carnegie Units and grades and class standings and, for a 5-year period, accept the graduates from these 30 schools almost solely on the schools' endorsements. Practically every accredited college in the country agreed to participate. The experiment, which became known as the Eight-Year Study, became a major lesson in the meaning of standards.[5] The study tracked the graduates— over 1,500 in all—of the high school classes of 1936 through 1939 through their 4 years of college and determined how these graduates of informal programs performed in college in comparison to matched individuals of similar ability and background from conventional high schools who were also attending the college. And then the participating high schools set about releasing their programs from the bonds of grades, courses, and distribution requirements. Some accomplished the task better than others.

The study found that the graduates of these progressive high schools generally performed in college as well as or better than their counterparts from more conventional high schools. The major exception to this general theme was foreign languages, where graduates of conventional high schools performed better. Furthermore, the graduates of the most unusual of the 30 high schools—the programs that were most different from the conventional—performed noticeably better than those from the less unusual programs among the 30 schools.

The great irony of the Eight-Year Study is how little impact it had on the practices of the American high school.[6] How is it that a study of such scope that yielded results so counter to the conventional wisdom of its day could be so unknown today? Two explanations present themselves. First, the results were published in 1942 at the height of World War II, a time when the nation's attention was understandably diverted from educational matters. Then, at the end of the war the progressive education movement, along with a host of other liberal causes, became ensnared in the cold war and McCarthyism. Some old guard progressives, people such as George Counts and Harold Rugg, were socialists who were disfigured into communists in the foment of the times. The red-hunters viewed the "loose practices" of the schools these men espoused as the nation's soft underbelly, vulnerable to communist infiltration. Rather than using the postwar years to build on the work of the insightful teachers in these 30 schools, the body politic turned its attention to requiring loyalty oaths of them. The years that have passed since have not been sufficient time to regain what was swept away.

The kids of the Eight-Year Study were demonstrably ready for college. Open School kids do just fine in the real world, too, as do the graduates of hundreds of other informal high schools across the country. Indeed, at last count Open School students have been accepted into 60 different colleges and universities, including several Ivy League schools.[7] If we must have reasons not to allow more schools such as these to develop, we must look not to the colleges for an excuse, but within ourselves.

Conclusion

THE OPEN SCHOOL AS EXEMPLAR

The Open School is not for everyone. No single conception of high school is. But, certainly, we could use more schools that embrace its values and that have as clear a sense of their mission as this school has. Before that gradual transformation can take place we have to break the big comprehensive high school's hold on our thinking. How do we begin to view it as the problematic institution that it has become? An example may illustrate the difficulty of the task.

I recall the experience of a friend who taught phys ed in a rural Illinois high school. My friend, Ellen, got to know this big kid, a junior, who one day confided to her that he didn't know how to read and there seemed to be no way to get help with his problem. Ellen could scarcely believe him so she began checking around, finding out how her school dealt with the problem of a high school kid who couldn't read. It turned out he was right; there was no mechanism for helping him. The mass delusion was that everybody learns to read in elementary school— junior high at the latest—and nobody could even function in a high school without being able to read. Therefore, Ellen's high school needed no program to teach kids to read. She ended up teaching the kid to read during lunch each day, and by the end of the year he was coping nicely with his schoolwork. With Ellen's help he had solved his problem.

But how can Ellen's school solve *its* problem when it engages in a deception so pervasive that it can't even recognize that it has a problem? To do so people must somehow jump out of the elaborate system of fallacy they've constructed for themselves—no easy feat. Douglas Hofstadter (1979) relates a visit to a computer chess tournament. The contest featured computer programs trying to best each other at chess. One program, the weakest of all, impressed the experts present by quitting lost games long before they were over. Rather than continuing, machine-like, to grind away at a lost cause it would—like a good human player—quickly and rather elegantly resign. The high school hasn't yet been able to acknowledge that the game is lost.

American education can learn something about lost causes from the Pony Express, a major reform of the mail delivery service of the 1850s. The Pony Express was the embodiment of a technology—transporting information by horse—that had been advanced to its inherent capacity. Men and horses were pressed to their physical limits to make a familiar concept meet the increased demands of an expanding country. The Pony Express was more than a system of mail delivery; it had a romance about it—a rider and horse at full gallop, hell-bent for the next way station—that remains frozen like a Remington bronze in our minds. But the Pony Express lasted barely a decade. It was replaced— almost overnight—by a very different means of delivering information: the telegraph. A message that had taken days of extreme effort to deliver on horseback suddenly could be delivered in seconds, literally with the flick of a finger.

As those who frame educational policy attempt to meet the needs of a changing society, they might be advised to consider the Pony Express. Almost all of the current effort to reform the high school is being expended in attempts to improve the current technology. It is a quest for faster horses. That we should cling to a familiar idea is understandable; the high school is deeply embedded in our social fabric. The Friday night game, the Prom, the impressive buildings are compelling cultural icons. They distract our attention as we attempt to consider the high school as a place of learning. But if we think of the big high school as a technology pushed to its inherent limits, the current debate about reform—especially all the pointing of fingers at "ill-prepared" teachers and "aimless" students—takes on new meaning. Current pronouncements and fact-finding reports begin to sound too much like calls for more way stations so that the horses will be fresher and faster. The debate prompts me to jump out of the system, to seek a solution so different from current practice that it might well be termed a new technology. That search took me to the Open School.

A School for Teachers

At the heart of any good school are good teachers, but high schools have become terribly difficult places in which to *teach*. One critical way in which any new conception of the high school must improve immeasurably on current practice is in the manner in which it supports teaching. Teaching is not easy at the Open School but it is distinctive from teaching in many other schools in that one can regularly see results from one's effort.

From the very first day of staff meetings as people talked enthusiastically about new activities that they had planned for the year, I was struck by the sense that this was a staff on which almost every individual was an active learner. One reason that the new classes and trips that they were planning were exciting for the staff was that each represented a new opportunity for *them* to learn. The staff's camaraderie and its unconditional support of individual interests were often evident in staff meetings. Each staff member was ready to support the pursuits of the others even when they might have competed for students with a personal pet project or posed a personal philosophical conflict.[1] Annie Hazzard noticed it, too. Annie was an artist and a single mother in her mid-thirties who was retreading herself as a teacher. Annie called the group "a rare staff."

> I have never seen—in an institution or even a family—a place where there is so much heartfelt concern and humor and love and honesty and a sense of safety and security that allows people to really say what's on their minds. I know there's a problem here with individuals having so much power [that the decision-making process sometimes bogs down], but on the other hand it's so important for everybody to have input and to have it respected. (Int. 5/88)

We speculated about what to make of the staff's effective performance. I asked her the chicken and egg question: "Do you think this is a collection of super-teachers that has created a super-school, or do you think the Open School's an environment in which a group of okay teachers, through the whole process of empowerment that goes on here, has been able to expand its capabilities?"

Annie's guess was that these individuals "were extraordinary teachers elsewhere," but that their "extraordinariness," as she put it, began to blossom when they came to the school. "They had opportunities to really stretch and grow," was how she put it.

I described my somewhat different view. I told her that I had tried in my mind's eye to imagine various staff members in a regular high school and that, while I didn't see anyone on the staff who would be a bad teacher in that setting, I saw many people, including myself, who would have trouble teaching in a regular high school. "In that sense," I said, "I guess I attribute more to the Open School's setting than you do."

Annie agreed "wholeheartedly" with this different way of looking at the issue. "Their style of teaching—the whole way that they communicate and bring students more fully to learning—is totally enhanced at this school," she said. And if she, like I, tried to imagine them teaching at a regular school, she saw them having "a really hard time." Annie added that she couldn't imagine them teaching at the Open School and then going back to some of the schools that she had seen recently. "I tell my teacher friends what's going on here. They *cannot* believe it," she said. "They have to be *so* careful about what they say and whom they say it to. There are major repercussions in their lives—on the job—if they don't walk on eggs."

I saw repeatedly the staff's extraordinariness, as Annie would put it. The Open School's staff worked wonders in everyday practice, occasionally even pulling off the magical. But they may have been at their best in crises. The resourcefulness they displayed in trying circumstances probably resides in most good teachers, but I think the responsiveness of the Open School's setting allowed that resourcefulness to come into play in ways that seldom are available even in good, but more typical, schools. Most schools, in their headlong rush to achieve time-on-task standards, to meet quotas for increasing scores on achievement tests, and to cover the textbook, have difficulty finding ways to respond to kids' more personal dilemmas. Deeds that simply would be *expected* of an Open School teacher would be considered, in most schools, extraordinary acts. Occurring as they would in an environment that provides almost no support for such actions, they would rightly be labeled "beyond the call of duty." Kids' lives are sometimes turned around by the right conversation with the right adult at the right time. By providing time to talk, the Open School allowed many more of these moments to be consummated. That makes all the difference. It is at these times that caring human beings become great teachers.

Our best opportunity to develop schools with environments that support this sort of teaching is to create schools that can truly be governed by their teachers. But why should it be so important that a school be a good place for teachers? Schools are supposed to be good places for kids. Teachers are paid to be there. It's their *job*. In myriad ways public education is slowly suffocating in its own dreary tedium. Giving teachers control of their schools is central to the gradual improvement of the conditions of teaching, conditions that the Carnegie Task Force on Teaching (1986) termed abysmal. As we have abandoned small personal schools, two related circumstances have evolved. The role of administrators has increasingly gained our attention, and we have gradually wrested control of schools from teachers. The degree to which support for teachers has waned is evident not from what administrators and board members *say* about teachers, but in what they *do* about them.

> There are many people in policy-making roles and administrative positions who mouth pat phrases about the importance of teachers and teaching—and then proceed to undercut teachers by creating conditions of work that blunt their enthusiasm and stifle their creativity. [Such actions constitute] a kind of "neutering" of teachers. Neutered teachers lack physical strength and energy, enthusiasm for their work, and motivation. (Frymier, 1987, p. 9)

We shouldn't be surprised to find talented individuals, or even untalented ones for that matter, fleeing such conditions.

None of this dismal picture existed at the Open School. At least one change occurred in the staff almost every year, but the overall feeling of the staff was one of stability, in part because almost any new teacher had already worked in the school in some capacity. Most staff members were long-termers. Jeff and Susie had been with the school from the start. Ruth had joined the staff a year later. Most of the staff had been around for 6 or 8 years.[2] With one or two exceptions all the staff members felt that they had found their teaching home. Rick was one of those exceptions. The unproductivity of kids still learning to use the freedom of the Open School drove him a little crazy. He'd tried to get the staff to tighten its standards for what students must do to remain in the school but all the staff's decisions were by consensus. Its inability to reach a consensus on tightening the structure of the program was a major frustration for him and he left the school.[3] For most of the staff, though, their commitment to the school probably was stronger than their commitment to teaching. Several said that if it weren't for the Open School, they would no longer be teaching.

An Exemplar or a Devil's Island?

That no single exemplar solves all of the problems of the high school becomes clear as one observes the differing reactions of both professionals and lay people to the Open School; outsiders view the school through many different lenses. Take, as an example, the librarian from another Jeffco school who upon reading Judy Sherbert's name badge at a district workshop exclaimed, "Oh my! You *are* a brave woman!" It was just one of several interesting reactions that Judy's badge drew during those 2 days of staff development meetings in the Old World.[4] Judy's badge read, innocently enough:

JUDY SHERBERT
OPEN SCHOOL

This librarian apparently viewed the school as some sort of penal colony—a Devil's Island—to which the school district banished its most troublesome students. Her comment was representative of one view of the Open School held by a portion of Jeffco's educators. It may have been the dominant view but that was difficult to assess. But it wasn't the only view. No discussion of the Open School as an exemplar would be complete without some description of how differently different people viewed the school.

I found many instances in which the Open School was viewed quite positively within the district. Take, as an example, the high school counselor who told Ruth that the Open School would be a perfect environment for a gifted student with whom she worked, or the elementary teacher who misunderstood the program to be exclusively for gifted students. Then there was a particular meeting of Jeffco's high school principals that managed to move beyond its typical agenda of budget problems and changes in attendance boundaries to a discussion of what ought to constitute a high school education for Jeffco's youngsters. As Ruth's big-school colleagues lamented the resistance they were encountering from their teachers as they worked to install effective advising programs and to resuscitate suffocating curricula, they regularly qualified their generalizations about Jeffco's high schools with remarks like, "Of course, Ruth, you're already doing that."[5] Particularly in the mountain region, the school's home ground in this sprawling school district at the time of the study, the Open School enjoyed a balanced, perhaps even positive, reputation.[6]

In contrast to these hopeful anecdotes were the many that the staff heard that suggested that the school often was seen as a good place for bad kids. Amy Foster's mother, an elementary teacher in the district, was told by a high school counselor that Amy was throwing away her education by transferring to the Open School.[7] Jeffco Superintendent John Peper's view of the school carried understandable importance. Once, in the middle of a conversation that had taken on the tone of a debate, he asked me what I thought of the school. Emboldened by the competitive discussion, I'd said that I thought the Open School was one of the best high schools in the country; the school *was* in my opinion an exemplar. He shared his view: The Open School was a good school that still had improvements to make if it was to be a model of the open philosophy it espoused, but it was certainly no exemplar. If any Jeffco school merited consideration as the best high school in the country it would be Wheatridge High.[8]

The prophet is unknown in his own camp, goes an old adage. Public alternative schools often have horrendous reputations within their districts—much worse than the reputation that the Open School has within Jeffco. Local educators see their alternative schools as pariahs more often than as paragons. This status seems to be the product of two factors. The first is mostly the problem of the Old World misunderstanding the New World: The Old World views those people over there as being just a little crazy and out-of-control. The degree to which these image problems are internal to a school district—while the very same school may be viewed as an exemplar elsewhere—might be taken as evidence that journeys to the New World are travels in time, into the future of schooling, more than they are travels in space.[9]

Foxfire, an internationally recognized high school journalism program, has also experienced this proximity-induced resentment. The program, located in Rabun Gap, Georgia, motivates kids to do their best by having them publish a magazine on the lore of the local mountain people. Through the vehicle of the magazine the kids learn about their roots as they preserve their mountain heritage. More important, they learn that they are capable human beings. Foxfire has been so successful that it now boasts a large international subscription list. The best of its articles have been compiled into, at last count, 10 widely sold books. The royalties from these books have transformed Foxfire into a multimillion dollar foundation that funds college scholarships for Rabun Gap kids and finances its historical preservation efforts. One would think that Georgia's journalism teachers would flock to the school to learn about the program, just as kids and teachers from as far away as Alaska do. Some do. But more of them organized an effort to prohibit the program's founder, certified as a teacher of English rather than journalism, from working with Foxfire (Wigginton, 1986).

The Open School attracts hundreds of visitors each year. I have counted as many as 27 on a single day.[10] About half of them are prospective students and their parents who are asked to visit the school before a final decision to attend is made. Most of the rest come from other areas of Colorado but some are from other states and occasionally from Canada and Mexico. On the day that 27 people visited, 11 were students, teachers, and parents from a California school, spending most of a week at the Open School. Two other visitors were teachers from Washington state. Except for Ann Brady, the assistant superintendent for the mountain area, the school had almost no visitors from Jeffco's professional ranks. John Peper visited the school just once, early in his 7-year tenure as Jeffco's superintendent.[11]

The second reason a school district may tend to malign its alternative schools is what, for lack of a simpler term, might be called dissonance reduction (Festinger, 1957). If I am an Old World educator struggling to shepherd kids along the path to adulthood, I have to make sense of my occasional failures. If I am using well-established, time-proven, Old World practices, it's hard for me to conclude that *I'm* doing anything wrong. If my up-to-date school is operating correctly, then the problem has got to be the kids or parents or society or something else; that being the case I can conclude that we've got to get these problem kids out of this otherwise okay school. Since kids can no longer be expelled easily, the alternative school becomes the depository for them. It has the reputation of taking *anybody*, and the district still gets state money for them. (The Open School kids, for example, occasionally told stories of administrators who used the school as a bogey man, threatening to "send" them there if they didn't get in line.) If the alternative school proves to be successful in working with these castoffs, its practices may well be judged suspect.

I have already noted that, at the time of the study, the Open School's waiting list grew by about one applicant each school day; it had been as high as 230 kids.[12] Most of these students, in consultation with their parents, had decided to try the Open School. Others were referrals of one sort or another and, since schools seldom refer their best kids somewhere else, most of these referrals were troubled kids. Early in the year, for example, the staff discussed the steady increase in the proportion of entering students who had been "staffed," Jeffco's term for students who were receiving some form of special services. Poz, the school's specialist in such matters, worried at the time that the district, through its pattern of referrals, was gradually turning the Open School into a special ed school.[13] But given that even teachers inside the Open School worried about possible imbalances within their student body, it's unfair to condemn Old World educators' similar views of the school. It was natural for them to view a school that they saw as being loaded with crazy, out-of-control, problem kids as a crazy, out-of-control, problem school, a Devil's Island where only the bravest of librarians could survive.

In fairness to Jeffco's high school counselors and administrators, they had very limited options in finding a proper placement for the growing number of mismatches they encountered between Old World programs and kids with modern-day problems. The Adult High School and the Vocational School were also options, but at the time of the study, the Open School was the only school available to Jeffco's over 18,000 high schoolers that most people would describe as being philosophically distinct.[14]

Contrast these local images with the school's national reputation. On April 5, 1988, NBC aired nationally a profile of the school. The segment appeared on *Main Street*, an after-school program that was cast in a TV news magazine format and geared to an early-teen audience. NBC had learned of the Open School from an east coast professor and asked to do a piece on the school. A film crew flew to Florida and followed the Tallahassee Work Trip for a day as the kids built an animal habitat. Later, the crew spent another day filming in Evergreen. The final 7-minute segment was a tightly edited montage, laced with testimonials from kids and with snippets of life in the school and on the trip. NBC didn't show everything. Gratefully, they omitted footage of Bert Lucas asleep in the hall. (Bert arose before 5:00 A.M. each day to begin his $3\frac{1}{2}$-hour commute to the school; occasionally, as it did that day, the regimen subdued him.) Most of the school community thought NBC represented the school about as well as one could in so short a time segment. Perhaps the network was attracted to the school not because it was good but because it was different and visually interesting. But it is also possible that NBC, too, thought it had found an exemplar.

We call phenomena that arouse divergent feelings in people controversial. John Peper and NBC and Judy's librarian friend and a professor spending a year in the school can quite conceivably all hold very different, even contradictory, views of the school and, in a limited way, all be right about it. Like the old anecdote about the blind men describing the elephant, each possesses different information about the Open School. Rather than put Bert on public display, NBC chose to place the viewer's hand on a different part of the elephant by showing hard-bitten Angie Sieboldt, standing with hammer in hand in the Florida sun, making a glowing statement about what the Open School was doing for her. She talked about "feeling gypped in her former education. They taught me the same things over and over," she said, "not what I needed to know to be able to do what I wanted to do. This school's trying to teach me what I *want* to know, plus the other things that I *have* to know."[15]

The Open School was no Devil's Island, and it's hard to envision a set of circumstances that could transform a program as powerful as the school's into one. The staff was too convinced of the rightness of what it was doing and too committed to seeing it continue to allow that to happen without a Herculean struggle. But many forces outside the school would likely carry it in that direction if the staff's sense of purpose and vigilance should waver. Our first impulse upon confronting anything new is not to try to learn from it but to transform it into something we understand. Columbus understood Indians—or so he thought—and so the strange new people he encountered became Indians. The path of educational change is strewn with victims of the Old World's formidable power to perform such transformations not only successfully but almost effortlessly.

The Feasibility of Very Small Schools

To those who would dismiss the idea that the solution to the problems of the high school lies in the development of very small schools because they are too expensive, I recommend the following exercise: Imagine a school district modeled not on the practices of General Motors but on those of a cottage industry. The average per-pupil expenditure in this country is about $5,260 a year.[16] Envision a small, highly autonomous school, given that funding level. If the school has 200 kids in it, its annual operating budget is over $1,050,000. Return 20% of it—$210,000—to a trimmed-down central administration for its reduced services and for bus transportation. Imagine a low student/teacher ratio, say 20 : 1. Pay your 10 teachers well, say an average of $45,000 a year (including fringe benefits). Hire a head teacher and pay him or her $60,000. Find an appropriate building for your program in your community and rent it at $7,000 a month plus another $3,000 for utilities. Hire a secretary, a custodian, and a cleaning person at $20,000 each. Budget $1,000 a year for supplies for each of your teachers and $3,000 for the central office. Put aside $10,000 to buy books each year and $20,000 for computers and A-V equipment. If the idea of trips is appealing, lease three vans, each at $5,000 dollars a year. That's probably enough to cover maintenance of them, but include another $3,000 just to be sure. Put $12,000 into a mileage budget. Now comes the fun: figuring out what to do with the more than $70,000 that has yet to be spent.

When I play this little game with people, they invariably look for the catch. Like a con game it's too good to be true. We all *know* that small schools don't work because they're too expensive. There is a catch of sorts, of course; some of this money is inextricably mired in the interlocking bureaucracy of special interests. But the exercise also suggests that the expensive part of a transition to small schools is the cost of maintaining the big-school, big-bureaucracy infrastructure (school districts currently employ approximately one administrative staff member for every two-and-a-half teachers) while giving small schools their fair share of the resources.[17] Remember, also, that we've used the national average as a baseline in our exercise. Envision the school that is possible for a couple of hundred impoverished inner-city kids in Washington, DC, for example, where the expenditure per kid is half again as much as the national average.[18]

School as a Place of Inspiration

If we have learned anything in the last 30 years of efforts to reform the high school, it is that we don't solve the problem by throwing money at it. Good schools move us in ways that don't carry price tags. The late Joseph Campbell (n.d.), interpreter of the myths of the world's cultures and religions, once said:

> The seat of the soul is there where the inner and the outer worlds meet. The outer world is what you get in scholarship, the inner world is your response to it. And it's where these come together that we have the Mythos. The outer world changes with historical time—the inner world is the world of Anthropos. It is the world constant to the human race and so you have throughout the mythical systems a constant and you always have the sense of *recognizing* something. And what you are recognizing is your own inward life and at the same time the inflection of history.

Many visitors to the Open School sense something mythic in its makeup in the sense, I think, that Campbell used the term. They recognize, some in only a few minutes, their own inward life. The school somehow feels right. It took Annie Hazzard 10 minutes to "fall in love with the school," to decide that the Open School was the kind of place where she needed to be not just for the 8 weeks of her student teaching but for the rest of her professional life. "I think it was the emotional level of the school," she told me. "You could sense the commitment from people about why they were here. They were here for their own reasons, not because they had to be" (Int. 5/88). I like to think that this "feel" of the school stirs something in our collective memory about what education ought to be. The late architect, Louis I. Kahn (1973), was very much in touch with the essence of school.

> Schools began with a man under a tree, a man who did not know he was a teacher, discussing his realizations with a few others who did not know they were students. The students reflected on the exchanges between them and on how good it was to be in the presence of this man. They wished their sons, also, to listen to such a man. Soon, the needed spaces

were erected and the first schools came into existence. The establishment of schools was inevitable because they are part of the desires of man. Our vast systems of education, now vested in institutions, stem from these little schools, but the *spirit* of their beginning is now forgotten. (p. 71, emphasis added)

To many, that spirit is evident in the Open School. But even some who sense it are nevertheless suspicious of Campbell's inner world. They would believe what others have taught them to *think* — the outer world of scholarship — rather than what they *feel* when they visit this strange little school. We must somehow get these people to at least allow others — those among us who not only feel but accept the power of an Open School — to create more schools like it throughout the country. The disbelievers must allow the believers to make such schools available to those who are ready for them. No one else need be required to attend these new schools in order for them to fulfill their evolutionary role in the Darwinian sense of the term. We desperately need exemplars, workable prototypes that abandon the industrial model of schooling that has brought us to schools bankrupt of personal relationships and enamored with the status of bigness. The Open School and other schools like it are compasses that point the way to these new schools. The smaller, more personal schools that may develop in the coming years will not all be alike. The Open School is just one of many different ways to reconceive the public high school. What other wonderful surprises are in store for us once teachers, working in small groups, are freed to dream — as the Open School's staff has — of different kinds of schools?

The kids would tell a visitor from the Old World, without too much prodding, that the Open School wasn't perfect, that it had its problems. But they usually would also say in one way or another that even with its flaws the school remained a place in which people — kids *and* teachers — learned to believe in themselves, were challenged to dream great accomplishments, and were empowered to transform their dreams into reality. In these ways, this is a high school that works.

Details of the Study

I first obtained permission to conduct the study from the Open School and then from the Jefferson County Schools' Department of Program Evaluation. I employed a participant/observer research design, but conducted few *formal* observations, indeed, many fewer than I'd planned. Early in my year in the school I came to feel so much a staff member and to sense the benefits of that level of acceptance, that I elected to mute the public face of my role as researcher as much as possible. I avoided obtrusive acts — among them, entering the Open School's small, informal classes just "to watch." Rather, my observations of the school became the stuff of my day-to-day work in it. I often saw other staff members teach, but it was usually in the context of classes we were conducting jointly. My field notes are consequently the sporadic recollections of events that had occurred hours, sometimes days, earlier rather than detailed accounts written as the events unfolded. My approach had its pitfalls. In two cases my recollection of an event was not corroborated by a staff member who also experienced it, and no field notes existed to support my memory. In each case, after discussion with the staff member failed to resolve our divergent views, I removed the description of the event from the book.

I have already summarized, in the Introduction, the interviews that were conducted. Most of the student interviews were conducted by the research team that I assembled from within the school community and trained in standard interviewing techniques. The team and I then constructed a three-part interview guide (see Figure A.1) containing eight general questions that ensured that each interviewee's views on several key issues would be collected.

Informed consent was obtained from all interviewees or, in the case of minors, from a parent or guardian. I attempted as much as was possible to protect interviewees' anonymity, and the consent form made it clear that they owned their data. It stated that interviewees would have opportunities to inspect drafts of the developing book, including the final draft, and that they had the right to request modifications. If I could not agree to the changes, I would remove from the

FIGURE A.1 Outline for a Student Interview

Preliminary Comments:
- Make sure informed consent has been established.
- Ask if it is okay to tape the session. Don't use tape if interviewee seems at all concerned about it. Also offer to turn the tape off temporarily anytime the interviewee wishes.
- Re-emphasize the point made in the informed consent form, that the interviewee owns his or her information and that I will not use anything with which he or she is uncomfortable.

The Interview:
1. Please give me a brief biography. I'm especially interested in your schooling experiences, your family, and interesting events in your life.
2. How did you come to be a student at the Open School?
3. Please describe your period of adjustment to the school.
4. Why is this school important to you?
5. What are the important differences between the Open School and other schools you've attended?
6. Is this a demanding place to go to school?
7. What are the big issues (perhaps problems is a better term for them) at the Open School right now?
8. What do you think a book about the Open School should be sure to include?

Closing the Interview:
- Can you suggest a student whom we might interview who you think would have a view of the school that is very different from yours?
- Would you be willing to have a follow-up interview if we decided that one would be useful?
- Thank you for participating.

---

book the material they found problematic. Few changes were requested beyond those that I would describe as corrections of errors of fact. The deletion of one sentence that would have surely raised a controversy within Jeffco (a statement that I had deliberated about removing myself) was the school's sole act of what most individuals might construe as censorship of the manuscript—that is, removal of material acknowledged to be factual. In this instance I believe any benefit denied the reader by this deletion is far outweighed by the damage its inclusion might have caused the school.

Almost all interviews were tape-recorded and then transcribed into typescripts. (Notes were also taken.) Interviewees understood that the recorder could be stopped, temporarily or for the remainder of the interview, if they wished to share particularly sensitive or confidential information. Only on rare occasions did an interviewee exercise this option. I read and unitized the typescripts—several hundred pages in all—into major themes. I also searched the typescripts electronically for terms used widely in the school, terms such as Walkabout, trips, empowerment, achievement, Advising, and Beginnings. Segments of typescripts identified in this manner were then electronically compiled into separate documents—some as long as 20 pages—to be scanned for themes.

The research team met about every 2 weeks from the time it was formed in November through April, when the schedules of the graduating seniors on the team became very hectic. The group functioned as a hermeneutic circle, helping me understand the significance of particular events or practices. Members read and discussed early drafts of several chapters of the book, thus ensuring that my emerging view of the school would have a certain congruence with their long-term understanding of it. Team members were paid a stipend for their work. Students on the team were paid the same amount as staff members.

The five New World Seminars were not a part of the original research design but rather a serendipity. They became an efficient and potent way to collect staff members' contrasting views (their collective construction of phenomena). The order in which they actually occurred is different from the order in which they appear here; I have noted those differences as I presented the seminars. Except for the first seminar, each was grounded in my direct experience in the school and the questions raised by that experience. Shortly after a seminar I would circulate within the staff a draft of my often heavily edited version of the discussion. I took care to see that each individual who was quoted in a seminar read and corrected my edited version of his or her statements. An important element of the seminar process was the informal collection of private views in the days following the seminar. Eventually, I also made these additions available to the staff and invited their reactions to them too.

The absence in the book of detailed accounts of what transpired in classrooms may puzzle some readers; a description of a school can hardly be called complete without them. Early on, I judged most classroom activity at the Open School to be not very different from what I had seen in the more informal classrooms in many conventional high schools. I decided that there were more interesting places to focus my attention, and as the growing length of the book became a factor, I chose to not expend precious pages on the classroom. As it is, much that I think would interest and inform readers about other aspects of the school has been left out.

I employed a number of measures designed to heighten the trustworthiness and authenticity of my account of the Open School and to minimize its distortions (Lincoln & Guba, 1985, 1986). Primary among these safeguards was the length of my stay in the school; for an entire academic year I *was* a staff member at the school. The prolonged immersion in the setting may have been crucial in attempting to study a school with a culture so different from the norm that I would come to think of it as a New World.

Extended immersion in a setting also presents the opposite danger, of becoming too involved, of going native. To those who may have heard at times the rustle of a grass skirt in these pages, let me acknowledge that the glowing nature of much of my account of the school warrants this suspicion. I am not the first observer of the Open School to wonder if his highly positive representation of the school was accurate. Bert Horwood (1987, pp. 9–11), for example, became concerned that his own "favorable disposition" arising from his many "pleasant and happy encounters in the school" might be casting an unrealistically rosy hue on his reporting. Horwood conducted a word count of all the adjectives students had used to describe the school in their interviews. The count confirmed the appropriateness of his very positive portrayal. As my own rebuttal to the suspicion that I went native at the Open School, I offer the New World Seminars. These dialogues with the staff are perhaps the most visible artifact of what several staff members described as my role as resident skeptic. They commented about the utility of my questioning attitude or the degree to which they thought I functioned as a "conscience" for the staff.

Trustworthiness and authenticity were also guarded through my efforts to triangulate views that individuals held of specific events or issues: Were they idiosyncratic or universal? Some triangulation was quite purposeful, involving follow-up interviews with individuals to collect their personal views of particular events or issues, or consciously seeking out others who might hold opposing views. The sample of students selected for interviewing by the research team was, for example, purposely diverse in terms of the students' motivations for attending the Open School and the length of time they had spent in it, and included students from all four of the groups identified in the external audit team's report that was discussed in Chapter 17. The standard closing question to our interviews was to ask each student to nominate another student who held a very different view of the school than his or her own. Many of the names offered were already on our interview list. Those that weren't were added.

Much triangulation was more subtle; I fine-tuned my account as the Open School community reacted first to early drafts of chapters and then to the final review copy. Individual staff members and students were often asked to be the first to read sensitive material about them or some event or person that they had described to me. I apologize publicly for the occasions when something slipped through this informal safety net.

Except for the one understandable instance I've already related, I never felt the hand of censorship operating here. Rather than asking that a negative portrayal be removed or softened, staff members typically suggested that it be balanced with a related positive event. Indeed, I was impressed—as others have been—with how open the staff is to criticism and the degree to which its basic nature is to be self-critical. In 1987, for example, the external audit team commented that in its visit to the school it did not encounter one weakness worth noting that the staff had not already identified in its self-study (Smith et al., 1987).

I also had hoped to conduct a final formal hearing at the school after the staff and students had reviewed the entire manuscript, what I considered a final, comprehensive step in establishing the account's authenticity. I was unable to obtain the funding to conduct this final check, however. Instead, I collected individuals' final suggestions for changes by mail and by phone.

An important final check of the trustworthiness of this account would have been the execution of a final audit. My plan was to invite either Bert Horwood or Mary Ellen Sweeney—both of whom know the school and qualitative research methods—to visit Bloomington for a few days to assess the congruence of the final account with the original data sources: the audio tapes, typescripts, and field notes. Unfortunately, the study's funding period expired long before the final manuscript was completed, and the funds for an external audit were withdrawn.

Notes

Prologue: Can This Be a Public School?

1. With one exception, all students' names are pseudonyms. By unanimous consent of the staff, all staff members bear their real names.
2. The number of required courses was reduced to one in 1986.

Introduction: The Study and the School

1. Team members read Guba and Lincoln's (1981) suggestions for conducting interviews, and I used them as a guideline for training team members in interview techniques. The team originally included a fourth student who withdrew from the project after training, but before interviewing started.
2. Arnie Langberg made reference to this North Central Association accreditation evaluator's assessment in informal conversation with me.
3. See Schrag, 1965, p. 244. Schrag places the merger in 1951, a date in some conflict with the district document I used as a source, which cited 1950 as the date of consolidation.
4. At the time of the study, Tanglewood was a preschool through ninth grade elementary/middle school that was also a part of the Jefferson County School District. In September 1989 Tanglewood and the Open School merged, both moving into a former junior high school building in Lakewood, to become the Jefferson County Open School, offering preschool through twelfth grade.
5. John Peper, Jeffco's superintendent at the time of the study, suspected that while an accurate figure was unattainable, the 70% estimate was probably not far off.
6. Rick related this estimate to me in informal conversation.
7. Most of the historical information about Evergreen is drawn from "Remember When," a historical supplement to the *Canyon Courier & High Timber Times*, February 22 and 23, 1989.

Chapter 1: Saddle Up

1. The attitudes and feelings attributed to Inge in this chapter were collected in interviews with her in January and February 1988.

2. Inge's view of Adult High was certainly not universal. The school's general reputation, at least within the Open School, seemed to be favorable.

3. Although the waiting list reached 191 applicants during the summer, many students' personal circumstances had changed by August, resulting in reductions in the list that allowed the Open School to admit every applicant who was still interested in attending the school.

4. Other advisors' advisee loads at the beginning of the school year ranged from five to 21 students, with 14 being the average.

5. The tragic death of these high school students apparently had become a significant event for many school people. Arnie had heard a number of administrators in the Denver area cite the event as justification for disallowing a variety of school activities in the nearby Rockies.

6. See Lesson II and Chapter 5 for a detailed explanation of the school's six Passage experiences and the Walkabout curriculum of which Passages are the central element.

7. Staff members paid for their own food on school trips but not for bus transportation. If public transportation—plane, train, or bus—was used for a trip, staff members, including volunteer adults and parents, paid their own fares.

8. This view was Ruth Steele's impression, formed over several years of informal conversations with checkers and sackers at the store and with other community people, of how the kids were viewed by the supermarket's personnel.

9. Students played important roles on some of the school's committees. For example, a hiring committee was formed each year to review applications and interview prospective staff members. At some point in each interview all adults would typically leave the room and allow the students on the committee to interview the applicant without adult influence. Typically, no vote of this committee was taken unless a student majority was present. When the position being filled was covered by the professional contract that Jeffco and the teachers' union had negotiated, the committee's actions were governed by those hiring rules. On rare occasions these rules thwarted the school's attempts to hire what it judged to be the best person for the job. Rick Lopez, for example, had worked in Jeffco's conventional schools for 13 years when the Hiring Committee selected him for a position as counselor/teacher. The decision was overruled by the central administration because a teacher with more seniority in the district was also an applicant. Rick—and the school—spent two frustrating years while the wrong person for the job made enough mistakes to be pushed out of the position. Most often though, the school figured out ways to get the people it wanted, as it eventually did in Rick's case.

10. The student identified as Tony did not smoke again until 6 months later. He had no particular reason or physiological urge to start smoking again; he just decided he would.

Chapter 2: F.A.C.

1. I roomed at the Langbergs' home during my year in Evergreen.

2. See Deal and Kennedy, 1982, for an explanation of the several roles that help maintain the culture of an organization.

3. I never told Carol about the All-Stars. I decided to let her learn of it as she read this book.

4. The name of the owner of Kelly Place, like all other persons mentioned who are not staff members, is a pseudonym. Kelly Place, however, is the correct name of this educational center located in the Cortez, Colorado area.

5. This annual trip to the Tallahassee Junior Museum combines biology (each student becomes an "expert" on one of the museum's animals and teaches the rest of the group about it) and carpentry (the group builds a new animal habitat for the museum).

Summing Up Lesson I: Getting Started on the Right Foot

1. The staff verified this statement in a staff meeting on March 16, 1988.

2. Ruth made this statement in March 1988. Sam Laumann, whose Wilderness Trip ended after 2 hours, eventually lent credence to this statistic by leaving the school in mid-year.

3. These goals were reconstructed not only from casual conversations but also from an information document the school provides parents and students.

4. In a March 12, 1990 letter to me, Ruth reported that in 1986 only 16 of Tanglewood's 33 sixth graders (48%) moved down the hall into Tanglewood's junior high program. The figure improved somewhat in 1987, when 22 of 37 sixth graders (60%) stayed in the program.

5. The school had a chronic problem tracking what happened to kids who left the program. Many finished their high school educations elsewhere, often via the G.E.D. certificate. A full accounting of what happened to the 45 early leavers of the year of the study is given in the Summing Up to Lesson VI.

6. Almost every student interviewed as part of the study described this period of adjustment as being difficult. (Asking students to describe their early adjustment was a standard step in the interview process.)

Chapter 3: Giving Students Control of Their Education

1. The complete list of the 49 competencies can be found in Gregory and Smith, 1987, pp. 104–106.

2. Distinctions such as freshman, sophomore, and junior make little sense in a school as individualized as the Open School. The school community did, however, use the term "senior," particularly the term "graduating senior," to refer to those students who were in the final sprint to finish the last of their Passages and complete the writing of their Transcripts.

3. Related to me in a May 1988 interview with one of these three staff members.

4. Sharon's early view of me was confirmed by her in a February 1989 interview.

Chapter 5: Walkabout Day

1. The details of the incident were corroborated by Dan McCrimmon in a July 1990 phone conversation.

2. From the student's paper for the Passage wrap-up.

3. From the student's paper for the Passage wrap-up.

4. From an excerpt that appeared in the school's newsletter.

Summing Up Lesson II: School as a Place of Empowerment

1. Students had the prerogative to participate on the teams of their "home" high school—the school they would have attended if they hadn't enrolled at the Open School—or on the teams at Evergreen High School, the school closest to the Open School. A handful of students exercised this option each year. During the year of the study an Open School student playing for Evergreen High was named the outstanding female soccer player in the county.

2. Related to me in an interview with one of the three students.

3. Most of Don's thoughts portrayed here were collected in an interview shortly after the Cortez trip in the fall of 1987.

Lesson III: Community

1. I conducted most of this social climate research with Gerald R. Smith. See Chapter 2 of *High Schools as Communities: The Small School Reconsidered*, 1987, for a discussion of cliques.

Chapter 7: Toby May

1. The events described in this chapter are a reconstruction of the accounts received in interviews with two students, here bearing the pseudonyms Inge Pedersen and Ritch Hahn, who made the trip to Central City with Toby. One staff member was also interviewed. Linda May (also a pseudonym) reacted by letter to an early draft of the chapter and volunteered much information about Toby that has been included in the final version. Toby, to whom this book is dedicated, is the only student who bears his real name.

2. From a May 1988 interview with a staff member.

3. From a May 1988 interview with a staff member.

4. It was never firmly established that Randy Ledbetter (a pseudonym) was at a bar at this time. He did admit to having been at a bar earlier in the afternoon. He claimed to have been at his girlfriend's house at this time. From conversations with Randy, Linda May thinks the account presented here is more accurate than Randy's official version of the story.

5. Related to me by Linda May in a letter on November 9, 1989.

6. From a May 1988 interview with a staff member.

7. Taken from a *Rocky Mountain News* article (March 19, 1988, p. 38) in which Ledbetter's sentencing was reported.

8. The march took place on a drizzly Saturday morning a few weeks later. The kids did an extremely capable job of organizing the event. One hundred and sixteen people—students, friends of Toby's, and concerned citizens—took

part. The Governor's office was represented and the march was covered by news teams from every major television station in Denver. Russ Molby documented the entire enterprise, which formed the core of his Global Awareness Passage.

9. Toby's wishes for his funeral were described by Linda May in a November 9, 1989 letter.

10. Related to me by Ruth in informal conversation the following day.

11. Most of the qualities in this list are from Linda May's letter of November 9, 1989, but many of them were also shared by friends at the funeral.

Chapter 8: The Second New World Seminar— The Individual and the Community

1. The seminar occurred in March 1987. While it is presented here as the second seminar it actually was the third such discussion that occurred during the year. The process that I adhered to for all but the first seminar involved preparing a written statement that laid out an issue, distributing that statement a day or two before a staff meeting, and discussing the issue for about a half hour as an agenda item of the staff meeting. For all seminars including the first one I tape-recorded the discussion and then prepared an edited abridged typescript of the discussion. The typescript was then shared with the principal participants in the discussion for their revisions and approval. This review process sometimes involved more than one iteration.

2. Susie Bogard and a visiting volunteer had a total of about $50 stolen from their belongings while they were out of the room for a few minutes. Some vandalism to the room also occurred. The incident was notable in part because of the rarity of theft and vandalism in the school.

3. Twenty-seven of the school's 238 students were legally classified as requiring special services. While the entire staff worked with all of these kids and various staff members were advisors to many of them, it was Poz's primary responsibility to see that each of these students' programs was appropriately structured. The only difference that I could perceive in these programs was that the students were often required to take certain classes called Skills Labs, which were taught by Poz. Just as we all worked with the special ed kids, Poz also worked with all the other kids. During the year, he taught cooking (New Orleans cuisine), a film class, and a literature class—or, more accurately, an American studies class—on the topic of baseball. That class culminated in a trip to Kansas City to see a Royals–Yankees series. Poz completed his doctorate in 1989.

4. Advisors were so strongly linked to the work of their advisees that a phrase like this wasn't at all usual in the parlance of the school.

5. Futures was a student/staff committee that was responsible for the ongoing reshaping of the curriculum.

6. The Caulkathon was a community service project in which the whole school participated. It usually occurred in the fall. Teams of students would

spread out over the Denver area, winterizing (especially caulking) the homes of low income senior citizens.

Summing Up Lesson III: Community as an Organizing Principle for a School

1. The estimate of one student per school day was Rick's, the staff member charged with maintaining the list. At this writing the school is a Pre-K–12 school with a waiting list that exceeds 1,000 students. The Jeffco administration continues to deny the school's requests to begin a second, similar school in the district, but parental pressure to do so is building.

2. Instead, these teachers became members of what I came to call the farm team. The analogy began to form in my mind on my first morning in Evergreen, as I had breakfast with Roberta Page, newly hired as a one-year replacement teacher for Judi Justus who was spending the year on sabbatical leave. Roberta described the list of over 20 applicants for the position, all people who had worked in the school in some capacity over the previous few years. I became aware that teaching at the Open School had become so prized a professional plum that almost no one who had not worked in the school—as an aide, a volunteer, or a one-year replacement teacher—stood much of a chance of being hired for a permanent position. As Roberta described the pool of candidates, I began imagining it functioning like a baseball farm team. These people had each found their way into the school and had become smitten with it, as Roberta and I had. Most of them were working at a variety of other jobs—some even teaching in other schools—but they shared a common goal: to be called up to the big team.

Chapter 9: Lost on a Dark Mountain

1. The account given here was constructed from two of Bruce's tellings of the tale. One was a recount of it to the entire staff at the first staff meeting after the trip; the other was given to me in private for the express purpose of detailing it here. The student identified here as Cindy McPhearson left the school a few weeks after the incident, before she could be interviewed. Bruce was uncertain that she would have granted me an interview anyway, since she would not discuss the incident with anyone.

2. Bruce used the term in private conversation with me and I recall him using it in the privacy of staff meetings. I don't recall hearing him use the term in conversation with students, although I can imagine him doing so. Both his typical playful banter with his kids and his propensity to challenge them to reach beyond their current grasp might lead to his invoking it in certain circumstances.

3. Those who have taught teenagers likely understand the dynamic operating here: that students, unwilling to readily accept the advice of adults, must learn some lessons on their own. If, indeed, an individual did not have

sufficient warm clothes, other group members would be asked to share their extra apparel with that person. In doing so, they would be helping to solidify the group.

Chapter 10: The Third New World Seminar—
Limits and Boundaries

1. While this seminar is presented as the "third," it actually occurred second.

2. Here, I make reference to an incident that I don't relate in the book. At the retreat a boy and girl stole into the room next to mine for the presumed purpose of having a sexual liaison, which I interrupted before much of anything could happen.

3. The Fight occurred 2 or 3 weeks before this seminar and ended with the boy pinning the girl's shoulders to the ground with his knees and spitting tobacco juice in her face. The Fight remained a topic of discussion in part because of the concern of some staff members that the boy, who was the clear aggressor in the incident, had received—in the eyes of some staff members—too light a punishment for his deed.

4. This event in Western Civics is discussed again in the Fourth New World Seminar (Chapter 15).

5. Related to me by Arnie in a conversation on March 12, 1988, several weeks after the seminar.

Summing Up Lesson IV: Expanding the Envelope

1. Jeff and Susie Bogard, who both participated in the trip, verified the details of this account in a July 1992 telephone conversation.

2. Holding a parent information meeting was a requirement of every trip. Trip staff members had to make it a point to talk by telephone with parents who couldn't attend the meeting to ensure that no student was going on a trip without a parent knowing its details.

3. Some trips had special requirements. On the Mazatlan Trip, for example, we flew commercially and lived in Mexican homes. Because it was an international trip, we had to have passports or official birth certificates for every student and for the trip staff: Fitz and me. To ensure that we were not abducting teenagers and transporting them to Mexico, the Mexican customs authorities also required that we present notarized letters in which parents gave us permission to take their child to Mexico. If the parent's surname was different from his or her child's, as many were in a county with an unusually high divorce rate, we had to have a second notarized letter explaining why the surnames were different.

4. These three strategies were enumerated by Arnie in a panel discussion at the United States Office of Education's regional conference on Choosing Better Schools held in Denver on November 16 and 17, 1989.

Lesson V: Experiential Learning

1. Information provided by Ruth.
2. I also participated in the Wilderness Backpacking Trip, which, because of its size and circumstances, was conducted in a different manner from the school's other extended trips.
3. Information provided by Ruth.
4. Shared by Jeff in an informal conversation in November 1989.

Chapter 12: A Discovery in Dinosaur Land

1. This event was related to me by Judith Miller-Smith, who then helped me refine early drafts of the description of the incident to improve the story's accuracy. Judith went on to take a position at Tanglewood and eventually was reunited with the Open School staff when the two schools merged in 1989.

Summing Up Lesson V: Learning *in* the World

1. All the examples of processing that are presented here were retrieved from audiotapes of the Navajo Work Trip's four processing sessions.
2. Both the student's comments and the trip staff's reactions to them were taken from the self-evaluation of the student identified here as Bert Lucas.
3. Collected in informal conversation in February 1988 with the student identified here as Josey Fink.
4. Collected in an informal follow-up conversation in November 1989.

Lesson VI: Standards

1. This is sometimes termed studying *off* of the problem. I think of it as being similar to the fresh perspective one gains of one's own country through an extended stay in a foreign country. Jerry Smith and I discuss the issue of control throughout our book, *High Schools as Communities: The Small School Reconsidered* (1987).

Chapter 13: The Fabulous Five

1. The first portion of a staff meeting that I relate here is really a composite of parts of the first agenda item—which was always the fabulous five—of several meetings. The identities of the students being discussed have been guarded in several ways. Besides my usual practice of using pseudonyms for all students, I have, in most cases, changed the students' advisors and occasionally the gender of some members of the students' families or friends, and have altered details of the circumstances of their lives that might otherwise reveal their identities.

Chapter 14: The Hall Lounge

1. Words to this effect *were* said in Governance that day. These particular statements, however, are a paraphrase of excerpts from a March 1988 interview with a graduating senior.

2. Designs for refurbishing the student lounge never moved beyond preliminary sketches and discussions.

Chapter 15: The Fourth New World Seminar—
The Culture of Classrooms

1. I don't mean to imply by this observation that classes in most high schools today don't share this problem; indeed, abundant evidence supporting that contention exists. See, for example, Theodore Sizer's *Horace's Compromise* (1984); Arthur Powell et al.'s *The Shopping Mall High School* (1985); Ernest L. Boyer's *High School* (1983); and Michael W. Sedlak et al.'s *Selling Students Short* (1986).

2. From a November 1987 conversation in which I was a participant. While this seminar occurred in February 1988 the stimulus for it was written and distributed to the staff in early December, which explains the use of the word *recently*.

3. Some other movies screened in Poz's film class were: Pakula's *Parallax View*, Kazan's *On the Waterfront*, and Truffaut's *Small Change*.

4. This incident was first discussed in the Second New World Seminar (see Chapter 8).

5. Most evaluations at the Open School started with students evaluating experiences they'd completed, including how they'd performed during them. The teacher or person in charge (which occasionally was a student) then responded to the students' evaluations.

6. Leadership was a class open to any student in the school. The class functioned as an agenda committee for Governance meetings and the students in the class led Governance on a rotating basis.

7. Observation made by a staff member who co-taught some of these seminars.

Chapter 17: The Fifth New World Seminar—
Responding to Demands

1. The four populations identified in the external audit (Smith et al., 1987) were: (1) kids coming to the school directly from Tanglewood who may already have been philosophically attuned to the program; (2) kids who had been successful elsewhere but were interested in self-directed learning; (3) kids who had found conventional education inappropriate or dysfunctional but may also have been unprepared for the Open School's self-directed learning; and

(4) students with severe personal problems for whom the school fulfilled a therapeutic function.

2. This was one of the school's most coveted trips, with more students, especially graduating seniors, wanting to go than could be accommodated.

3. Dan wrote a proposal in 1978 for a federal grant for this approach to teaching music for another Colorado school. The proposal was funded but the school got cold feet and backed out. With lots of money and nowhere to spend it Dan approached Arnie, looking for a job. He could scarcely get a brief description of his idea out before Arnie said yes. I have encountered several kids over the years who have said that they came to the Open School specifically to take part in this unusual music curriculum.

4. Triads were explained in Chapter 5.

5. See Coleman, 1972, for one explication of this observed condition of today's youngsters.

Chapter 18: Moving On

1. *Dineh* is the Navajo word for the Navajo people.

Summing Up Lesson VI: Standards for Individuals

1. See Sizer, 1984; Powell et al., 1985; and Sedlak et al., 1986 for discussions of how treaties work in classrooms.

2. Each fall the staff held a weekend retreat. The facilitator working with the group the year before the study became aware of the differences within the staff on this issue and asked individuals to physically place themselves on a continuum, an imaginary line running through several rooms of the house in which they were meeting. The discussion that ensued apparently turned into a heated argument, with at least one staff member feeling attacked and leaving the retreat early. I had volunteered to help plan what was the next retreat and I learned of the incident through advice I received from several independent sources: No more continuums!

3. Information that Linda May shared with me in a January 1991 phone conversation. Several of the kids who had been in the accident with Toby and had maintained contact with Linda related the incident to her. I had no way to verify the accuracy of the story.

4. Information obtained from Rick Lopez. These figures represent the status of the student body as of May 3 of the year of the study. Several additional students—unaccounted for in these statistics—may have left the school in June and, of course, more students would have changed their educational plans over the ensuing summer.

5. See Aiken, 1942, for a summary of the Eight-Year Study, one of the most comprehensive studies ever conducted of American education. Four colleges did not participate in the study: Harvard, Haverford, Princeton, and Yale.

6. See Thomas, 1990, pp. 275–286, for a discussion of the study and its obscurity.

7. This figure was obtained from a 1992 list provided by the school.

Conclusion: The Open School as Exemplar

1. The support also could be more than psychic. During the years when Dana worked in the school as a teacher's aide she was four courses shy of being a certified teacher. Her husband at the time was insecure in their relationship and jealous of Dana's enthusiasm for the school. Though he was earning good money—as Dana put it—he wouldn't give her the tuition money. Dana was earning so little as an aide that she couldn't afford the tuition to take the courses. Seeing her predicament, the staff contributed its own money to pay for the courses at Denver University, perhaps the most expensive school in Colorado. The money wasn't a loan but a gift to Dana for everything she'd given the school. Dana earned her teaching certificate and assumed a teaching slot that opened shortly thereafter. (Anecdote related to me by Arnie in casual conversation and corroborated in an interview with Dana.)

2. The figure is summarized from staff biographies that were a standard part of staff interviews.

3. Rick joined the Tanglewood staff, working with junior high kids, the year after the study. After the two schools merged he rejoined the Open School's secondary level staff but after 2 more years with the school again elected to leave.

4. Overheard by me and then corroborated in an interview in November 1987.

5. This anecdote was related by Ruth during the staff meeting of May 4, 1988.

6. Most of the evidence for these generalizations was drawn from the anecdotes of the staff. As such, they are most accurately described as these insiders' perceptions of how the outside world views the school.

7. Related to me by the parent, here called Mrs. Foster, at an open house meeting.

8. From a June 1988 interview. John Peper waived all rights to anonymity, saying, "*All* my statements are public statements."

9. Some suggest that alternatives such as the Open School are not so much glimpses of the future as they are throwbacks to the past, to the Progressive Education era.

10. Monday was visitors' day. Besides teachers and students from other school districts, visitors included teacher preparation students from nearby universities. The visitors' day attendance of 27 was achieved on May 2, 1988. Weekly figures of a dozen or less were more typical.

11. Information offered by Marilyn Wittebort, the school's secretary throughout those years. John Peper left Jeffco's superintendency in 1989.

12. Now that the school is a prekindergarten through twelfth grade program, its waiting list exceeds 1,000 students.

13. Comment made by Rick Posner at an August 24, 1987 staff meeting.

14. In 1985 the staff made a concerted effort to establish another school "down in the flatlands," which would have been something of a clone of the Open School. The plan had half of the staff moving to the new school and half staying at the current one. The described plan struck me as the biological dividing of a cell with each new half "growing" the new staff members it would need to become whole again. Planning efforts with parents were curtailed abruptly when central administrators learned of the activity. The administration told the staff that the existing range of alternatives was sufficient to meet the needs of the district.

15. From the videotape of the NBC segment.

16. The figure seems high but it encompasses all costs, including buildings, which are not typically part of such estimates. According to statistics compiled by the National Education Association (1991, p. 59), the 1990–91 average of the state averages was $5,261. New Jersey at $9,159 had the highest average of the states. The lowest was Utah with $2,993.

17. Unpublished data from the U.S. Department of Labor's "Current Population Survey, 1986–87," cited by Darling-Hammond, 1990.

18. The 1990–1991 figure for Washington, DC, was $8,210. See National Education Association, 1991, p. 59.

References

Aiken, W. M. (1942). *The story of the Eight-Year Study*. New York: Harper & Row.

Boyer, E. L. (1983). *High school: A report on secondary education in America*. New York: Harper & Row.

Campbell, J. (n.d.). *The hero's journey* [Transcript of television program]. San Diego: KPBS, San Diego State University.

Canyon Courier & High Timber Times. (1989, February 22 & 23). Remember when [historical supplement].

Carnegie Task Force on Teaching as a Profession. (1986). *A nation prepared: Teachers for the twenty-first century*. New York: Carnegie Forum on Education and the Economy.

Coleman, J. S. (1972, February). The children have outgrown the schools. *Psychology Today, 5*(9), 72–75, 82.

Coleman, J. S. (1987, April 21). *Families and schools*. Address presented at the annual meeting of the American Educational Research Association, Washington, DC.

Colsgrove, M., Bloomfield, H. H., & McWilliams, P. (1976). *How to survive the loss of a love*. New York: Bantam.

Comer, J. P. (1989). *Maggie's American dream*. New York: Plume.

Darling-Hammond, L. (1990, December). Achieving our goals: Superficial or structural reforms? *Phi Delta Kappan, 72*(4), 286–295.

Deal, T. E., & Kennedy, A. A. (1982). *Corporate cultures: The rites and rituals of corporate life*. Reading, MA: Addison-Wesley.

Festinger, L. (1957). *A theory of cognitive dissonance*. Palo Alto, CA: Stanford University Press.

Fields, R., Weyler, R., Magraski, R., & Taylor, P. (1984). *Chop wood, carry water: A guide to finding spiritual fulfillment in everyday life*. Los Angeles: Jeremy P. Tarcher.

Frymier, J. (1987, September). Bureaucracy and the neutering of teachers. *Phi Delta Kappan, 68*(1), 9–14.

Gibbons, M. (1974, May). Walkabout: Searching for the right passage from childhood and school. *Phi Delta Kappan, 55*(8), 596–602.

Gregory, T. B., & Smith, G. R. (1983, April). *Differences between alternative and conventional schools in meeting students' needs*. Paper presented at the annual meeting of the American Educational Research Association, Montreal.

Gregory, T. B., & Smith, G. R. (1987). *High schools as communities: The small school reconsidered.* Bloomington, IN: Phi Delta Kappa Foundation.

Guba, E. G., & Lincoln, Y. S. (1981). *Effective evaluation.* San Francisco: Jossey-Bass.

Herndon, J. (1971). *How to survive in your native land.* New York: Simon & Schuster.

Hofstadter, D. R. (1979). *Gödel, Escher, Bach: An eternal golden braid.* New York: Vintage Books.

Horwood, B. (1987). *Experiential education in high school: Life in the Walkabout Program.* N.p.: Association for Experiential Education.

Hout, P. (1983, April 13). Remarks made during a presentation to the annual meeting of the American Educational Research Association in Montreal.

Kahn, L. I. (1973). *The notebooks and drawings of Louis I. Kahn* (R. S. Wurman & E. Feldman, Eds.). Cambridge, MA: Massachusetts Institute of Technology Press.

Lincoln, Y. S., & Guba, E. G. (1985). *Naturalistic inquiry.* Beverly Hills, CA: Sage.

Lincoln, Y. S., & Guba, E. G. (1986). But is it rigorous? Trustworthiness and authenticity in naturalistic evaluation. In D. D. Williams (Ed.), *Naturalistic evaluation* (New Directions in Program Evaluation No. 30, pp. 73–84). San Francisco: Jossey-Bass.

Locke, R. F. (1986). *The book of the Navajo.* Los Angeles: Mankind (Holloway House) Publishing.

National Education Association. (1991). *Rankings of the states, 1991.* Washington, DC: Author.

Peters, T. J., & Waterman, R. H., Jr. (1982). *In pursuit of excellence.* New York: Warner.

Powell, A. G., Farrar, E., & Cohen, D. K. (1985). *The shopping mall high school.* Boston: Houghton Mifflin.

Schrag, P. (1965). *Voices in the classroom: Public schools and public attitudes.* Boston: Beacon.

Sedlak, M. W., Wheeler, C. W., Pullin, D. C., & Cusick, P. A. (1986). *Selling students short: Classroom bargains and academic reform in the American high school.* New York: Teachers College Press.

Sizer, T. R. (1984). *Horace's compromise: The dilemma of the American high school.* Boston: Houghton Mifflin.

Smith, G. R., & Gregory, T. B. (1982, Winter). The impact of social climates: Differences between conventional and alternative schools. *Educational Horizons, 60*(2), 83–89.

Smith, G. R., Gregory, T. B., & Pugh, R. C. (1981, April). Meeting students' needs: Evidence for the superiority of alternative schools. *Phi Delta Kappan, 62,* 561–564.

Smith, V. (Chairperson) & seven others. (1987, March 13). Jefferson County Open High School external audit [Unpublished school document].

Steele, R. (1987). Self-study of Jefferson County Open High School for the external audit process [Unpublished school document].

Strother, D. B. (1990, October). Cooperative learning: Fad or foundation for learning? *Phi Delta Kappan, 72*(2), 158–160, 162.

Sweeney, M. E. (1983). *An exploratory structural-functional analysis of American urban traditional and alternative secondary public schools.* Doctoral dissertation, Portland State University.

Tenenbaum, S. (1951). *William Heard Kilpatrick: Trail blazer in education.* New York: Harper & Brothers.

Thomas, B. R. (1990). The school as a moral learning community. In J. I. Goodlad, R. Soder, & K. A. Sirotnik (Eds.), *The moral dimensions of teaching* (pp. 266–295). San Francisco: Jossey-Bass.

Wigginton, E. (1975). *Moments: The Foxfire experience.* Kennebunk, ME: Institutional Development and Economic Affairs Service, Inc.

Wigginton, E. (1986). *Sometimes a shining moment: The Foxfire experience.* Garden City, NY: Anchor Press/Doubleday.

Wilson-Schaef, A. (1986). *Co-dependence: Misunderstood—mistreated.* New York: Harper & Row.

About the Author

Tom Gregory has taught at Indiana University in Bloomington for the past 24 years. He conducts research on, consults with, and writes about alternative public education. He is co-author (with Jerry Smith) of *High Schools as Communities: The Small School Reconsidered* (Phi Delta Kappa), a 1987 book that describes the power of alternative public high schools and argues for the transformation of all schools into very small, close-knit communities. His other books are *Encounters with Teaching: A Microteaching Manual* (Prentice Hall) published in 1972 and *Teaching Is . . .* (Science Research Associates), a 1974 book that he co-authored with Merrill Harmin.

Tom was director of Indiana's Alternative Schools Teacher Education Program from 1978 until the program closed its doors in 1982. He has received Indiana University's Distinguished Teacher Award and has been a Lilly Teaching Fellow. He spent his fellowship year on the staff of the Open High School, collecting the impressions that would form this book. More recently, he has led a small group of students, classroom teachers, and university faculty in the development of *The Community of Teachers*, the only performance-based teacher education program in the state of Indiana. The program, which began operation in the spring of 1993, is modeled on the core principles and processes of the Open High School.

Tips and Traps
When Buying
a Home

Other McGraw-Hill Books by Robert Irwin

Robert Irwin

Tips and Traps When Buying a Home

McGraw-Hill Publishing Company

New York   St. Louis   San Francisco   Auckland   Bogotá
Caracas   Hamburg   Lisbon   London   Madrid   Mexico
Milan   Montreal   New Delhi   Oklahoma City
Paris   San Juan   São Paulo   Singapore
Sydney   Tokyo   Toronto

Library of Congress Cataloging-in-Publication Data

Irwin, Robert
  Tips and traps when buying a home./Robert Irwin.

    p.   cm.
  Includes index.
  ISBN 0-07-032138-8—ISBN 0-07-032140-X (pbk.)
    1. House buying.   2. Real estate business.   I. Title.
  HD1379.I67   1990   89-39202
  643'.12—dc20   CIP

    7890   DOC/DOC   9876543

ISBN 0-07-032138-8

ISBN 0-07-032140-X {PBK.}

*The editors for this book were James Bessent and Jim Halston, the designer was
Naomi Auerbach, and the production supervisor was Suzanne W. Babeuf. This
book was set in Baskerville by the McGraw-Hill Publishing Company Professional & Reference Division composition unit.*

Printed and bound by R. R. Donnelley and Sons.

 This book is printed on recycled, acid-free paper containing a minimum of 50% recycled de-
inked fiber.

*For more information about other McGraw-Hill materials,
call 1-800-2-MCGRAW in the United States. In
other countries, call your nearest McGraw-Hill office.*

Contents

Preface

This year over three million people will buy either a new home or a resale. For many of you it will be your first home purchase. For others it will be a transaction the likes of which they do less than half a dozen times in a lifespan.

Buying the home—finding it, inspecting it, learning about the new laws concerning its purchase, dealing with the broker, the seller, the attorney, the escrow officer, the lender and, of course, the documents—can be a confusing, difficult, if not frightening experience. Even though I have purchased more houses than I care to remember, I can still vividly recall the first home I bought more than three decades ago, so strange (to me at the time) was the transaction.

It was with this concern for buyers and with the knowledge that most buyers are totally lost when purchasing a home, that I undertook to write what I hope is a book filled with answers. I have tried to anticipate the landmines and the swift currents and prepare you, the buyer, to deal successfully with these. I've put in several lifetimes worth (mine and many associates) of advice on how to effectively deal with agents, sellers, and all the other interested parties you'll meet. I've attempted to give you guidelines to follow and to warn you in advance of traps.

I hope you the reader will find this book enlightening as well as helpful and that it allows you to more easily and confidently purchase the ideal home of your dreams.

There were many people who participated in the preparation of this book, but I would especially like to thank two: Phillip Perry of *Real Estate Today* for his research help, and Martha Jewett, formerly senior editor at McGraw-Hill, for her editorial support.

Robert Irwin

Tips and Traps
When Buying
a Home

Introduction: The Right Time and Reason to Buy

How's Your Timing?

Is there a right time and a wrong time to buy a home? Are there right and wrong reasons for buying?

Yes, there is and there are. Let's begin with timing.

Here's **Tip No. 1** for this book. The right time to buy your home is in December, preferably during the last two weeks of the month when everyone is fussing about the holidays.

Historically, there have been fewer home sales in December (by a wide margin) than any other month of the year. Sellers who must sell because of personal or business reasons are desperate in December. There are so few buyers that motivated sellers will often grab ridiculously low offers, just to get out of the property. If you want to save money, buy your home in late December.

There's also a wrong time to buy. It's in late spring and early summer, specifically the months of May and June. Between 15 and 20 percent of all homes sold (new and resales) will be sold during those two months. They are the peak selling times.

A lot of the reason why May and June are such good sales months has to do with school schedules. Children tend to be getting out of school then, and families feel it is an optimum time to make a move. It also has to do with appearance. After the cold and/or wet winter, houses tend to look fresher and more appealing in spring. Sellers, of course, know this and spruce up the places even more to lure in buyers.

It's a seller's market in late spring and early summer, and if you want to pay top dollar and have the slimmest selection, buy then. Otherwise, wait until the cold of December when you normally have a bigger selection and better prices.

Consider Some of the Most Common Personal Reasons for Buying

There are also personal reasons for buying a home. While there aren't really right or wrong personal reasons, some are better than others. Do you fit in here?

Reason #1: I want to buy a new home to get more room.

This is usually a trap. If your major motivation is to get more room, meaning you're basically satisfied with your current house and neighborhood, you're probably better off adding on. Remember, the closing costs of a new house purchase plus moving expenses can amount to almost eight percent of the price you pay. On a $150,000 house, that can come to about $12,000. This is money that is essentially thrown away, although some of it may be deductible—see Chapter 10 on tax consequences. For $12,000 you can get a pretty good room addition even in this day and age.

Reason #2: I want to buy a new home to get a better neighborhood, better schools, better shopping, etc.

This is the best reason. Remember, in real estate the most important factor in the value of property is location. If your primary reason for moving is to get to a better location, you can only improve your financial condition. Go, move...but plan to pay far more than your current rent or mortgage payments.

Reason #3: I want to buy a new home to move to the country.

Again, a trap. Surprisingly, this is a reason very frequently quoted in today's market. Faced with urban blight, gangs, crime, and crowding both in cities and in suburbs, many families are opting to leave it all and head for the country. Country property in many areas of the nation is booming as more and more people flock to it.

Why, then is it a trap? Have you ever lived in the country? Can you take the "homey" and "backwoods" attitudes of many of the residents? Can you handle the lack of cultural activities such as plays, theatre, even movie theatres which frequently don't exist in the country? Remember, there are few malls in the country. Can you make a living there? If you can't, can you stand a long commute?

Interestingly enough, the divorce rate in the first three years for couples who move to the country is surprisingly high. Often the outdoorsperson of the family loves it while the other spouse misses old friends and urban activities. It's certainly something to consider before making such a move.

Reason #4: I want to buy a new home to get closer to work.

Sometimes a trap. Nobody I know likes to commute, and the longer the commute the less anyone likes it. On the other hand, it is seldom the case that buying a home closer to work will cost you less than your present rent or mortgage, or that it will put you in a better neighborhood. If you can get a cheaper property in a better neighborhood closer to work, then by all means move!

It might turn out that, yes, you'll get a shorter commute. But each evening you'll come home to an older house with associated problems, a more crime-ridden neighborhood, poorer schools, and, conceivably, a higher mortgage.

Perhaps alternatives such as a shared apartment closer to work or even a change of jobs should be considered.

Reason #5: I want to buy a brand new home.

Often an excellent reason. Many people consider brand new homes to be traps because of the added expenses. Not only do you have to buy the home, but often you have to buy new fencing, put in yards, pay for carpet upgrades, and so forth. In addition, new homes often cost significantly more than resales of comparable size in adjoining neighborhoods.

Nevertheless, new homes usually pay off. A new home which is well located will often appreciate faster than a neighboring resale. That means you'll get your money out more quickly, and there'll be more of it than with a resale.

In addition, new homes don't have to be constantly fixed. A trap that many home buyers overlook is the annual cost of fixing resales. It's a fact that any home older than seven years is going to cost, on the average, $1500 a year or more in repairs and maintenance: new roofs, furnace and plumbing problems, carpet replacement, painting, etc. It's a mistake to think that you only get additional expenses when you buy a new home. You inevitably get additional expenses when you buy any home.

Should You Buy at All?

As we've seen, timing a purchase is important, and buying for the right reasons is also important, but the simple fact is that most people don't pay much attention to either. There are over 60 million home owners in this country, and in an average year between four and five million homes are bought and sold. Buying a home, in fact, might even be described as a national pastime.

That being the case, if you're considering buying a home, new or resale, you owe it to yourself to get the best home in the best location for the best price and terms that you can. That's where this book comes in. This book is dedicated to showing you the tips that will benefit you as well as the traps that can ensnare an unwary buyer.

Tips and Traps When Buying a Home shows how to avoid expensive problems before they occur. It gives you sound advice on dealing with agents, spotting home defects, negotiating, understanding contracts and closings, and all the other complex issues associated with buying a house. It, literally, points out the traps to avoid, and gives you helpful tips so that your buying experience will be pleasurable both financially and personally.

Who Should Read This Book?

If you are any of the following, you are going to find this book very helpful:

- First-time buyer
- Moving up (selling an existing home to buy another)
- Buying a brand new home

- Buying a resale
- Buying a vacant lot with the intention of building
- Becoming involved with real estate as an investor

This book will show you how to get the best deal for your money and circumstance.

1
Everything Is Negotiable

This whole chapter is just one tip and here it is: *Everything is negotiable when buying a house.* The trouble is that most buyers either don't believe it or don't like it.

Here's a partial list of what's negotiable when you buy a house:

Price

Financing

Closing costs (except where specified by financing or law)

Occupancy (when you get the key and can move in)

Painting (will the seller repaint a portion of or the entire house?)

Repairs (will the seller repair the roof, plumbing, windows, etc., and what kind and quality of repairs will be made?)

Yard (will the seller remove unwanted trees, bushes—put in desired landscaping?)

Fixtures (which lights, fans, appliances, etc. stay and which go?)

Wall coverings (do the drapes stay or go?)

Dog house (does it stay or go?)

Dog or cat (does it stay?)

Furniture (will seller throw in certain pieces?)

Prepaid taxes and insurance (will the seller credit you with these?)

And *everything else.*

While it's true that custom suggests that in certain areas certain things are paid for by the buyer and others by the seller, such as title insurance or escrow costs, or that certain items, such as personal property, do not go with the house, you can throw custom to the winds. Everything, with only rare exceptions, is up for grabs when you buy a home. How much you grab for yourself and how much the seller grabs depends on how well you negotiate.

Of course, that's the rub. Many of us feel at a loss as negotiators. In the back of our minds we know we're going to come out second best and we just don't want to bother. That's the trap.

Negotiation gives the buyer incredible power in making a favorable transaction. It can also place him or her in a position of immense weakness. The fact is that how you negotiate determines whether you get the home of your dreams...or whether those dreams end up being a nightmare.

Negotiating from Weakness

I once had a friend who had an absolute abhorrence for traveling in Mexico, even though her business obligations required that she routinely go there. "Why?" I asked her on one occasion. "Why don't you like traveling in Mexico? The people are friendly, the scenery in many areas is spectacular, and the currency exchange rate for Americans is almost always very favorable. So, what don't you like about it?"

She glowered at me for a moment, then replied, "You never know what the price of anything is in Mexico." She waited for that to sink in, then continued, "You want to buy a pair of shoes. The price written on them may be 65,000 pesos, but you know you should be able to get them for about half, probably 30,000 pesos."

"You try to bargain and the seller gets upset and starts yelling, accusing you of trying to steal food from the mouths of his children. He says you're trying to cheat him and demands the full price. It gets embarrassing. I end up being upset and I don't enjoy myself. Why don't they just ask for 30,000 pesos to begin with?"

I nodded understandingly and said, "But don't you see? The negotiation for the price is a kind of ritual. It's expected that you'll offer less and pay less than the asking price. The seller's insults and threats are just a way of trying to coerce you into paying more. *There's nothing personal in it.* In fact some sociologists have suggested that it's a part of the Latin culture, an opportunity to demonstrate personal strength in a safe and accepted fashion."

She nodded, "Maybe that's why I feel so embarrassed when I end up paying 65,000 pesos for a pair of 30,000 peso shoes."

I told my friend she shouldn't take it so personally. I indicated that when I'd visited Mexico I'd seen a buyer and seller haggle for nearly an hour over the price of some small trinket, hurling accusations of thievery and insults relating to family origin. All of which were immediately forgotten the moment the sale was concluded, at which time both buyer and seller embraced each other as though they were bosom buddies. "Negotiation for price and even terms of sale is the accepted practice in probably 75 percent of the world. It is an ancient and honored tradition."

My friend scowled at me. "It's not a tradition in the United States. When I go into a department store, I know what the price is. There's no shenanigans, no arguing, no negotiations. If a pair of shoes in Macy's is listed at $65, that's the price—no ifs, ands, or buts!"

It was the end of our conversation. My friend was absolutely convinced that negotiating was the bane of third world countries and that it had no place in advanced societies such as our own.

How wrong she was.

Negotiation for price or terms of sale always has been and always will be the rule in any capitalist society. The appearance of fixed prices found in stores in the United States and other industrialized countries is simply a thin veneer of marketing. Most stores, from grocery stores to clothing stores are simply outlets for manufacturer's products. Each store represents a price level. If you don't like that price level, then try the store across the street...or your neighborhood discounter, or super-discounter, or manufacturer's outlet, or catalog store...or.... The price for almost any product will vary depending on the store you are in.

In the United States, where unskilled sales clerks are often the rule, the prices are set per store as a convenience not to you the buyer, but to the seller. Want a different price? Go to a different store. Where skilled sales personnel are employed, such as auto dealerships, negotiation is as alive in this country as it is in the heart of Mexico.

Negotiating in Real Estate

Which brings us back to buying a home. Here, as we've seen, everything is negotiable and the most important variables are usually the price and the terms. If you're a good negotiator, you may end up paying as much as 25 percent or more below what the seller is asking. Or, in some markets, in order to get the home you want you may end up paying 5 or 10 percent more than is being asked, and congratulate yourself on your fine deal!

Negotiation is an inherent part of buying real estate, and if you're going to participate you should plan on learning the basic skills.

Relying on the Agent

At this point, I'm sure some readers are saying, "Hold on, I worked with an agent when I bought my last home. The agent did my negotiating. The agent saw that I got a good price."

I doubt it. I doubt it very seriously. You may have gotten a good price, but if you did, it was largely because of your own efforts. The agent in the vast majority of cases is the *seller's* agent, with a fiduciary responsibility to the seller to find a buyer. In most states it is unethical, if not outright illegal, for the agent to even suggest you offer less than the seller is asking.

This doesn't mean that agents don't, in fact, do this. In my experience many agents do. But, they often couch their suggestions in language such as, "The sellers have indicated that they are anxious to sell and that they'd be agreeable to an offer of a little less than the asking price."

Indeed. The sellers may be desperate and may be willing to take an offer of 25 percent less than the asking price. But, the agent can't come right out and tell you that, because in most cases he or she represents the seller. In addition, the agent doesn't really want you to make a low offer. The lower your offer, the harder it is for the agent to get the sellers to accept, and the less chance there is of getting a commission. The agent only gets a commission when there's a sale. On the other hand, if you offer just a *little bit less*, the sellers will accept your offer in a flash. The agent will be thrilled to make such an easy commission.

So, instead of offering $25,000 less than the asking price, you offer $5000 less...and get it. The sellers are happy, the agent is happy, and you, you big dummy, are happy because you think you got yourself a "good price."

The point is that you can't rely on anyone but yourself when it comes to negotiation. If you are working with a good agent, he or she can handle the actual mechanics of speaking for you to the seller, and that's certainly a big plus. But it's ultimately up to you to determine what the parameters of the negotiation are going to be. You set the price, the terms, and all the other conditions of sale that you will accept.

Embarrassed by Negotiation

Which brings us back to you. Most house-hunters, particularly house-hunters who don't regularly invest in real estate, are worried about hurting the seller's feelings, about insulting the agent by offering a price far lower than the asking price, and most important, about doing anything that would appear foolish.

If that's the way you feel when you open negotiations for the purchase of your next home, you are a gone goose. Remember the example of buying shoes in Mexico? The seller and buyer in third world countries often trade insults for a very long time in haggling over the price. But then, when all is said and done, they shake hands and become bosom buddies.

Well, you may not end up bosom buddies with the seller, but remember that when negotiating for real estate you are participating in that same age-old ritual of bargaining. You are back there under the tent in the wilderness relying on your own cleverness and personal will power.

If you are weak and susceptible to the influence of the seller, or the seller's agent, you could be talked into paying a higher price, getting less favorable terms, or worst of all, accepting a house that you really don't want. On the other hand, if you are a good "horse trader" you are going to get a good deal all around.

Negotiating on a New Home

A few exceptions are in order here. Sometimes you're buying a brand new home instead of a resale. The builder-developer has a set price written in ink on the brochure. Either you pay that price, you are told, or you don't get the home. Right?

It depends. If the market is hot and new homes are selling as fast as they can be put up, yes, you'll have to pay the set price. In fact, in some areas of California people regularly camp out in front of builder-developers' offices for days, just for the privilege of paying full price for a new home!

On the other hand, if the market is slow, there's no reason you can't offer a builder-developer a lower price ... and get it. Just remember that builder-developers often have a relatively small profit margin, and they may not be able to accept a severely reduced price. See a later chapter on buying a brand new home from a builder-developer.

Negotiating with Sellers Directly

Sometimes sellers will bypass the use of an agent and attempt to sell their homes themselves. (In the trade these are called FSBOs—For Sale By Owners.) The temptation is to think that because no agent is involved, the seller doesn't have to pay a commission and, hence, can offer a lower price.

Maybe. On the other hand, you now have to not only set the parameters of your negotiations (price and terms), but you also have to carry out those negotiations face-to-face.

If you're a good horse trader, and if the seller is too, things should go fine and no agent may be needed. But, unfortunately, in our country most of us have been inured to thinking in terms of fixed prices and not in terms of negotiation. Hence, when you offer the seller far less than he or she is asking, you could be asked to leave in not so pleasant terms, and further negotiations might be impossible.

Or, if the seller is a good negotiator and you aren't, when your low offer is rejected, accompanied by suggestions that you've insulted the seller's integrity, you may be put off and leave without realizing that it was all part of the game.

As a result, for the vast majority of people, buying direct from sellers is more difficult and less likely to result in a good price and terms, than dealing with a broker-agent. This is contrary to what the TV "get rich quick" gurus of real estate push. I'll have a lot more to say about working with broker-agents in later chapters.

Learning to Negotiate Successfully

In the old days in real estate, as late as the 1950s, the Latin expression, "caveat emptor" was often quoted: "Let the buyer beware."

Since that time consumer protection laws have swelled to the point where today's buyer who knows how to take advantage of these laws is protected as never before. However, when it comes to the actual negotiations, there are no protections for the buyer. You are at your own mercy: you can make a good deal, or you can get yourself into terrible trouble.

The question naturally arises, therefore, of how a person who is not a real estate professional can negotiate successfully in what may be a den of wolves? How do you avoid cheating yourself by your negotiation inexperience?

The answer is to acquire knowledge. Having read this chapter you've already learned a great deal that you may not have known before. You now know that everything is negotiable. When the agent says, "There's no way you can ask for the refrigerator. It's personal property and goes with the seller automatically." You can stand back, take a deep breath and say with confidence, "Either I get that damn refrigerator or there's no deal!"

Grumbling, the agent will write into the contract that the refrigerator goes with the house, knowing full well that he or she is going to have to fight the seller for hours to get an agreement.

You should now know that there's nothing embarrassing about submitting low offers and making your agent struggle to get the seller to sign. There's nothing wrong with insisting on terms which are totally favorable to you. You should also now know that it's a mistake to let the seller's agent "assist" you in determining the price to offer.

Finally, you should now know that there's nothing foolish about getting down on the ground and scrambling for price and terms. It's an ancient tradition that, regardless of your particular background, is your human heritage. You were born to do it!

Knowledge Is Power

Ultimately, how you fare when buying a home is going to be a direct result of the knowledge you have. The more you know, the better position you'll be in to negotiate from strength.

How do you get that knowledge? In the next chapters you will discover those common and not so common traps that most buyers fall into. You'll also be given tips on what to look for and how to find exactly what you want in a home. Perhaps for the first time in your househunting experience, you will have a tool in hand that is completely dedicated to working for you. The following information aims to see that you get what you want when you buy a home. You'll find no sympathy for agents, sellers, or lenders in this book.

There is only one way to negotiate, and that is to negotiate from strength. There is only one way to get strength—through knowledge. Read on.

2
What You Can and Cannot Afford

Everything is too expensive!

That's been the lament of home buyers for the past forty years. The good news is that isn't true, necessarily. Chances are you can find a house you can afford. The question is, is it the house you want to buy?

What you really need is perspective, a feel for the market—what's available in your general price range.

Tip

You've probably already looked, but the first place to get an initial idea of the market prices in your area is your newspaper. Check out the "house for sale" ads. They will quickly give you an overall feeling for the general cost of homes.

Trap

Don't associate the prices you see in the paper with accurate descriptions of property. Real estate advertising is full of puffery. A "Magnificent Tudor home with guarded grounds" may mean that there are brown wooden slats on the garage and there's an ugly cyclone fence surrounding it. A "Rustic ranch house with enough acreage to spread around" may mean it's in total disrepair and situated on swamp land. You won't be able to associate prices with property until you personally see it. Just use the ads to get a feel for overall pricing.

How Much Can You Afford?

Checking the newspaper ads for homes is often a disquieting experience. Prices usually seem too high. You can't possibly afford to buy a house...or can you? The real question, of course, is what can you actually afford to pay? A price is too high only if you can't afford it.

Tip

Most people can afford to pay far more than they initially believe they can. As we'll see in the next chapter, it's to your advantage to *stretch* when buying a home—trying to get into the most expensive house you can afford usually pays off later on when your income increases and property values appreciate.

There are three elements that determine how much you can afford to pay for a house. They are:

1. Down payment—You will need to have some cash to offer as a down payment.

Tip

Don't even dream about "no money down" purchases. With certain rare exceptions, they never have existed as economically realistic alternatives. The whole concept was dreamt up by marketers to sell books, tapes, and seminars.

2. Mortgage qualifying—In today's market, no one (okay, almost no one) pays cash. Ninety-nine percent of buyers secure mortgages or trust deeds in order to finance their purchases. Therefore, the biggest determiner of how much you can afford is how much you can borrow. The more you can borrow, the bigger the house you can buy.

3. Closing costs—These are almost always present and can be significant, sometimes as much as 5 percent of the purchase price.

We'll consider separately each of the elements that determines how much you can afford.

Down Payment

How big a down payment will you need to buy a home, and where will you get it? The actual down payment requirements will vary depending

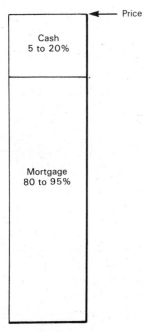

Figure 2-1.

on how the deal is structured and the type of financing you secure. In a typical conservative, conventional loan, without government guaranteed or insured financing, the down payment is 20 percent. If you are buying a $100,000 house, that means you need to come up with $20,000...cash.

From here, we work down. How do you reduce the cash requirement to 15 or 10 or even just 5 percent? There are ways. See Fig. 2-1.

Private Mortgage Insurance

If you have an excellent credit history, and if the house itself qualifies by being in a good neighborhood, in good condition, and considered "prime" by lenders, you may be able to get private mortgage insurance (PMI). This insures the lender against loss in case you default. With PMI you may only need to put 10 percent down or, in some cases, as little as 5 percent.

PMI insurance, however, adds an additional one-quarter percent in interest to your mortgage. Almost any bank or savings and loan can arrange a PMI loan.

Portfolio Lenders

Another alternative is to secure financing from a savings and loan or other lending institution which carries its own portfolio. Most lenders "sell" their loans on the secondary market. That means they recoup 95 percent of the money they originally loaned and just get a small percentage of the interest. A portfolio lender keeps the mortgage and gets all the interest.

Portfolio lenders are allowed by government regulation to reduce the down payment on a small percent of their total loans to 10 percent and in some cases to 5 percent, although most don't do this. Thus, if you can find a portfolio lender, you may be able to secure a lower down payment.

Tip

How to find a portfolio lender? Call. Get your phone book, look up savings and loan associations, also called thrift associations in some parts of the country, and start calling. Ask to talk to a loan officer and ask if they make 5 or 10 percent down loans. If they do, they'll let you know immediately.

Another way to find portfolio lenders is to contact a local broker. In most urban areas brokers receive weekly lists of all lenders indicating their requirements and their offerings, including down payment. A broker with such a list can immediately tell which lender is offering what in terms of down payment and interest rates that week.

Government Assisted Financing

There are several government programs available. The most common is the standard FHA (Federal Housing Administration) loan on single family dwellings. The FHA insures a private lender under this program, and the down payment may be as low as 5 percent. The trouble with FHA loans is that as of this writing the maximum amount of the mortgage is $95,000. In addition, they require you to have excellent credit and to live in the home.

Trap

FHA loans were extremely popular at one time. Recently, however, the FHA has had to take back enormous numbers of properties through foreclosure and as a result has tightened up its requirements. One of these requirements is that the borrower pay the insurance fee for the loan *up front*. In the past this fee could be paid monthly over the life of the loan. The fee can be quite substantial.

Tip

To make this more palatable, the FHA has been allowing lenders to add the fee to the loan amount. You still pay it, but at least it doesn't have to be paid in cash out of your pocket.

The Veteran's Administration also has a loan program (VA loans) which guarantees loans to lenders. It offers true "nothing down" financing. To qualify, however, you must be a veteran having served during certain specified periods. You must also meet strict requirements. Since the times of service change fairly regularly, as do the actual requirements, you should contact the Veteran's Administration to determine if you would qualify for a VA loan.

Seller Financing

Finally, there is always the seller. Oftentimes a seller will be willing to carry a second mortgage, or other level of mortgage, in order to make the sale. You may be able to secure an 80 percent mortgage from an institutional lender and then get another 10 percent from the seller in the form of a carry-back mortgage. Figure 2-2 demonstrates this.

Trap

The basis for much of the "no money down" nonsense that was popularized in real estate a few years ago was to get sellers to carry back all of the down payment—20 percent or more. This put the sellers at a real disadvantage in terms of collateral, and today few if any sellers are foolish enough to consider this. In addition, most institutional lenders will not offer a mortgage unless you put down at least 10 percent with no more than a 10 percent second mortgage on an 80 percent first mortgage. To get around this, a few unscrupulous real estate people suggested lying to the institutional lender and securing a 20 percent or greater second mortgage "under the table" from the seller.

Yes, it can and has been done, but you as a buyer open yourself to enormous liability if you participate in such a scheme. Most institutional lenders are federally insured, and that means that if word ever gets out, the federal government, Treasury or FBI, investigates. Enough said that the penalties for securing a mortgage under fraud are quite severe.

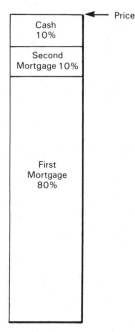

Figure 2-2.

These are your basic alternatives with regard to a down payment. Suffice it to say you will need some payment amount but how much you will need depends on how tenacious and inventive you are in locating lenders willing to make higher percentage loans.

Of course the question now becomes, "Where am I going to get the money for the down payment?" It would be nice if we could simply write out a check. However, most of us are always pressed for cash. Other than a checking or savings account, here are some sources of cash for a down payment which you may not have considered before.

Tip

Sources of cash:

1. Cash value of life insurance (borrowing on it)

2. Refinancing or selling an auto or boat

3. Sale of other physical assets to generate cash

4. Sale of stocks, bonds, or other securities

5. Sale of present home

6. Gifts or loans from relatives or friends

7. Refinancing investment real estate you already own (Must be obtained before applying for loan)

8. Income tax refund

9. Letter of credit or credit line from a bank (Must be obtained before applying for loan)

10. MasterCard, Visa, or other credit card (Must be obtained before applying for loan)

11. "Sweat equity"—offering to fix up a house in return for a reduced down payment

12. Accumulation of funds from your regular income between date of purchase and close of escrow (insist on a long escrow—three months or more)

13. Personal loan on hobby materials, jewelry or furs, cameras, etc.

14. Business loan (must be obtained before applying for loan)

15. Passbook loan (must be obtained before applying for loan)

Trap

Many of the sources of cash listed involve borrowing. However, a requirement of all government insured lenders is that the down payment *not come from borrowed funds.* If you indicate that you are borrowing the down payment, it is almost certain to disqualify you from normal financing.

Tip

Borrow the money *before* you enter into a transaction to purchase a home. That way, you'll have the cash in hand, and borrowing will show up as an existing loan against your credit. There is no restriction against doing this. Be aware, however, that an extra loan against your credit will decrease your ability to borrow on a home. You will be tying up some of your income to pay off the loan. That income won't be available to help you qualify for a home mortgage.

Mortgage Qualifying

The tendency when buying is to think in terms of price, "How high a price can I afford?" A better way to look at it is, "How big a mortgage can I afford?" There are no price restrictions you have to face. But there are mortgage restrictions. You can only get as big a mortgage as you can qualify for. Of course, the size of the mortgage determines the highest price you can pay, unless you can come up with more cash down payment.

Therefore, a big consideration is not price, but mortgage amount. There are a variety of ways to determine just how big a mortgage you can really afford.

Prequalifying Interview

What's become popular recently are prequalifying interviews with lenders. Essentially this just means that you contact a lender such as a savings and loan. A loan officer then does a screening interview. The screening interview is usually one of two forms, informal and formal.

The Informal Screening

This takes about twenty minutes or less. You tell the lender what you make, how much money you have in the bank, and what your credit is like. The lender does some quick calculations and tells you how much money he will lend you toward the purchase of a home.

Trap

In an informal screening you may exaggerate. You may not even know the true answers to some of the questions asked and may guess at them...and end up being quite inaccurate. On the other hand, the lender is in no way committed to anything he or she may say. In other words, the whole interview is an exercise in fantasizing. Yes, you may get a ballpark figure for how much of a loan you can get, and therefore, how big a house you can afford. But, chances are you will be off so significantly that it could lead you to search for a house that is either too high in price for you or one which offers far less in amenities than you want.

The Formal Screening

Here the lender takes a written loan application from you. You are asked to fill out information on every aspect of your financial life going back a good many years. Some of the questions may seem personal. They are. Just grin and bear it. If you want the money, you have to bare your soul.

Once the application is in, the lender may ask for money. You may be asked to come up with around $50 for a credit report.

Trap

If the lender asks for more than $50, for example for prepaid points or document fees or other costs, run, don't walk out of the office. You're being had. On the other hand, a very few lenders don't even require the fee for the credit report, but pick it up themselves!

After you pay the credit report cost and turn in the completed and signed mortgage application, in some cases you may be asked for additional documents. If you're self-employed you may be asked for two years of tax returns. You may be asked for signed statements from banks showing your deposits or a statement from your employer showing your job status. You'll have to turn these in anyway if you end up getting the loan. Most lenders make a commitment assuming that what you've told them is accurate, but some still do insist on actually seeing the documents.

Finally, usually a day or so later, you'll be notified of the size of loan you qualify for from your formal screening. This is a fairly hard commitment. You can usually bank on it. Now you can seriously go househunting.

Tip

Formal screening to prequalify is extremely useful in a hot market where houses are selling as fast as they come onto the market, and sometimes for prices which are higher than the seller is asking. You are at an advantage if you can go into such a transaction with your financing already arranged. You may beat out an equally qualified buyer who doesn't have financing in hand.

Trap

Prequalifying only means that you are assured of a mortgage *from that particular lender.* It may turn out that some other lender may offer better terms. Unless speed is of the essence, you are usually better off waiting until *after* you have signed a purchase agreement and had it accepted by the seller to look for financing. You increase your chances of getting the best financing terms this way. Except in hot markets, you can put a contingency clause in the purchase contract that allows you out of the deal in the event you can't find financing. Most sellers allow this and it's discussed in a later chapter.

Note: For more on mortgage qualifying, see the separate chapter on financing.

Qualifying Yourself

Thus far we have considered how a lender may qualify you for a mort-gage. However, you don't have to go to a lender for this. If you know the parameters you can just as quickly and easily qualify yourself. That's what we're going to do now. The following requires some simple math—percentages, addition, and subtraction. If that's a problem for you, stick with getting qualified by a lender. Otherwise, get your pencil.

To begin, fill out the simple worksheet provided in Fig. 2-3.

The worksheet is deceptively simple and surprisingly accurate. The answer you get should give you a figure fairly close to what a lender would come up with. For example, Fig. 2-4 shows how a typical couple might answer the worksheet.

Tip

If you want to raise the mortgage amount you can qualify for and hence the mortgage amount, pay off credit card and other long-term debt first. For example, you may owe eight more installments on your wash-ing machine. Pay off three installments, now you only owe five. It has changed from long-term to short-term debt.

YOUR MORTGAGE WORKSHEET

Determining your maximum monthly payment

Your combined monthly gross income	$ _____
Less any long-term debt (such as car payments)	− _____
	= _____
Multiply by 0.34 (for an 80 percent loan)	× _____
Multiply by 0.28 (for a 90 percent loan)	× _____
Maximum monthly payment you can afford	$ _____
Less insurance and taxes on the property (an-nual amount divided by 12)	− _____
Maximum monthly mortgage payment you can afford	_____

Figure 2-3.

YOUR MORTGAGE WORKSHEET

Determining your maximum monthly payment

Your combined monthly gross income	$	3000
Less any long-term debt (such as car payments)	−	350
	=	2650
Multiply by 0.34 (for an 80 percent loan)	=	901
Multiply by 0.28 (for a 90 percent loan)	=	742
Maximum monthly payment you can afford	=	$901 or $742
Less insurance and taxes on the property (annual amount divided by 12)	−	150
Maximum monthly mortgage payment you can afford	=	$751 or $592

Combined income—This is both spouses' gross income—the total on your paystubs *before* taxes and other deductions.

Long-term debt—Any debt that is going to take you more than six months to pay off. This includes credit cards.

Figure 2-4.

Multiply by 0.34 or 0.28—These arcane sounding numbers are figures that lenders use to determine your ability to repay. Typically, according to lenders, you can't afford to have a mortgage for more than 28 percent of your gross income if it's 90 percent of the purchase price, or 34 percent of your gross income if it's 80 percent of the purchase price.

Tip

Don't believe it for a minute! People who are good money managers can handle debts as high as 50 percent. Bad money managers can't handle debts as low as 20 percent. The 0.28 and 0.34 numbers lenders use came out of studies done for the Federal Housing Administration in the 1930s and 1940s. They are arbitrary. The easiest way to recognize this fact is to ask why the same person could afford 34 percent of gross income on an 80 percent loan, while only 28 percent on a 90 percent loan? Shouldn't you be able to afford a set amount regardless of the size of the loan?

The reason for the percentages lies in the risk to the lender. Presumably, at 28 percent you are more easily able to make the payment and less of a risk. Nonsense! But, it's nonsense you must abide by in order to get a lender to give you an institutional mortgage.

Non-conforming Loan

You can avoid this problem by getting a "non-conforming loan" from some lenders. This is a loan for 75 percent or less of the value of the property and nobody cares how much you make or what you can qualify for. But beware, non-conforming loans have higher interest rates and often shorter terms.

Private portfolio banks and thrifts sometimes make non-conforming loans, but for the most part they are made by private mortgage lenders. Check your phone book under "Mortgage Lenders."

Trap

Private mortgage lenders are usually private individuals or groups of individuals who are very familiar with the real estate business and who are willing to take risks. While they must be licensed in most states and must abide by many rules and regulations, they are not nearly as well regulated as banks and savings and loans. In addition, they don't have the fancy stone buildings and the highly visible images to protect. Consequently, they may try to stick you with excessive costs, higher than necessary interest rates, and other restrictive or undesirable mortgage terms. When dealing with a private mortgage lender, *always have a real estate attorney working for you.*

Less Insurance and Taxes on the Property

Before calculating the final mortgage payment you can afford, you must take into account taxes and insurance. If you already have a property in mind, find out from the owner, agent, or county assessor what the taxes *will be* when you buy. Find out what the insurance amount will be from an insurance agent. Usually these are given annually. Divide by 12 to get the monthly amount.

Trap

Don't rely on the *current* tax or insurance bill. In many states, property is reassessed when it is sold (Proposition 13 in California). Although this procedure is being challenged in the courts, as of this writing it remains in effect. That means that your property will have a new assessed valuation and, more than likely, higher taxes when you become owner. Also, the present owner may not be insuring the property for full value. You'll want to do that, so your insurance bill also may be higher.

Tip

If you haven't found a property yet, use the following "guestimates" for taxes. First figure the maximum house price you can afford.

In states with low taxes—2 percent of house price

In states with medium taxes—3 percent of house price

In states with high taxes—4 percent of house price

Any agent, escrow officer, loan officer, or real estate lawyer can tell you whether you live in a high, medium, or low tax state.

Maximum Monthly Payment You Can Afford

Be sure you understand this clearly. This is not necessarily the maximum payment you can afford in reality. It's the maximum payment that the lenders think you can afford.

Determining the Maximum Mortgage You Can Afford

Once you know the maximum payment that you can afford, it's relatively simple to determine the maximum mortgage. The chart shown in Table 2-1 gives mortgages for various interest rates based on the monthly payment. The chart works backwards—usually you know the mortgage amount and then use the chart to determine the monthly payment. Here we know the monthly payment and from it the maximum mortgage.

Determining the Maximum House Price You Can Afford

Once again we work backwards. Usually we know the price of the house and then calculate the maximum mortgage. Typically it is 80 percent of the house price.

Table 2-1. Finding Your Maximum Loan

To use the chart, locate the maximum payment you can afford on the left side. Once you have found your maximum payment, read across the top of the chart to the current interest rate. Where the current interest rate intersects with the maximum payment you can afford you will find the approximate mortgage you can afford. (Assumes 30-year loan.)

Monthly pay-ment you can afford	Current interest rate for mortgage loan						
	9%	10%	11%	12%	13%	14%	15%
$ 300	$ 37,284	$ 34,185	$ 31,501	$29,165	$27,120	$25,319	$23,726
$ 400	$ 49,712	$ 45,580	$ 42,002	$38,887	$36,159	$33,759	$31,634
$ 500	$ 62,140	$ 56,975	$ 52,502	$48,608	$45,199	$42,198	$39,543
$ 600	$ 74,568	$ 68,370	$ 63,003	$58,330	$54,239	$50,638	$47,451
$ 700	$ 86,995	$ 79,765	$ 73,503	$68,052	$63,279	$59,078	$55,360
$ 800	$ 99,423	$ 91,160	$ 84,004	$77,773	$72,319	$67,517	$63,269
$ 900	$111,851	$102,555	$ 94,504	$87,495	$81,359	$75,957	$71,177
$1,000	$124,279	$113,950	$105,005	$97,217	$90,399	$84,397	$79,086

We now add taxes, insurance, and down payment. Using Table 2-2, we can calculate the maximum price.

Table 2-2. Finding Your Maximum Price

Find your maximum monthly payment on left, the interest rate on mortgage across the top. Where two figures meet is the *approximate* maximum price you can afford.

Monthly payment	Interest rate				
	9%	10%	11%	12%	13%
$ 500	$ 62,000	$ 58,000	$ 54,000	$ 50,000	$ 48,000
$ 750	$ 92,000	$ 86,000	$ 80,000	$ 76,000	$ 72,000
$1,000	$124,000	$116,000	$108,000	$102,000	$ 96,000
$1,250	$154,000	$144,000	$136,000	$126,000	$119,000
$1,500	$185,000	$172,000	$162,000	$152,000	$142,000
$1,750	$215,000	$202,000	$188,000	$176,000	$166,000
$2,000	$245,000	$230,000	$214,000	$201,000	$190,000

Chart assumes a fixed-rate, 30-year mortgage, 20 percent down payment, 34 percent of income for mortgage payment and taxes, and insurance of 2 percent annually.

Getting the Interest Rate Down

It should be obvious that the amount of mortgage you can afford for any given payment rapidly goes down as the interest rate you have to pay goes up. For example, if you can afford $1000 a month, then at 9 percent you can afford roughly a $125,000 mortgage. However, at 15 percent you can afford approximately an $80,000 mortgage, all at the same monthly payment.

The interest rate on the mortgage is not something you have a whole lot of control over. The cost of borrowing money fluctuates widely, and a lot depends on the timing of your purchase. As recently as 1987 interest rates on owner-occupied homes were as low as 8 1/2 percent. By 1988 they had risen to almost 12 percent.

If interest rates are high when you decide to buy, one alternative is an adjustable rate mortgage. Typically, these offer low initial interest rates as an inducement to make the purchase. Thus far we have only been considering "fixed" interest rates, which are the true interest rate. For adjustable mortgages this rate may be considerably lower.

For example, at a time when fixed rates are at 12 percent, it is not uncommon for adjustable rates to be at 9 or even 8 percent. Think of how much bigger a mortgage and how much bigger a house you can afford with an adjustable at 8 percent than with a fixed rate mortgage at 12 percent.

It's not quite that easy. While lenders were allowed to qualify buyers at their initial rates for adjustable loans in the past, this resulted in many foreclosures when the adjustable rates rose and buyers couldn't make the payments. Today most lenders qualify buyers somewhere between their initial rate for an adjustable loan and the fixed rate. For example, if the fixed rate were 12 percent and the adjustable rate were 8 percent, you might be required to qualify at 10 percent. Even this, however, would mean a bigger mortgage and bigger house for you.

Trap

Adjustable rate mortgages, in general, are traps. They contain numerous pitfalls that the average borrower just isn't aware of. For example, when you get an 8 percent adjustable rate mortgage, the true rate may be 11 or 12 percent. What does that mean? It means that even if interest rates don't go up within a few adjustment periods you'll be paying at the 12 percent interest rate. To put it another way, even if rates don't go up, your monthly payments could increase by 30 percent!

Another trap has to do with negative amortization. Some of the adjustable loans keep the monthly payments down by adding the interest to the principle. In other words, you end up owing more than you borrowed!

There are other pitfalls with adjustable rate mortgages, and these are covered in a separate chapter on financing.

Where to Look for Financing

Thus far we've discussed how to qualify yourself for a mortgage. There remains the question of to whom you go to get that mortgage? Here are some answers:

Savings and Loan associations (thrifts)

Banks

Mortgage bankers (those who fund mortgages themselves)

Mortgage brokers (those who act as agents for lenders)

Credit unions

Insurance companies (usually accessible through mortgage bankers or brokers)

Corporate financing (for transferees through your company)

Letters of credit (from banks or individuals)

Private lenders

Farmers Home Administration

Sources for all of the above can be found in the yellow pages of your telephone book. Check under financing, mortgages, home loans, or related categories.

Closing Costs

Most buyers simply overlook this very real cost. Don't. Closing costs are expensive. Typically they are around 5 percent of the purchase price of the house. If you pay $100,000 for a home, expect to pay about $5000 in closing costs.

These are cash costs. You need to come up with them *in addition* to your down payment. They include:

Points (percentages of the mortgage paid to the lender to compensate for a lower interest rate or for the "work" of making the loan)

Title and escrow charges and document fees

Attorney fees

Other costs.

(We'll examine closing costs much more closely in a separate chapter.)

Tip

There are several methods of reducing, eliminating, or deferring closing costs. One is to have the mortgage amount increased to cover the closing costs. Check with your lender to see if they will do this.

Another is to negotiate the closing costs with the seller *before you commit to the purchase.* Remember, closing costs are negotiable. You and the seller can agree between yourselves that as part of the deal the seller will pay your closing costs.

What are the chances of a seller agreeing to this? Pretty good in a buyer's market where the seller is desperate to unload a house. Not so good in a sellers' market where houses are moving rapidly.

Also, keep in mind that negotiability extends to all areas of the transaction. If you're getting a terrific price the seller is less inclined to pay part or all of your closing costs. On the other hand, if you're giving the seller pretty much what he or she wants in price and the market isn't too tight, then maybe reduced closing costs are possible.

How Much House Can You Really Afford?

As we've seen, the amount you can afford is pretty much arbitrary. It's a function of your ability to repay. The more you can repay, in terms of the monthly payment you can afford, the more house you can get.

Keep in mind that another function of getting a mortgage is your credit rating or your track record in repaying loans. Here, we've assumed right along that it's excellent. If it's not, then most lenders won't make a loan regardless of how much money you make. An exception is a non-conforming loan where only the property has to qualify.

Most people have a ballpark figure in mind when they start house hunting. If you've worked through the worksheets provided with this chapter, you should have a much closer idea. Now, get out there and start looking!

3

How to Find the Right House

It isn't like looking for a needle in a haystack. It's more like looking for one certain piece of hay.

Once you've determined how much of a house you can afford, it's time to start the hunt. You'll want to marshal all the resources at your command to locate the perfect house, particularly since you'll normally have an enormous selection to choose from. However, simply darting about here and there won't do it. You have to set certain parameters. The following is a list of the items you should consider.

Your House Hunting Parameters

1. How many bedrooms are minimum?

Tip

Most houses are three or four bedrooms. You'll probably have to pay a premium for five or more bedrooms. Houses with less than three bedrooms are often more difficult to resell.

2. How many bathrooms are minimum—one, two, three, or more?

Trap

Don't buy a house with only one bathroom. It's particularly difficult to resell.

3. Do you want a newer house with all the amenities of newness, such as better insulation, plumbing, heating and electrical sys-

33

tems, along with fewer repairs? Or will you settle for the comforts of an older home, such as a more established yard, garden, and neighborhood?

4. Are there any special features that you must have? These include: breakfast nooks, work areas in the garage, skylights, wood paneling, etc.

Tip

Try to be as flexible as possible. The more you must have, the more it's going to cost you.

5. Is there a particular school district you want to be in? What about being close to a shopping center?

6. If you're going to commute, what is the *maximum* distance you are willing to drive?

Tip

Get a map. Indicate those areas which are within range, or those which are too far out.

7. Do you want your house to be a two-story, three-story, split-level, or ranch? Or will you accept any format?

8. What about colors? If you can't stand a blue house or a green house or a yellow house, you better recognize this fact up front.

9. Do you want a fireplace? What about a pool? Air conditioning?

Tip

You'll pay substantially more for a pool house. A fireplace and even air conditioning, in many areas are standard equipment these days. Expect to pay less for a house without them.

10. Do you want a big lot? Does it have to have a view? Do you mind being on a busy street? What about a corner lot?

Trap

Big lots are supposed to be better and cost more, but in reality they require much more time, effort, and money to maintain and frequently are harder to resell. A view lot will *always* cost more, but it will bring more on resale. A corner lot means street noise on two sides which is often objectionable. Being on a busy street makes a house almost twice as hard to resell as being on a quiet street.

Getting Started

Okay, you have an idea of what you want, and you're ready to look. Where do you begin? You actually have a limited number of sources for finding just the right house. They include:

1. Checking the paper

2. Driving around looking for "For Sale" signs

3. Talking and working with agents

4. Checking bulletin boards

5. Talking to friends, acquaintances, people at work

Trap

The important thing here is not to reinvent the wheel. When you begin looking for just the right house, what you're really doing is gathering information. You want to learn which neighborhoods you can afford, what those neighborhoods look like, what the traffic and public transportation are like, what about schools and shopping and so forth.

It's a lot of information, and you want to get it the quickest and easiest way possible. One way is to go around investigating by yourself. In a few weeks you'll turn up most of the answers.

An easier way is to contact a good agent. An agent's career involves learning this information. In a single conversation, an agent can impart to you information it would take you weeks to gather on your own. Agents can also be an excellent source for directing you to others who may have knowledge that they don't possess.

Tip

Always, always carry a map with you. When a broker says that the "Maple Heights" and "Laurel Park" areas are affordable, ask for the price range of those areas and then mark it on your map. You'll be surprised how ten minutes later you can't remember whether it was Maple Park or Laurel Heights or what. When an agent tells you about schools or malls or public transportation, mark them on the map. Unless you're very familiar with the area, the information will go in one ear and out the other in moments.

Sniffing Out the Areas

Once you get a broker to whittle down the general areas that are in your price range, do some investigation on your own.

1. Drive the areas. You should look for how people keep up their properties. Are all the lawns nicely mowed? Or are their broken cars and autoparts strewn across lawns? Watch for broken fences, strewn trash, and graffiti; a sure sign the neighborhood is going downhill.

2. Check the public transportation. Stop at the bus or train station and talk to people. Find out how long it *really* takes to commute. If you're going to be driving on a thruway or freeway, wait until rush hour and then drive it yourself. Use a watch to determine just how long it takes you. You may be surprised.

3. Check out libraries, fire stations, police departments, and hospitals as well as malls and grocery stores. Are they convenient and well-located?

4. Once you whittle down the areas even more based on the the items you discovered by driving around, stop, park your car, and start walking. Talk to anyone you meet. Ask about problems in the area, about schools, about bad neighbors. When you're doing this you can also ask if they know of any house not yet listed that might be coming on the market soon. We'll have more to say about this later.

Closing In on the House

By now you should have narrowed down the neighborhoods. You want to live between Ethel Street and Oak Boulevard or in the Pinewood or Horizon Hills or Wildfield tracts. You're ready to find the house. What you need to do is to quickly get a handle on *every* house in your price range in those areas.

Isn't that an overwhelming task? Not really. Be aware that in most areas, 95 percent of the homes are listed with agents. The reason is simple—the vast majority of sellers don't have the time, expertise, or energy to sell their property themselves. Also, it's a fact that buyers rarely purchase a home they "drop into" because of a for sale sign. They often have to be directed to the right home.

So, start with the agents. Have an agent show you the listed houses in your area. We'll go into detail on the best ways to do that in the next chapter.

In addition, check out the FSBOs in the area.

FSBOs

FSBO stands for *For Sale By Owner*. There are always some available in any neighborhood. When the market is hot and houses are selling well, sellers try to avoid paying a commission by selling themselves. When the market is cold and houses aren't selling, sellers eventually give up on agents and try to sell by themselves.

You can drop in on the FSBOs, although sometimes it's best to call first if that's what the sign in front says. Almost always you'll be courteously shown around the property. The troubles don't start until you begin asking about price, terms, and financing.

Trap

Many FSBO sellers have only a vague idea of what their house is really worth in terms of the market. Most often they are asking too much. If you suggest this to them, they may be insulted. In addition, very often they have no idea of how to arrange financing for you. You'll have to handle this yourself. Finally, and most importantly, it is very difficult to negotiate terms or price reductions with them because of the one-on-one relationship between you, the buyer, and them. Unless you're well versed in real estate, it's difficult to deal with FSBO sellers.

Tip

One way of handling FSBOs is to prearrange to have an agent help you out. When you find a FSBO that you like, the agent will step in and handle the negotiations. For this, you will pay the agent a flat fee, usually far less than a full commission, often in the $500 to $2500 range. Or the agent may arrange a partial commission from the seller. Many agents will accept these terms if their only requirement is to negotiate and if you and the seller will sign statements absolving them of responsibility for the ultimate disposition of the deal. See the next chapter on selecting an agent.

My own experience with FSBOs has not been particularly successful. As a buyer, I have walked the streets stopping at FSBOs and talking to sellers. I have tried to buy them for myself. Unless the seller is just trying to sell by owner for a few weeks before listing, the results have almost universally been dismal. Typically a determined FSBO seller wants too much for the property or is inflexible when it comes to the terms. In other words, I can make a better deal on a listed property.

Finding Properties Prior to Their Being Listed

There is another category of property which, though rare, offers great financial opportunities to you, the buyer. That is a property which has not yet come onto the market.

Sellers have a world of reasons for selling. Sometimes it is a well thought-out decision determined over a long period of time. In other cases sudden events such as job-change, illness, or death may cause a quick decision to sell.

Regardless of how it happens, there is always a period of time between when the seller makes the decision, or is close to making the decision, and when she actually lists the property with an agent. I call this the "golden time."

The Golden Time

During the golden time the seller is willing to sell, but hasn't yet fully committed to an agent or anyone else. If you can come in at that point with a reasonable offer the seller is very likely to accept. She will be thinking about all the hassles of selling that you will save her: no agents to deal with, no commission to pay, no time spent showing the property and waiting for buyers. You're a life-saver if you come during that golden period.

Unfortunately, the golden time only lasts a few days to a few weeks. Also unfortunately, it's very hard to learn about sellers who are in that golden time.

Often it's only through friends, acquaintances, or associates at work that you learn that Jim is considering selling his home or Mary is planning to list her property. When you learn of this, act immediately. Contact Mary or Jim that very day or evening at the latest. Tell them you are actively looking to buy a home and would very much like to consider theirs. Will they just let you come over and look?

Then go. Chances are the house will be in a terrible location or will be too small or too big or too crazy. But, every once in a while, it's just right. When it is, strike a deal right there and then. Presumably by this time you know what houses are going for in the area and you know what a good price is. Come to terms and have your agent or attorney handle the paperwork later.

By getting to a house before it gets listed or goes up for sale, you can often save a lot of money and get superior terms.

The Fixer-Upper

There are two reasons people look for fixer-uppers, run-down houses that usually sell for less because of their condition. The first is as an investment. The idea is that you'll go in, do the fix-up work, and sell for a profit.

The second is that a fixer-upper will sell for less in any given neighborhood. Hence, you might be able to get into the neighborhood you want by buying a fixer-upper when otherwise you'd be excluded because of price.

Both reasons are valid. I've bought more fixer-uppers than I'd care to remember and most of the time I've gotten good prices and made a profit on resale. But not always. The most common problem with fixer-uppers is that the buyer, particularly the inexperienced buyer, *underestimates* the costs of repair.

"I'll do it myself!"

The four most invidious words with regard to a fixer-upper are, "I'll do it myself!" "I'll fix: the ceiling, the plumbing, the holes in the wall, the torn wiring, the broken sink and toilet, the gutters, the holes in the roof, the cracked foundation, the broken windows, the leaking pool and pool pump and filter, the doors, the plaster, the...everything!"

The truth is, the most successful fixer-uppers are those who can, in fact, do it all themselves, saving fortunes on repair costs. Unfortunately, the most unsuccessful are those who realize, usually too late, that they don't have the aptitude, knowledge, or tenacity, to do it themselves. Putting in a water heater by yourself, the simplest of fixer-upper jobs, should cost no more than $150 including the water heater and parts. The same job hired out to a plumber will cost upwards of $300 or more. Repairing a roof yourself could cost $1000 in shingles or $2500 to hire someone to do it. Installing floor tile could cost $250 in tile and glue or $1000 to hire it out. See the point?

If you are a fixer-upper person, by all means give it a try. But, if you don't know the working end of a screwdriver or how to strip wire for a plug, forget it. You don't have a chance. If you have to hire it out, the money you saved on the purchase of a fixer-upper will be spent many times over getting the place fixed up.

Tip

Go partners with a renovator when buying a fixer-upper. You'll agree to live in the house for a set period of time, say two years. During that time your partner will fix up the place, then you'll sell for a profit that you'll split. The trick is to find a handy person who's looking to make a few bucks on the side fixing up a property. Of course, you'll have to tolerate living in a house that's never quite finished, but your partner may help with the down payment and the monthly payment, and you could end up living in a property you'd never be able to afford by yourself.

Trap

Be sure you're getting a terrific price when you buy a fixer-upper. In tight markets and in good neighborhoods, run-down houses often go for nearly as much as properties in good condition. That's a rip-off for you, the buyer.

When buying a fixer-upper, be prepared to spend no more than 75 percent or less of the market price of comparable houses. If you spend more, you're not getting a good deal and ultimately you'll probably lose money.

Beware of Over-Built Homes

You're looking at houses in a neighborhood that typically has three and four bedroom, single-story homes. Suddenly you come across a house with two stories and six bedrooms. The owner has "added on." There's an extra bath, a remodeled kitchen. In fact, the house looks like a palace. And the price is palatial.

Nevertheless, it offers so much that you're thinking of some way that you can get into it. Sell the car, the boat, the dog? Work an extra two jobs? You'd do anything to get this wonderful house.

Forget it. The house is a loser, a white elephant. The only reason it looks so terrific is that it's a BMW surrounded by Fords. Put it with other BMWs, Mercedes-Benzes, and Rolls Royces and it'll look common.

There are relatively few things that an owner can do to add on to a house and still recoup the money invested. Remodeling a kitchen is one.

But start adding floors and rooms, and very quickly the house becomes overbuilt—the neighborhood doesn't justify the work that was done.

Typically in such a situation, the owners are asking far less than the actual expenses incurred while remodeling, but far more than surrounding houses cost. It's going to take them a very long time to find a buyer, and if you're that buyer, it's going to take you a very long time when you want to resell.

Trap

Buyers look for location first, the building second. If a house is too big or overbuilt for a location, it becomes a problem. You don't want to purchase someone else's problem.

Tip

Buy the least expensive house in the most expensive neighborhood. If you do, you multiply your chances for making money later on when you resell.

Househunting Hints

As you go from house to house, remember that a big factor is exhaustion. It's not just being physically tired, it's the fact that after a while all the houses start to look the same. Therefore, it's a good idea to keep in mind the following:

1. *Always take a notepad and map with you.*   Mark the location of the house on the map and write down special features on the pad. If the owner offers you a fact sheet, *save it*, even if you don't seem interested in the house at the time. Later on, you may think about it and realize it had more appeal than you at first thought.

2. *Never look at more than three houses at one time.*   After that, you're no longer being careful. You're just running through, not paying attention to the details that could make you fall in love with a place.

If you need to see a lot of houses, take big breaks. See three in the morning, then stop and have lunch. See three more, then stop and do something else. See three more in the evening. Nine houses in one day is the absolute capacity of almost any prospective buyer. Even with nine, the features of one will begin to blend in with the features of another.

3. *Get a camera and snap pictures of the houses that appeal to you.*   A picture is worth a thousand words. You'll instantly remember the fea-

tures of a house once you see a picture of the outside or some room inside. Frequently agents or owners will provide you with photocopied pictures.

4. *Sketch floor plans that you like on your notepad.* It helps you to remember and is also a good means of comparing one house with another.

5. *Don't be afraid to ask questions.* Many buyers worry that they'll be thought foolish if they ask about drain pipes or washrooms or taxes or something they think everyone else knows about. There are no foolish questions, only foolish buyers who don't ask questions. A seemingly simple question may open up a whole line of concern that you weren't aware of.

Tip

It's far better to ask about the problems of a house before you buy than to be stuck with them after you own it.

4
Picking the Right Agent

Most people think picking real estate agents is like picking apples out of a barrel. There are going to be a few shiny ones here and there, a few bad ones on the bottom, but overall they are going to be pretty much the same. Unfortunately, that's simply not true. Yes, there are always a few bad apples, but the real distinction has not so much to do with ethics but with competence. Some agents are competent, but many are not.

It's important to understand what I mean by competent. I'm not talking about understanding the laws of your state with regard to licensing of agents or the selling of real estate. Today most states have strict tests that agents must pass as well as continuing education to make sure they understand what their legal and fiduciary responsibilities are. In this sense the overwhelming number of agents are able. It's when it comes to serving your needs that most fall down.

My father, who was a successful agent for over 30 years, used to say, "When I first got my license, I thought I was ready to sell real estate. It wasn't until 10 years later that I finally learned how to really be an agent."

To understand what he meant, it's important to understand just what's involved in being a real estate agent. Once you see the selling of property from the agent's perspective, you'll get a whole new view of how to pick the right agent.

What It Means to Be a Real Estate Agent

According to Hollywood, the real estate agent drives a Mercedes or at worst a Caddy or BMW. He or she, most agents are women, meets clients over cocktails, attends flashy parties with lenders, and makes oodles of money —certainly into the six figures.

The truth is somewhat less exciting. According to several surveys, the average agent in 1987 made under $20,000 a year. In addition, out of that $20,000 the agent paid for:

A business automobile

Gas and maintenance for that car

Phone

Dress clothes for work

Other expenses involved in operating a business

In other words, after expenses, the average real estate agent was pretty close to, if not below, the poverty line in terms of income *from real estate.*

"How can that be?" I'm sure you're asking. The agents you've met always seem so successful.

The truth? It's mostly a front. A lot of agents simply work hard at looking good.

You also have to understand that real estate is actually a second or part-time career for many individuals. It attracts an enormous number of people who are looking for less than full-time work. Typically these are people who have retired from another profession such as teaching, the military, government, or large corporations, and are now on a pension and looking to pick up a few extra bucks. Often these people have dabbled a little in real estate and are in an office as much to look for bargains for themselves as to service you or other clients. These people in the trade are called "inactive" agents.

The real trouble is that because an inactive agent often has another steady source of income, he isn't "hungry" enough to get out there, find the really good houses, and negotiate the toughest deals. After all, whether he makes a sale or not, he knows he'll survive...because of his pension.

How many inactive agents are out there? The easiest way to tell is to remember the 80/20 rule. Every real estate broker, and I was one for many years, knows that 20 percent of the agents sell 80 percent of the property. The corollary is that 80 percent of the agents are only selling 20 percent of the property. That big 80 percent represents the "inactive" group.

The Hot 20 Percent

On the other hand, let's talk about that 20 percent who are making the vast majority of deals. These are the "active" agents. Typically they are aggressive, often relatively young individuals who have no means of support other than real estate. To put it bluntly, if they don't make deals, they don't eat.

If you were to isolate this group of individuals, you would find that they typically make over $60,000 a year, and probably half of them make well into six figures. They are out there beating the bushes from dawn till dusk. They look at *every* new house that comes on the market in their area. They are constantly "farming" (talking with potential sellers) to get listings. When they get an offer, they go in there and negotiate all night if necessary to get the seller to either accept or compromise.

Is this the agent you want working for you? You bet it is!

Separating the Active from the Inactive Agents

Okay, you want an active agent. How do you get one?

First off, remember that an active agent is *active*. He or she should:

1. Have a number of properties listed

2. Be always working tirelessly—evenings and weekends

3. Be extremely familiar with the market in your area

4. Be ready and able to show you numerous sales made *in the past few months*

5. Be busy with real estate—but not too busy to show you houses

Tip

Recommendations by friends is a good method of finding the active agent. If your friend has had a good experience with an agent, it's a good sign. But, remember, it's not a guarantee. Your friend might have just been lucky and fallen into the perfect house. The agent's efforts could have been incidental. Even with a recommendation, you need to be sure you've got an active agent.

Active vs. Inactive Offices

Just as there are two types of agents, there are also two types of offices: the active office where sales are constantly happening, and the inactive office where the agents sit around and commiserate with one another about the slow (to them) real estate market.

There are a few good ways to tell the two types of offices apart:

1. An active office almost always advertises heavily. Check the ads in your local paper.

2. An active office usually has quite a few agents, and they always seem to be scurrying around, not sitting at their desks drinking coffee and reading the sports section of the paper.

3. An active office usually has promotions going on to induce greater activity from agents. Walking in, you will often see "sales person of the month" and "lister of the month" awards, TVs or trips to Hawaii for the best producer of the season, and so forth.

4. Other agents will know of the active offices and often will speak grudgingly of them as people who are always getting the deals done.

5. This is just a personal observation, but I have found that active offices usually have a secretarial staff. The agents are out there selling, the staff handles the paperwork. In an inactive office, without many sales or much revenue, it seems the agents are stuck with all the secretarial duties.

Just keep in mind that the 80/20 ratio still applies even in an active office. It's just that in an inactive office, the hot 20 percent aren't there.

How to Find an Active Agent in an Active Office

If you walk into an active real estate office chances are eight to two against your getting an active agent. The reason is that all agents "pull floor time." This is time they are allowed to sit in the office and pick up potential clients who come over the transom. You walk in and you get the current floor agent or, if there's a receptionist, the next agent who is "up."

You'll immediately know this person. How? While other people in the office smile at you, they'll quickly come up, introduce themselves and ask how they can be helpful.

Since almost all agents, active or inactive, are people oriented, they almost certainly will be polite, charming, and apparently helpful. But, if this person is an inactive agent he or she is wasting your time.

Tip

When you walk into a real estate office cold, don't accept the first agent that comes to see you. Rather, say that you are waiting to see someone, an agent, but you can't remember the name. Now, while the receptionist or the floor agent begins listing the names of the agents in the company, *look around the walls of the reception area.* As noted, a great many active companies will have "agent of the month" awards hanging there. Very frequently, the award for the past 10 or 12 months will have gone repeatedly to one agent. Just point to the plaque and say, "That's her," or, "That's him." You'll be quickly introduced to the most active agent in the office.

Tip

If there are no awards, then *ask to see the broker.* It's important to understand that all real estate offices are organized around one person, the broker. Everyone else is an associate agent. Other brokers may even have their licenses subordinated to the main broker.

In a small office, the broker acts as a salesperson. In a larger office, however, the broker typically sits somewhere in a back office and handles closings and other difficult work. In a very large office, the broker frequently may be out making big deals while subordinate brokers handle the day-to-day work.

When you ask to see the broker, you are usually asked in response, "Will your name be recognized by our broker?" In other words, do you have an appointment?

Just reply, "My business concerns one of your agents. I only want to speak to the broker."

Just the hint that there could be some problem will get you an audience. Real estate companies dread complaints or angry clients. Most will bend over backwards to avoid any kind of dissatisfaction.

When you are ushered in to to see the broker or the person who is in charge at the moment, in the case of a very large office, carefully explain that you have not yet talked to any agent in the office. This avoids the problem of having one agent or another claim that you are their client. Tell the broker you are going to be buying a house in the very near future and you want to deal with *the most active agent in the office* in terms of sales. No one else will do.

The broker may chuckle at your boldness but in most cases will tell you who that agent is. And, you're on your way. If the broker refuses, leave. There are almost as many real estate companies to choose from as there are houses for sale.

Trap

Don't be misled into picking your agent on the basis of the real estate company's name and supposed reputation. Over the past few decades franchising has proliferated in the real estate market. But a real estate franchise is no better and no worse than a fast food franchise such as McDonald's or Burger King. All that you are assured of in a fast food franchise is that you will get a certain *minimum* quality of hamburger and service. The same holds true for real estate franchises.

In nearly every state each real estate office, regardless of the franchise name, is individually owned and operated. What you're dealing with is the local broker and agents who have adopted the sign, the coat, and the procedures of a franchising company. Ultimately, the franchise office is neither better nor worse than a non-franchised office in providing you with good, active agents—it just has name recognition, more advertising clout, and, sometimes, nicer jackets. Agent for agent, I don't feel there's a significant difference. Some franchises offer their own financing and escrows which can be a sort of plus. But typically their financing comes from a lender who's allowing them to use the lender's name, and, in my opinion, it's always better to use an independent escrow.

It's important to remember that real estate, almost more than any other business, is highly personalized. The deal you get will depend mostly on the one person with whom you deal. You can get a great active agent with a non-franchised company just as well as you can with a franchised company.

After You Find the Active Agent

Once you find an active agent, you must decide whether or not she is right for you. Watch for obvious problems such as personality clashes or basic differences in outlook. In addition, you want to be sure that the agent isn't so aggressive that she overwhelms you. You want to be able to control your agent, not the other way round. Remember your agent influences your decision by what she does or does not say. Be sure that the agent isn't using this power to manipulate you into something you may not want.

Tip

Try to work with several agents, but only *one at a time*. If you are going to be looking at property on Saturday and Sunday, work with only one agent on Saturday. Then on Sunday, use a second agent, being up-front by telling that second agent with whom you've already worked and the properties you've already seen. Ask the second agent if he has something different to show you.

There are two reasons for doing this. First, while nearly all properties listed by agents are put on the Multiple Listing Service (MLS) where nearly all agents can work on them, some really good properties are kept as "pocket listings," often against MLS rules. Unless you work with several agents, you won't be exposed to these pocket listings.

Second, understand that the agent who first shows you the property you eventually buy may be entitled to a portion of the commission even if a different agent eventually makes the sale. This could cause hard feelings or even problems later on should a different agent submit the offer. Instead of working hard to negotiate the best price and terms for you, the various agents could get into a squabble over who gets what portion of the commission.

Work with only one agent at a time and tell that agent the properties you've already seen and who else you've worked with. It will save you time and possible problems later on.

Trap

Years ago, before the consumer protection movement was even dreamt of, I knew an agent who had a very aggressive style. He would get his clients in his car, which was connected with his office by two-way radio—this was before cellular phones. He would then take them out looking at properties.

After he had exhausted his immediate list of properties, he would call his office and his secretary would look up other properties for them to see. This impressed some clients.

They would continue to look until the clients were exhausted and asked to be taken back to the office where their car was located. He would refuse! Oh, he wouldn't exactly say, "No!" Instead he'd tell them about some other house that was just around the corner and was just right for them. He literally kept them prisoner in his car until they finally agreed to make an offer!

Of course, they could have made him stop and then gotten out. But more often than not they were new to the area and had no idea where they were.

While some clients did get angry and refuse to consider anything until he brought them back, a surprising number actually were coerced into making offers. The agent formerly worked for a used car dealer where he would tell prospective buyers that their present car was blocking a driveway and that he'd move it. When they handed him the keys, he'd throw the keys on the roof of the building and then tell them that their only way home was with a new car.

Fortunately, today such actions are unheard of, but the story illustrates an important point. Some agents are more actively aggressive than you want or can handle. If that's the case, run, don't walk away. They'll coerce you into bad deals every time.

The Agent's Responsibility May Not Be to You!

This is a most important point that most buyers simply don't understand. Let's say that you've found an active agent whom you like and with whom you can work. You must now come to grips with the fact that in most cases this agent *does not work for you*. She is the agent of and works for the seller.

It doesn't matter that your agent shows you around to many houses listed by other agents in the Multiple Listing Service where agents pool their listings. It doesn't matter that the house you decide to make an offer on has a separate agent who listed it. This can be confusing to buyers, particularly when very often there is one agent (yours) who shows you a house and who takes your offer, and another agent (who listed the property) who seems to represent the seller. Usually the agent who shows you around is the "subagent" of the agent who listed the property. In other words, they are very often *both* the agents of the seller.

The law of agency in all states is quite clear. It requires that an agent maintain a *fiduciary* relationship with whomever that agent represents. In most cases, that's the seller.

Thus, if the "subagent" who's been showing you around takes an offer from you and presents it to a seller, who is represented by a listing agent, both of these people still have a fiduciary relationship not with you, but with the seller.

What does having a fiduciary relationship mean? It means that the agents owe the seller, "integrity, honesty, and loyalty."

That translates into this:

1. Unless the seller has authorized it, your agent can't disclose how much less than the selling price the seller might take, even if the agent knows of a specific figure. This isn't to say that many agents don't hint at this, but they can't come right out and tell you, for example, that the seller said, "My price is $100,000, but I'm so desperate to sell, I'd take $75,000, *but don't you dare tell that to any buyer!*"

2. The agent can't disclose that the seller might accept terms more favorable to you, unless the seller has authorized the agent to tell you.

3. On the other hand, if you tell the agent that you're desperate to buy, that even though you're offering $75,000, you'd be willing to pay $80,000, the agent is *obligated* to tell the seller what you said. Working with a seller's agent is almost like having an enemy spy in your camp.

Of course, in actual practice there is some bending of the rules. The Realtor's Code of Ethics, that is supposedly adopted by all agents who join that national organization, stresses that the agent will work fairly for both buyer and seller.

Nevertheless, in today's world where consumers are so litigious, many agents are hesitant to do anything which a seller might construe as violating the fiduciary relationship, and which might result in a law suit against them. Hence, when you work with a seller's agent or subagent, don't expect to get advised on how to get the best terms or price.

Tip

When you're working with a seller's agent, even one you consider on your side, button your lips. Don't tell the seller's agent the highest you'll go on an offer. Don't let the agent know the best terms you'll give the seller. Think of the agent as the seller's earphone. Don't whisper anything in the agent's ear that you don't want the seller to hear. Keep your own confidences.

Dual Agents

There is no easy solution to the problem of agency for buyers. One answer, however, that is gaining increasing popularity in some areas of the country is to have a "dual agent."

A dual agent represents both buyer and seller. This agent owes both the sellers and you, "Integrity, honesty, and loyalty." However, the dual agent still *may not tell you if the seller will accept a price less than the property is listed for.* However, to compensate for this, the dual agent may also not tell the seller that you'd be willing to pay more than the price you offer. The same generally holds true with terms.

Thus, while the dual agent really isn't 100 percent on your side, he also isn't 100 percent on the seller's side either.

Trap

Don't assume that just because your agent isn't the lister of the property, that he or she is a dual agent. Your agent could be the subagent of the lister.

To be sure that you are dealing with a dual agent, that agent should give you a written letter stating exactly the relationship. Many states require a formal disclosure as part of their agency law. California, for example, requires dual agents to give a signed statement to that effect to both buyer and seller.

Tip

An agent *cannot* generally perform as a dual agent unless she has the express written consent of *both* buyer and seller. Without that express written consent, the presumption is usually that he or she is the agent of the seller.

Buyer's Agents

As if it isn't confusing enough already, there is yet another designation of agent, a buyer's agent. This is an agent who truly works for you, the buyer. After all, if sellers can have their agents, why can't buyers?

There's really no reason. It's done all the time in large investment deals. The only problem, usually, is one of cost. If you want a buyer's agent, you may have to pay the commission yourself.

At this point I'm sure some buyers are ready to hurl this book out the window. Pay a commission when you buy? In addition to the cost of the house, the down payment, the closing costs, and on and on...add to that the cost of a buyer's agent's commission? That's crazy!

Not really. There are advantages and, sometimes, there are ways to avoid paying anything more than you'd otherwise pay on a purchase.

The advantages are that a true buyer's agent has a fiduciary responsibility to you, not to the seller. The agent must tell you everything to your advantage known about the property and about the seller, including any information about the seller's willingness to accept a lower price or better terms. You might save the commission or more on just this information.

In addition, the buyer's agent's fee is usually half of a full commission. If the commission rate in your area is six percent, the buyer's agent's commission may be only three percent. Often a deal can be worked out where the seller agrees to pay your agent half the commission and the seller's agent the other half. Thus, it may not cost you any more than if you hadn't worked with a buyer's agent.

Tip

Agents who are willing to represent buyers tend to be few and far between, but they do advertise in phone books and in newspapers. In addition, regular seller's agents in almost every area know of them and usually are willing to at least let you know who they are, if not recommend them to you, once you make it plain that's what you want.

Further, buyer's agents are adept in working out the commission with the sellers. As a result, very frequently, it doesn't cost you any more to use a buyer's agent than to use a seller's agent or a dual agent.

Should you use a buyer's agent? The vast majority of buyers don't, and that's unfortunate. The only way to get an agent really on your side, is to use a buyer's agent. I wholeheartedly suggest you look for one when you get ready to buy.

The Bad Apples

As noted earlier, there are always a few bad apples. These are agents who are either outright crooks or who are so unaware of real estate laws that they can cause you harm in a deal. How do you avoid these?

Fortunately, in most cases the bad apples don't last long. After a few deals they often mess up so badly that there are letters of complaint to the state real estate regulatory body. This body either revokes the license or disciplines the agent. The danger is that you might run into one of these before they get thrown out. How do you protect yourself?

I wish I had a surefire answer. Here are some standard tips for picking any person to whom you give your confidence in financial dealings:

1. Find out how long the agent has been in the business. Even if the salesperson has only been in business a few years the office should have

been around a long time. Only do business with an agent or office that has a long track record, five to seven years at the least.

2. Work with a national franchisee. While earlier I stressed that this is no guarantee you'll get an active agent, it does give you some assurance of at least minimal quality in terms of procedures. Besides, if the agent should be truly incompetent and negligent, you can always appeal to the national office of the chain.

3. Ask to see the agent's real estate license. In all states, agents *must be licensed* and that license must be prominently displayed in the agent's office. He or she will be pleased to show it to you.

In truth, most buyers are only going to consider the above three suggestions, plus recommendations of friends. However, if you're really concerned, here are some additional steps you can take to find out about an agent's background:

4. Check with the local Better Business Bureau or, in an extreme case, the local district attorney's office to see if there are now pending or have ever been any complaints against the agent or the office.

5. Call the state real estate department and ask if the agent's license has ever been revoked or suspended or if the agent has ever been disciplined. This is public information to which you are entitled.

Quite frankly, few buyers will ever do this. In most cases we tend to accept a friendly smile and a solid handshake as evidence of competence and honesty. And in most cases things work out just fine. Remember, however, we are now considering those very few bad apples.

Trap

The worst thing that you can do is to find out you've been dealing with a bad agent after something has happened—after you've made an offer that has somehow gone awry and it has resulted in a money loss to you or the threat of a lawsuit from the seller or some other injured party. A few calls may quickly tell you that this agent has been in hot water since getting a real estate license. Then you'll say to yourself, "If only I had investigated first!"

Remember, it only takes one or two phone calls to the right people and perhaps fifteen minutes of time to at least get a minimal background check on the person who is going to advise you on what is probably the biggest investment you'll make in your life.

Trap

The truth is, you can never be completely sure. I recently learned of an agent who was falsifying loan documents. This person was telling buyers they could get financing that they obviously could not qualify for, and was getting it. We'll call him Jim. Jim was securing false verifications of employment, which your employer fills out giving your salary, and false verifications of deposit, which a bank or S & L fills out giving the cash that you have on hand for a down payment. A lender bases a loan on both these verifications. Since most loans today are sold in the secondary market to government agencies, to falsify them is a federal offense investigated by the Federal Bureau of Investigation or the Treasury department. Fraud here is a serious offense.

Jim was blithely falsifying these documents for buyers, telling them not to worry, it was done every day, that it was just a formality and that they'd never have anything to worry about. The interesting thing is that Jim had been doing it successfully for over seven years. He was considered one of the most successful members of the real estate profession, a pillar of the community.

Perhaps he might have gone on another seven years, but circumstances eventually did him in. As it turned out he was doing more and more deals with more and more people who couldn't really qualify for mortgages, and the lenders never suspected fraud until there was an upturn in interest rates. Since in Jim's case the vast majority of mortgages he was placing involved adjustable rates, where the interest rate and monthly payments vary according to the economic climate, an upturn in interest rates meant the people to whom he had sold houses were suddenly faced with higher payments. Since they hadn't really been qualified at the original payments, the higher payments were overwhelming. Many of them couldn't pay and their mortgages went into foreclosure.

A secretary for one of the secondary lenders who was going through paperwork happened to notice that a lot of foreclosures in the area involved borrowers who had originally purchased homes through Jim. An investigation was quietly launched. It was a simple matter to go back several years and check on the verifications of deposit with banks and S & Ls and the verifications of employment with employers. It quickly became clear that outright fraud had been committed.

As a result, Jim, in disgrace, was brought to trial and his real estate business shut down. But what was worse, the buyers were likewise charged with fraud. That meant that they were personally subject to any losses that the lenders incurred in the foreclosures, as well as subject to civil and criminal penalties.

The moral of this story is that a bad apple once in a great while can appear to be a shiny, bright apple. Of course, as P.T. Barnum and later W.C. Fields were heard to say, "You can never cheat an honest man." If those buyers had really thought it through they would never have allowed Jim to falsify their verifications.

Picking the right agent is certainly the second most important decision you'll make, after picking the right house. Take the time to make that decision wisely.

5
Inspecting
the House

Thus far we've detailed what to look for in selecting a house. Now, we're going to spend more time going over evaluating the house you select. After all, just because it's standing doesn't mean that it isn't ready to fall over.

In the past the dictum, "Let the buyer beware!" was the rule in house-hunting. Today, however, consumerism has turned the tables. Today it's, "Let the seller beware." Sellers in many areas of the country must present to you, the buyer, a disclosure listing any and all faults with the house *before you make a purchase offer*. While sellers may know many of the home's problems (such as bad neighbors or leaky plumbing) they may know next to nothing about the house's heating system or even its foundation. For that reason many sellers hire a house inspector to issue a report.

If you get the seller's disclosure statement coupled with the report of a professional housing inspector (described in an earlier chapter), you have a pretty good idea of the condition of the property. But what if you don't? What if your state doesn't require such elaborate disclosures? Or what if the seller simply fills out the disclosure and doesn't bother to hire an inspector?

You can always simply go through with the purchase and if anything major turns up later on, sue the seller and the agent—a decidedly poor approach. Or you can hire an inspector yourself and make that a condition of the purchase. Or, you can inspect the property on your own.

The last of these options is definitely the cheapest, but not necessarily the best, since you may not be particularly skilled in determining problems. However, if you do decide to do it on your own, here is a checklist of items to look for.

Note: Many of the items on this list require the eye of a skilled workperson to determine if they are a problem. You may want to enlist the services of various skilled workpeople, particularly with the electrical and heating systems.

Tip

Make an inspection before you make a purchase offer. The home inspection checklist that follows will guide you through your inspection step by step. If you want to make it after a purchase offer has been accepted by the seller, make this inspection a "contingency" of the offer. See the next chapter for an explanation of contingencies.

Home Inspection Checklist

Drainage

Drainage problems can lead to cracked foundations and slabs. They can cause a house to shift, particularly if it's located on a hillside, and in extreme cases, can cause the actual collapse of the home.

The correction of drainage problems is best left to experts, however, even a beginner can usually tell where drainage problems exist:

	YES	NO
1. Is there dampness under the house? (The basement should be dry as dust.)	[]	[]
2. Are there footprints or ribbed patterns in the dirt under the house indicating that when it rains, water creeps in?	[]	[]
3. Is there mold (black or green) on wood under the house indicating heavy moisture?	[]	[]
4. Does the ground outside slope away from the house? (If it slopes into the house, you've got serious problems.)	[]	[]

Foundation

The concrete foundation is what supports your house. Usually there is a peripheral foundation which goes around the entire edge of the home. Within this peripheral foundation there may be concrete blocks supporting the floor in a wood floor home or a concrete slab in a cement floor home.

The peripheral foundation, also called footings, extends upward perhaps a half-foot or more from the ground to where the wood frame of the house begins. It also extends downward into the soil. The further down the foundation extends and the wider it is, the better. In areas with expansive soil (the soil swells when wet) or other soil problems, a minimum depth for the concrete foundation should be 16 inches by 8 inches wide. In areas with freezing weather, this may need to go even deeper.

In addition, there should be steel rods in the concrete. The steel holds the concrete together. Cement by itself will crack easily.

Cracks in the foundation can lead to uneven floors inside the house. It can also lead to slippage down a hillside as well as to broken windows and cracks appearing in walls and ceilings.

Some breakage of foundations happens naturally over time. However, severe breakage indicates a problem which could get worse.

	YES	NO
1. Do you see cracks in the foundation when you walk around the exterior of the house? (Hairline cracks always occur and should be disregarded.)	[ ]	[ ]
2. Are the cracks wider at the top than at the bottom? (This indicates actual breakage, a serious problem if the top of the break is a 1/4 inch or more.)	[ ]	[ ]
3. Is there an actual separation in the foundation? (This indicates not enough steel reinforcement was used when the foundation was built.)	[ ]	[ ]
4. In a slab house, does the floor feel uneven when you walk over it indicating cracks hidden under carpets or tiles?	[ ]	[ ]
5. Under a house, do any of the girders sag? This indicates that the foundation has slipped.	[ ]	[ ]

Roof

The purpose of the roof, besides providing an aesthetic look, is to keep rain and snow out of the house. The cost of repairing a roof can be high, of replacing a roof enormous ($3000 to $10,000 as of this writing). You want to be sure that the roof is in good shape. If it's not, you may want to have the seller fix or replace it or make an adjustment to the price.

Some general information on roofs is in order.

Wood Shake Roofs. Depending on the thickness of the shake, they can last 20 to 30 years. If the house you are buying has a wood shake roof and it's 20 years old or older, check the roof very carefully. (Note: Shake roofs are banned in some areas because of the fire hazard they pose.)

	YES	NO
1. Are there pieces of the roof lying on the ground around the house? (This is an obvious bad sign.)	[ ]	[ ]
2. Using binoculars can you see missing shingles anywhere on the roof?	[ ]	[ ]
3. Are there any signs of leakage in the ceiling or walls inside the house?	[ ]	[ ]

Composition shingles. Made of tar or some similar composition, they have a lifespan of from 15 to 30 years, depending on the quality.

	YES	NO
1. Is the *color* of the shingles good or are they starting to fade (a sure sign of wear)?	[ ]	[ ]
2. Are the edges of the shingles curling up? (A sign of wear in hot climates.)	[ ]	[ ]
3. Are there any bare spots on the roof?	[ ]	[ ]
4. Are there any signs of leakage in the ceiling or walls inside the house?	[ ]	[ ]

Aluminum shingles. These have a lifespan of 50 years. Generally they don't wear out unless they have been damaged.

	YES	NO
1. Are there signs of fading or peeling of their color? (The shingles may continue to keep the weather out, but will look terrible.)	[ ]	[ ]
2. Are there any dents or separations in the shingles indicating someone has walked on them?	[ ]	[ ]
3. Are there any signs of leakage in the ceiling or walls inside the house?	[ ]	[ ]

Tiles. Tile roofs last indefinitely (80 years or more). However, they can easily be broken and once broken, loose their ability to keep the weather out.

	YES	NO
1. Are any of the tiles broken?	[ ]	[ ]
2. Have any fallen off?	[ ]	[ ]

3. Are there any signs of leakage in the ceiling or walls
inside the house?   [ ]   [ ]

Paint

Interior.   In a resale, don't expect to get a house that doesn't require
repainting. As soon as the seller's furniture gets moved out, you're going to see whole areas that need repainting. The only question is, will
you do it or will the seller?

	YES	NO
1. Are there marks on the walls?	[ ]	[ ]
2. Is the current paint in good condition or is it flaking indicating it will have to be sanded before new paint can be applied?	[ ]	[ ]
3. Are the colors light? (Covering dark colors may require two or more new coats.)	[ ]	[ ]

Exterior.   Weathering is the problem here. Even the best paints usually don't last more than five to seven years. Repainting the exterior is
often more expensive than the interior since it often requires removing
chipped and peeling paint.

	YES	NO
1. Is the paint chipped or peeling?	[ ]	[ ]
2. Are the colors faded? (Faded colors indicate paint that is aging.)	[ ]	[ ]
3. Is the caulking around windows starting to fall out?	[ ]	[ ]
4. Is the aluminum siding firm, not becoming detached?	[ ]	[ ]
5. Are the gutters falling? Is the paint on them peeling?	[ ]	[ ]

Plumbing

In general, you need an expert to tell you if there are serious plumbing
problems. There are, however, some telltale signs you can check for:

	YES	NO
1. Is the plumbing copper instead of galvanized steel? (Galvanized steel lasts about 30 years, sometimes less—copper lasts virtually forever.)	[ ]	[ ]
2. Are there leaks at the joints of galvanized pipes? (These are usually visible under the house or in the garage; they indicate electrolytic action may be cor-		

roding the pipes and they may need to be replaced—
$5000 or more.)   [ ]   [ ]

3. Are there leaks under the sinks in any of the bathrooms or in the kitchen? (Possibly a minor problem,
but why should you have to fix it?)   [ ]   [ ]

4. Is the water heater old? (The date is sometimes
stamped on the label—a water heater rarely lasts
more than seven years.)   [ ]   [ ]

5. Does the water heater have a safety valve? (This is vi-
tally important. If you're not sure what a safety valve
is, have a professional check it out.)   [ ]   [ ]

In addition, the gas supply line needs to be checked. A professional
should do this.

Wiring

This is the venue of the professional. Don't attempt to make a judgment
on the wiring unless you're an electrician. Some danger signals to watch
for include:

	YES	NO
1. Do switches or sockets spark when used?	[ ]	[ ]
2. Are there inoperative lights or switches?	[ ]	[ ]

Heating

Even more than in the case of wiring, a professional needs to check it
out. If you're using gas, you need to be sure that there are no leaks.
Here are some telltale signs to look for:

	YES	NO
1. Does the flame in the furnace turn yellow and rise high above the burners? (A bad sign indicating a ruptured combustion chamber—a new furnace is needed—$1200 or more.)	[ ]	[ ]
2. Do you smell gas around the furnace? (A very bad sign—call the gas company immediately.)	[ ]	[ ]
3. If there is radiant heat or heating that requires plumbing, are there any leaks?	[ ]	[ ]

Fireplace

Most people figure that there's little to go wrong with a fireplace. Unfortunately, that's not the case. The bricks in a fireplace can crack and
the fireplace itself can pull away from the house (something which hap-

pens in earthquake country). This can lead to a dangerous situation in which the house can catch fire if the fireplace is used.

	YES	NO
1. From the outside, is the fireplace tight against the house or can you see a separation? (A separation is a big danger sign—have a professional check it out.)	[ ]	[ ]
2. Are there any visible cracks in the external bricks of the fireplace?	[ ]	[ ]
3. Are there any cracks in the firebricks inside the fireplace?	[ ]	[ ]

Tile

	YES	NO
1. Are there any cracks in the tile of the kitchen or bathrooms? (Cracks can be caused simply by dropping something heavy on the tile or can be symptomatic of house movements and a cracked foundation.)	[ ]	[ ]
2. Are floor tiles cracked? (Replacing cracked floor tiles when there is a problem with the floor simply means that the new tiles will soon crack. Fixing the floor problem could be very expensive.)	[ ]	[ ]

Termite Report

When you get a new loan, the lender almost always requires a termite clearance. This is a report from a registered termite company which states that the house is free of infestation.

It's important to understand that the report is of limited value. In areas where termites are endemic, there will always be some infestation. The reports usually state the house to be clear of termites for 60 days—the inspectors know that after that the termites will be back.

In order to get a clearance, repair work must often be done. In some cases this is minor involving the replacement of some wood and, occasionally spraying. In other cases it is major, requiring the tenting of the house.

In most cases the termites chomp away at the wood structure of the home and are of little consequence. The real problem is that over 30 or 40 years, they can eat enough of the wood to make the house collapse.

	YES	NO
1. Is there a termite report?	[ ]	[ ]
2. Are you getting a termite clearance?	[ ]	[ ]

3. Will the seller pay for all repair work? (Normally the
   buyer pays for any preventative work.)   [ ]   [ ]

Hazards

Thus far we've been dealing with ordinary run-of-the-mill problems
that you can look for in any home. There are, however, additional problems which are of a hazardous nature. You should be aware of these
and have a professional check for them.

                                                              YES   NO
1. Asbestos ceilings?   [ ]   [ ]

Prior to about 1980, blown in ceilings contained asbestos which would
then float down in invisible fibers. These ceilings should be scraped, removed, and then repainted or reblown with a non-asbestos mixture.
The cost for doing this is high.

                                                              YES   NO
2. Wrapped asbestos pipes?   [ ]   [ ]

   In some parts of the country, heating pipes under the house or in the
basement were wrapped in asbestos insulation. This needs to be removed by experts and the pipes need to be rewrapped.

                                                              YES   NO
3. Leaded copper pipe joints?   [ ]   [ ]

   Prior to about 1986 the solder used to connect copper pipes in houses
was made of a mixture of tin and lead. It was discovered that the lead
would leach into water that sat in the pipes. Modern solders use a different non-lead mixture. There is little that can be done about this short
of resoldering all the copper joints. After about five years the leaching
process tends to become minimal. It's mostly a problem in houses between two and five years old. (You can run the water a while before using it to reduce the risk of lead poisoning.)

                                                              YES   NO
4. Smoke alarms?   [ ]   [ ]

   These should be installed on all floors and near kitchens and fire-
places.

                                                              YES   NO
5. Insulation?   [ ]   [ ]

This isn't really a hazard, however, if you're in cold country without adequate insulation, you can be mighty uncomfortable. In most cases, in an older house the roof insulation can easily be brought up to modern building requirements. When insulating walls, in some areas, holes were cut and a formaldehyde based insulation was shot in. The formaldehyde itself is a health hazard, and where this has been done, sometimes the walls must be cut open and this insulation removed.

6
Making a Successful Offer

Chances are that if you're over 16 years old you've had the experience of making an offer on an automobile. Perhaps the car was at a dealer's lot. You told the salesperson that you'd like to buy it, and after much coaxing you agreed to name a price. He said something like, "Fine, let's write it up."

If your experience is like mine, a very short time later you were in a cubicle in the dealer's inner offices. You might have been pressured by the salesperson to maybe offer a bit more to get the car. Then you signed the offer, perhaps gave the salesperson a check for a hundred dollars, and waited.

Fifteen minutes later a new salesperson entered the office with your offer, shaking her head and saying what a shame it was, because the car was so nice, yet the dealer had paid more for it than you were offering. You couldn't really expect the dealer to lose money on the sale, could you? Couldn't you come up with a bit more?

So, by now quite interested in the car, you offered a bit more and then waited again.

This time another individual came to see you. He said he was the sales manager. Yes, your new offer was better, but the dealership had "detailed" (cleaned) the car and had put on new tires, new brakes and done other work. That had to be paid for.

You argue back and forth, the dealer agrees to take off the new tires and put on some older, but still perfectly safe tires, and you come up with a few more bucks. The sales manager leaves and then you wait some more.

Finally, if you're really getting the full treatment, the "owner" (or someone who says she's the owner) calls on a phone. She sounds angry. She sounds as though she's insulted because you're offering so little. She gives you a price below which she won't sell the car. It's substantially higher than the price you offered. She says it's the best she can do and hangs up.

A few minutes later the sales manager walks in with a bright smile and congratulates you on your fine negotiating. Now just sign on the dotted line for the price the owner demanded and you'll get your car.

But you're stubborn. You're not going to pay that much. After some not entirely friendly arguing, you get up and leave. You'll find another car elsewhere.

Just as your feet touch the pavement outside the dealership the original salesperson comes running up. "What happened?," He says. "I thought you were going to buy the car?"

You start telling this friendly, interested person a tale of woe, and he says maybe he can do something. After all, his commission is on the line. "Just come back into the office and wait a minute..."

You go back and wait a few minutes, and then the whole group, except for the owner, appears in the office. They all seem in earnest. What's the highest price you'll go, they want to know?

Feeling intimidated, you name a price between your last offer and the owner's ultimatum. They shake their heads, say that it can't be done. Won't you come up with a few dollars more?

What the heck, you've already invested five hours in this. You offer a hundred dollars more. They all disappear. A few minutes later the original salesperson appears. Okay, your offer's accepted. Let's get down to the paper work.

Question: Did you get a good deal? Or did you get snookered?

Answer: Chances are you got snookered. In some car dealerships, the whole thing is an act, carefully choreographed and planned out ahead of time. You never know what the lowest price the dealer would have sold the car for might be, unless the dealer refuses to sell at your best offer and let's you walk away. Unless this happens, you'll never know if your offer was really low.

This, of course, is why many Americans hate buying cars. It's the feeling that you're being manipulated. Of course, in many cases, you are.

Buying real estate has its similarities. In real estate there usually isn't a troop of agents trying to get you to sign, although in difficult negotiations you may not only meet and have to deal with the agent who showed you the property, but also with the listing agent and the broker of each company involved.

In addition, there are going to be demands on you to come up with a better price, unless you're already offering full or close to full price. Just as in buying a car, pressure will be applied to try to get you to move as close to sales price as possible in order to make a deal.

However, there are significant differences when comparing buying a house with purchasing a car. With a car the pressures tend to be pretty obvious. With a house, they tend to be more subtle. The real estate agent realizes this may be the biggest investment of your life and handles you very carefully so as not to let your fear of the the size of the deal outweigh your desire for the property. Nevertheless, the pressure is there. How well you recognize it and respond to it will determine how good a deal you get. Pressure occurs in three areas:

1. Determining price

2. Deposit size

3. Terms

We'll cover each separately. Let's say you've found the house of your dreams and you're now ready to make an offer. How much should you offer?

How Much Should You Offer?

If you ask your agent you may not get the lowest price the seller would accept. Remember, as noted in an earlier chapter, the agent is usually working for the seller, unless you're using a dual or buyer's agent. In addition, the agent doesn't get a commission unless the sale is made, and the more you offer the greater likelihood of acceptance by the seller. Consequently, in many ways when you ask your real estate agent how much to offer, you're in a position similar to asking an automobile salesperson how much to offer. *You're asking the wrong person.*

Who should you ask?

You can rely on a variety of people to find out what might be the best price to offer on the home of your dreams. Here are some of them.

Rely on Yourself

If you've been looking at homes for a while, you should have a pretty good idea what similar houses are listed for. This gives you a good idea of the price range of your prospective house.

Tip

Selling prices and listing prices are different. Houses rarely sell for what they are listed. Ask your agent to let you see the *selling prices* of similar homes going back at least a year. Any agent worth her salt has these figures readily available from the MLS. Pick out all sales for similar houses, then try to get as close a match as possible (same number of bedrooms, bathrooms, pool, amenities). In an active market you'll find half a dozen sales or more.

Now, look at the *lowest sales price*. If it's more than 5 percent lower than the next lowest price, ask the agent why it was so low? Was the house falling down? Did it need a new roof or driveway? Was there some reason for the extremely low price?

If there was and that same reason does not apply to your house, discard that lowest price. If not, *my suggestion is that you then offer the lowest price that any similar house has sold for in the past year, or less.*

Trap

Your agent may strongly object to offering such a low price. She may say that the seller certainly won't accept. Maybe the seller *owes more than you're offering*. Maybe the seller has added features which make the house more valuable.

Consider these arguments. It's most unlikely a seller will take less than is owed on the house. Added features, such as a new kitchen, bathroom, or other remodeling, do add somewhat to the value of the house. Remember, don't buy a white elephant by purchasing an overbuilt house...also, don't reimburse the seller for the entire costs of remodeling. Except, perhaps, for a kitchen, it just isn't worth it.

If these arguments make sense, you may want to increase your offer more. On the other hand, if they don't hold water then stick to your guns. If the listing shows that the owner does not owe more than your offer, the additions really aren't worth it.

Tip

With a "lowball" offer, some agents get adamant. They say something like, "I can't take this offer to the seller. You'll just have to offer more."

Baloney! The seller's agent has to take every legitimate offer to the seller. A legitimate offer is an offer in writing accompanied by a deposit. Your agent may not like it, but will do it. On the other hand, if the agent is reticent to submit the offer you'd do better by finding a different agent who is more willing to try to get your price for you.

Ask a Different Agent

Another way to determine an appropriate price is to consult with an agent who is in no way involved in the transaction. By the time you get ready to make an offer you will undoubtedly have worked with several agents. Go back to one who didn't show you the house you're now considering and have a friendly chat. Make it perfectly clear at the onset that you're going to make an offer through another agent. All you now want is advice.

Remember, agents only make a commission when they are involved in the sale. Thus, this outside agent, who didn't show you the house and who won't write up the offer, has no way to make a commission on this sale ... unless he can talk you out of making an offer or into making that offer through him.

Thus, you're suddenly going to hear a whole different story. You're going to hear why the property isn't as good as you first thought. You're going to hear how maybe you ought to offer less, a lot less. You'll hear how this agent can get you a better deal than you might otherwise get through the other agent. You're going to hear things that an agent confident of a sale might not care to say.

Listen, but take it all with a grain of salt. Remember, the agent's motivation remains to get a commission. If you listen between the lines, you might hear what a good offer really should be.

Tip

If you are using a "buyer's agent" as described in the last chapter, it is incumbent on that agent to give you the best price the seller is likely to accept. You can rely much more heavily on a buyer's agent's advice than on a seller's agent's or a dual agent's comments.

Ask the Seller

This may come as a surprise to many buyers. "You mean I can talk to the seller?"

Of course you can. The worst the seller can say is, "I'm not discussing the sale. Talk to my agent."

The best the seller can do is to tell you how desperate he or she is and how urgently a sale is needed ... and how low an offer might be accepted.

Tip

Your agent isn't likely to encourage you to talk to the seller. That bypasses the agent and arouses all kinds of suspicions (like maybe you're trying to finagle a deal to avoid paying a commission). Don't worry.

They won't put you behind bars for talking to the seller. Just remember, the seller is only a phone call away.

Trap

Don't try to bypass the agent to avoid the commission...even though a seller may suggest this, offering to split the cost of the commission through a lower price.

If an agent showed you the property, then almost certainly the house is tied up by an exclusive listing. The only way for the seller to avoid paying a commission is to wait until the listing has expired. Even then, most listing agreements provide that a commission must be paid to an agent for months after the listing expires if the buyer was shown the house during the the listing period by the agent.

You would have to wait months in order for this finagling to be effective, and during that time chances are someone else would come along and buy the property out from under you.

Hire an Appraiser

The trouble with this route is that it usually takes too much time and is too expensive (typically $150 to $300). But, if you have the time and want a sometimes realistic figure for the true market value of the property, you can hire an appraiser.

Tip

Appraisers usually work on a fee basis for lenders. Chances are that if you're going to get a mortgage on the property, you'll need an appraisal anyway. This way, you'll just get it sooner.

Trap

Not all appraisers are approved by every lender. If you intend to save money on an appraisal by using it for both setting the price and obtaining a mortgage, be sure you know in advance which appraiser your lender uses. Also, cut a deal with the appraiser so you don't get charged twice. Finally, remember that even if you ultimately don't purchase the property, you're still liable for the cost of the appraisal.

Appraisers can be recommended by lenders. They are also listed in the yellow pages of your phone directory. Those who have M.A.I. (American Institute of Real Estate Appraisers) or S.R.E.A. (Society of Real Estate Appraisers) designations are members of professional appraisal organizations and have completed usually extensive courses in appraising.

Tip

You can make an offer with the price contingent upon an appraisal. In other words, you'll agree to accept whatever the appraiser says the property is worth if the seller will likewise accept it. Usually there are "outs" included which provide that if the price is above a certain point, you won't accept, or if it's below a certain point, the seller doesn't have to go through with it.

This procedure is sometimes done with investment properties, though done rarely with houses. Nevertheless, if you have sellers who are convinced that their price is right and won't budge, it's another alternative. Just be sure that you agree in advance on who the appraiser is and who is to pay the appraisal fee.

How Should You Handle the Deposit

Once you've settled on the price, the next consideration for most buyers is the deposit. This is unfortunate since the deposit is usually the item of least consequence in an offer. Nevertheless, since most buyers worry about it, let's consider it now.

The deposit is money that you put up at the time you make an offer on a piece of property to show that you are in earnest about buying it. You're putting your money where your mouth is, so to speak. Hence the deposit is actually "earnest money." It demonstrates to the seller that your offer isn't capricious. From a seller's perspective, if you say you'll buy a property, it's one thing, but if you say you'll buy it and put up $5000 cash, that's something else.

Tip

An offer can be made without a deposit; however, it may not be binding upon the seller. The deposit, the transfer of money, helps guarantee that the seller is bound to the offer once it's accepted.

Agents, almost universally, insist that you put up a big deposit. They argue that this will convince the seller that you are in earnest about buying the property and that it will help make the deal. While there is a germ of truth here, there is also a lot of chaff.

How Big Should My Earnest Money Deposit Be?

You can offer *any amount* as a deposit. Sellers often insist that you offer 5 percent of the purchase price. On a $100,000 property that's $5000. This is, of course, ridiculous. All that the seller wants is to get you as committed as possible to the deal so you won't back out later on. Remember also, that the agent in most cases is working for the seller.

With one exception, which we'll note shortly, it's to your advantage to offer *as little as possible* in a deposit. The reason is simple: the money you put up as a deposit is at risk, the less you put up, the less you have at risk.

The exception is when there is a hot market and you're competing against other buyers. A seller faced with two offers which are essentially the same except that one has a big deposit while the other a small one, is more likely to accept the offer with the big deposit.

When I buy property, I rarely put up a deposit of more than $1000 *regardless of the price*, unless, of course, it's a hot market. A thousand dollars should convince a seller that you're sincere.

Tip

Many purchase contracts provide that once the seller has accepted the offer and once financing has been arranged, the buyer will put up an additional amount of money. You can thus put up a larger deposit once you're assured the deal has every chance of going through.

Also, a deposit doesn't have to be in the form of cash. It can be a promissory note, a check that all parties agree not to cash, or even personal property such as the title to a car or boat. Cash, however, talks the loudest when you're trying to convince a seller to accept an offer.

Trap

Sometimes sellers will specify in a listing agreement that they will accept no offers with less than a $5000 deposit, for example. If that's the case, then the agent isn't required to submit offers with less than $5000 as a deposit. Most agents, however, will submit any and all offers.

At this point, I'm sure some readers are wondering, why not put up a bigger deposit? Why not simply go along with the agent's advice?

To answer that you have to understand how risk is involved in deposits. Too often buyers simply put their faith in their agent and assume that everything is bound to turn out okay. In most cases, it does, but if things go bad, they can go very bad very quickly, particularly in terms of the deposit.

There are two problem areas you should know about:

1. Who gets the deposit?
2. How do you get it back if the deal falls through?

Who Gets the Deposit

The seller is entitled to the deposit. However, the seller is the last person in the world you want to give the deposit to. The seller might immediately spend the money, then later on, if the deal falls through, might not be able to refund it to you, even if you're entitled to get it back. It could require the services of an attorney and a lawsuit to secure the return of the deposit, and that could be prohibitively expensive. In other words, giving the deposit to the seller is like dropping it down a bottomless pit.

You want the deposit to go to a neutral party who will not frivolously spend the money and who will have it on hand to pay you back, if necessary. The most likely candidate here is the agent.

Real estate agents are required to maintain trust accounts for any money they receive. In other words, they can't commingle your money with their own, but must hold it in a separate account in trust for you. The agent, in theory, is supposed to give the deposit to the sellers—it's their money. Most agents, however, will hold the money in trust until the offer is accepted.

Tip

In most states the most common reason for real estate license suspension or revocation is the commingling of funds in a trust account. It's not that agents are dishonest, it's that they are sometimes lousy accountants.

However, to insure that they don't lose their licenses, they will almost always bend over backwards to repay any money kept in their trust account. Further, many states have special recovery funds. If you lose money through the carelessness, or fraud, of an agent, you may be able to recover it from the state, even though it could take years. Check with your state's department of real estate.

Trap

Today, many very good agents realize that accepting a check for a deposit puts them at great risk. If the deal doesn't go through, both the buyer and the seller may demand the money, leaving the agent in the middle. To avoid this, shrewd agents suggest you write the deposit check out to an escrow company which, you agree in advance, will handle the escrow of the property once the seller accepts.

There is a peril here. It is that after the seller accepts, the deal can fall through *due to no fault of your own.* If that happens you could have trouble getting your money back.

The reason is that escrows are simply neutral parties who handle the documents and funds in a transaction. In order for an escrow to operate, *all parties involved* must agree to the escrow's instructions. If, for example, you tell the escrow to return your money and the seller tells the escrow to hold onto it or to turn it over to him or her, there's no agreement. And your money remains in limbo.

This affects you far more than the seller, after all, it's your money. Many sellers are content to let the money sit in an inactive escrow for months just to "punish" a buyer for a deal that falls through.

Fortunately, calmer minds often prevail, and sellers usually will agree to release your funds once they become convinced there's no way they can get them, and that to continue to hold them might result in a lawsuit against them.

Nevertheless, while making your check payable to an escrow does insure that it goes to a neutral party, it doesn't insure that you'll get it back any easier.

How Do You Get the Deposit Back If the Deal Falls Through?

What must be obvious by now is that putting up a deposit is a fairly tricky thing with some significant consequences. How do you get the deposit back if the deal doesn't go through?

There are two considerations here. First, why didn't the deal go through? If it's your fault, you may not be entitled to a return of the deposit.

Second, if you are entitled to a return, how do you get the funds transferred back to you.

Tip

A little over a decade ago I wrote a book on this subject and then I suggested that all a buyer had to do was to use one of several suggested clauses in a purchase contract to ensure a return of the deposit. Since then, however, times have changed. Today, the chances of getting a deposit returned to you if a deal goes sour are much more complicated and are fraught with all sorts of legal entanglements.

Therefore, operating on the principle that the time to consult an attorney is before you need one, my advice is to seek the services of a professional real estate lawyer at this juncture. Chances are you're going to need one anyway before the deal is concluded, and by bringing him or her in at an early stage, you could avoid much grief. Most lawyers who deal in real estate have set fees that are much lower than for general legal work. Ask the lawyer *in advance* what the fees are.

1. *The return of the deposit if the seller doesn't accept your offer.* If the seller does not accept your offer, you're entitled to your deposit back. It's just that simple.

The seller has to agree to your *entire* offer including any terms you propose. If the seller agrees to the price, but not the terms, and counters with different terms which you don't accept, there's no deal and you're entitled to your money back. If the seller accepts your terms, but counters with a different price which you don't accept, the deal's off and you're entitled to your deposit back.

The moment the seller "counters" (proposes a deal different in some way no matter how small), your original offer has been declined. Unless you accept the seller's counteroffer, you're entitled to your deposit back. We'll have more to say about what constitutes acceptance and what doesn't, shortly.

Trap

Once in a very great while an unscrupulous agent will say something such as, "Even though the seller didn't accept, I made a good faith effort to get the deal through. Therefore, I'm entitled to half the deposit. I'll return half to you and keep the other half."

No way. The agent gets a commission *only if the deal is consummated*. If the seller never agrees, no commission is due. Politely tell the agent you want all of your deposit back immediately or you will report him or her to the state department of real estate. That should do it.

2. The return of the deposit if the seller accepts and the deal falls through due to the buyer's fault. There are lots of reasons the deal might fall through and it may be your fault. For example, you could be counting on Aunt Harriet to give you the money for the down payment. You get the seller to sign an offer, secure financing, and poor Aunt Harriet has a heart attack and dies. Her money will be tied up in probate for years. Sure, you didn't do anything intentionally to quash the deal, but you don't have the expected money to perform. As far as the seller is concerned, it's your fault.

Or, you get cold feet. You take a look at those huge monthly payments and you decide that you can't go through with it. You want out, period.

Or, you find another house that is really perfect. You want to get out of this deal so that you can get the other.

Or...

There are lots of reasons, good and bad, why you might not want to or be able to perform on your end of a purchase agreement. The point here is, however, that for whatever reason, it's your fault the deal doesn't go forward. What are your chances of getting the deposit back?

Put simply, your chances are not good.

In fact, you could be in hot water and liable for a lot more than just the deposit, as we'll see shortly.

Most sales agreements provide that if you default, the seller is entitled to keep the deposit. Separately, agreements between seller and agent specify that they will split the deposit in the event of your default. Thus, at least in theory, as soon as you default on the deal, your deposit is lost. Unfortunately, it may not end there.

In addition, the seller may sue you. After the seller accepts your offer and you default (refuse to buy), the seller can sue you for *specific performance.* That means the seller can sue to force you to buy. Since, for practical purposes, this is most unlikely, it's hard to force someone to buy something, the seller could sue for money equivalent to the price of the property...as well as damages...and possibly win.

In the past when a buyer defaulted, a seller occasionally did sue for damages, thus tying up the courts and causing long-term problems for everyone concerned. As a result, liquidated damage clauses for residential real estate (buyer occupied) have come into use and are accepted and even codified in many states.

Basically these liquidated damages clauses state that if you and the seller agree in advance, the deposit, or a portion of it, will constitute the entire damages the seller is entitled to in the event of your default. In other words, you agree in advance that the seller can keep the deposit providing she agrees not to sue you for additional damages or specific performance.

Many states put limitations on liquidated damages. In California, for example, the maximum the seller can keep under this clause is 3 percent of the selling price. If the seller wants to keep more, he has to prove that it's reasonable to hang onto the money in a court of law. If you want to get the 3 percent back, you have to prove why it's reasonable for you to get it. Either way, for practical purposes, the seller is usually satisfied, and unless you're litigious by nature you probably are too. Of course, both seller and buyer can agree to virtually any amount as liquidate damages, though it's normally not to your advantage as buyer to agree to a higher amount.

Tip

The moral here is simple. If you default, plan to lose all or part of your deposit. Don't enter into a contract to buy real estate unless you plan to perform. If you have doubts, leave a way out for yourself via a "contingency clause," to be discussed later.

What potentially can or cannot happen may seem quite dire. However, what actually happens in practice can be somewhat different. If you simply back out because you change your mind or find a better house, chances are neither agent nor seller is going to be sympathetic and you stand an excellent chance of losing your deposit.

However, if circumstances cause you to default, such as death of your aunt on whom you were counting for money, or you get sick or injured or something happens which is truly beyond your control, then it's a different story. Here, you are truly relying on the goodwill of the agent and the seller. In almost every case I've seen where this has happened, the buyer has gotten the deposit back.

Agents are not in the business to make money on deposits. Sellers are interested in selling, not keeping the deposit of a person who falls on ill times. I have seen agents bend over backwards in these circumstances to get the seller to give the deposit back. I have seen sellers gladly return the deposit, sometimes over an agent's objections. Of course, you could get the bad apples, but goodwill is everywhere, and if you default due to circumstances beyond your control, chances are you'll get most if not all of your deposit back.

3. *The return of the deposit if the seller fails to go through with the deal.* Why would a seller fail to go through with a deal, once signed? Simple, you offer $150,000 for a house and the seller accepts. Two days

later another buyer comes in with an offer of $175,000. Wouldn't it be wonderful if the seller could get out of your deal and accept the new one? The seller would stand to make an additional $25,000. That's plenty of reason to default.

In these circumstances you are fully entitled to the return of your deposit. In addition, you may want to sue the seller for specific performance, to force him or her to sell to you. After all, you could then resell for the higher price and keep the profit!

When the seller defaults, there's not much concern about getting the deposit back. Usually the seller is more than happy to do everything to get that deposit back to you in the hope that you won't take further action.

Tip

You can refuse to accept the deposit back. Tell the agent you insist on buying the property and that you'll hold the seller to the exact terms of the deal. This should tie up the property at the least.

If you're really not all that interested in the property, however, the worst you might do is get a cash settlement from the seller.

Remember, however, as a practical matter it's difficult to force a seller to sell a house when she or he is determined not to sell, even when you're in the right. It's also iffy to press a law suit since there could be "outs" the seller might find in the purchase agreement.

Rather than drag the whole thing into litigation which could take years to resolve and in which there is no guarantee you'll prevail, it might be better to simply take your deposit back (and any settlement the agent and seller may offer) and look elsewhere.

4. *The return of the deposit if it's not one's fault, but the deal just can't be made.* There are a lot of reasons why a deal might not go through: you may not be able to secure adequate financing, the title to the property may not be clear, there could be extensive termite damage, or it could turn out the house is in the middle of a flood plain.

The reasons are endless and they crop up in perhaps 25 percent of all deals. In most cases there's a way to work them out: other financing is secured, the seller clears the title, the termite damage is fixed, you agree to accept the risk of flood damage for a lower price, and so on. In other words, the problems are negotiated.

However, sometimes it just doesn't work and there's no deal to be made. What happens to your deposit then?

If you've given it to an agent who has kept it in a trust account, you can demand it back, and in most cases the agent will immediately return it. If the conditions of the purchase agreement can't be met, you're entitled to it back, and most agents don't want to argue the point.

On the other hand, if it's been deposited to an escrow account, it takes both buyer's and seller's agreement to get it out. Maybe the seller is angry that the deal fell through and says, "I'm not signing anything."

There your deposit sits, even though you're perfectly entitled to it. Unless the agent can prevail and convince the seller to release it, it could remain there for a very long time!

For practical matters, however, as soon as another buyer comes along the seller will be forced to release it or it could jeopardize a later sale.

Tip

One possible method of avoiding the tying up of the deposit in escrow if the sale does not go through is to insist that the escrow instructions provide that should the deal not be consummated within a specified period of time (90 days, for example) because any of the conditions of sale cannot be met, the escrow will automatically return the deposit to you.

Thus, if the deal doesn't go through, you automatically get your money back.

The trouble is, most sellers see this as a way for you, the buyer, to weasel out of the deal and will refuse to go along with it. It's a great method to use, if you can. However, your choice may often be between insisting on such a clause and losing the deal or just allowing your money to go into escrow and taking your chances.

All of which brings us back to my original point. The money you put up for deposit is *at risk*. The less you put up, the less you risk.

Tip

If the seller insists on a large deposit, offer to *increase* the deposit at a later time. For example, once you and the property have qualified for a mortgage and the seller has proven clear title, you'll agree to increase the deposit. That should only take a few weeks and should satisfy the seller's concerns over a small deposit.

What Terms Should You Offer?

The terms of a purchase are often more important than the price. Thus, this is an area of vital concern to you, the buyer.

Tip

Sellers are often hung up on price. Offer them their full price and they may give you ridiculously favorable terms.

Your agent is likely to insist that you offer terms which basically protect you. For example, he or she may want to include a clause that allows you to receive your deposit money back and to get out of the deal if you cannot secure financing. Usually this is a wise idea.

On the other hand, the agent is not likely to want to include terms too much in your favor which would allow you to back out of the deal anytime you wanted. The agent's goal, particularly if you're dealing with a seller's agent, is to tie you into the deal as strongly as possible. Remember, the agent only gets a commission if the deal is consummated.

Financing Terms

Most of the terms of a purchase agreement are going to revolve around the financing. Will you get the mortgage money from an outside lender? Will you want the seller to finance all or part of your purchase? What interest rate and terms will you insist upon for the mortgage?

Tip

It's not enough to simply provide that you must secure a mortgage or there is no deal. It's important that the terms of the mortgage be spelled out. For example:

1. The mortgage will be for $100,000 (or whatever amount)
2. The interest rate will not exceed 11 percent (or whatever rate is current)
3. The term of the mortgage will be for 30 years (or 15 or whatever)
4. It will be a "fixed," "adjustable," or some other type of mortgage
5. Other specifics

Indicating exactly what type of mortgage you are to get protects you and gives you a way out should financing not be available.

We'll have a separate chapter on financing, but for here, it's important to point out that the more "contingencies" you add regarding the mortgage, it's less likely the seller will go along with the deal. Consider the case of two buyers interested in the same house: the first offers *all cash*, meaning that the buyer is going to find her own financing and guarantees to conclude the deal. The second is your offer which is for 20 percent down with the sale contingent on your securing financing.

Which is the stronger offer? If you were the seller, which would you take?

If I were the seller I'd surely take the first offer. There the buyer is saying that she is not worrying about financing and it's not contingent on the sale. In the second you are saying you don't know about financing. Maybe it can be secured ... and then, maybe not. The first offer is a sure deal, or at least an almost sure forfeit of deposit if the deal doesn't go through. The second deal is a maybe, until you're able to secure financing.

Tip

As noted earlier, in a hot market, a wise buyer will obtain preliminary approval for financing from a lender before looking for a house. Then when the house is found, in order to knock out competitive buyers, may come in with an "all cash" offer as indicated above.

This remains risky, because you never know for sure that you'll get financing until the money is funded. However, it impresses sellers immensely.

Another way to knock out competition in a hot market or even to get better terms in a normal market is to offer the seller full price. As noted earlier, sellers are almost always hung up on price. If they think they're getting their price, then they're happy, no matter how unfavorable the terms may be.

After offering full price, insist that the seller carry back a second mortgage (or first) at a lower than market interest rate for longer than a normal term. For example, write in a second mortgage for 8 percent when the going rate is 12 percent, for ten years when the normal term is five. Why would a seller agree to financing so favorable to you? Because you're offering full price.

Tip

The few thousand dollars you don't get knocked off the price may be more than offset by far lower payments over the term of the mortgage.

Time

There are other terms of serious importance to you. One of the most crucial is time. How long do you have to secure financing, to come up with the down payment and closing costs, to close the escrow?

Time is often negotiated. Perhaps the seller wants 90 days before moving out. That suits you fine, so there is immediate agreement.

On the other hand, perhaps the seller wants to close escrow in 30 days, but you feel you'll need 90 to raise the cash for the down payment. Now, time is a negotiating point. You compromise: you'll take a chance on coming up with the cash in 60 days, but the seller has to be willing to lower the price $1000 or throw in the refrigerator.

The sellers balk and say the most they can go is 45 days, but they'll lower the interest rate on the second mortgage they're carrying from 11 percent to 10 percent and throw in the refrigerator. Is it okay with you?

Now you have to make a judgment call. The agent may suggest a "bridge" loan to cover the extra time you'll need. This is temporary financing until you can get your cash. But this costs you extra money.

In the final analysis, you'll have to weigh all the factors regarding time. Just remember it's a negotiating card—one which only you can play.

Other Terms

There are a host of other terms in a real estate transaction, almost all of which are negotiable. For example, you may agree to pay full price for a property *if* the seller agrees to pay your closing costs.

Or, you'll only buy if the seller agrees to pay both for the termite inspection as well as any repair work.

Or...?

Throughout all this you can generally rely on the real estate agent to see that you don't get into anything that would really hurt you. After all, that might result in problems for the agent down the road. On the other hand, you can't expect the agent to fight too hard to help you get very favorable terms, particularly if it's a seller's agent. The more the terms favor you, the harder it is for the agent to get the sellers to agree. I've never met an agent who wanted to work hard.

Thus, it's up to you to get the best terms.

As noted earlier, the time to consult an attorney is before you need one. At this juncture a real estate attorney can prove extremely useful. An attorney can create a purchase agreement that protects you and gives you the most favorable terms.

Trap

Beware of attorneys who work too hard for your interests. In general, real estate agents dread attorneys, not because they protect people, but because they tend to muck up deals. There's an old saying amongst real estate agents that says the fastest way to have a deal go sour is to bring in an attorney.

Yes, you want your rights protected and you want the most favorable terms, but you also want to be able to ultimately purchase the house. An attorney can create a sales contract so favorable to you that no seller will accept it.

As with the ancient Greeks, moderation is in order. Allow your attorney to correctly draw up the terms, but use your own common sense when it comes to which terms to include.

Contingency Clauses

A "contingency clause" is essentially any clause in a contract that says the offer depends or hinges on some other event or action. For example, wording that says, "This offer is contingent upon the buyer's winning the state lottery" is a legitimate contingency clause, one that obviously no seller would accept.

I used to know a builder whose advice was, "No matter what the contract, always be sure that somewhere in it, it says,'subject to.' I don't care what comes after the 'subject to,' just as long as it's in there."

The words "subject to" have a meaning similar to contingent. They make the sales offer hinge on some event or action. What my builder friend meant was that as long as those words were in it, he could get out of the contract if he had to. He had had many experiences fighting subcontractors, land owners, and others, and I firmly believe that he could get out of any contract with those words in it. For your purposes, however, a contingency clause is very useful to protect you against an unforeseen change of condition.

Some contingencies are absolutely necessary for the sales agreement and few agents would hesitate to put them in. For example, you might have a contingency clause that would read: "This offer contingent on the Buyers completing the sale of their current home at 123 Maple St., Ft. Wayne, Indiana for $100,000 within 60 days of seller's acceptance of this offer." (Note: Do not rely on this language—consult your attorney.)

The idea here is that if you the buyer don't sell your current house, you aren't committed to purchasing the new one. To make sure this is fully understood, the following language is sometimes added, "If this condition of sale is not satisfied within the specified time, Buyer may cancel agreement and receive deposit back. Cancellation is to be by written notice. If no such notice is given, this condition shall be considered waived."

The obvious purpose here is to protect you as much as possible. Keep in mind, however, that many sellers *will not accept such contingencies.*

After all, why should they tie up their house while you're trying to sell yours? Of course, if the market's slow, they may be willing. But in a hot market, forget it.

Trap

I once was working with another agent in the sale of my own house and the purchase of another. I wrote in a contingency clause similar to the one noted above. The agent objected. She said, "You'll never get the seller to sign. Besides, the market's hot. You'll sell your house. Why worry? Just agree to buy the other one without the clause."

Fortunately, I refused. The seller didn't and the deal was made.

As it turned out, I did sell my house nearly two months later, but found it would take an additional 45 days for the sale to be completed (a total of about 100 days). The contingency clause was for only 60 days. Near the end of the 60 days I sent a letter to the sellers saying I had not completed the sale of my house and I was canceling the agreement. However, I did have a buyer for my property and if the seller would give me an additional 45 days, I could conclude the sale.

The sellers fumed and ranted, but what could they do? I had every right to cancel the deal. On the other hand, if they agreed to an extension, they would still sell their house. Of course they agreed.

On the other hand, consider what would've happened without that contingency clause. I'd have been forced to try to make the purchase of the new house without the sale of my existing property or face losing my deposit and potentially having to pay damages. The sellers would be under no pressure to give me an extension of time.

The agent advised me badly. She only wanted a quick sale. Since the contingency weakened the sale, she advised against it. Whose interest was she looking out for in this case?

Tip

Unless it's otherwise already covered in the sales agreement, you may want to insist upon your approval of a professional house inspection as a contingency (see the last chapter). A house inspector (they are listed in the yellow pages of your phone book and should belong to the American Society of Home Inspectors, ASHI) can go through and tell you if there are any problem areas in the house such as plumbing, electrical, heating and air conditioning and so forth.

The cost is usually only a few hundred dollars and in most cases, the sellers may be willing to pay for it. The sellers are willing because it protects them against hidden problems when they warrant the house to be in good condition.

Just be sure that you have *approval* of the inspection and/or that the seller agrees to correct any problems, otherwise you could find out that there's trouble and still be committed to purchase without it getting fixed!

Frivolous Contingency Clauses

As buyers have become more aware of contingency clauses, they have tried with increasing frequency to have them inserted into purchase agreements.

Tip

Whenever possible, leave yourself a way out of a purchase agreement. You never know what's going to happen and you might need it.

The trouble is that at the same time sellers have become increasingly wary of such clauses in agreements. Sellers want to know that their property is sold. They don't want to take it off the market on a presumed sale only to learn two months later that the buyer is backing out, without penalty, because of a contingency clause.

Thus in today's market only realistic contingency clauses are likely to be accepted, not frivolous ones. What are frivolous contingency clauses which sellers are unlikely to accept? Here are a few:

"This purchase is contingent on the Buyer's grandmother inspecting and approving the property." (Two months later grandma looks at the property and disapproves—no deal.)

"This purchase is contingent upon the buyer securing a first mortgage at 8 percent per annum." (The current rate is 10 percent—no deal here.)

"This purchase is contingent on the buyer's approval of a soil and structural inspection of the property." (The buyer can simply disapprove even a good inspection.)

I hope you get the idea. Whenever the sale is contingent upon some outside event that the buyer controls, it's really a wide open deal from which the buyer can back out at virtually any time. In the real world sellers rarely accept such contingencies.

However, smart sellers *will accept* frivolous contingencies by limiting them. The most common form of limitation is time. Yes, you can have your grandmother look at the property or have an inspection. But, it must be done *within 7 days* of the seller's acceptance. If you haven't given the seller written notice of disapproval within 7 days, it is assumed you have approved and the contingency is removed.

What this does is give you, the buyer, some time, but not limitless time. In this case once the 7 (or however many) days have passed, either you bite the bullet and purchase the property or walk away from it.

Help on Contingency Clauses

Your real estate agent will help on contingency clauses. However, for safety they should be written by a competent real estate attorney.

Also, remember your agent is trying to close the deal, to be sure there is a sale. The agent's interests may not be in giving you as many "outs" as possible. They may be quite the opposite. An attorney you hire, on the other hand, will be most interested in seeing that you have as many options as possible.

7

Understanding the Sales Agreement

The sales agreement, also called the deposit receipt, is the document used by you to make an offer on the property. Once the offer is accepted, it becomes the agreement for the sale.

In the old days of real estate the sales agreement was usually just one page long. It had very little printed material and was mostly composed of empty spaces that the agent filled in. That has changed dramatically.

Over the years dissatisfied buyers and sellers (a very small minority, but with important implications) have gone to court fighting over various issues such as specific performance, deposits, or damages. What was discovered was that very frequently the sales agreement, drawn up not by an attorney but by a real estate agent, did not hold up. Suits were lost because the agreement was defective. This resulted in additional suits against agents, almost all of whom now carry a form of malpractice or errors and omissions insurance.

It also resulted in a new kind of sales agreement. The new agreement is frequently four to six pages long. Almost all of it is printed out—the agent typically only checks boxes or fills in dollar amounts.

In fact, there are very few places that the agent even has the opportunity to write anything out. The whole emphasis is on seeing to it that relatively few terms can be added for fear that they may void or weaken the agreement.

About the only place that the agent can add anything is in the realm of contingency clauses as explained in the last chapter. Usually there are only a few lines left for this near the end of the document.

A sales agreement is a legally binding document. As noted, once the seller signs it, it binds both you, the buyer, and the seller to its terms regarding the sale of the property. *You are encouraged to have your real estate attorney explain the legal ramifications of it to you before you fill it out.*

In addition to legal considerations, however, there are also some practical ones, and that's what we're going to look at in this chapter.

The Process of Buying a Home

Before we look at the sales agreement it may be helpful to see the role it plays in the purchase of your next home. Here are the steps involved in making a purchase:

1. You find the home you like.

2. You make an offer. It is written on a purchase agreement.

3. The seller accepts. (If the seller doesn't accept, start over with 1.)

4. Your agent or you open *escrow*. An escrow is used today in most states. It is a licensed and bonded company which acts as a neutral third party. The escrow receives all funds, makes sure that all documents are properly executed, and when all the conditions of the sales agreement and of the lender have been met, transfers title to you, records the mortgage in favor of the lender, and gives the sellers their funds.

Trap

In some states, particularly along the eastern coast, it is traditional for a real estate attorney to handle the function of the escrow. The attorney does what licensed escrow companies do in most other states. There are those who swear by this procedure and others who swear at it. If it's my money, unless the attorney is state licensed and bonded, I'll use a state licensed, bonded escrow company every time. I've heard of too many complications arising when an individual, even an attorney, handles the functions of an escrow.

5. You secure your financing if you haven't already and fulfill any other obligations you're committed to as part of the sales agreement—such as adding extra cash to the deposit or approving a contingency.

6. During the same time the sellers fulfill their obligations such as providing a termite clearance, clear title, and clearing any contingencies they may have.

7. The lender agrees to fund your mortgage.

8. You inspect the property.

9. You sign the final documents, the escrow records the documents and transfers funds.

10. You get possession and the keys.

Figure 7-1 is a time line that shows roughly how long the process takes and when the various steps occur.

Now that we've covered the procedure, let's return to that document which allows it to happen, the purchase agreement. Remember, this is both an offer to buy and, if accepted, the agreement on which the sale is made.

A typical real estate sales agreement, also called a "deposit receipt" or "purchase agreement," will include language covering the following areas (if it does not cover these areas, you should ask your agent or attorney, why it doesn't):

1. Price, down payment, and deposit

2. Specific terms for all financing

3. Street improvements or bonds—if any, who pays for them

4. When you will be given occupancy (discussed below)

5. The term of the escrow (how long it will be open)

6. How you will take title (tenants in common, joint tenancy, community property, etc.—see your lawyer for this—there are important tax and legal ramifications for how you take title)

7. Liquidated damages (discussed in the previous chapter)

8. Arbitration in case of disputes (discussed shortly)

9. Who will hold the keys and when they will be turned over to you (normally when you take possession at the close of escrow)

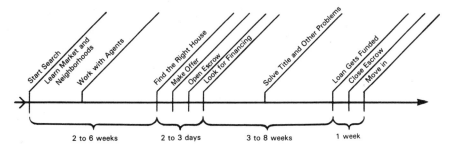

Figure 7-1.

10. Any personal property involved (discussed shortly)

11. Foreign tax withholding (applies only if seller is a foreigner)

12. Seller's statement of the condition of property

13. Seller's warranties

14. Physical inspection (discussed below)

15. Termite report (required by most lenders, if the lender doesn't require it, you should)

16. Soil or geological tests (found in areas with earthquakes or other soil problems)

17. Flood or water hazards (noting if the property is in any flood hazard area)

18. Zoning problems (indicating if the property is in a special zone, such as a "coastal zone," which could affect your ability to build or add on)

19. Home protection plan (which pays for damage or problems with the heating, plumbing, electrical, etc. systems—discussed below)

20. Energy retrofit requirements (local or state ordinances requiring additional insulation be placed in the house when the property is sold)

21. How prorations will be handled (discussed below)

Occupancy

The question here is, when will you take possession of the property? The most common answer is at the close of escrow after title has been recorded in your name.

Trap

The danger with occupancy is that the sellers won't move out. There are many reasons the sellers might not move: a new house they are planning to move into might not be ready, or there might be illness in the family and a family member might not be easily moved, or they could just be ornery.

Whatever the reason, if they don't move, it spells trouble for you. If the sellers are still in possession of the house once you get title you can't easily have them removed. In the old days "self-help eviction" was allowed—you could go in and physically throw them out! That's been taboo for quite a few years now.

To get them out you might need to conduct an "unlawful detainer" action through the courts. This usually takes about a month, may cost upwards of a thousand dollars and require the services of an attorney.

Tip

There's an easy way to insure that there is no problem with occupancy. It involves two steps:

Step 1: Most sales agreements state when occupancy is to be given. Be sure yours says that it is to be given at least one day before the close of escrow.

Step 2: In order to close escrow, you normally have to sign a whole series of documents as well as deposit the down payment into escrow. These are loan agreements for the lender as well as other papers. These may be signed and the down payment deposited as close as *one day before escrow is set to terminate.*

Quite simply, if it were me, I'd refuse to sign until I was convinced that the sellers had completely moved from the property. If the sellers aren't gone, or close to it, one day before the close of escrow, and the transfer of title to you, it isn't likely they'll be gone the next day.

Be sure your refusal to complete escrow is understood by the agents and the seller. You have the down payment money, you are ready, willing, and able to sign. But you won't until the seller moves. If there is a clause in the contract that specifies the sellers are to be out one day before the close of escrow, you should be on steady ground.

It may seem a harsh thing to do and may result in some temporarily hurt feelings, but you'll save yourself an incredible hassle which could result if you take title with the sellers still in possession of the property.

Final Inspection

This has become commonplace across the country. You see the property before you make the offer. Then there's a wait of up to several months while financing is arranged, title is cleared, and so forth. How do you know that the property is the same as when you first saw it? How do you know the seller hasn't smashed holes in the walls and broken the appliances? This is unlikely, but it does happen.

You know by insisting on a final inspection, also sometimes called a final "walk through." Before the deal closes you once again examine what you are buying to be sure it's as you first saw it (or reasonably close).

Trap

Sometimes agents will suggest that a date for the final walk through be written into the sales agreement. This is usually a bad idea. You don't want a specific set date because you don't know when escrow will close and you'll get occupancy. The final inspection should be immediately before escrow closes, the day before, if possible.

Also, if you inspect the property too early, the seller may still be living in it, and furniture and carpets not yet removed may conceal potential damage. *Try to be sure the seller is out before you have your final inspection.* This helps solve the problem of occupancy noted above.

Finally, *be sure the gas, electricity, and water are on* when you have your inspection, otherwise you won't be able to tell if any of the house's systems are broken.

Tip

Don't expect the property to look as clean as it did when you first saw it. If the seller was living in the property when you first saw it, carpets and furniture will hide a lot of marks and scuffing. Once the furniture and carpeting are removed these stand out like sore thumbs. Dark scratch marks on walls and scrapes on floors are common. Indentations in carpeting where heavy furniture stood are also common, as is some slight discoloration. Most of this carpet indentation will disappear within a few days on its own.

There's very little you can do about normal wear and tear, unless one of the contingencies of your sales agreement was that the seller would repaint and clean the carpets—something to consider.

What you need to look for is any major damage that was not there before and *that the seller did not disclose in the sales agreement or accompanying documents.* What specifically should you look for? Consider this list:

1. Holes in wall.

2. Broken plaster.

3. Broken windows.

4. Inoperative or broken appliances such as stove, garbage disposal, or oven.

5. Faulty or broken water heater ($300 to repair), gas heater (upwards of $1200 to repair), or air conditioner ($1000 or more to repair).

6. Gashes, slashes, or marks in wood floors which will require sanding and revarnishing.

7. Damaged or inoperative light fixtures.

8. Broken or inoperative heating or air conditioning thermostat (upwards of $150 to fix).

9. Faulty plumbing. Copper plumbing is usually best, except for concerns over lead toxicity caused by lead solder used to seal joints. Galvanized steel plumbing in older houses may corrode due to electrolytic action. Look in the garage for rust at pipe joints—it's a dead giveaway of these problems.

10. Faulty electrical system. Older houses in some cases used aluminum wire. There is visually nothing wrong with this except that it requires special handling at connections.

11. Damaged carpet—This is one of the trickiest areas. There are three things to look for:
    a. Excessive wear—Look for "bald spots" particularly in heavily trafficked areas.
    b. Dirt—Before the carpet has been cleaned, this is easily seen. Cleaning, however, may cover it up for a few weeks and then it could come back.
    c. Cat or dog urination—This is the worst. In some cases carpets can be treated to neutralize the urine, but in many cases the carpet must be removed and destroyed, including the padding. Since carpet is frequently the most expensive item in a house ($15 and up a yard to replace), it's important that this be discovered. How do you discover it without moving in and noticing that acrid odor after it's too late? I know of no method other than getting down on your hands and knees and sniffing. It may seem undignified to do this in each room, but believe me, it can save you incredible cost and problems later on.

Professional Inspection

What should be apparent if you've just read the previous section is that a lot of the things you need to look for when buying a house require technical expertise, particularly in terms of structure, plumbing, heating, electrical, and so forth. Most of us simply aren't qualified to handle this.

Thus, it may be worthwhile to pay to have a house inspector go through and give a report. House inspectors are listed in the yellow pages of your phone book. Look for one who has the ASHI—American Society of Home Inspectors—designation. (See the last chapter on contingency clauses for more on home inspectors.) This should be done prior to your own final inspection. Corrective work should also be done prior to your inspection. That way, you can go through the house on your inspection with the list of problems and see that the work has been corrected.

Home Protection Plan

These are plans offered by several national and a few local companies which give you some protection for the major systems of your home. Typically they cover plumbing (including water heater), heating, air-conditioning, electrical, appliances, and so forth. The idea is that for a set period of time after you move in, should there be a problem, the home protection company will cover it. The cost is usually nominal, a few hundred dollars for a year's worth of coverage. And most are renewable.

Trap

In order for most home protection plans to be effective, the *seller* must warrant that all systems are operating and in good condition at the time of the sale. Thus, you want to be sure that the home protection plan is included as part of the sales agreement, that it is purchased prior to sale, and that the seller gives the appropriate warranties. If you wait until after title transfers, you may either not be able to get the plan or may find that you have to warrant the condition of the various home systems only to find that some aren't working.

Tip

When these plans first came out, I was strongly opposed to them. It seemed a needless waste of money. If the plan cost $300 and you kept it in force for five years, it would cost you $1500. In addition, each time you used it there was typically a fairly high deductible, between $30 and $50. I felt that for far less than $1500 over five years you could cover the cost of a water heater which was the item most likely to need replacement.

In addition, the primary reason that these plans originally gained popularity was that real estate agents used them to protect themselves. It was becoming a too common tale that a house would be sold, the water heater would go out, and the buyer would threaten to take the seller and agent to court.

Sellers typically would say, "Drop dead!" to the buyer, and to avoid litigation and hard feelings the agent would end up paying for the water heater replacement. With home protection plans the cost was covered and the agent would not be bothered.

Thus I originally felt that they were a waste of money; however, since then the price of everything had skyrocketed, particularly on older homes. I recently had to replace a furnace in a rental that was not covered by a home protection plan, I had owned it for many years. A new furnace, which 10 years ago might have cost $250, today cost $1250.

The same is true for everything else in a home. Thus, particularly if the home is over seven years old, a home protection plan may be an excellent idea. *Just insist that the seller pay for the first year's coverage.* Either party can pay, and there's no reason you should since during the first year it's actually protecting the seller's warranty of the property.

Arbitration

Some sales agreements contain arbitration clauses. Typically these refer only to the deposit, but in some cases they may refer to other areas. Basically what they say is that if there is a disagreement, you will submit it to binding arbitration—you will go along with whatever an arbitrator says.

Trap

You could be giving up significant rights if you sign an arbitration agreement. You could lose the option of suing the seller for damages or even specific performance.

On the other hand, the seller could be giving up the same rights, meaning that you could be avoiding the risk of being sued.

If you agree to arbitration, just remember that for it to be effective *both the buyer and the seller have to agree.* If just one agrees, it won't work.

Tip

Be sure that you know who the arbitrator will be. Many arbitration clauses specify that the arbitrator will be a member of the American Arbitration Association (local members listed in the yellow pages of your phone book). This is fine, since such members are skilled at arbitration. But, they are also quite expensive. It really doesn't make much sense to use an arbitrator when the fee may exceed the worth of the item being arbitrated.

Prorations

Typically there are always some items that are "prorated." This simply means that items such as taxes, fire insurance, or impounds are adjusted in proportion to your use.

For example, a fire insurance policy is usually written and paid for three years in advance. However, the house may be sold after the policy has been in effect for only one year. You, the buyer, are taking over the policy. In this case the seller may want to "prorate" the cost of the insurance policy. In other words, you would pay him back for the two years you are going to be using the policy.

The same applies to prepaid taxes or taxes that are owed. Adjustments are made in your favor or the seller's favor, depending on when payment was originally made and what the date of proration is.

There are only two questions with regard to proration—what will be prorated and on what date. In general all items that are affected by time are prorated. Normally the proration date is the close of escrow.

Tip

You can make proration a contingency on the sale of the property. For example, property taxes may be due in full by March 15 and paid through July 1. You buy on April 1, thus, in theory, you owe the seller for three months of prepaid property taxes. But, you insert a contingency clause that insists there is to be no proration of taxes. The seller is desperate to sell and so agrees. You've gained three month's worth of taxes.

Making prorations a contingency is most often seen when there are "impound accounts." An impound account is where the lender collects 1/12th of the annual taxes and fire insurance on the property each month as part of the monthly payment. Since payments for taxes and insurance are made either annually or semiannually, such funds can add up to a substantial amount of money. Typically on a sale, the buyer owes the seller a prorated portion of the impound accounts.

However, many buyers insist that the impound accounts be transferred to them with no prorations. If it's a hot market with lots of buyers, the seller will haughtily refuse. But in a tight market, the seller may feel pressured to accept. If the seller does, you may have made yourself as much as several thousand dollars!

Personal Property

When you purchase a home, you are basically buying "real property." Loosely defined, real property is the land, the house and anything that's permanently attached to it. For example, the windows in the house are real property.

Personal property, on the other hand, is everything else. Furniture is personal property as are dishes, clothes, and most things that you can take with you.

For most things the definition of what's personal and what's real property is easily grasped and readily agreed to. However, in some circumstances the line between personal and real becomes very fine, and that's when you can run into trouble.

For example, wall-to-wall carpeting that is tacked down is normally considered real property—it's permanently attached to the house. But what about a rug that is thrown over the floor and not attached? Normally, it would be considered personal property.

Drapes which are hung on rods are usually considered personal property if you can take them off without in any way damaging the house. But the rods that hold the drapes which are affixed by screws into the walls of the house are usually considered real property.

Can you see where problems could arise? You see a house and you fall in love with it. It is completely carpeted and draped. You buy it. But on your final walk-through all the carpeting is gone as are the drapes. What happened?

"Why," the seller remarks innocently, "those were my personal property and I took them along with the furniture."

Is the seller allowed to do that? Probably, if they weren't permanently attached and if no mention of them was made in the sales agreement.

Tip

If you're ever in the situation described above, you can always say you were led to believe by the seller and the agent that the rugs and drapes were going with the deal, and you're not going to complete the purchase until you get them. You may not get them all, but a compromise will probably be reached in which you get some of them.

Trap

Don't assume anything when it comes to items such as rugs, drapes, and even appliances. Yes, appliances—most stoves and ovens just pull out and unplug, and unless they are included in a mortgage, a seller may feel they are personal property too. Assume they are personal property unless you are specifically told they are not.

It is because of the confusion between personal and real property that today most sales agreements include a clause which states something such as, "all wall coverings and floor coverings are included with the purchase except _____ ," and a space is left to write in any exceptions. Another clause should include all appliances and light fixtures. Look for these clauses in the sales agreement and if they are not there, ask your agent and/or attorney why they are not.

Tip

What should be fairly obvious is that the distinction between personal and real has many gray areas. Sometimes you can take advantage of these in-between spots.

For example, you look at a house and you are impressed with the kitchen. It has been redone and is truly beautiful. There are impressive oak cabinets and a special wall cabinet into which a large two-door refrigerator fits perfectly. You ask about the refrigerator and are told that it, of course, is the personal property of the seller. It's not included in the sale.

But, you think to yourself, where in the world am I ever going to find another refrigerator to fit so perfectly in there? Isn't it a shame that it doesn't go with the house.

Well, of course, *you can make it go with the house.* When you write up your offer to purchase, indicate that one of the conditions of sale is that the refrigerator goes with the house. No refrigerator, no deal.

What you have done here is convert a piece of personal property into real property through the use of the sales agreement. Will the sellers accept?

It depends on how anxious they are to sell. If you're the first serious buyer to come along in months, they'll probably grab it. On the other hand, if they've been getting offers every few days, they'll probably turn it down.

Remember, what you're actually doing is offering the sellers a reduction in price equivalent to the cost of the refrigerator, at least that's the way the sellers will see it. You may want to let the refrigerator go and simply get a lower price.

The sales agreement (purchase agreement, offer to purchase, deposit receipt) is where you make your deal. It is, of course, simply a piece of paper, but it legally binds you to the seller. More than that, it's the place where you get a good deal, a mediocre one, or a deal you'll be kicking yourself about for years to come.

Don't rush into the sales agreement. Take your time. Check with your attorney. Be sure you're getting all that you can. Be sure you're making the best deal possible.

8

Counter-Offers—The Art of Bargaining

I once had a friend who was a master at making offers on houses. She would make the offer favorable to her in all areas—price, terms, time, contingencies, personal property—every area you could name. There was nothing left to favor the seller.

Almost always her offers got turned down. But also almost always the sellers *countered*. They came back with a compromise offer. What was interesting was that often the compromise the sellers came back with was more favorable than this buyer could have hoped to get in an original offer. She had mastered the art of compromising.

Often you may be able to get what you want in price or terms not by demanding it up front, but by compromising in the counter-offer. The counter-offer can be your most important bargaining tool when used correctly. It can get you the best deal when nothing else can.

Countering Procedures

"Counter-offers" occur when the seller turns down your original offer, but then sends back to you a sales agreement that offers different price, terms, or virtually anything else different from your original offer. The procedure is quite simple. Assuming you're using an agent:

1. You'll make an offer which the agent and/or attorney will write up.
2. The agent will present the offer as soon as possible to the seller.

3. The sellers will either accept the offer exactly as presented or will turn it down.

4. If the sellers turn down the offer, they may make a counter-offer to you.

5. You may now accept their counter-offer or turn it down. If you turn it down, you may counter back.

6. This countering can go on almost indefinitely. Sometimes it gets down to arguing over a washing machine or repainting one wall of a living room.

7. The deal is made only when both you and the seller accept the same counter-offer.

Tip

Whenever a seller counters with any kind of change at all, it automatically means that your original offer is turned down. You now have the option of walking away from the deal with your deposit and no strings attached.

Countering Strategies

The Terrible Offer

In the opening example of this chapter we talked about a buyer who purposely made very unfavorable offers to sellers in the hopes they would counter with a compromise offer that was still fairly unfavorable to them. This is a strategy which sometimes works. However, it is also fraught with peril.

Remember, the seller may simply turn down the offer and not counter. When that happens, what do you do?

The buyer noted above would simply forget the property and move on. Her philosophy was that there were many more houses for sale than buyers and a better deal was always waiting just around the corner.

If you can feel that way about the house you're offering on, then perhaps the "terrible offer" is the way for you to go. The trouble, however, is that most of us fall in love with a house. Once we decide to make an offer, we've committed ourselves to getting that house no matter what. Thus, what happens when you make a "terrible offer" and the sellers turn you down cold? Now either you give up on that house, or you eat humble pie and make a better offer. If you really want the place you have to come back with a better offer.

This, however, lets the sellers know something that you want to keep very secret. It lets them know that you are desperate to buy the house. Otherwise, why would you come back with a stronger offer after they've turned you down cold? Now the sellers are likely to hold out for better terms, price, and just about everything else. The "terrible offer" strategy has painted you into a corner from which there is little escape.

The Wonderful Offer

Okay, the point is well taken. You really want the house, therefore you should make the very best offer you can, right? Figure out what is the highest price you can pay, the best terms you can offer, and so on. In other words, you offer the most favorable offer to the sellers that you can.

Great, except that unless you're offering full price and the exact terms the sellers want, you probably won't get the house. Why? It's simple.

No matter what you offer, if it's less than exactly what the seller is asking, you'll probably get a counter-offer.

The sellers will counter with a bit higher price, a bit better terms for them and then where are you? You've already given everything you can give. There's nothing left. You can't offer more money or better terms. The best you can do is send the agent back with your original offer saying, "take it or leave it—the buyers can't do better."

Depending on the market, lots of sellers will leave it.

The Compromise Offer

Somewhere in between the "terrible offer" and the "wonderful offer" is the compromise offer. This is an offer which you don't expect the sellers to accept, but which you hope will set the stage for a bargaining process that will get you the property at a price and terms you can afford and are willing to pay.

Tip

Don't expect the agent to lead you to the compromise offer. In my experience most agents suggest the buyer make the "wonderful offer." The agent is thinking in the back of his mind that this is most likely to get the seller to sign, or at least counter, and when the seller counters, the buyer will always be willing to come up with more. In other words, the agent may be manipulating you to spend more than you can or want.

How do you know what to put into the "compromise offer?" What price, terms, and so forth should it be? We discussed this at some length in terms of actual figures in an earlier chapter. Now, however, in terms of strategy, here's what I suggest.

Try to make the lowest offer to which the seller will make a serious counter.

The Art of Countering

The easiest area to demonstrate countering is in terms of price. We'll say the sellers are asking $120,000 for the property. Similar houses are selling in the $115,000 to $125,000 range. If you offer $100,000 the sellers are going to think you're trying to steal it and either may not counter-offer, or may simply counter at, perhaps, $119,500, very close to full price.

On the other hand, if you offer $110,000, for example, you're very close to the bottom range for houses in the area. The sellers may realize that what you're doing is trying to determine if they are willing to accept the lower end of the price range or about $115,000.

To most sellers this will seem a serious offer to which they should make a serious counter. Of course they could simply hold to their price, or if they're serious about selling, they might counter at $116,000.

Now you're getting somewhere. You may simply want to accept this counter-offer and end the dickering. However, if you're really inclined to get the most, now you'll up the ante, but only a bit. Perhaps you'll offer $111,000. The sellers have come down $4000, you've gone up $1000.

The sellers very quickly will see where this is going—$5000 separates you. They may suspect that you want them to come down another $4000 while you'll go up only $1000 more, settling on a price of around $112,000.

This will upset most sellers, and very likely they will now make their best counter-offer. It might simply be $115,000, the lower end of the price range for their type of house. Or, they might split the difference offering $2500 less or $113,500. In any event, this is likely to be as low as they go.

What should you do?

When the compromising reaches this stage, my suggestion is to accept the sellers' offer if you're in love with the house. It may indeed be as low as they will go. If you try to counter again, they may simply wash their hands of it, and you may end up not getting the property.

Trap

Don't paint yourself into a corner. If you only make counter-offers that favor you, you could lose. Once in a while, a seller may accept. But, if you're determined to have the house, you're better off making a counter that that contains enough bones for the sellers so that if they don't accept, at least they'll counter back.

Tip

The goal in compromising is to keep the ball in play. You always want there to be a counter-offer somewhere enroute. The moment either you or the sellers stop countering, the deal is dead.

Acceptance

There are a few technicalities about offers and counter-offers that you should know if only to understand what's happening. Sometimes, however, these technicalities can save you money, if not a deal.

Timing for the Offer

When you make an offer to a seller, it is open-ended. That means that you've written down the price, the terms, and any other conditions that you want and that *you agree to be bound by them.* If the seller accepts and communicates that acceptance to you, you're on the hook.

However, things change. The house you're in love with today may not be so appealing tomorrow. Yet another home may come along that really turns you on next week. Your financial condition could change. Therefore, you don't want to make this open-ended offer last forever. You want to set a time limit on it. The offer is good, for example, for one week only. After that, it's null and void.

The sales agreement normally will include a space where you can fill in the time limit for the offer. Be sure *not* to leave this space blank.

Trap

Sometimes agents will encourage you put in a long period of time—four to five days—for acceptance to take place. They may say that it will take that long to convince the seller to sign.

This only makes sense if the sellers are out of town and even then it may only be marginally good advice. The reason is simple. The more time the sellers have to think about it, the more time they have to find reasons *not* to sign.

In addition, some scheming sellers may simply hang on to your offer and not sign hoping that before the time limit expires a different and better offer will come in.

Giving the seller a lot of time to accept is simply cutting your own throat.

Tip

One of the most successful real estate agents I knew used to insist his buyers give the sellers only one day and that was the same day that the offer was made. In other words, if you made the offer at five o'clock that evening, the sellers had only until twelve o'clock that same night to sign, otherwise the offer was no longer valid.

Buyers used to protest saying, "What if the sellers want to think about it?"

The agent would respond, "The more the sellers think about it, the more likely they are to find reasons to not sign."

Buyers would ask, "But doesn't that put the seller on the spot?"

To which the agent would reply, "Certainly. That's the whole point. The short time *forces* the seller to make a decision here and now."

Finally, buyers would worry, "Won't the seller think the offer is frivolous, being made with such a short time for acceptance?"

"Quite the contrary," the agent would reply, "A short time period for acceptance shows you mean business. It implies that if the seller doesn't accept the offer right away, presumably as written, you'll go elsewhere."

You know something? That agent was right. He got more buyers' offers accepted without changes or with only minor counters than any other agent I ever knew. Think about it.

Withdrawing Your Offer

It's important to understand that although your offer is open-ended, and although it has a defined time limit for acceptance, you do not have to keep it open. *Anytime before the seller signs and that acceptance is conveyed to you, you can withdraw the offer.*

You make an offer at five o'clock that the agent will present to the sellers at eight o'clock. At 8:30, you call the seller's house and ask the agent if they've accepted. He says he's just presented it, and they're thinking about it. They'll probably sign in a few minutes. You instruct him to withdraw the offer. The offer is no longer good.

Why would you want to withdraw an offer? There are lots of reasons. Soon after submitting an offer, you find a better house at a better price. You want out of the offer immediately.

Or, perish the thought, you or a family member has a car accident or you discover that you have a debilitating disease and you don't want to go through with the deal.

Or, you're simply being fickle.

It doesn't matter. You don't have to have a reason. You can withdraw the offer anytime before acceptance is communicated to you.

Communicating Acceptance

Remember, it's not good enough for the seller to have signed your offer. That acceptance *must be communicated to you.* In practice this is done two ways. Usually the agent will immediately call you to tell you the seller has accepted your offer and shortly thereafter follow it up by presenting a copy of the offer to you that has been signed by the sellers.

Technically, communication isn't complete until you get that copy signed by the sellers, but in the real world, calling and telling you usually is what is done by most agents.

Keep in mind that the offer is accepted *only if it is unchanged.* If even one word or one dollar has been changed, *the offer has been rejected.*

Trap

Many buyers are unaware of the important subtleties of unaccepted offers. I have seen agents get sellers to make a counter-offer, then call the buyer and say, "Congratulations...your offer was accepted! Only the seller made a few changes which I'll need to drop by and have you initial. I'll explain it to you when I get there."

That's wrong. If the seller changes anything, the offer is rejected—totally and completely.

A counter-offer is just that. It's a new offer that the seller is making. *You are under no obligation to accept a counter-offer, no matter how close to your original offer it may be.*

Sellers are at great risk when they make counter-offers because they are, in effect, rejecting your offer and substituting another for it. When this happens the tables are turned. The sellers must give you a time limit to accept their counter-offer, and you can do with it what you will.

Just remember, if you counter the counter, once again the ball's in the other court.

The Form for a Counter

In the old days sales agreements had so little printed on them that it was a simple matter to "X" out the undesirable conditions and then write in new ones. In other words, there were plenty of open spaces available. Frequently, a counter-offer that had gone back and forth a number of times had so many changes and buyers' and sellers' initials scribbled on it that it was hard to read and difficult to determine what the final conditions were.

That was the trouble. Should there be a dispute later on, the sales agreement, which is the document that makes the deal, wasn't reliable.

As a result, as noted earlier, today's sales agreements have very little room on them to write in anything. Most is printed material and boxes that can be checked or have dollar amounts entered. It is very difficult to write a counter on such a document.

Tip

It is good strategy to make the counter-offer (either your own or the seller's) on the same document as the original offer. The reason is psychological. When the sellers counter on the same document, even though you may know that their counter rejects your original offer, using the same document makes it somehow seem like you're closer than before.

Similarly, when you counter the sellers' counter-offer, putting it on the same document does the same thing for the seller.

Counter-Offer Alternatives

There are basically three alternatives for the form of a counter-offer. The first is to write up a new offer on a new document. This is the least desirable alternative for the reasons stated in the previous tip.

The next alternative is to scribble changes on the sales agreement itself. This also is not a good idea because of the way the forms are created today. They very quickly become illegible.

The third and usually best alternative is to turn the form over and write the counter-offer on the back of the original. If this is impossible, use a special counter-offer form which can then be attached to and made a part of the sales agreement document.

Most agents are quite adroit at doing this. A typical counter-offer form would have the seller *sign the front of the sales agreement* and then have a clause by the signature which would read something like this:

"All of the terms and conditions set out on the face of the contract are acceptable to the seller in their entirety, with the following corrections or changes: 1. _____ , 2. _____ , etc."

Remember, this is a *rejection* of your offer. It is a counter-offer which you may or may not want to accept. But you are not bound to accept it.

When to Stop Countering

Sometimes you and the sellers are so far off on price or terms that it becomes obvious that there is no real room for compromise. For example the best offer you can make is $112,000 and the best counter the seller can make you is $120,000. Sometimes you have to accept the fact that not all deals can be made.

Tip

Refusing to counter can be a bargaining tool. After several counter-offers you're still apart on price or terms. Instead of accepting the sellers' most recent counter, you send it back. You include a signed statement to the effect that your last counter-offer (the one before the sellers made their most recent counter) is your last and best offer. You'll give the sellers until midnight to accept it or you're no longer interested in the property. Further, you're not interested in any more counter-offers from the seller.

The idea here is to decide the deal on a single throw of the dice. It's all or nothing. You're tired of bargaining. Either the seller accepts what you've offered or you'll go elsewhere.

I've personally used this technique many times and it works more often than it fails. You just have to be prepared to give up the house in case the sellers remain adamant.

9

Getting the Right Financing

In today's market there are many financing options. You can get fixed rate or adjustable rate loans. You can get terms of 30 years, 15 years, or less. You can even get repayment schedules that are monthly or bi-weekly.

The whole point is that while your agent and accountant may advise, it's up to you to get the right financing for yourself. Only you can determine which payments are going to be most comfortable.

To help you make an intelligent decision, this chapter summarizes many of your financing options as well as the pluses and minuses of each. Just remember, you want to make your financing decisions *as early as possible* in the buying process to allow yourself the greatest flexibility. (For more detailed information on financing, I suggest my book, *Making Mortgages Work for You*, McGraw-Hill, 1987.)

Interest Rates

For most people their first consideration with regard to a mortgage is the interest rate. Higher interest rates translate into higher payments. Consequently, most people want the lowest interest rates possible.

Trap

Don't hunt for a mortgage only by interest rates. Some mortgages, such as adjustables, begin with a very low interest rate that quickly, within months, climbs higher than other mortgages. Shopping by interest rate alone is fool's game.

113

The best way to shop for interest rates is to compare *like-kind* mortgages. You don't want to compare apples and oranges.

Today there are basically two kinds of conventional (non-government insured or guaranteed) mortgages available. The "fixed rate" where the interest rate does not change for the life of the mortgage, and the "adjustable rate" where the interest rate changes on a prearranged schedule. When you compare mortgages, be sure you compare fixed rate to fixed rate and adjustable to adjustable. Of course, at some point, you'll also want to compare adjustable to fixed, but that's a much more complex calculation as we'll see shortly.

Fixed Rate Mortgages

Each lender who offers fixed rate mortgages (not all do anymore) posts the current interest rate. These rates are often printed weekly in local papers. Also, in many areas a newsletter service gathers them all up and sends them off to brokers. Thus, you can usually find the rates for all the local lenders with one stop at your agent's office.

Here's what a typical list of lender's fixed-rate mortgages might look like:

ABC S & L	10 + 3 + 50
Amalgamated Bank	11 + 300
Jones Mortgage Bankers	10.3 + 1 + 250
Associated Lenders	10.7 + 1 + 300
WW S & L	10.5 + 1.5

At first glance this list of interest rates might seem fairly complex. What, after all, are all those pluses for? Isn't interest just interest?

Not really. In addition to the actual interest rate to be charged over the life of the mortgage, nearly all lenders of fixed rate mortgages also charge "upfront fees."

Upfront Fees

There are two basic upfront fees. (The lender may tack on many more—see the chapter on closing costs.) The first is "points." A point is a single percentage of a mortgage. Thus two points on a $100,000 loan equals $2000. Four points would equal $4000 and so forth.

Points are an additional charge you must pay at the time you secure the mortgage. Thus, if your mortgage is for $100,000 and two points, the lender actually only funds $98,000. You must come up with the difference ($2000) in cash yourself at closing.

Points are the lender's way of discounting the mortgage. Yes, the interest rate may say 10 percent, but if the mortgage has two points, the true interest rate is closer to 10.3 percent, as revealed on the APR (Annual Percentage Rate) statement that must be given to you.

Why not simply ask a higher interest rate and forget the points? That would be too simple and logical. Lenders prefer to play games with mortgages and borrowers, sticking to an older, arcane system that uses discounts to make it appear that the interest rates are really lower than they are.

The second up-front cost is a "loan fee." This is typically expressed in terms of dollars—usually between $50 and $500. It is used to cover the lender's costs in preparing the mortgage documents, setting up the repayment account, and other bookkeeping functions.

Tip

In the old days there were no "loan fees." Rather, the lender absorbed these costs from the interest payment. Today, however, most loans are sold on a secondary market to government organizations such as Fannie Mae or Freddie Mac, and there is little room for such absorption. Thus, the fees. You can argue with them, but unless they are unreasonable (see the chapter on closing costs), you're stuck with them.

Thus, when you see a mortgage rate posted as, "10 + 3 + 50," what it's really saying is that the loan is at 10 percent with three points plus a $50 loan fee.

10 = 10 percent (first number)

3 = 3 points (second number)

50 = $50 loan fee (third number)

Now, when you compare fixed rate mortgages you have something to compare them against.

The real question is what is the best combination? If you are primarily interested in interest rates, and thus your monthly payment, check the first number. However, be aware that lenders with low interest rates often make up for it by jacking up the points, the second number.

If you want to reduce your closing costs and can stand a bit higher monthly payment, look for low second and third numbers (points and loan fees). Often a lender with a higher interest rate will offer significantly lower points and loan fees.

Ultimately, you want the *lowest combination* of all three numbers. There is a very complex method for calculating all three numbers to see what the true interest rate is. This is done for you once you apply and are given your APR statement. Initially, however, you can pretty much eyeball the rates and choose the two or three best for you. Then, ask the lender for the true APR in each case.

Adjustable Rate Mortgages

Adjustable interest rates are given much in the same fashion as fixed rates except that occasionally the points and loan fees may be much lower. In addition, the interest rate shown for comparison on adjustable rate mortgages is frequently much lower than for fixed rate mortgages.

This is, of course, the appeal of such loans. They appear to be giving you a better deal. We'll have much more to say about this shortly.

Adjustable rates often also show two other columns, the "caps," or the maximum amount that the interest rate can rise over the term of the loan, and the adjustment period. For example, a summary of different lenders might look like this:

	Interest Rate	Caps	Adjustments
AVD S & L	8 + 1 + 100	5	6 months
Mary's bank	9 + 2 + 50	3/1	3 months
City S & L	9 + 1	7	monthly

The interest rates we've already gone over. The caps mean the maximum amount the interest rate can rise during the loan period. For AVD S & L, for example, the interest rate can rise a maximum of 5 percent (from the current 8 to 13). For Mary's bank the rate can rise a maximum of 3 percent (from the current 9 to 12). Mary's bank has a second figure (/1) which indicates that it also has a "payment cap." In other words, regardless of how high the interest rate cap may go, your payments can't rise more than 1 percent (in this case) per adjustment period.

Trap

Payment caps are a real trap since they often lead to "negative amortization" which, simply put, means that you end up owing much more than you originally borrowed.

Tip

Generally you want to look for the *lowest* interest rate cap. The lower the cap, the less the interest rate can rise during the term of the mortgage.

The adjustment periods can vary enormously. They can be anywhere from monthly to every three years. The more frequent the adjustment period, the more volatile your mortgage payments. The longer the adjustment period, the more stable your monthly payments.

Tip

Generally speaking, look for the longest adjustment period possible. This will give you more time between monthly payment changes, although when they do come, they can be more dramatic.

You've now seen how interest rates are shown for fixed and adjustable rate loans. Just remember, don't compare apples with oranges, fixed rate with adjustables. We'll see why, shortly.

Term

Your next consideration with regard to a mortgage should probably be the term. The most common mortgage has a 30-year payback period. However, in recent years mortgages with only 15-year paybacks have come into vogue. Often you have your choice between these two terms.

Tip

The shorter term means you pay less interest. The reason is simple, you borrow the money for a shorter period of time on a shorter term mortgage.

Tables 9-1 and 9-2 can be used to compare two $100,000 mortgages at 12 percent interest. One is for 30 years, the other is for 15. Note that

Table 9-1. Amount to Principal vs. Amount to Interest on a 30-Year Mortgage

Monthly Payment of $1028 on a $100,000 Mortgage at 12 Percent

Month	Balance	Interest	Principal
1	$99,971.30	$1000.00	$ 28.62
12	99,636.30	996.69	31.93
24	99,226.30	992.63	35.99
36	98,764.10	988.05	40.57
48	98,243.30	982.89	45.73
60	97,656.40	977.08	51.54
72	96,995.30	970.54	58.08
84	96,250.30	963.16	65.46
96	95,411.00	954.85	73.77
108	94,465.10	945.49	83.13
120	93,399.30	934.93	93.69
132	92,198.50	923.05	105.57
144	90,845.80	909.65	118.97
156	89,320.30	894.55	134.74
168	87,602.00	877.54	151.08
180	85,665.80	858.37	170.25
192	83,484.10	836.76	191.86
204	81,025.60	812.42	216.20
216	78,255.60	785.00	243.62
228	75,133.90	754.09	274.53
240	71,616.30	719.26	309.36
252	67,652.60	680.02	348.60
264	63,186.70	635.80	392.83
276	58,154.80	585.98	442.64
288	52,484.70	529.84	498.78
300	46,095.60	466.58	562.04
312	38,896.10	395.30	633.32
324	30,783.50	314.98	713.64
336	21,642.10	224.47	804.15
348	11,341.40	112.48	906.14

Final payment = $756.38
Total interest = $270,016
Total payments = $370,016

with the 15-year mortgage the total interest paid is about $116,000. With a 30-year mortgage the total interest, however, is $270,000—more than twice as much at the same interest rate.

Of course, you may be saying to yourself that this is all well and good. Yes, you save more than half the interest, but you probably more than double your payments!

Table 9-2. Amount to Principal vs. Amount to Interest on a 15-Year Mortgage

Monthly Payment of $1200 on a $100,000 Mortgage at 12 Percent

Month	Balance	Interest	Principal
1	$100,000	$1002	$ 198
12	97,461	977	223
24	94,601	949	252
36	91,377	917	284
48	87,745	881	320
60	83,652	840	360
72	79,040	794	406
84	73,844	743	457
96	67,988	685	515
108	61,389	620	580
120	53,954	546	654
132	45,575	463	737
144	36,134	370	831
156	25,496	264	936
168	13,508	146	1055
180	0	12	1188

Total interest = $116,032
Total payments = $216,032

Not at all. The difference in payments between the same 15- and 30-year mortgage is only about 15 percent. On a $100,000 mortgage at 12 percent, the payments are $1029 for 30 years and $1200 for 15 years—a difference of only $171 dollars a month. Yes, it really does work out that way. It's all in the way mortgages are calculated.

Trap

From the above discussion, the most likely conclusion to jump to is to get a 15-year mortgage—look at all the interest saved. The problem is the 15 percent higher monthly payment. What if during the time you're paying back the mortgage, you become ill or lose your job? It's a lot harder to repay $1200 a month than $1029.

The solution is to get a 30-year mortgage *with no prepayment penalty*. Many modern mortgages don't require penalties for early repayment. No prepayment penalty means that you can repay more than your monthly payment at any time.

Then, instead of repaying the $1029 that is your regular payment each month, add $171 to it and repay at the rate of $1200 a month.

You'll now pay off the mortgage in half the time, 15 years. In addition, if you ever get into any trouble, you can fall back and repay at the slower $1029 schedule. It's just some added insurance for you.

Another new feature offered in some mortgages is a biweekly repayment plan. Instead of paying your mortgage each month, you pay it every other week. The result is that you actually pay an extra month each year because there are 12 months, but 52 weeks in a year. Over the long haul, that extra month means you end up paying less interest. This works for either a 30- or a 15- year mortgage.

Tip

The problem with these types of mortgages is that you can be forever writing checks. Therefore, the only realistic way of handling them is to have the money taken out of your account automatically every two weeks.

Trap

This mortgage is designed to repay interest more quickly and definitely benefits the lender. As seen it can also benefit you, provided you are not someone who is self-employed or who gets paid irregularly. An unstable cash flow can cause real problems when you have a mortgage payment every other week.

Indices

Adjustable rate mortgages are all geared to different indices. These indices rise and fall along with other interest rates and, accordingly, so does the rate on your mortgage. Ideally you want an interest rate which has the least volatility. On the other hand, frequently the lender wants a more volatile interest rate to protect money that has been loaned.

The most commonly used indices include:

1. Six-month T-bill rate

2. One-year T-bill rate

3. Three-year T-bill rate

4. Cost of funds for the lender

5. Average of fixed rate mortgages

6. Average rate paid on jumbo CDs

Tip

Historically the cost of funds index has been the most stable. However, as we move into new economic climates that could change. Lenders will provide you with a chart showing changes in the index for your loan. Be sure you ask for a chart that includes the period of 1979 through 1981 so you can see how the index performed in unstable economic conditions.

Trap

Keep in mind that the index rate is *not* your interest rate. Typically, the lender adds a margin of two to five points (percent) to the index. Thus, if the index is at 7 percent and the margin is 3 percent, your interest rate is actually 10 percent.

Discounts

Most ARMS are discounted. This means that the rate at which you initially get the loan is only an introductory rate. The true rate (what the interest rate should be based on the index and the margin) is often much higher.

Trap

Discounts are really "come ons" to get you to sign up for the ARM. Often they are several percent below the true rate. What this means is that in the first few adjustment periods, your effective interest rate will rise *even if the index does not.*

As an example, the discounted rate may be 8 percent and the true rate may be 10. You get the ARM at 8 percent. However, it has three month adjustment periods with a maximum adjustment of 1 percent in interest each period. Thus, if the index does not change, your interest rate automatically will go up 1 percent the first three months and 1 percent the second three months so that six months after you get the loan, you are paying 10 percent instead of 8 percent.

Note: The introductory rate is only *temporary*. Don't be fooled into thinking that it is the true rate of your mortgage. In some cases both the introductory and the true rate are given when you apply for a mortgage—unfortunately, this tends to be the exception rather than the rule.

Negative Amortization

As mentioned earlier, this happens when the interest rate goes up and your monthly payment does not. In this case you may not be paying enough each month to meet the interest on the mortgage, let alone repaying the principle. The excess interest is then *added to the principle* and you end up paying more than you originally borrowed. Current law generally allows the lender to increase the principle of the mortgage to 125 percent of its original amount through negative amortization.

Tip

You only have to worry about negative amortization *if* you have a cap on the payment of your mortgage. If you have no payment cap, assuming it's a normal loan, you don't have negative amortization.

The Adjustable vs. the Fixed Rate Mortgage

We've already covered adjustable and fixed rate mortgages in terms of how to compare them separately. Now it's time to compare apples and oranges. The first comparison is in terms of interest rates. Be sure you compare the *true interest rate* of the ARM, as explained above with the interest rate of the fixed rate mortgage. Chances are you'll find that they are within a point of each other.

Tip

This comparison ignores the introductory discount. That's fine, as long as you plan to hold the property for more than just a year or two. If, however, you plan to sell very soon, then take advantage of the introductory discount. By all means get an ARM with as long an adjustment period as possible. You can hope the interest rate won't rise to the true level until you're ready to sell. Thus, during your period of ownership, you'll have paid the introductory rate, or close to it, and saved yourself a considerable amount of money.

Also compare points and loan fees. If cash is a big consideration and ARMS have lower initial costs, they may be a real option for you.

Finally, consider the interest rate cap on the ARM and the future economic climate of the country. If you think that times are going to be steady, with no big rise in interest rates in the foreseeable future, then an ARM may be for you. On the other hand, if you see interest rates rising, grab a fixed rate, even if it appears high to you today. There's no nicer feeling than knowing you're locked into 12 percent when everyone else is paying 15 percent.

Trap

Remember that ARMs are adjustable. That means that if interest rates go up, so do your payments. This may occur even after a rates have peaked and started to come down. Because of your adjustment period, you may play "catch-up" for months after the downturn. You can't call your lender later and say, "I can't handle a $200 increase in my monthly payment!" Your lender isn't going to be sympathetic and will threaten you with foreclosure if you don't pay. The time to consider a big monthly increase is *before* you get that mortgage, not afterward.

Tip

Look for an ARM that is "convertible" to a fixed rate. Many allow a conversion at a set date, three or seven years, for example, in the future. Just be sure the conversion is guaranteed at the lowest interest rate at the time of conversion.

Other Mortgages

There are a variety of other mortgages available on the market today.

FHA

FHA mortgages are insured by the government although they are offered by most lenders such as banks and S & Ls. Generally the interest rate is a bit lower, although the points can be higher. The problem is that the ceiling or maximum rate for FHA loans is relatively low, close to $100,000 as of this writing.

Trap

If you get a new FHA loan you'll have to pay the insurance premium for the loan upfront. The premium is fairly high, close to 4 percent of the loan amount. You can, however, add the premium to the loan, although this does increase your monthly payments.

Additionally, you are required to occupy the property as your residence, and the property itself must pass a strict qualifying appraisal.

Tip

There are generally no prepayment penalties for FHA mortgages and they are partially assumable. That means that the buyers must qualify as if they were getting a new FHA loan. However, generally they can assume the existing interest rate.

VA

These are loans which are guaranteed by the Veteran's Administration. The guarantee is not to you, but to the bank or S & L which makes the loan. These mortgages offer competitive interest rates, reduced costs, and in many cases, *no down payments.*

In order to get a VA loan you must have been on active duty in the armed forces during certain periods of time which change periodically—check with the Veteran's Administration for the current requirements. In addition, the property must pass a rigid appraisal. Finally, you must plan to occupy the property.

Tip

VA loans, in general, are fully assumable. You can sell the property to someone else, and they can pick up the loan at the existing interest rate.

Trap

Once you get a VA loan, you are on the hook for that loan for as long as it is on the property. Even if at some later date you sell the property, you may still be responsible for the loan. If the future buyer defaults, the VA could come looking to you for repayment.

Graduated Payments

This type of loan can be incorporated with almost any other including government loans. It involves having a graduated instead of a fixed payment schedule. Generally it means that you pay less when you first get the loan and are least able to pay. Then, as your income goes up, so to does the monthly payment.

Trap

Don't get this kind of loan unless you're quite certain you're going to have an increase in income. If your income remains the same or declines, you could be in big trouble.

Second Mortgage

This is generally a fixed rate loan. It can be obtained from an institutional lender such as a bank or S & L or, often, from the seller.

The second mortgage typically has a higher interest rate than the first and is for a shorter term.

Trap

Beware of "balloon payments" on seconds. This results when the mortgage is not fully "amortized"—the monthly payments do not fully pay off the principle. At the end of the term, you could end up owing a substantial amount of money. For example, if you borrow $10,000 at 10 percent, *interest only*, for seven years, at the end of the term, you still owe $10,000! Remember, the mortgage was for "interest only" meaning that the monthly payments only covered the interest.

Some seconds have payments which only partially return all the principal. This is frequently the case with a mortgage that is "amortized for 15 years, due in five." That means that the monthly payment is high enough to pay back the loan in 15 years. But, you owe it all back in five years. When the fifth year comes around, most of your principal is still owing. Now you must either dig deep into your pockets or refinance.

There are a number of other mortgages out on the market such as "reverse equities," where the lender pays you a monthly amount and the mortgage builds up over the years. But these are generally specialized mortgages rarely used.

When you look for a mortgage, just remember that knowledge is your best ally. The more you know, the less likely a lender is going to be able to take advantage of you.

10
Keeping Closing Costs Down

Closing costs used to be called "hidden costs." They were called that because they often appeared unexpectedly, just as you were about to close the deal. Suddenly, you had to come up with thousands more than you anticipated. The "hidden costs" were unwelcome arrivals.

That's rarely the case today. The reason is that "Truth In Lending" laws require lenders to give you preliminary estimates of the closing costs long before the end of the escrow. In addition, in order to be sure that the sale goes through, nearly all agents go out of their way to inform you of what your closing costs will be.

In this chapter we're going to look at your typical closing costs. We're going to get a feeling for what you should be paying and what you shouldn't.

Tip

The actual use of these preliminary estimates is to let you know well in advance *the nature of the charges the lender will make.* Be sure the charges are reasonable (as described below). Otherwise, you'll want to go to a different lender.

Typical Closing Costs

The following are some of the things you might have to pay for at the closing.

1. Insurance

   Policy of fire insurance
   Home-owner's insurance
   Home warranty

2. Taxes

   Prorations
   Tax service contract

3. Mortgage

   Assumption fee
   Document preparation fee
   Loan fee
   Account set-up fee
   Impound set-up/service fee
   IRS filing fee
   Attorney fee
   Collection set-up fee

4. Attorney

   Document preparation fee
   Services rendered fee

5. Recording

   Deed
   Affidavit of value
   Encumbrance (or release of)
   Assumption

6. Escrow

   Document preparation fee
   Escrow fee
   Interest proration
   Taxes proration
   Rents proration
   Insurance proration

7. Title insurance

   Title insurance fee
   ALTA fee
   Other fee

It's obvious there are a lot of fees that you could be charged for closing costs, and, for the average person, they seem written in a foreign language. After all, what's an "ALTA" fee or an "impound set-up/service fee" or any of the dozens of other fees? Are they all legitimate? How much should you expect to pay?

Tip

Remember, everything is negotiable. The fees noted above are typical buyer's fees. But, if you negotiate for it, there's nothing to say that a seller can't pay them.

Insurance

Let's consider the fees by headings. The first heading is insurance. As the buyer of a home (new or resale) you will want to carry fire insurance. The lender, in fact, will demand that you do as a condition of the financing.

Trap

Don't think you can get out of insuring the property. If you don't, the lender will put its own, usually more expensive policy on the property and bill you for it. If you refuse to pay, you could be placed in default and the lender could foreclose.

While you are required to pay for fire and basic hazard insurance, you are not required to carry a "home-owner's policy." The home-owner's policy runs almost twice as much as the basic fire/hazard policy, but it's usually a good investment. It protects you against a wide variety of losses including liability if someone gets hurt on your property.

A home warranty package is absolutely optional. It typically costs from $250 upwards, depending on the quality of coverage.

Tip

If your agent insists on your getting a home warranty, it's probably more to protect the agent's interests than your own. My suggestion is that *you insist* the agent pay for it. Some agents will.

Taxes

It's the only thing that's certain, besides death. You will have to pay property taxes. The escrow company prorates your share of them. (See an explanation in an earlier chapter.)

If you are getting a new loan that does not have a tax impound account, the lender may also require that you pay for a "tax service contract." The fee is usually around $25. What this contract does is that it hires a company to watch your property's taxes. If you fail to pay them, a report is sent to the lender who then pays the taxes, adds the amount onto your mortgage and, often, begins foreclosure.

Mortgage

This is usually the most costly area for the buyer. If you get a new mortgage, you're going to have to pay a lot for it. Often the costs of closing the mortgage can come to 2 or 3 percent of the total amount.

Assumption Fee

If you're assuming an existing mortgage, you have this to pay. It's typically in the $100 or less range.

Trap

Most mortgages are *not assumable*. They are written with "due on sale" or "alienation" clauses which prevent you from assuming them. Today the only really assumable mortgages are FHA insured and VA guaranteed loans and even these may have qualifying conditions. Some ARMS (Adjustable Rate Mortgages) are quasi-assumable. That means that, yes, you can assume the indebtedness. But the interest rate is often hiked up to the current market rate and you may have to go through a qualifying process similar to that of any new loan. Don't be misled into believing you can *automatically assume* a mortgage.

Document Preparation Fee

This is a fee paid to the lender for preparing the loan documents. It can be anywhere from $50 to $600.

Trap

This is a *phony fee*. The lender has to prepare documents for the mortgage anyway. To charge you for the preparation is unconscionable. Some lenders add in this fee simply as a way to acquire additional funds from you in exchange for making the loan.

You can refuse to pay this fee. The lender, however, can refuse to fund the loan, so, in the end, you may have to pay it anyway. The best thing to do is to find out *in advance* if the lender has a document fee and how much it is. At that time, you can always walk away and find a new lender.

Points

A point is equal to 1 percent of the mortgage. If the mortgage is for $100,000, two points are equal to $2000.

Lenders charge points for a variety of reasons, usually to offset a lower than market interest rate that you may be getting. The amount of points you pay varies according to the market. I've seen points as high as 10 and as low as zero. Be sure you shop around for the lender offering the lowest points before you secure financing. (See the chapter on financing.)

Tip

Sometimes the points you pay to get a loan are considered interest and may be deducted from your income tax. The rule for this, however, seems to change annually, so check with your tax accountant to see how much, if any, may be deductible.

Loan Fee

This is an up-front charge in addition to points. Many lenders, for example, will charge "two points plus $200." The $200 is the loan fee and usually goes to cover such work as preparing documents and funding the money.

Trap

It's preposterous to pay both a loan fee and document preparation fee. To avoid this you must get a good lender before you get to escrow. It's usually too late to start screaming about such charges at the closing.

Account Set-up Fee

This is another absurd charge. Here the lender is charging you to set up the pay-back account—the little payment book you'll get and the book-keeping entries made when you pay.

Trap

Again, it's usually too late to complain at the close of escrow. Determine well in advance the charges your lender will make.

Impound Set-Up/Service Fee

Some loans require you to pay one twelfth of your taxes and insurance each month. This is a charge to set up the lender's account that handles this. "Impound" simply means the holding of tax and insurance money for you and then paying it out appropriately.

Trap

Again an absurd fee. This should be part of the service that the lender performs.

Attorney Fee

This is a fee that you pay to the *lender's attorney* for checking over the mortgage documents and the transaction.

Trap

Another rip-off. Unless the deal is extraordinary, the lender should have attorneys on staff (virtually all do) who automatically check documents and deals. It should be part of the lending service.

Collection Set-up Fee

This is usually used if part of the property is a rental and rents need to be collected and paid directly to the lender or if your payment is going to be paid directly out of your paycheck or checking account to the lender.

This fee is atypical and shouldn't appear unless there are special circumstances discussed with you in advance by your lender.

Attorney Fees

You will probably want to have an attorney representing you. She should interact at various stages during the transaction. The attorney should be at the closing to explain the various documents you will be asked to sign as well as the various closing costs noted here.

One of those closing costs will be the attorney's fee. This may be a single fee or may be broken down into several areas such as document preparation, legal advice, services rendered, and so forth.

Tip

The attorneys who work in real estate usually have set fees for standard transactions. These fees are normally under $500 and frequently under $250. *Be sure you discuss your attorney's fees before hiring her.* Remember, the attorney's fees, like everything else, are negotiable.

Recording Fees

These are charges from the escrow company for recording documents. The typical cost to record a document is $7 to $12 per *document*. If the fees are any higher than this, be sure and ask for an explanation.

Escrow Costs

Assuming that you are using an independent escrow company, and you certainly should, there will be a separate charge. The cost usually varies according to the price of the house. A minimum of $250 is often the case.

Tip

The party (buyer or seller) who pays for the escrow costs is usually determined by custom in a particular area. Typically you will split these costs with the seller. However, there is nothing to keep you from demanding at the time the sales agreement is signed that the seller pay them. You are on very shaky grounds if you make your demands at the time escrow is set to close.

As part of the escrow charges there may also be prorations of interest, taxes, rents, and insurance. Just be sure that you're only paying your fair share.

Trap

Items typically are prorated at the close of escrow. However, if you are not getting possession of the property until a later date (probably a bad idea, see an earlier chapter on offers), then it's unfair for you to have to pay interest, insurance, and taxes until that date. If you're taking possession later than the close of escrow, be sure that prorations are made as of that later date.

Title Insurance

No lender will offer a mortgage without title insurance. Even if by some miracle you should find one who did, you shouldn't ever buy a property without title insurance. It is what guarantees that you actually have what you purchased.

The cost of title insurance varies according to the price of the property. A $100,000 property might cost you anywhere from $300 to $600 depending on the area of the country and the title insurance company.

Tip

There are lots of title insurance companies. Typically the escrow company or the agents will prefer a specific company. That's usually because the title company is giving them perks if not downright kickbacks for referring business. (Perks might be something as innocuous as free stationary to something as serious as free vacations.) The relationship between the title company and the agent should be disclosed to you.

Since for practical purposes one title company is as good as another, it really shouldn't matter to you...except in the case of fees. If one title company is *cheaper* than another, insist on the cheaper company. *You must do this at the time escrow is opened.*

A standard policy of title insurance protects you. However, lenders will often insist on your obtaining additional insurance called an ALTA

(American Land Title Association) policy. It gives the lender additional assurances including, often, an inspection of the property. In some states the ALTA has a different name. In California, for example, a CLTA (California Land Title Association) policy is usually accepted in lieu of an ALTA policy.

Tip

Usually the seller pays for the standard policy, guaranteeing you clear title. The buyer normally pays for the additional ALTA policy. Just be sure that you don't end up paying for both policies. In some areas it's customary for buyers and sellers to split title insurance costs.

These, then, are the typical closing costs you will encounter and what's normal and abnormal about them. Just remember that in real estate closing costs are high and getting higher. There have actually been proposals in various states to tax the sale of real estate. A 1 percent sales tax, for example, could impose an enormous additional cost. Fortunately, to my knowledge none of these taxes has passed at the present time.

Just be sure that with closing costs you pay your fair share—not a dime more.

11
Buying a Lot and Building Your Own House

It's the dream of many couples to buy a lot, design and then build their own home. It might be a vacation home in the woods, or it might be in a suburban location. The common theme, however, is doing it yourself. Somehow, we all think if we can just get the chance to build we'll do it better than anyone else.

I know my wife and I shared this dream and recently we made it a reality in the north woods of California. The lessons we learned, as well as those of other self-builders with whom I've talked, can be extremely helpful if you're just starting on this course.

Tip

You can do it. It doesn't take as much money as you think. It doesn't take as much specialized knowledge. What it takes mostly is time and determination.

Trap

Chances are you can't do it better than builders whose profession is putting up homes. They know materials and labor, design and construction, as well as where to cut corners and where to be lavish. But what you can offer that they can't is your own unique approach.

Everyone should build their own home, *once*. It's an experience you'll cherish and never forget. And the home you produce will always have a warm spot in your heart.

The Lot

The first thing you must do is find a lot. These days most people who construct their own home do it in rural or vacation areas, developers having already built up most suburban areas. Lots are for sale everywhere, but good lots are hard to find. Here's a checklist of what to look for in a good lot:

Good Lot Checklist

Location

Everyone knows that location is important in real estate, but it is doubly important in rural or vacation areas. The reason is simple: these properties take much longer to sell, frequently years. If you want to resell, you're going to need a prime location so you can get out relatively quickly. Does your lot have the following: These are listed in order of importance.

	YES	NO
1. Close to urban/suburban area?	[ ]	[ ]
2. Waterfront (river or lake)?	[ ]	[ ]
3. View?	[ ]	[ ]
4. Level building site?	[ ]	[ ]
5. Easy access roads?	[ ]	[ ]

Lot Amenities

These are the features of the particular lot that you find. Some lots are grand while others are not so grand. Does your lot have:

	YES	NO
1. Many trees?	[ ]	[ ]
2. A lot of room? (a minus in the city, but a plus in the country)	[ ]	[ ]
3. Good soil? (more difficult to build in "rock country")	[ ]	[ ]

4. A lot of level ground? (harder to build on a
mountainside)   [ ]   [ ]

Water

In the city it's something you take for granted, but building in the country it's a prime consideration. Does your lot have:

	YES	NO
1. A well?	[ ]	[ ]
2. A water company? (better)	[ ]	[ ]
3. An irrigation system? (for gardening)	[ ]	[ ]

Sewerage

It's something important to consider before you buy. Does your lot
have:

	YES	NO
1. Access to a public sewer system? (how much will it cost to hook up to it?)	[ ]	[ ]
2. A requirement for a septic tank? (with enough room for a leach field?)	[ ]	[ ]

Power

Yes, many rural or mountain lots have not yet been accessed by the
power company. It's a very big negative.

	YES	NO
1. Does your lot have electric power?	[ ]	[ ]
2. If not, is it coming soon?	[ ]	[ ]

Drainage

This can be a big factor later on, although it's something few of us remember to consider when we buy. Does your lot:

	YES	NO
1. Drain adequately?	[ ]	[ ]

	YES	NO
2. Have soft, wet areas indicating heavy water build-up?	[ ]	[ ]
3. Need drainage ditches before you build?	[ ]	[ ]

Title

Buying a lot is not quite the same as buying a house. You have to worry about all kinds of restrictions.

	YES	NO
1. Can you get clear title?	[ ]	[ ]
2. Are there any easements (to power companies, water companies, etc.) on your lot?	[ ]	[ ]
3. Are those easements just where you want to build? (if they are, you won't be able to)	[ ]	[ ]
4. Are you in any kind of a restricted area that would impair your ability to build:		
a. Coastal preserve?	[ ]	[ ]
b. National forest?	[ ]	[ ]
c. Wildlife preserve?	[ ]	[ ]
d. Other?	[ ]	[ ]
5. Is there a building moratorium in your area?	[ ]	[ ]

Environmental Concerns

This is an important issue which you usually have to dig for.

	YES	NO
1. Is your area facing any kind of environmental impact control?	[ ]	[ ]
2. Is there something occurring in the area which would severely damage the value of your property:	[ ]	[ ]
a. Draining a lake?	[ ]	[ ]
b. Changing the course of a river?	[ ]	[ ]
c. Lumbering activity?	[ ]	[ ]
3. Is your lot located in a geologically unstable area (earthquake)?	[ ]	[ ]

Tip

Leach fields are something new to many first time home builders. When you have a septic system, it is composed of two elements, the tank which holds the solid sewerage and the leach field which drains out the liquid sewerage. A tank only take a few dozen square feet. A leach field, on the other hand, requires hundreds of square feet, usually in a *flat* area. Be sure you identify the location of your leech field as well as your building site when looking at a rural lot.

Trap

Beware of lots that have their own wells. Chances are you'll be required to put in a septic tank for sewerage. Unless the lot is *very* large, the septic leach field may interfere with the well water. In short, it may be difficult to secure a building permit, and, even if you do, you stand the chance of poisoning yourself.

Also, many buyers look at their future lot in only one season. In the fall, for example, the lot may be dry and covered with beautiful foliage. However, in the spring it may be a swamp from stagnant winter run-off.

Be sure to talk to local residents to get a picture of what your lot is going to be like all year long. Also, look for ditches that neighbors have dug as well as natural water run-offs—these indicate the drainage of the lot. Beware of flat areas with no run-off as they could become pools of water (or ice) in other seasons.

Finally, the quality of soil is a critical factor when building. Ideally you want soil that allows water to percolate yet retains its shape. Expansive soil (mostly clays) expand when its gets wet and this can easily lead to cracked foundations. Sandy soils can more easily wash away. If there is any doubt at all, get a soils report from a qualified engineering company.

Financing the Lot

Generally lots are paid for either in cash or with a mortgage carried back by the seller. This is usually for a term of under 10 years at prevailing interest rates. It would be a mistake to buy a lot thinking you can refinance it through a bank or savings and loan. S and Ls generally won't loan on bare land. Banks, when they will loan, generally will only give 50 percent or less of the appraised value.

Tip

Don't be hesitant to make a bold offer on financing of a lot. For example, you may offer 10 percent down with the owners to carry a 15-year mortgage for the balance at 2 percent below the current interest rate. Remember that lots are hard to sell and that frequently the people who own them, own them free and clear. You're not going to get such a favorable offer accepted every time, but you will get it accepted more often than you think.

The Plans

Once you have your lot, the next step is to get a set of construction plans. This can be a very expensive or very inexpensive task. At one end are the ready-made plans which are available through the mail from building magazines (just check your newsstands). At the other end of the spectrum you can hire an architect to draw up a set of plans just for you.

Mail-Order Plans

This is definitely the cheapest way to go since a set of plans can be obtained for just a few hundred dollars. There are literally thousands of these available. Be sure you check to see that they are appropriate for your area of the country and that the building material list doesn't involve some overly expensive timbers or metal.

Trap

Be careful if you buy "through the mail" plans. A "working set" includes all elevations as well as details of all unusual construction. Some of the plans which I have seen sent through the mail are simply a front view and an inside view. It definitely gives you enough to see what the house will look like, but it's a far cry from being detailed enough for you or a builder to work with. Be sure that if you order through the mail there is a full "money back" guarantee. In addition, as soon as you get the plans, take them to a builder to see if they are adequate.

Tip

Even if you order plans through the mail, you will probably have to modify them to accommodate your building site. Why not hire a local architect on an hourly basis to modify these plans? The cost can be a fraction of what drawing up a set of plans from scratch would be.

Custom-Made Plans

This is the most expensive way to go, but you can arrive at a unique and well-built house. You hire an architect to draft a set of plans for you.

Typically the cost is 3 to 5 percent of the cost of building the house. If it costs $100,000 to build the house, figure $3000 to $5000 for the plans.

A good architect will visit the building site and design the plans to fit the contour of the land. In addition, he or she will listen carefully to your desires for a home and incorporate those features that you want.

Finally, a good architect will be aware of building codes and of building materials costs in your area and will design a house to take advantage of whatever cost savings that are possible.

Tip

Interview the architect as you would any other person you are hiring. Ask to see plans that she or he has previously done. Sometimes you can save money by modifying an existing set of plans. Find out who the architect has designed houses for and then call up those owners. Did they like the work? Did the architect take advantage of cost savings wherever possible? Would they recommend the person?

Trap

Find out first what the costs will be. Some architects work on an hourly basis, others a set fee. Don't assume that the costs will be minimal. They can be very expensive.

Do-It-Yourself Plans

In most areas of the country if you agree to live in the property for at least a year, you are permitted not only to do all of the construction yourself, but to also draw up the plans. No, this is not an impossible task. I've done it myself and I have no background in architecture or drafting.

What I did was to study the lot and then design a house that took advantage of the view. I then hired a draftsperson to create a set of working construction plans based on my rough sketches. Finally, I hired an engineer to determine the required loads. The total cost to me was under $1000. You can do it too.

Tip

Work with your local building department, not against it. Find out in advance what special requirements they have (snow load, wind resistance, insulation, sewer systems, etc.). Incorporate these features into your plans at an early stage.

Get to know your local building inspector and ask her or him for advice. This person may save you hours of time and thousands of dollars by suggesting approved methods of building that you may not have thought of.

Picking a Builder

Of course, you can build it all yourself, if you happen to be a relative of Hercules. However, some of the work is extremely hard, such as pouring concrete or lifting heavy timbers. Some requires skills such as soldering plumbing or plastering. And some is just plain tedious, such as putting up siding or sheet rock.

The alternative is to hire workpeople and/or a builder. Unless you plan to do 75 percent or more of the work yourself, you're better off striking a deal with a builder.

Trap

Many builders are only interested in making a set profit on each job. When you submit a set of plans to them for a bid, they simply add up the square footage, multiply by a predetermined price ($30 to $70 a foot) and that's your cost.

If you plan to do some of the work, finish the house for example, you need to find a builder who actually does cost estimates. These include finding out what the materials and labor will actually cost and then calculating profit on top of that. In the house I recently built, two builders went the first route, the third builder the other course. The third builder's price was 30 percent lower than that of the first two!

Tip

If you do most of the work yourself you can hire workpeople to do the remaining chores for you. You can do, essentially, what the builder does. You can hire carpenters, plumbers, roofers, tapers and so forth.

However, those you hire typically work on a "per job" basis instead of an hourly basis. They will want to see your plans and then will "bid the job." If they see you're inexperienced, they may give you a high bid.

To avoid this, be sure that you get at least three bids for each job.

Builder's Checklist

	YES	NO
1. How many years has your builder been in the business *in the area of your lot* (three is usually considered a minimum)?	_____	
2. Is your builder state licensed?	[ ]	[ ]
3. Have you called the state licensing bureau to see if there are any complaints against your builder?	[ ]	[ ]
4. Have you called the local Better Business Bureau or District Attorney's office to see if there are complaints?	[ ]	[ ]
5. Have you visited other houses your builder has constructed?	[ ]	[ ]
6. Did the construction look solid?	[ ]	[ ]
7. Did the owners voice any complaints?	[ ]	[ ]
8. Did you call the local building supply company to ask if your builder was ever late making payments?	[ ]	[ ]
9. Is your builder ready and able to get started, or will you be put off?	[ ]	[ ]
10. Do you get along well with your builder?	[ ]	[ ]

Trap

Most builders will want you to sign a building agreement with them in which you agree to pay them a series of payments out of which they will pay their workers and their material suppliers. However, if you *pay the builder* and the builder *does not pay the workers and suppliers,* you could still be liable for full payment to those workers and suppliers. They could file mechanic's liens on your property and take it away from you unless you pay, even if you have to pay twice.

Your only recourse, in such an event, is to sue the builder, who may have filed for bankruptcy.

Tip

You can protect yourself by asking your builder to supply you with a completion bond. Most builders balk at this, however, because they tend to be expensive and difficult to qualify for.

If you are securing financing in order to build, generally the lender will check out the builder and will withhold payments until the builder supplies proof of payment for labor and supplies. You can demand this proof in the form of mechanic's "releases" too. Again, however, it's a hassle for the builder and many don't like doing it. In addition, sometimes the mechanics will give releases and then still file liens later on saying that the release was given on the builder's check, the lien filed when that check bounced.

The greatest protection you can get is to insist on paying subcontractors and materials suppliers yourself. The builder submits a "chit" or authorization and you issue the check.

Again, however, builders don't like doing this because it allows you to see exactly how much they are paying for labor and materials and how much profit they are making off you.

The Construction Itself

Finally, you've bought the lot, had the plans drawn up, secured a builder, or hired subcontractors, and are ready to go.

Once construction starts, plan on being there a great deal of the time or on having a builder or someone knowledgeable there to handle things.

There are always questions that pop up. What does that little squiggle on the plans mean? The plans call for a three-foot foundation, but there's a seven-foot hole in the building site—what do we do? Where do you want the electrical switches? And on and on. Somebody has to be there to handle the questions.

Trap

Don't count on the local building inspector to insure that everything is done right. Building inspectors are notoriously lax. If you don't know how it should be built, hire someone who does to supervise the job.

Tip

Plan on spending more time than you first estimate. Workers won't show up on time. Building materials are delayed getting to the site. The weather turns against you. To be perfectly safe, use a rule of two. It takes twice as long to do anything as you think it will.

Buying a lot and building your own house is a wonderful experience. But as anyone who has done it will tell you, it's the sort of thing you only want to do once.

12

When You Buy a Condo or Vacation Home

The old adage was, "Those who can, buy houses. Those who can't, buy condos. And those who won't, buy vacation homes!"

Times do change, however. Today, condos are considered the first choice by many buyers instead of an unappealing second. And vacation property is no longer the realm of the rich or the radical, but is instead becoming increasingly important as the second home of many middle-income families.

Thus making the right move when buying a condo or a vacation home is a prime consideration. We'll consider each separately.

Condos

A condominium, as most buyers know, is a kind of shared ownership. Typically you end up separately owning the inside of the unit while sharing in common with the other owners all the grounds, walkways, recreational facilities—in short, everything outside. Another way to look at it is as if you were renting an apartment and then decided to buy your rental unit. Indeed, many condos are converted apartment houses.

It's sometimes useful to know that there are really at least three separate kinds of condominium type ownership. The first is the one which most people are familiar with—you could be on the fifth floor of a building and you own only that airspace that your unit occupies.

The second is sometimes called a "townhouse," technically known as a

PUD or Planned Unit Development. Here units are not arranged one on top of each other. Rather, each unit has its own ground space below and airspace above. You actually own the ground beneath your townhouse. You do however share common walls.

Finally, there's the "co-op" or cooperatively owned property. This is a different sort of ownership in that you, as an individual, don't actually own any separate airspace or ground space. Rather, you own a share in a company which owns the entire property. While you have the exclusive right to use a particular unit, you don't actually own it in the sense of being able to sell it. To sell your unit, you must sell your share in the company.

Each of these types of ownership has its pluses and minuses which we'll consider shortly.

Privacy

When you buy into condominium ownership, you are actually trading off a portion of your privacy in exchange for reduced price, guaranteed maintenance, and shared lifestyle. Condominium ownership is very much like living in an apartment. Your neighbors are only a thin wall away.

On the other hand, you usually, though not always, pay significantly less for a condo. Typically their prices are cheaper than single family houses. In addition, since all the areas outside your unit are commonly owned, it is normally the responsibility of a Home Owner's Association (HOA) to see to their care and grooming. And finally, often there are recreational amenities such as a swimming pool, rec room, tennis courts, regular parties, and so forth that go along with condominium living.

Trap

Regardless of what condominium promoters say, the fact is that during boom periods condos are typically the last to see price appreciation, and during slumps they are the first to see price drops (except for urban condos noted below). This is primarily due to the perception of most Americans that condominiums, while not quite second-class living, are still not as good as owning your own single-family home. I'm not saying that I agree with this perception—only that's it's an important factor in the marketplace.

Don't be fooled into buying a condominium *because it's cheaper than a similarly sized and located single family home.* Yes, it may be cheaper to buy, but chances are it will not appreciate as fast as a house, and you'll have more trouble finding a buyer when it comes time to sell.

Tip

On the other hand, condos offer an opportunity to those who can't afford to buy a well-located single family house. What you quickly learn when you first go house-hunting is that it's a very expensive proposition and often that first house is the hardest to afford.

A condo can provide a marvelous first house. The price is often reasonable, the financing roughly the same as for single-family houses, and you can get into good locations. Many first-time buyers purchase a condo and then live in it a few years building up their equities. When they sell, they have a small nest-egg that they can then apply toward a house.

Urban Opportunities

Thus far we've been speaking primarily of condos which are located in the suburbs. However, in extremely high-priced urban areas, such as Manhattan, virtually no well-located single-family residences may be available. When that's the case, then condominium living has a different appeal.

Tip

Well-located urban condos have seen some of the greatest price appreciation in recent years. Such units in Manhattan, Boston, Washington, as well as parts of Chicago and Los Angeles have gone up in price faster, on the whole, than single-family units in surrounding areas.

In addition in urban areas particularly on the east coast, the co-op has been a popular vehicle of ownership. This has added a feature of exclusivity to the attractiveness of communal living. In a co-op, it is often the case that you cannot buy a share of the property unless and until the current owners vote you in.

While this has resulted in some excesses, many of which have been addressed by federal fair-housing legislation, what it has done is create the impression of a private club. Some co-op owners in Manhattan, for example, are able to charge millions of dollars for their units because of this perceived exclusivity.

Problems with Condos

There are some problems that go along with condo and coop ownership. Besides the loss of privacy, these include the fact that you aren't

"Lord of all you survey." You normally can't paint the outside of your building or change the flower arrangement in front of your door. Even if you want to alter the interior of your unit, with the exception of simply changing the paint, you may have to get approval from the Home Owner's Association.

Tip

Expect to spend some time on the Home Owner's Association if you buy into a condo. If you don't, you'll find that the HOA board is always doing something you consider ridiculous or something you don't like. If you're a member, you'll want to be a part of decisions that affect your home and its value.

Trap

Beware of HOA burn-out. This comes after you've been a member of the board for a year or two and found that you can't get done what you want to get done. Oftentimes, owners will get discouraged and will sell their unit. If you're at least aware of this possibility, you may be less inclined to make such a drastic move when it does occur.

Vacation Homes

Vacation homes are really quite different from condos; however, they do share some of the problems. Vacation homes, for most of us, are second homes.

At one time second homes were the exclusive realm of the rich. However, in recent years many middle-income families have purchased a vacation home, even if it's only a cabin in the woods. Spurred by the need to get away from the crowding of cities and lured by the thought of acquiring some potentially valuable land, many have spent the time and money to buy these second properties.

In the chapter on building your own home, we discussed many of the problems and opportunities of buying a lot and building your own vacation home. Here, we're going to concentrate on economic issues.

Second homes are expensive, very expensive. Assuming you finance the purchase you will have an additional set of mortgage payments to make. Plus you'll have a second set of taxes and insurance to worry about. Then there's utilities, upkeep, homeowner's dues (if you're in a country-club setting), fire protection, and a host of other concerns.

Quite frankly, *from a strictly economic perspective,* a second home makes little financial sense.

Tip

Often you can rent out a second or vacation home. The tax laws are written in such as way that if you rent out the property *for only two weeks a year,* you can keep the income without declaring it.

On the other hand, if you use the property yourself for *more than two weeks a year,* you probably can't claim it as income property. (You can't get a deduction for depreciation and you can only offset your expenses against your income.)

Note: The tax rules for vacation homes are fairly complex. Consult your tax accountant or attorney.

Trap

If you rent out your vacation home, don't expect the tenants to take as good care of it as you would. This is particularly the case with rapid turnover—when you're renting on a weekly or monthly basis. You won't want to have good furniture in the place or anything you consider precious. These factors make many people regret the fact that they rent out their property.

Then there is the matter of reselling. Unlike suburban or urban homes, vacation property, particularly rural vacation property, is highly illiquid. All real estate is illiquid, but vacation property more so.

If you have a house in a tract near a city, there's always going to be a buyer for it. In a bad market you may have to lower your price or offer seller financing. But, if you make the property attractive enough, a buyer will come along and take it.

With vacation property, however, that's not the case. During boom periods, particularly when people are feeling good about the economy and want to find places to "get away" to, vacation property thrives. Buyers are almost knocking on your door.

On the other hand, during economic slumps when people are more concerned about keeping their jobs than vacation, you find that *there are no buyers.* That's right. It may not matter how low you reduce your price or how favorable the terms—there may simply be no buyers at all available.

Tip

Only consider the purchase of a vacation or second home as a long-term proposition. Once you buy, figure you are going to be stuck with the property for a minimum of three years. Tell yourself that if you want to sell, it could take you one to two years to find a buyer. That's not an exaggeration in many areas.

Of course, you could have buyers lining up outside. But *don't count on it*. If you figure that the day you buy is the worst day of the worst month of the worst year for vacation property, you won't go far wrong...and you could end up doing quite well.

Vacation property—a second home—is a risky venture. As noted, in the past it was for the rich, who could afford it. Today, it's for everyone, including many of us who can't afford it.

Before you jump in, take a long hard look at your financing, particularly several years down the road. Will you need the money you invest for something else? If so, will you be able to get it out?

On the other hand, we don't live by bread alone. Life in the city can be too competitive, too noisy, too crowded. Sometimes the only answer is a second or a vacation home.

13
Buying a New Home from a Builder

In an average year there are close to a million new residential units built in the United States, most of them single family residences or condos. While this is only perhaps a third or a fourth of the number of sales, the vast majority being resales of existing homes, it still represents a large group of buyers. Perhaps you are considering the purchase of a new home instead of a resale. Are there different things to watch for? Are there special benefits as well as pitfalls to avoid?

The answers are all yes. While there are similarities, buying a new home is substantially different from buying a resale. It is a different market which requires you to have specialized knowledge.

The Appreciation Question

A question frequently asked by buyers is, "Where will I get the greatest appreciation—in a new home or in a resale? In other words, if I had a choice between two houses, a brand new one and a resale each worth $100,000 and both in similar neighborhoods, which house would make me the most money over the next five years?"

In the distant past the answer was generally the resale. The existing house had developed neighborhoods, schools, shopping, gardens, etc. It had all the amenities already in place, and for that reason resales tended to appreciate more than new homes and to cost more as well.

Over the past decade, however, the tables have turned. Today, in many areas of the country, *but not all*, the price appreciation on new homes is far and away greater than on resales. In addition, for the same

153

number of square feet, a new home costs more than a resale. That only stands to reason—with inflation it costs more to build the same house today than it did five or ten years ago.

Today, if you're looking to make money on your house, buy a brand new one in the most expensive suburb of the city. Chances are that's the house that's going to appreciate fastest. However, also be prepared to pay considerably more for buying that home, as much as 150 percent per square foot more than for an existing home in a nearby tract.

Trap

Real estate is a *localized* market. That means that you cannot say that something is true at any given time for all parts of the country. For example, during the mid 1980s, the northeast saw price appreciation of as much as 300 percent. This was at the same time as the midwest and southwest saw prices decline as much as 35 percent (in oil patch or agricultural areas such as Texas, Oklahoma and parts of Colorado). During this same period, on the west coast, prices were fairly flat.

By the end of the 1980s, however, prices in the northeast were declining some 5 to 15 percent, had leveled off in the midwest and southwest, and were nearly doubling on the west coast.

With regard to new homes, generally, in a hot market the new houses will indeed appreciate faster than existing houses as noted above. However, in a stagnant and particularly in a *declining* market, new homes may not even hold their sales price, and large numbers of unpurchased, vacant homes (sometimes vandalized) can ruin the reputation of a new tract.

Finding the Right New Home

If you've determined to buy a new home, be prepared to spend a lot of time looking. In most areas of the country, there are new home tracts springing up all around. Many areas have new homes "buyer's guides" which are small magazines detailing the houses, their price range, and giving maps showing how to get there. The Sunday real estate section of any major newspaper almost always has ads depicting the new homes.

Picking the Right New Home

Here's a checklist of items to look for when choosing a brand new home:

New Home Checklist

1. Number of bedrooms—Three is ideal for resale, two may restrict your ability to quickly resell, four could make the house overbuilt for the area. _____?

2. Number of bathrooms—Two is minimal, three is better, four is overkill. _____?

3. Ceilings—High ceilings are in vogue. A better house will have at least one room with vaulted ceilings, usually a living or family room. _____?

4. Kitchen—Large and well-equipped kitchens sell houses. If your kitchen has an island in it complete with a stove, all the better. Is the oven self-cleaning?_____?

5. Garage—A two car garage is a must. Three car is better._____?

6. Additional rooms—A plus, if they don't force the price out of sight. They include: library, nursery, computer room or even a sound studio. _____?

7. Yard—Small yards are the rule today given the high cost of land. Many families prefer small yards to avoid having to do extensive yard work. Large yards are considered luxury items in expensive homes. _____?

8. Central air conditioning—More and more considered to be a necessity rather than a luxury. _____?

9. High quality insulation—Check with the builder. The "R" rating should be the minimum required for the weather in your area. Higher "R" ratings will decrease your heating and cooling costs. Ask if the house was "wrapped" with a vapor/moisture barrier. It helps the insulation do its work. _____?

10. Glass—Are the sliding glass doors, bathroom windows and other windows easily accessed by children made of "safety glass?"_____?

11. Electrical outlets—The standard in most construction is one outlet every 12 feet of linear wall space. Extra outlets in kitchens and baths are a plus. _____?

12. Floor coverings—Wall-to-wall carpet is the rule in most new homes. Tiles are a plus. Hardwood floors are an additional plus, but remember, you'll have to buy carpet to put over them. _____?

Picking the Right Neighborhood

Here's a checklist to help you evaluate a neighborhood for a new home.

New Neighborhood Checklist

		YES	NO
1.	Is shopping nearby?	[ ]	[ ]
2.	Are the local schools good?	[ ]	[ ]
3.	Are the schools nearby?	[ ]	[ ]
4.	Are there day-care facilities nearby?	[ ]	[ ]
5.	Is the police department responsive?	[ ]	[ ]
6.	Is there adequate fire protection?	[ ]	[ ]
7.	Is there a hospital nearby?	[ ]	[ ]
8.	Is the neighborhood "quiet?"	[ ]	[ ]
9.	Are posted speed limits slow?	[ ]	[ ]
10.	Is there a high-traffic street nearby?	[ ]	[ ]
11.	Is there a park nearby?	[ ]	[ ]
12.	Is public transportation available?	[ ]	[ ]
13.	Is there adequate off-street parking?	[ ]	[ ]
14.	Are the lots "private" enough?	[ ]	[ ]
15.	Is the tract landscaped?	[ ]	[ ]
16.	Is there danger of future erosion?	[ ]	[ ]
17.	Does the water system provide pure drinking water?	[ ]	[ ]
18.	Are there any special assessments that you'll have to pay (street improvement, sewer tax, etc.)?	[ ]	[ ]
19.	Are there any nearby hazards or nuisances (factories, swamps or rivers, oil tanks, hazardous waste facilities, etc.)?	[ ]	[ ]
20.	Are you connected to a sewer system (Septic systems are less desirable.)?	[ ]	[ ]

In addition to the features of the house itself as well as the neighborhood, there is the additional factor of the marketplace. The housing market is volatile with many ups and downs. Here's what to look for in a variety of different markets:

Buying a New Home in a Stable Market

In a stable market, with no rapid price appreciation or depreciation, there are more new homes than buyers, and builders are anxious to sell them off. The ads for the homes are placed in all papers, there are signs along the major roads directing you to the new tracts, and there are almost always models available to see of all the homes.

While the salespeople in the office try to get you to make a quick decision, you have plenty of time. You can leisurely shop around going from tract to tract until you find just the right home for you. Once you find it, you can often negotiate more favorable terms from the builder (reduced price, a buydown on the loan—where the builder pays part of your interest for a few years—free amenities such as fences, yards, and so forth). This is the ideal market in which to buy a new home. In a sense, it's a "buyer's market" and you're sitting in the driver's seat.

Tip

Try to buy the medium-sized home in the best located tract you can find—this property will appreciate the fastest. (The smallest home may simply be too small for many buyers and could be a white elephant; the largest home is often too expensive when it comes time for resale.)

Buying a New Home in a Down Market

You'll know this market if you're in it. Builders will have enormous ads saying such things as "Prices slashed 10 percent on all homes!" or "Rent before you buy!" or "Must sell out this month—we'll make any deal!"

The ads for the new homes sound like ads for used cars. Of course, if the ads don't alert you, there are other signs of a down market:

1. Statistics available from brokers and published in the business section of the local papers indicate that home sales are off from last year.

2. The numbers of houses advertised for sale (both new and resale) in the newspapers is enormous.

3. There are numerous "repos" advertised. For example, the FHA (Federal Housing Administration) or the VA (Veteran's Administration) may take out large ads indicating where auctions of foreclosed properties will be held.

4. There's difficulty getting financing from lenders because of the many houses already in default.

5. Tracts of new homes are fully built with the houses standing vacant and unsold.

Tip

Don't buy a new home in this market! In a down market you can find "steals" on existing homes as desperate sellers fight to get out. On the other hand, builders are limited in how much they can drop their prices. They generally operate on thin margins and the houses are financed for most of their value. You'll get a far better deal on a resale in a down market than on a new home.

Trap

If you must buy a new home in a down market, spend a lot of time investigating the market. In Phoenix, for example, which had a down market for most of the 1980s, some new housing tracts often would deteriorate into virtual slums as buyers couldn't keep up the payments and lost their properties. As a buyer of a new home, you could frequently go around into the tract past the models and find identical six-month-old resales being offered for *less than the price of the brand new homes!*

These tracts might have spawned fine yards and beautiful developments in an up market. But in a down market, they are a patchwork of well-kept homes, foreclosed and run-down properties, and unsold new homes. Chances are it will be years before this tract stabilizes and more years before you will get any price appreciation.

On the other hand, at the same time there may be resales nearby in tracts that were developed years earlier and which are attractive and fully occupied. These resales may cost less than the new tracts, yet, because of being fully developed, offer a greater chance for resale at a profit.

Buying a New Home in a Hot Market

This may be the most difficult sort of home to buy. Hot markets have occurred on both coasts at various times over the past decade. Generally the hot market doesn't last for more than 18 to 24 months. But during that time, it's like living in a different world.

What happens in a hot market is that there are more buyers than there are homes available for sale, both resales and new. The reason for this is that prices are perceived to be going up and speculators enter the market as well as people who buy with the intention of occupying the property.

In a hot market prices go up for both resales and new homes. However, they go up faster for new homes. I have seen *numerous* new housing tracts in southern California where the price of the home has gone up by $50,000 *between the time the buyers put down the deposit and the time they gained occupancy* (often a period of three to six months)! Is it any wonder that speculators want to get their hands on these houses? They can buy and resell for a huge profit in just a few months.

When buying a new home in a hot market the odds are set against you. You are competing against other buyers for relatively few homes. Builders don't need to advertise since buyers are beating the woods looking for new homes, so it's hard to locate the tracts. And frequently the prices of the new homes are so high that it's scary.

The Early Bird Gets the Worm

I have a friend who recently wanted to buy a brand new home in Danville, a suburb of San Francisco. This was at a time when the market was almost too hot to touch.

This friend, we'll call him Jerry, was, however, determined. Each day after work he would cruise the roads of Danville looking for signs of new construction—lots being bulldozed, houses being framed, even signs indicating that a builder was going to develop a tract on a certain piece of land.

Eventually Jerry located a tract he liked. It was the second phase of a builder's earlier development. When Jerry found it, the lots were just being bulldozed. No construction had started.

There really was no one there to talk to. So Jerry flagged down a bull-dozer driver and asked where he could find the construction foreman. From that person he learned who the developer was and called the developer's office.

The developer told him that while she had plans for the houses being constructed, she hadn't yet finalized plans for their cost. She took his name and promised to call him back as soon as she had calculated how much they would sell for.

Jerry didn't take any chances. He called her every week for two months until finally she gave him a price list and indicated that the construction company would begin accepting offers to purchase on June 10th, one month hence.

Jerry got a copy of the plans (the models weren't yet built) and went around to the building sites deciding finally on a particular lot and design he preferred. The cost was $35,000 more than he thought he could afford, however, he borrowed from his parents in order to be sure he could buy the house.

Four days before the builder was going to accept offers Jerry, complete with cot, sleeping bag, thermos and ice chest filled with food, set up residence in front of the builder's office. Mind you, this was four days early.

Jerry was the first one there. However, within hours of his arrival a half dozen other people showed up and camped out behind him. By the next day the line had swollen to over two dozen. Two days before the houses were going on sale, there were over 50 people in line. Keep in mind, there were only going to be 28 houses sold.

To help keep things orderly, Jerry made a list of who was in line in what position and gave it to the developer who agreed to honor it.

Finally the fateful day arrived. Jerry was the first one in, the first to give his deposit, the first to sign a sales agreement. There obviously was no haggling on price or terms…Jerry accepted whatever the builder dictated. Then he went home to the first decent night's sleep in nearly a week.

It took six months to build the homes. Finally, after some harrowing troubles with qualifying for the lender (Jerry borrowed extra money from relatives), he got the house and moved in. His house came with no fences, no yard, and very few amenities inside. He paid $50,000 more than he wanted to. But he was in.

Question: Was it a good move for Jerry?

He thinks so. The end of this true story is that three months after Jerry moved in, *he was offered a $55,000 profit* if he would sell. He hung on to the property hoping to make much more on it down the line.

Tip

In a hot market the builder-developer really doesn't need to bother with marginal buyers. Be sure you have the necessary down payment lined up in advance and that you can qualify for the financing.

In Jerry's tract there were some 83 people who wanted to buy 28 houses. That meant that for every house sold, there were at least three "back-up" offers. (A "back-up" offer is a buyer who was too late to make a purchase, but puts up a deposit and agrees to buy the property if the earlier buyer can't qualify for the financing or for any reason refuses to go through.) In this situation not having a sufficient down payment ready to go or having a blemish on your credit rating that you haven't taken care of can cause you to lose the deal. Remember, in such a market with other people lined up behind you to buy the property, the builder isn't going to feel particularly inclined to go out of her way to give you extra time to solve your own buying problems.

Buying Built vs. Yet-to-Be-Built New Homes

As we've seen from the prior examples, in a hot market you often don't have much of a choice. You have to be prepared to buy a home when the house has barely started construction in order to have any chance of buying at all.

On the other hand, in a down market, you don't want to buy a home unless the tract is fully built and 90 percent of the homes are sold, occupied, and there are no foreclosures.

However, in a stable market, which is the most typical, you oftentimes have a choice. You can pick from a few homes that are finished, or you can wait to buy a home yet to be constructed which can be built to your specific needs.

Does it make any difference? Is there any advantage one way or another?

Yes and yes. Whenever possible, *always* buy a home that is already built. This has two advantages for you: First, you can see what you're getting. Second, you know it's going to get built.

Will You Really Get the Home You Buy?

I have another friend who wanted to buy a home in a tract in Orange county, south of Los Angeles. Jill, we'll call her, loved the location and fell in love with one of the models. There were several homes already constructed and ready for sale, but not the model she wanted. This was during a stable period in between two hot periods in the area. The builder told Jill her model would be available in the "next phase." He took a $500 deposit from her and signed an agreement explaining that she would be required to fill out a sales agreement as soon as the house was built. The $500 merely reserved it for her. He guessed that it would be ready in three and a half months.

Four months later the builder hadn't even broken ground. Jill, and a number of others, were haunting his offices trying to find out what the problem was. All she could get were vague answers. She was told that the lenders would not agree to the financing because of some title problems. Or there was a permit difficulty with the city. Or the builder was waiting until material costs came down. Or something else.

Finally, five and a half months after she paid her deposit, work began. It took another five and a half months to finish her home.

During the building period, she visited the home whenever she could, sometimes several visits a week. She didn't notice any problems until the house was almost completed and the wall boards put up. Then she realized that the floor plan was not exactly the same as the model. The windows of the living room didn't face the hills, the one feature she admired most about the plan.

She confronted the builder after he missed three appointments to see her. Yes, he explained, the plans were changed. Building costs had changed and he was just adjusting to them. A few corners had been cut here and there so that he could deliver the property at the agreed upon price.

What could she do? She continued to wait.

Finally, the building was completed. It wasn't at all what she hoped it would be. But after all the waiting (nearly 10 months), she was glad she would be able to move in.

When she went to sign the sales agreement, however, she found that the price had gone up by $11,000!

How could that be, she wanted to know? She had agreed upon a price with the builder. He pointed out that the price he agreed upon was the price of 10 months earlier. Costs had gone up since then not only including building materials and labor, but the interest he was paying on his construction loan. He pointed to a clause in their agreement which clearly stated he could adjust the price to reflect any increased costs.

In the end, it wasn't the house Jill wanted at the price she wanted to pay. She got her $500 deposit back and began to look elsewhere. However, she had lost nearly 10 months not to mention all the hassle.

Yes, this is a true story. No, it doesn't happen all of the time. It probably doesn't happen most of the time although price and plan changes are legend in construction. But it does happen enough that you should be aware of it and at least plan on the possibility.

Fences, Yards, and Upgrades

Have you noticed that when you buy a new car you almost never get it for the base sticker price. Invariably, you end up paying more for extras. Buying a new home is not dissimilar.

When you buy a new home there are lots of extras. These fall into two categories—extra items (such as fences) and upgrades to a better quality of item (such as carpets). Here's a list of some of the extras and upgrades you can expect to pay for:

1. Larger or view lot
2. Any changes in the basic construction plan
3. Fences
4. Landscaped yard
5. Upgrade of roof
6. Upgrade of exterior walls
7. Upgrade of carpet or tile

8. Air conditioning (now standard on many homes)

9. Additional mirrors or windows

10. Upgrade of insulation

11. Upgrade of appliances (stove, oven, dishwasher, etc.)

12. Upgrade of plumbing fixtures (toilets, sinks, tubs)

13. Larger water heater

Many builders have a list of upgrades that they strictly adhere to. For example, you have your choice of three grades of carpet and that's it. Or you can choose from six tile patterns, three of which cost extra, no changes allowed.

There are several reasons that builders limit the changes and upgrades you can make. One is cost. They get guaranteed estimates from a few distributors and they know what it's going to cost to purchase a particular product. That makes it easy for them to stick with that product.

Also, there's the cost of labor as well as materials. Some materials require extra labor costs. For example, some Japanese tiles are irregular (when compared to American or European tiles), and there may be an extra labor charge for installing them. To avoid hassles here the builder may simply limit the selection to half a dozen patterns, all because he knows he can control the labor costs.

The real question you should ask yourself is which upgrades and extras are worthwhile and which are not. Here are some clues:

Larger or View Lot

The price isn't usually that much more. For example, a lot with a view may cost $5000 more than a lot without. A larger lot may cost $1500 more than a standard lot.

Tip

If you buy a view lot, it's the best money you can spend. You'll get it back times over when you sell.

Trap

If you buy a larger lot, beware. Unless you landscape it so that it requires little to no maintenance work, it could be a drawback when you resell.

Fences

In those areas of the country where fences are common, you're going to need a fence.

Tip

It's often simpler to let the builder put it up at the time the house is constructed than to put it up yourself, particularly if there are architectural or building restrictions.

However, that may not be the cheapest route. Often an independent fence contractor can beat the builder's price. Finally, if you're handy, you can beat both prices substantially by doing it yourself.

Carpets and Floor Coverings

Usually new homes come with wall to wall carpet, tile and/or finished wood. But the quality of these often leaves much to be desired. This is most obvious in terms of tile and carpets. The model home may have luxurious, thick carpeting while the actual carpeting that comes with the home may be short and threadbare. The model may have colorful Italian tiles while the standard home comes with ordinary white tiles.

Tip

It usually doesn't pay to upgrade to the most expensive tile or carpet, but it usually does pay to upgrade to a medium quality for two reasons: First, at least in terms of carpet, it insures that the floor covering will last more than just a few years. Second, it helps to insure that the carpet will look good, a particularly important point if you want to resell in a few years. Carpets make the biggest impression on potential home buyers— don't you look at them first? Besides, upgrading carpet isn't usually that expensive as the difference between medium and low grade is often less than $10 a yard.

Trap

Be careful of upgrading tiles. The cost of tiles varies enormously. Some tiles may only be a dollar a square foot. Others may be $100 a square foot or more. Colorful tiles are nice, but for resale, clean, unbroken regular tiles will usually do just as well.

Yard

Some builders will put in yards, front and back, for you if you wish. Except for one case, explained shortly, this is usually a trap. The cost for putting in yards can be very expensive. On the other hand, if you do some of the work yourself and hire out only the difficult tasks like installing the plumbing and planting large trees, you can do it for significantly less.

Trap

The one exception is the front yard in tracts which have architectural control. The CC and Rs (Covenants, Conditions, and Restrictions) which govern the tract may require a certain type of front yard. Certain bushes, certain arrangements, or certain watering patterns may be required.

Often, when architectural control of front yards is required, the cost is automatically included in the price of the house and the builder automatically puts in the yard. But not always. Sometimes you have the option of paying the builder or doing it yourself.

My advice is that in this case, let the builder do it. You will save hassles arguing with the architectural committee, sprained backs (as you try to put in a pineapple tree that weighs three times as much as you do), and possibly even money.

Air Conditioning

If this is offered as an option instead of a standard feature, get it. The climate appears to be changing for the warmer in most parts of the country. Today, just as in automobiles, air conditioning is considered to be a standard feature. You may find that you have trouble selling your house later on, if it doesn't have air.

Trap

All other options and upgrades (roof, exterior walls, mirrors or windows, added insulation, appliances, larger water heater, etc.) are usually a waste of your money. You'll have trouble getting the investment back later on when you go to resell. (The exception is when the appliances that come with the house are especially shoddy.)

The Perils of Shoddy Construction

One of the advantages of buying a resale is that you pretty well know what you're getting. If the home has been standing for five, ten, or more years, chances are it will stand another thirty or forty.

On the other hand, when you purchase a new home, you're buying something that is as yet untried. If there are defects, they could show up in the first few years of usage.

But, I hear many readers saying, aren't new homes fully inspected by city or county building departments. Don't they have to meet strict health and safety guidelines?

Yes...and no. All modern buildings are inspected at numerous times during their construction. In most cases the inspector catches problems and forces their correction before a "certificate of occupancy" is granted. You can't occupy the home without this certificate—in most areas you can't even connect to water, power or gas without it.

However, there may be only one or two building inspectors and hundreds of houses to inspect. Further, while in most cases the inspectors are well trained and experienced, they often are not expert in every area of construction. And in a few cases they simply are not very well qualified.

The upshot of all this is the fact that regardless of the area of the country, shoddy construction goes on all the time right next to excellent construction. For example, in one housing tract in Southern California, the builder decided to use a Spanish tile roof. This consists of red, curved tiles interlaced to form a very attractive roof line.

The trouble with the tiles is that they aren't very good at holding out water. In a wind driven storm, the water sweeps up under the edges of the tiles and through the roofs. In the old days (the 1700s) Spanish tile roofs were used extensively in California. However, in those days a kind of mortar was applied to the roof and the tiles carefully set into it. This effectively water-proofed them.

Today the use of this mortar would be unattractive and expensive. So instead, roofers lay down layers of heavy, waterproof felt before placing the tiles. It acts as an effective water barrier.

However, in this particular tract the roofer had never before laid Spanish tiles. No felt was placed beneath them. The building inspector, also unfamiliar with the need for felt, didn't catch it.

You're right, the first rain the roofs leaked—every roof in a tract of over 60 houses!

About two-thirds had been sold and the water damage forced the occupants out. Needless to say they were furious and everyone looked to the builder for repairs.

The builder was an honorable person, but not particularly wealthy. All of the tile on the roofs had to be removed and felt placed back down. It meant reroofing over 60 homes, a very, very costly thing to do. The builder simply couldn't handle it and declared bankruptcy.

The homes that hadn't been sold were taken back by the lender, who corrected the problem. But the two-thirds that had been sold ended up being the responsibility of the owners. It cost about $10,000 per house for the repairs.

This was shoddy construction. But no one was really trying to cut corners. It was just a case of a builder working in an area of unfamiliarity and a building inspector likewise being in the dark.

Unfortunately, this isn't an isolated case. In another tract of new homes in a neighboring state, the builder did not use approved metal fittings to join the heavy timbers that held the ceiling of the house to the beams that supported them. Again, for some inexplicable reason, the building inspector didn't catch it. As a result, within a few years (after the houses had all been sold out), they began shifting. Cracks appeared in ceilings and walls, and in one case a dining room ceiling crashed down onto the dining room table (fortunately, there were no injuries).

Complaints from home owners caused a thorough investigation by the city, which then condemned the houses and forbade anyone to live in them until the problems were corrected. The owners had to to move out. The retrofitting of the metal braces required cutting into walls and ceilings and cost thousands of dollars per house. Again, the builder declared bankruptcy and the owners were left to their own resources to make the repairs.

Of course, these are exceptions. Most buyers of new homes have no problems at all or small problems which the builder quickly fixes. But that doesn't mean that major structural problems in workmanship or even materials couldn't occur. In a way it's again like buying a car. Chances are the one you get will be wonderful. On the other hand, you could get a lemon.

Warranties

Many builders back their construction with warranties. According to a study by *Professional Builders* magazine, November 1985, 92 percent of builders were offering some sort of home warranty program. Even a builder who does not give you a written warranty may be offering you an "implied" warranty, depending upon the state in which you live. Today many states have strong consumer protection laws which allow you to take the builder to court for shoddy construction, and to win a settlement. (Of course, that's of dubious value if the builder has gone broke.)

Of that vast majority of builders who offer warranties, there are two groups—those who self-warrant and those who buy insurance.

Self-Warranted Homes

A builder who self-warrants a home will normally give you a certificate of warranty which states what is covered and what is not covered. Typically such a warranty says that if it's not specifically noted, it's not covered.

The Magnuson-Moss Act (1975) is a disclosure law which is handled by the Federal Trade Commission (FTC). Under Magnuson-Moss, a warranty issued by a builder must include the following:

1. The name of the person who is warranted (you) and *a specific statement of whether the warranty is transferable if you sell the property.*
2. Precise information on what is covered and what is excluded.
3. Exact language detailing what a builder will do to correct a problem that arises.
4. The length of the warranty.
5. The procedure, in detail, for filing a claim.
6. Any limitations on consequential damages. (Consequential damages result as a consequence of covered problems. The most common example is a water pipe bursting causing damage to furniture. The pipe may be covered, but is the furniture?)
7. Any reduction of implied warranties must be stated clearly.

Trap

As part of the warranty, some builders have the buyers sign a statement that they *waive all implied warranties.* In the states that permit this if you sign this statement you may give up more rights than you get since the implied warranties may be stronger than the builder's specific warranties. If a builder insists you sign this statement you may want to consider a different builder and house.

Under a builder's warranty, you have to go back to the builder to get satisfaction if a problem arises. It's to your advantage, therefore, to find a builder who is big enough to sustain the loses involved with any problems. We'll have more to say on selecting the right builder shortly.

Insurance-Warranted Homes

A different kind of warranty is offered by about a third of all builders nationwide. This is a warranty backed not only by the builder, but also by an insurance company.

The largest and oldest of the insurance companies that handle such warranties is the Home Owners Warranty (HOW) Corporation. Under HOW, the builder continues to warrant the house, but HOW backs up that warranty. In addition it offers a plan that changes with the years the house is in existence.

For example, in the first year, under HOW, the builder warrants the home to be free from defects in workmanship and materials in compliance with HOW's approved standards including major structural defects.

In the second year, the builder continues to warrant against major structural defects and against defects in wiring, piping, and ductwork.

In years three through ten, the builder carries insurance against major structural defects protecting you, the buyer.

Tip

HOW insurance is normally transferable; however, there are limitations and exclusions. Under the plan, your first recourse is to seek a solution to the problem from the builder. If the builder does not or is not able to comply, HOW picks up the tab for covered items after a one-time $250 deductible.

Although HOW has the vast majority of insurance warranties, there are other companies that offer competing plans. While the plans tend to be similar, there are important differences which you should determine by reading them closely.

Selecting the Right Builder

Most of us simply shop houses. We go from tract to tract trying to find the new home that will be just right for us. It's also important, however, to shop builders. It should be evident from the discussions on shoddy workmanship and on warranties that a lot depends on the builder. You want a builder who does good work and who has the means to back it up should any unforeseen problems arise.

Builder-Quality Checklist

Here's a checklist to help determine the quality of the builder:

1. How long has the builder been constructing new   _____
   homes? Longevity is always a good sign.

                                                              YES   NO
2. Can you get a recommendation (or a condemnation)
   from a relative, friend, or associate who's previously
   had dealings with the builder?   [ ]   [ ]

3. Check with the Better Business Bureau. This organization normally keeps complaints filed against businesses. Does this builder have complaints filed?   [ ]   [ ]

4. Check with any consumer groups active in the area.
   Also check with the local office of the National Association of Home Builders. Your builder should be a
   member of this group and they may be able to give a
   recommendation.   _____

5. Find out where the builder has previously built
   new homes. Go to the tract and knock on a few
   doors. Simply say you are going to be buying a
   home from the same builder and you would like to
   know if those who bought before had any problems
   such as shoddy work or reluctance to fix problems.
   Don't be embarrassed. Home owners love to talk
   about their builder. Either she's wonderful and has
   done a marvelous job. Or he's been a disaster for
   them. Just be sure you talk to more than one person to get a balanced viewpoint.   _____

Negotiating with the Builder

Now we come to the tricky part for many new home buyers—negotiating with the builder. Here many who purchase a new home are completely lost, signing anything and everything that is placed before them.

Tip

Just as with purchasing a resale, when buying a new home *everything is
negotiable*. The problem with new homes, however, is that the builder is
often tied into financing and labor and materials contracts so that he or
she cannot really offer the flexibility an owner of a resale can.

Typically, when buying a new home you are presented with a colorful
and expensive-looking brochure which gives the floor plans of the var-

ious models that the builder is offering. Along with these is usually a price schedule. For plan "A" the price is $85,000 until January 2nd when the price goes up to $87,500. For plan "B" the price is $135,000. For plan "C" it's $168,000 and so forth. In addition, there are higher costs for better lots as well as additional costs for upgrades as described earlier.

Thus, the prices are laid out in the same fashion as they are in a grocery store. You certainly can't bargain with the grocer over the price of a jar of mayonnaise, so how do you bargain with a builder over the price list for a new home?

Trap

It's important to understand that builders-developers like to create the impression that nothing is negotiable—either you take their price or you don't get the house. That's part of the reason for the elaborate brochures.

The truth, however, is that builders are sellers just like any other sellers. When builders need to get rid of homes they will negotiate down to the bare bones, regardless of what the brochures say.

The way you negotiate with builders is to say that you would "like to submit an offer on one of the houses." The salesperson should be a licensed real estate agent and, acting as a fiduciary for the builder, must submit all offers unless the builder has a written stipulation that no offers be submitted below a specific price—an unlikely possibility. The trick, of course, is to make the offer reasonable.

The easiest way to negotiate is to find a builder who already has houses up, then to accept the price and bargain over the "extras." Yes, you'll pay the price, but you want complete fencing around the property, you want an upgrade of carpet *at no additional cost to you* and you want a self-cleaning oven instead of the standard oven included with the homes.

In a flat market with already constructed homes, as noted earlier in this chapter, the builder might very well consider such an offer. After all, the builder gets the fencing, the carpeting, and the stove at wholesale. Why not pay the additional charges to get rid of a home that's costing that builder upwards of a thousand dollars or more a month in interest charges?

Tip

As noted earlier, don't expect the builder to budge in a hot market or where the houses haven't yet been constructed. In this case there's no leverage on your side. Why should the builder accept a lower offer when there are other buyers standing in line to pay full price, or when the builder hasn't even put up the houses and isn't paying interest on them?

Another bargaining point is terms. This is often the case when interest rates are high and it's difficult to qualify for mortgages. The builder may be willing to "pay down" the mortgage by several points. For example, when you get the mortgage, instead of paying the going rate of 12 percent, for the first three years you might pay 10 percent, the builder paying the other 2 percent. On a $100,000 mortgage, 2 percentage points can save you roughly $2000 a year in interest payments in this case.

Trap

Beware of builders who pay down the mortgage, then raise the price by an offsetting amount. In the above example, you would save close to $6000 over a three-year buy-down. But, if the builder raised the price of the property by $6000, where would your savings be? You'd be converting a lower payment into a higher price, and after the first three years you'd be paying interest on that higher price.

In most cases builders won't buy-down an interest rate unless their houses have been sitting there for a long time and the builder is anxious to get rid of them. If that's the case, by talking to those who bought six months ago in the same tract, you should be able to establish what the original pricing was. Thus you can determine if the builder has raised the price to pay for your buy-down.

Finally you can negotiate price with a builder, although your chances of getting a significant reduction are slim. Here's the reason why.

Builders usually operate on a fairly tight margin—10 or 15 percent profit is considered good. Let's consider a builder who is working with a 10 percent margin building homes that are priced to sell in the $100,000 range. The builder's profit is $10,000 meaning the house costs roughly $90,000 to construct (including land).

It's important to understand that the builder almost never puts up the entire $90,000 to build the home. Rather he usually buys the land and then borrows the money under a construction loan from a lender to erect the building. Let's say in our example that the land costs 25 percent of the selling price or $25,000. Thus the house actually costs $65,000 to build.

Building costs	65,000
Land	25,000
Profit	10,000
Selling price	100,000

The builder has a loan for $65,000 or more on the house on which interest must be paid monthly. In addition there are charges for taxes and insurance. Typically the interest charges as well as the costs for taxes and insurance during the building period and for perhaps a month or two afterward have been factored into the $65,000 cost of construction.

However, if the builder puts up the houses and they don't sell during that allotted period, then the cost for interest, taxes and insurance begins to come out of his pocket. Thus after the construction period, the builder, in this example, might be paying out close to $1000 a month while waiting for a buyer.

It's easy to see that after 10 months the builder would have used up all the profit. Thus, as time goes by he becomes increasingly anxious to sell. Your chances of getting a better deal improve the longer construction has been completed and the houses are sitting there.

On the other hand, the longer the houses are sitting there, the less the builder can lower the price. If the houses have been sitting for five months and the builder has paid out $5000 of the profit margin there is only $5000 in profit left to make. If you offer $5000 less than the selling price the builder will make no profit at all and is likely to turn you down. Perhaps a drop in price of $1000 or $2000 might be accepted, but the builder simply can't afford to take much less.

That's why it's not very likely that you'll be able to bargain a builder down in price. Better to go for extras, upgrades, or terms.

Tip

The higher priced the house, the more bargaining room a builder may have. If you're in the $300,000 price range or higher the profit margins may go up significantly. Some builders look for 20 percent profits or higher in these areas. Thus, the higher the price, the more chance you have of negotiating a lower price.

14
After the Close

You've found your house and purchased it. You've paid your money, gotten your mortgage, and escrow has closed. A set of keys has been delivered into your hands and there are hearty congratulations from all concerned. You're now the proud owner of a new home. What next?

Obviously there's the nerve-straining process of moving in to go through, but once that's completed, that's it, isn't it? The hassle is over—or has it just begun?

Most buyers feel that the problems with a purchase end with the end of escrow. In some cases that's true, but in other cases it isn't. In this chapter we're going to look at what might go wrong and how to correct it...after the close.

The Small Stuff

As soon as you're sure the deal is going to go through, you should establish utilities service to the property. You will want to contact:

Phone company

Gas company

Electric company

Water company

Garbage collector

Post office

Tip

Be sure and write your name on the mailbox. Some postal employees will not deliver to a home unless the addressee's name is on the mailbox, even though the address on the letter may be correct. Also, be sure and fill out "change of address" forms at the post office.

Trap

Be aware that many utility companies have been ripped off by people who have established service (usually tenants) and then, after a few months, have reneged on the bills. Thus you may be required to put up a service deposit of as high as a hundred dollars or more *per utility*. Try to avoid this cost whenever possible by "transferring" your service from your last residence instead of closing it out and opening new service at the new house.

The In-Between Stuff

As soon as you move in, it's a good idea to check around the property to be sure that everything is as it should be. You might not have noticed something in your final inspection or something could have changed since then. Here's a checklist when you buy a resale:

	YES	NO
1. Is all fencing up and in place? (This is a particular concern if you have pets or small children.)	[ ]	[ ]
2. If you have yard gate, does it close automatically? (A must if you have a pool.)	[ ]	[ ]
3. Do all the electrical switches, sockets, and appliances work?	[ ]	[ ]
4. Do you smell gas escaping anywhere, but particularly around heaters and stoves? (If yes, open all the windows and call the gas company immediately. Do not light any matches or try to find the leak yourself.)	[ ]	[ ]
5. Are there any water leaks at the water heater or elsewhere?	[ ]	[ ]
6. Is the paint and appearance of exterior and interior as you expected it to be?	[ ]	[ ]
7. Are there any cracked windows or windows that don't function?	[ ]	[ ]
8. Do all the doors close properly?	[ ]	[ ]
9. Has the previous owner left anything behind that should be returned?	[ ]	[ ]

10. Is there anything unusual or out-of-place that you
    might want to mention to someone?   [ ]   [ ]

All of the above are usually relatively simple problems. By that I
mean that they're probably not worth getting upset about. There's
bound to be some wear and tear on the property. It's to be expected as
are sticky windows and doors. After all, it's not a brand new house.

If the previous owners left something behind, give them or their
agent a call. If the water heater leaks, call up the warranty service
(which you probably bought) or the seller's agent. They'll most likely be
happy to take care of it for you. The same holds true for safety problems such as a gate that doesn't close automatically or gas leaks.

Tip

I use this rule of thumb when buying a new property: If the problem is
going to cost $50 or less to fix, I take care of it myself. If it costs more
than that, I complain to the seller or the seller's agent.

Remember, there are *always* going to be some problems when moving into a resale. If you expect them, they won't get out of hand.

The Big Stuff

And then there's the big stuff, problems which are major, serious, and
need your special attention. Here's a list of what to look for:

	YES	NO
1. Does the seller (or seller's agent) refuse to handle any of the small or in-between stuff?	[ ]	[ ]
2. Is there major damage?	[ ]	[ ]
3. Did the sellers lie about or omit something important regarding the property?	[ ]	[ ]
4. Is there a problem with the mortgage, the title, or the moneys involved?	[ ]	[ ]
5. Is there anything else wrong which keeps you from sleeping at night?	[ ]	[ ]

If you answer "Yes" to any of the above, then you've stepped out of
the ordinary adjustment problems that any buyers face when moving in,
and have entered the realm of big time problems. Let's consider them
one at a time.

1. The sellers (or their agent) refuse to take care of any of the little
things wrong.

Tip

My suggestion is that if the problems are little, still forget it. The hassle of fighting someone over a half dozen minor things isn't worth the upset stomach and potential heart attack you can get over it. I believe one of the best pieces of advice in the world is, "Don't sweat the small stuff."

Trap

On the other hand, add together enough small stuff and it can become pretty big. If the sellers won't listen to you, have your lawyer (the one you used on the deal), write them a letter. People respond surprisingly quickly to letters from attorneys. Even better, if the seller's agent won't listen, write a letter of complaint to your state's real estate regulatory body. But before you send it to the state, send a copy to the agent with a note that says, "Do I really need to send this, or can we settle this reasonably, now?" It's surprising how quickly agents respond when their license to practice real estate is threatened.

2. Is there major damage? What's major damage? *Broken beams, cracked floors, ruined carpets, drapes or paint, etc.* You'll know major when you see major.

Generally speaking, there are two kinds of major damage—disclosed and undisclosed. If the damage was disclosed to you before the sale was completed (usually a letter or a form that *you signed for having received*) you're probably stuck with it. You knew about it and you still accepted the property. The sellers aren't going to be the least bit sympathetic, and, chances are, neither is anyone else.

On the other hand, there's undisclosed damage. The worst I ever saw of this was when sellers left on a vacation about three weeks prior to the close of escrow...with two cats locked inside their house.

The cats had adequate food and water, but were not trained to use a small box of kitty litter left for their benefit. In those three weeks they ruined the carpet. However, to see the carpet was not to know the problem, because upon returning home, the aghast sellers immediately had it cleaned. The problem was odor which could not be removed from the carpeting.

For the final walk-though, the sellers used air fresheners and opened all the windows, so the buyers had no idea there was a problem.

It became quite evident to the buyers what the problem was, however, the first night they moved in. When it got cold in the evening they closed the windows and went to sleep. The odors welled up, causing allergic reactions in the children and forcing them to move to a motel.

What could the buyers do?

They demanded the sellers correct the problem. That is, they demanded all new wall-to-wall carpeting throughout the house, at a cost of over $12,000!

The sellers, at first, refused to pay...until it became evident to them that the problem would not go away and that they had not disclosed it. Then their attorney suggested they pay and move on, which they did.

3. Did the sellers lie about or omit something important regarding the property? Did they say the house was ten years old and you flip over the top of the toilet bowl tank and see that it's 25 years old? (The date of manufacture of toilet bowl tanks is almost always inside the lid. Since these are rarely replaced, it often gives a good indication to the age of the property.) Did they forget to mention that there was toxic waste in the drainage canal behind the house? (See "Your Courses of Action" below for what to do.)

4. Is there a problem with the title or the mortgage? Title problems are extremely rare. If you have one, however, hang onto that policy of title insurance you bought. It's your guarantee that either you'll get clear title or your money back.

Tip

Call the title company at once if there's a problem. If they refuse to fix it to your satisfaction, call the state real estate department or the appropriate agency in your state which governs title companies. They will investigate the problem for you.

The biggest problem with mortgage companies is that they sometimes get your loan payback account mixed up with someone else's. You owe $512 a month, but your payment book comes in and it says you owe $3200 a month!

Don't get excited...stay calm. Call the mortgage company. They'll straighten it out.

Tip

Don't expect the first person at the mortgage company you talk to will solve your problem. You may have to persist through several levels of management before you find someone in authority who can handle the problem. Eventually, however, it will get straightened out. The lender will insist on getting paid every penny owed, but won't take a penny more than is owed (else the lender could face enormous penalties including paying you up to three times the money you borrowed!).

Don't do the lender any favors.

One couple recently bought a home obtaining a new adjustable rate mortgage. The mortgage was supposed to be adjusted every three months. At the end of the fourth month the buyers noticed that the lender hadn't made an adjustment, even though interest rates had gone up. At the end of the fifth month, still no change had been made. Wanting to do the right thing, the sellers wrote to the lender explaining that the payments were too small.

Instead of thanking them, the lender immediately raised the payments, said the borrowers were delinquent in their fourth and fifth months (because they had paid too little), and put the property into foreclosure!

Yes, it eventually all got straightened out, but not before the lender insisted on and got an increase in those two months plus late penalties! I agree it's incredible, but it did, in fact happen.

On the other hand, if the sellers had never bothered to tell the lender of its mistake...? A close reading of their loan documents revealed that once the adjustment period had passed, the lender would have had no further recourse. If they hadn't said anything and another three months had gone by (the adjustment period), the lender would have had to bear the responsibility of its own incompetence.

5. If you can't sleep at night, you've got a problem. The sooner you get it resolved, the sooner you'll get your sleep. Here are some alternatives:

Your Courses of Action When There Is a Problem

1. Decide whether or not you can live with it.

2. If you can't live with it, call *your agent* and see if she or he can correct the problem.

3. If you get no satisfaction, call the sellers and their agent and demand a correction of the problem.

4. If you get no satisfaction, consider writing the state real estate licensing agency, but let the agent know first that you're planning to do this.

5. Call your attorney.

Index

About the Author

Robert Irwin has been a successful real estate broker for over 25 years and has helped buyers and sellers alike through every kind of real estate transaction imaginable. He has been a consultant to lenders, investors, and other brokers and is one of the most knowledgeable and prolific writers in the field. His books include *Making Mortgages Work for You, How to Find Hidden Real Estate Bargains, The McGraw-Hill Real Estate Handbook, The Handbook of Property Management,* and *How to Find and Manage Profitable Properties.* His latest book, *Tips and Traps When Buying a Home,* will also be of great interest to you if you are planning to buy a new house at the same time that you dispose of the house you currently own.